THE SERENE CINCINNATIANS

PUBLISHER'S NOTE

Another volume in the Society in America Series, independent volumes by distinguished writers devoted to the important cities and sections of the country. The aim of these volumes is to portray the individual characteristics, to underscore the idiosyncrasies, and to trace the growth of sectional societies with special emphasis on local traditions and on the personalities who embodied them.

Already Published

THREE GREAT LADIES OF CINCINNATI

MRS. CHARLES P. TAFT
(Annie Sinton)

MRS. BELLAMY STORER
(Maria Longworth)

MRS. THOMAS J. EMERY
(Mary M. Hopkins)

The Serene
Cincinnatians

ALVIN F. HARLOW

E. P. Dutton and Company, Inc.

NEW YORK   MDCCCCL

The Table of Contents

End Paper Design

CINCINNATI IN 1855

FROM AN OLD PRINT IN CINCINNATI PUBLIC LIBRARY

Frontispiece

THREE GREAT LADIES OF CINCINNATI

PICTURES FROM HISTORICAL AND PHILOSOPHICAL SOCIETY OF OHIO

THE SERENE CINCINNATIANS

CHAPTER I
Dynamic Serenity

THERE were cries of anguish and indignation along the middle Ohio River on a day in 1948 when a New York weekly news magazine, well known for its jocose laconicism and its deleterious effect upon the English language, remarked that "Dowdy, old-fashioned Cincinnati gets a new hotel this week." The Chamber of Commerce of that city, feeling a high degree of responsibility, suffered acutely. Some business men were of opinion that the fillip had been salutary; they had observed that two or three seedy-looking buildings which had had no attention for years, hastily called in the cleaners and painters. The city in general just fumed a little, and in Cincinnati fashion, grew calm again; while some of the mellow, well-seasoned older citizens and antiquarians merely smiled indulgently as at a typical reaction of the sort of mind which detects a slight musty odor about anything older than the day before yesterday's creation.

Cincinnati — where you can still buy a celluloid collar if you know where to look, and where they still have chimney sweeps, at least one of whom still wears a plug hat, an ancient badge of his calling — knows more about the facts of life than that. In its system of philosophy past and present are not worlds apart, antagonistic, but are one, a continuity; we are the immediate children of the past, and our traditions, as Woodrow Wilson observed, are our ballast; with a proper breadth of culture and vision, we may be mindful and appreciative of the past, yet receptive, even hospitable to the best in modernism. But Cincinnati holds to Viscount Falkland's dictum that "When it is not necessary to change, it is necessary not to change"; and remembering the costliness and futility of many experimental changes of recent years, one wonders whether he may not have been right.

Cincinnati is predominantly, and one ventures to say intelligently conservative. It has its individual Colonel Blimps, but it also has its sane conservatives, who teamed up with its liberals to rid it of bossism, to give it the city manager form of government and that cherished liberal device, Proportional Representation, a system of voting which no other American city of anywhere near its size, not even that great liberal stronghold, New York, has been able to make workable.

The very heart of the soul of Cincinnati being music, in its Symphony Orchestra its diastole may be watched and its tendencies studied. That orchestra stands firmly upon the unshakable classics, yet gives audition to anything in new music which carries a hint of promising young talent or a quality which may come to be accepted by the best taste of tomorrow. It has even gone far ahead of other orchestras in well-considered explorations into new fields. In November, 1948, Olin Downes, famous musical critic of the *New York Times*, journeyed out to Pittsburgh to hear a concert of that city's orchestra conducted by Victor de Sabata, artistic director of La Scala, Milan, and declared him to be "a foremost virtuoso conductor of today." He had not yet been discovered by New York, though he had long been famous all over Europe and in South America. The only North American community to give him an engagement previous to that time was Cincinnati, where he conducted the orchestra for half the season of 1927-28 — twenty-one years before any other city in the United States heard him! And slowly following Pittsburgh, at long last Chicago and New York enjoyed his spectacular artistry.

The $18,000,000 hotel and business building mentioned by the news weekly is in itself a rejoinder to the epithet, "old-fashioned"; a hint that a community which can so reverence the past, yet adventure further into the future than other cities, requires deeper study. Nowhere else will you find a big, tower-like hotel, not springing from the earth, but perched on top of a great, seven-story, *windowless* business building, so that no guest must sleep or try to sleep near street noises, being protected from them not only by height but by a setback of the structure; a hotel with new gadgets and opulence hitherto unknown in bedrooms, with its public room walls and ceilings splashed with some of the most wayward of surrealist murals by Juan Miro, and abstractionist fantasies which completely baffle the guests. It is as if Cincinnati were saying to the world, "We'll show you that we can be just as modern as anybody when we choose, and maybe a little more so."

But Cincinnati has in many ways been exploring untried paths for more than a century. Seeming to saunter in amiable tranquility, she has collected more "firsts" than her share; the first chartered municipal university and the first Jewish theological college in America; the first building in history erected as a dental college; the first air mail, carried out of Cincinnati by balloon, July 4th, 1835; the first really successful fire engine, built and put into service in 1853, more than four years before old-fashioned New York reluctantly accepted one (of Cincinnati manufacture) as a gift from a fire insurance company; the first salaried fire department, also established in 1853, twelve years before New York gave up its volunteers; the first railroad "club car" for suburban commuters in 1864, and the first after-theater train for suburbanites in 1876; the first annual municipal exposition in America, one so successful that when Philadelphia contemplated its great Centennial Exposition in 1876, it asked a Cincinnatian to plan and manage it; the first Turnverein in America; the first salaried baseball team in history, and the only one to go through a season without losing a game; the first and only major railroad in the world to be built and owned by a municipality. It pioneered in employees' profit-sharing and corporation ownership; it was the first large city (and is still the largest) to adopt the city manager plan of government, and the first to outlaw bossism permanently, though it must be confessed, after enduring it in malignant form for many years.

Yet paradoxically enough, in few or no cities of its size will you find so many accepted traditions, quaint customs and usages, such a habit of permanence and longevity —for there are as many persons aged sixty-five and over here as in Cleveland, which is fifty percent larger. Thus Cincinnati's serenity has in it the experience and philosophical composure of age, informed by historical consciousness, and with a strong blend of sound German imperturbability. Here you will find the world's only ten-thousand-year leasehold; an aboriginal Indian mound carefully preserved inside a big city; a century-old literary club of men, inhabiting a 130-year-old mansion, where it meets inexorably o' Monday nights; a gymnasium privately supported by memberships for ninety-eight years; some seventy-five centenarian (or older) businesses and industries, and others reaching or nearing that mark every year, a number of them still functioning (though much enlarged) on the very spot where they were born. Who would expect to find among them a mere yarn store, founded in 1845? And there is a plain old brick church — Wesley Chapel, one of several centenarian fanes — built in 1831 and protected since 1835 by a policy in a Cincinnati insurance company organized in 1826; a policy so old that the dividends have long been taking care of the premiums.

Reverence for tradition has led to some whimsical situations. Penetrating several yards into a downtown block, then turning at a right angle for a few feet more and halting, walled in everywhere by buildings, is a little, concrete-paved passage, unnoticed by thousands who pass its iron-gated entrance daily, and of whose meaning, even of whose existence, few people are aware. In the pre-sewer long ago, it was an easement, an access to eight of what the Earl of Chesterfield called necessary houses in the middle of the block, used by adjacent business men. Though it has been totally useless for decades, so dearly do the property holders still cherish these rights that when an effort was made a few years ago to buy that quarter of the block for building purposes, the value set on this little lane blocked the deal. Quite as curious is the case of a well, dug possibly a century and a half ago. All the stores and shops around it once used its water for drinking, and all adjoining property still has legal access to it in its deeds, though it has been covered and unused for at least seventy-five years. But when it was proposed to erect a twenty-story building on the spot, the would-be builders found that the well's sentimental (and if not sentimental, then what?) value was such that the project had to be abandoned.

It would seem that many Cincinnatians are at one with Walt Whitman, who once wrote a series of newspaper essays, pleading for the sanctity of old landmarks in Brooklyn. Any suggestion to move the Fountain, Cincinnati's pulsing heart for three-quarters of a century, for some absurd reason such as traffic easement, provokes a roar of protest that halts the proposition in its tracks. When the beautifully classic, columned structure of the centenarian Franklin Bank — whose organization had been absorbed and whose building was vacant and useless — was about to be razed a few years ago, the storm of popular disapproval actually delayed the operation for a while; and when the owners finally set their teeth and brought it down, they were marked in the minds of many citizens forever after as hard-faced vandals.

Longevity and skepticism as to the Oslerian theory, largely because it is daily disproven in Cincinnati, combine to produce long job tenures, 50 to 65 years being not infrequent; job dynasties such as the three-generation Stephan rule at the Zoo, industrial dynasties such as the Lawson four-generation, 134-year-old sheet metal works, commercial dynasties such as the Pioneer dry goods store — with three generations covering its 105-year existence, and with a tranquility often found here, content to remain just a modest-sized but soundly prosperous business—the Arnold 90-year-old bar and grill, with the grandson-proprietor still living in the top floor of the three-story building where it began, and a bathtub in one of the private dining rooms on the second floor, because once that was the family bathroom, and some thread of aversion to change gives it permanence. Even the patrons do not object to it, seeming to regard it as a part of the eternal scheme of the universe.

Such instances do not connote a general inertia or stodginess; for here is a city which has made itself the great bituminous coal market of America —and advertises it by its smoke; which created a huge, 25-building hospital so much better than all others in existence when it was built some years ago that it became a standard for others to aim at; which installed the most powerful radio station on the globe, only to have it quickly surpassed by one in Soviet Russia; which has the largest soap factory and the largest playing card factory in the world, the largest collective output of machine tools of any city on earth, one such plant disputing with another one or two for the honor of being the very biggest; which has built a modernistic railway terminal called by the *National Geographic Magazine* "one of earth's most overwhelming architectural feats." Yet it is a city which has not feared to reject, for its own reasons, great industrial plants which have been offered it.

For a century and more it has been doing things in its own whimsical way. Where else will you find grand opera with full Metropolitan casts presented in summer in a zoological park? And where else would such opera seasons be managed by the head of the local Musicians' union, to the satisfaction of the great majority of a cultured community?

Where else is a suburb like Glendale, where the carillon of the Episcopal Church notices its elder citizens' birthdays by playing their favorite hymns, and announces the birth of a baby in town with a program, beginning with the Long Meter Doxology, then revealing the big news with "Little Jack Horner" if it is a boy, or "Mary Had a Little Lamb" if a girl, continuing with two or three pieces perhaps selected by the parents and concluding with Brahms's Cradle Song? Every birth in the parish is thus announced, and any new arrival in the suburb may be included upon request. Even Catholics ask it and have the customary privilege of selecting the special music, aside from the three regular items. Whimsical requests are indulged; a Naval officer asked for the Navy Hymn, and a young Army veteran wanted "When the Caissons Go Rolling Along," if the baby proved to be a boy. And it was.

Where else will you find a thing comparable to the Good Friday pilgrimage of prayer by thousands of devout Catholics up a two-blocks-long stairway climbing the uppermost reaches of that near-Alp, Mount Adams — whose thickly-populated slope is remindful of a hill town in Italy — to a church on its brow, many of the faithful kneeling on every one of the 150 steps, neither rain nor snow nor sleet nor gloom of night nor umbrella-wrecking gale staying the progress of the penitents up the wind-swept crag; a procession beginning at midnight on Good Friday Eve, and continuing sometimes until the following midnight?

In a city of traditions, one is bound to find many sentimentalists and anniversary-minded folk. A suburban couple married in 1893 spent their wedding night at the Grand Hotel, then one of Cincinnati's greatest. For forty years thereafter, so sweetly did their old-fashioned romance endure, they celebrated every anniversary by registering at the Grand and occupying that self-same room, which the management came to reserve for them as a matter of routine. When the Grand, worn and outmoded, was demolished in 1933, they bought all the furniture of that room and installed it in a room in their own home.

Mrs. Trollope, Cincinnati's chief irritant to this day, was slightly contemptuous in 1828 when she saw business and professional men going to the street markets with basket on arm to bring home meats and vegetables. If she were around today and could visit Findlay Market on a Saturday, she would see much the same spectacle, though they come now mostly in automobiles; and some of those now shopping there are — as in a village in the Old Country—children and grandchildren of men and women who bought from parents and grandparents of the stallkeepers who serve them today. Findlay Market is a remarkable picture of the changelessness of some phases of Cincinnati. The Kunkel family have been making and selling pickles and sauerkraut there for more than half a century; you may see three generations of them at once in their stand, as also in the Kiskers' butcher shop. Ever since 1860 the Busches have been compounding and selling nearly fifty kinds of sausages here, while the Heintzes have been in cheeses for more than fifty years. In fruits and vegetables the fourth generations of Kruecks is now in harness, after more than seventy-five years.

But the most remarkable exhibit of Findlay Market is Mrs. Braun, slender, spectacled, tripping spryly about her butcher stall in white jacket and apron and small head-shawl, wielding knife, saw and cleaver. To look at her, she might be sixty, but she is much more than that for she herself said in 1949 that she and her husband were married and set up their shop there sixty-one years ago; he lived only seven years, and for fifty-four years this indomitable soul has carried on alone — alone, that is, on the first three market days of the week, though she has two men helpers on Saturdays. Her son, a prosperous business man, has tried to take his mother out of that stall, but she refuses to go. "Keeps me out of mischief," is her retort.

At the weekly tea of the staff of the Public Library, when it falls near Christmas Day, you will find the little German cookies of long ago served — *springele, lebkuchen, pfeffernüsse, plättchen, honig-kuchen* — which you may still buy at certain bakeries. The staff is not predominantly German; it's just that Cincinnati atmosphere.

Here is a city which from very early years had two well-defined halves in its character, the cultural side being as influential in shaping its personality as the material. One questions whether there was another city of its size in the nineteenth century that had as many clubs and societies, the majority of them aiming more or less directly at public or personal improvement. A remarkable number of them survive. This intellectual and artistic activity played a part in developing a stabilizing philosophy which, supplementing the balance and solidity of the material side, the numerous small industries and the extensive home ownership, has aided in protecting it from the worst effects of the financial and economic rocketing and plummeting that have cursed national life throughout our history. During the disaster period following the crash of 1929, it had only one bank failure — a minor one, out of which 83 per cent of the depositors' money was saved — and two small bank liquidations which paid the depositors in full; while of its numerous building and loan associations, not one failed, whereas in other states they were falling like grain before the reaper.

Cincinnati has always seemed a little mysterious to outsiders, an apparently inconsistent tangle of past, present and future. Its attitude and its thought-processes are unorthodox from an American point of view. You may count on the fingers of one hand

the American cities which are both progressive and really aware
of their yesterdays, and not only respect but cherish their traditions. Perhaps one reason why it seems old-fashioned is that it
seldom produces a scandal demanding far-flung headlines. It
prefers circumspect conduct on the part of public functionaries,
as certain Symphony Orchestra conductors have learned to their
cost. Once an inquisitive man jocularly mentioned skeletons to
a society dowager. "We haven't any," she twinkled at him. "We
Cincinnatians know each other so well that skeletons can't be
hidden in closets"; hence the more particular care not to have
skeletons. Once one of the nation's greatest whisky producers and
with some of the wildest night life, Cincinnati is now conservative
in its drinking, and the best society frowns upon sousing in youth.
It bans gambling, though not vehemently; you can bet on a race if
you do it demurely enough. Its ultra-sophisticates must cross to
the Kentucky shore for their night-club entertainment, incidentally supporting one such bistro on the hills back of Newport
which is finer than anything in New York. Again the paradox!

Cincinnati might bask — if it were not that she is too accustomed
to such praise to be moved by it — in kind words from many
visitors. It is criticism such as that of Mrs. Trollope and from *Time*
which upsets her poise. John Gunther, traveling *Inside U.S.A.*,
found Cincinnati "packed with charm. . . . Like all the river cities
partly German in origin . . . it has a certain stately and also sleepy
quality, a flavor of detachment, soundness and *je m'en fiche-
ism*. . . . For all its Germanness, it is one of the most truly American
cities in the Nation; it has a higher proportion of native-born
citizens than any city of similar rank."

George Sessions Perry sees Cincinnati as having "the straight-
forward simplicity of the Middle West, along with much of the
grace of its cross-the-river neighbor, the South. . . . Many of its
manners and menus, as well as its maturity of viewpoint, are
European. Its government machinery, to those accustomed to the
old toe-to-toe methods of two-party government, smacks slightly
of Graustark. . . .

"Cincinnati has a certain rhythm that must be sensed if the
city is to be understood. In the *dramatis personae* of American

cities, it is a curious, somehow Dickensian character. It is calm, and has a kind of simple poise which its most circumspect elements describe as serenity, and which its progressive forces call complacency. Though quietly merry, it is somehow deliberate and legalistic, instead of being either intuitive or impulsive. . . ."[1]

In these words are hints of the charm of this dingy, smoky, time-worn city, with its too-narrow but clean downtown streets — where the pedestrian has equal rights with the motorist — its untidy water front, its extensive slums, its kindly, courteous people, as Perry describes them, a blend of Cincinnati's own culture with Kentucky urbanity. There is also its comely situation, on seven hills, as the burghers are fond of saying, though it would puzzle the best topographers to count the seven. Daniel Webster called it "A beautiful example of cooperation between nature and art." Charles Daubeny, an English traveler of 1838, said, "There is nothing in all the Union so fine as its situation, with reference to the noble river which it commands." Lady Emmeline Stuart Wortley thought its location "truly magnificent"; while Harriet Martineau, enraptured by a sunset view from a hilltop in 1835, spoke of it as "that melting beauty which dims the eyes and fills the heart — that magical combination of hill, wood, lawn, river, with a picturesque city steeped in evening sunshine, the impression of which can never be lost nor even communicated."

The setting is an amphitheater, a circle of highland, the rim broken in four places, twice by the Ohio River, once on the south side by the Licking River, once on the north by Mill Creek. Inside the circle lies the business district of Cincinnati — the Basin, as it used to be called — and its Kentucky suburbs, Covington and Newport; whilst flowing along winding streets up to the hill-crests and over them are the more pictorial parts of the city, dappled with foliage. With growth and industrialization, some of the beauty of the picture is gone, though much is left. As a Cincinnati picture-book of long ago said, with typical classic elegance, "Industry invades, and Nature folds her tents. Daphne flees, not from Apollo, but from Vulcan." Travelers of earlier

---

[1] George Sessions Perry, *Cities of America*, (New York: 1947).

days found pleasure in the downtown street views, ending against the hillsides, "so that look up and down the streets whichever way you will," said Captain Frederick Marryat, "your eye reposes upon verdure and forest trees in the distance." "Improvement" has marred many of those pleasant vistas.

Perhaps the chief reason for the visitors' epithet, "Old-fashioned" is the presence in the Basin area of block after block of mid-nineteenth-century (or earlier) residences, packed shoulder to shoulder in unbroken array, yet with their own inner spaciousness, too, with semiclassical dignity of style and air of long-past gracious living, which, though it all may be outmoded, still confers distinction upon them. Sadly enough, many of them are now slum tenements; as for example, the West End, once a vast area of comfortable living, where many costly church and synagogue structures still stand, though long since passed from the original congregations, but which has for years been a poverty-cursed quarter. Here you may see in melancholy decline the house where young Rutherford B. Hayes lived when he was practicing law in Cincinnati, the birthplace and boyhood home of the great engineer, Joseph B. Strauss, builder of the Golden Gate Bridge, the first little Jewish cemetery, and other landmarks. There are some fine doorways, and many interiors with specimens of the elaborate and usually excellent wood-carving which was a fad in the days when all Cincinnati had the creative urge, and when a kit of carving tools was found in even wealthy homes. But these old houses, together with many worse tenements, are marked for destruction in the great slum clearance which has already begun. This will be a cleaner, brighter-faced city when the old-fashioned domiciles are gone, but it will have lost something which not only old citizens, but many tourists will miss.

Probably these buildings, so remindful of some parts of London, helped to endear Cincinnati to the English editor, E. H. Allen, of *The Teacher's World*, who visited it in 1925, and wrote, "It has a distinctive culture of its own, a political history in recent years that, to an Englishman, is romantic, and an educational organization that is not surpassed in America.

"Cincinnati reminded me most of England of all that I saw in

America. . . . To the Briton who is not pro-American . . . I would say, spend a month in Cincinnati, study its history and its schools, meet its leading citizens, and prepare to revise your opinion of one American city, anyway."

Another British journalist and author, Beverly Nichols, in his book, *The Star-Spangled Manner*, said that the Cincinnati businessmen whom he met "seemed more inclined to talk about modern English poetry than business; and when they did talk about business, they confined themselves to problems of international finance, which they discussed with vision and generosity . . . I have a particular affection for Cincinnati. I should like to call it an ugly city with a great soul, were not that phrase unpleasantly reminiscent of the style of the late Ella Wheeler Wilcox. It is, however, in spite of its grim energy, a city of deep and genuine culture."

As to discussing English poetry, Mr. Nichols must have met some exceptional businessmen in Cincinnati — which isn't saying that they aren't there. But the stranger will as a rule, one thinks, be more apt to meet businessmen and society women who will discuss with him the relative merits of Beethoven and Brahms and Tschaikovsky, or Wagner and Verdi and Puccini. For music is still the favorite art of Cincinnati; perhaps that is why it has retained so noticeable a measure of serenity.

CHAPTER II

Queen City of the West

FREDERICK JACKSON TURNER, author of *The Frontier in American History*, considers the "Great West" a more pivotal area in our history than the Atlantic Coast. Our most valuable contribution, he says, to "the history of the human spirit" has been our extension of the frontier into new regions and "in creating peaceful societies with new ideals" in the vast and varying wildernesses. Elsewhere he remarks that the influence of the frontier developed a pervasive "idealism," individual character and a "composite" nationality, all of which proves to be true in the case of young Cincinnati. These played prominent parts in its making, but the reasons for its peculiar personality and its rapid development into an outstanding cultural center are more complex.

As early as 1780, General William Lytle, a Pennsylvanian, fought Indians on what would now be the Cincinnati steamboat landing, and later came back to build a home a stone's throw away, and thus plant a famous name in the city's annals. The first construction on the site, however, was the little blockhouse erected by General George Rogers Clark in that same year and twice destroyed before the Pennsylvanian trader, Benjamin Stites, barging down the Ohio with hordes of other pioneers in the middle 1780's, first looked upon the land between the Great and Little Miami rivers with an eye that saw possibilities there. It was still untouched, most of the settlers so far preferring Kentucky. Returning East, Stites's talk spurred a New Jersey war veteran and former member of the Continental Congress, John Cleves Symmes, to come out and view the prospect o'er. Symmes wanted to patent all the land between the two Miamis, but finally compromised on 311,682 acres, all he could pay for.

Stites, as his associate, chose a spot near where the Little Miami empties into the Ohio, east of the present business center, and in 1788 christened his new-born settlement Columbia — now a Cincinnati suburb. Symmes himself went more than twenty miles downstream, almost to the mouth of the Great Miami, and named his townsite North Bend. His other associated adventurer, Matthias Denman, in partnership with two Kentuckians, Robert Patterson and John Filson, a Lexington schoolteacher, showed the best judgment of all by selecting 740 acres in the natural amphitheatre, "the Basin," facing the river between Columbia and North Bend, though nearer the former. That was a day or two after Christmas, 1788, and from that date Cincinnati reckons its existence, though the pioneers had purchased the land some months before.

It was a lovely, lonely domain then, thickly cloaked with forest, fat with sustenance — deer, bear, buffalo, turkeys, grouse, quail, pigeons, squirrels, rabbits, fish, bees laboring to provide the settler with honey, but with an occasional wolf or cougar, too, or worse still, an Indian, stealing through the coverts. The trees were thronged with birds, some now deplorably extinct — gorgeous green-and-gold parrakeets and beautiful passenger pigeons, most graceful of winged creatures, flying in incredible flocks often a hundred miles and more in length, but strangely vanishing from earth a century later.

Filson, the amateur surveyor, who was to plan the new city, had christened it before its settlement. As the spot was directly opposite the mouth of the little Licking River, he patched together L for Licking, the Latin *os* for mouth, *anti* meaning opposite, and, dropping into French, *ville* for city, though the compound was to be read in reverse — "city opposite the mouth of Licking" — in short, Losantiville. Then Filson vanished forever in the woods one day — the Indians could probably have explained that — and Israel Ludlow was engaged to survey the new town, his map covering only a small part of the present business district. He and his successors laid it out rectangularly for the most part, but with a fascinating number of jogs and offsets and little one-, two- and three-block-long streets sprinkled in among the major ones,

[22]

of all shades of narrowness, down to mere alleys, but even they edged with midget sidewalks. Oddly enough, a number of these minor lanes bear the names of prominent early citizens — Gano, Ludlow, Yeatman, L'Hommedieu, Longworth — which last-named finally became so notorious that it had to be changed.

The settlement went through the usual pioneer stages — logging, grubbing, cabin-building, planting, hunting, trapping, trading, spinning, weaving, making leather and homespun clothing, with a hoedown or a dash of Indian fighting now and then for spice. One man started a ferry across the Ohio, and two others opened a river-front tavern. When, in August, 1789, a major and a detachment of troops came down-river to build a fort in the Miami country, Losantiville was chosen as the most strategic location, and a death-blow was dealt to the ambitions of Columbia and North Bend. Fort Washington, a high stockade connecting five blockhouses and enclosing barracks and storehouses, was built, and exactly a year after the first settlement, General Josiah Harmar, arrived with 300 men, the fort's garrison. A few days later, General Arthur St. Clair, Governor of the Northwest Territory, appeared, laden with much prestige as an officer of the Revolution and later President of Congress. At a dinner given in his honor on January 4th, 1790, he announced a change in the name of the settlement. One version which some more rugged oldsters like, is that he had already changed it — and vigorously — when he stepped ashore from the flatboat. "Losantiville!" he boomed. "What an awful name! God damn it, call it Cincinnati!" honoring the Society of the Cincinnati, a commemorative organization of Revolutionary officers, of which he was a member.

If John Cleves Symmes did not originate the new name, he seemingly tried to claim credit for it. In a letter to a friend in New Jersey in 1791, he requested, "I beg, Sir, you will inquire of the literati in Jersey whether Cincinnata or Cincinnati be most proper. The design I had in giving that name was in honor of the Order of Cincinnati, and to denote the chief place of their residence; and so far as my little acquaintance with cases and genders extends, I think the name of a town should terminate in the feminine gender where it is not perfectly neuter. . . . I have frequent combats in this country on this subject, because most men spell it with ti, when I always do with ta." Does one find here the reason why so large a portion of its citizens – and some others, too – call it Cincinnata to this day? Charles Mackay, a British tourist of the 1850's, declared that "Americans generally pronounce the name of the city 'Sinsnahta.' "

Symmes, who soon became a territorial judge, may have been goaded into trying to steal credit from St. Clair by his troubles with that gentleman, whom the chronicler Charles Cist fifty years later compared to Cromwell and Napoleon for arrogance. The military and civil powers clashed frequently. Once when a young non-com named William Henry Harrison mistakenly punished a discharged soldier, a constable sent to arrest him was knocked sprawling by him with a cane. Young Harrison then appeared before a civil court and was given 24 hours' "imprisonment" at McHenry's Tavern. And there was William McMillan – first justice of the peace in the settlement and performer in 1790 of the first marriage ceremony – who was once ordered under arrest by the fort commandant, a sergeant and three men being sent to take him. The size of the squad was a hint of the high respect entertained for this big, two-fisted 'squire, who, nevertheless, was an intellectual and educated man, and later a territorial delegate to Congress. But even that small army wasn't enough, for McMillan knocked the sergeant and one man cold and put the other two soldiers to flight, badly battered.

The next two or three years were the hardest, what with Harmar and then St. Clair being disastrously routed by the Indians, with the loss of many Cincinnati citizens in battle. Practically all of the new-formed county – christened Hamilton – was put under martial law. Groups of settlers outside Cincinnati huddled together and built stockades and blockhouses which they called "stations," and which served as outposts for Fort Washington. Inside the fort, men sat in Presbyterian meeting, the first religious congregation, with rifles between their knees; and farmers tilled the fields with guns slung on their backs. St. Clair's defeat in 1791 was the worst disaster the territory had yet known. Many families who had come to Cincinnati the year before hurried away to Kentucky, and settlement in the Miami country suffered a set-back, from which it recovered slowly, even after General Anthony Wayne drubbed the Indians so soundly in 1794 that for Cincinnati the red menace was practically eliminated. The village had grown stubbornly despite hazards; births had begun in 1790, with local history unable to decide whether William Moody or David Cummins came first. When Moody died in 1879, he had seen the little clutch of cabins upon which he first opened his eyes grow to a city of 250,000.

In 1793 two great concomitants of civilization, a newspaper and a jail, appeared, though the jail was mostly for delinquent debtors rather than for misdemeanants; in fact, if a real robber or murderer had matriculated there, the debtor-prisoners might have refused to remain; for the mildness of their offense against society was tacitly recognized by the fact that they were not strictly incarcerated, but wandered around town during the day, only returning to be locked up at night, or "on the approach of the Sheriff," says Cist, "scampering home in a great fright, like so many rabbits to their holes." As for the tiny, four-page newspaper, *The Centinel of the Northwestern Territory*, it survived three years, and was succeeded by the *Freeman's Journal* ("Free, but not Licentious"), and in turn by the *Western Spy*, which was launched May 28th, 1799 and saw its publisher in prison for debt before Christmas, appealing to his subscribers to pay up, which explains why he was in his uneasy plight.

Cincinnati was briefly the capital of the Northwest Territory in 1795 — at least, the Legislature met there, but seems to have caused no great stir. A rough census taken that year indicated a population of about 500, living in 94 log and 10 frame houses. Already the lower streets had had a flood or two, and visitors from outside were predicting that the river would sooner or later sweep away the whole town. Plagues of squirrels, caterpillars and locusts or grasshoppers had in turn tested the community's patience and piety. Judge Jacob Burnet, one of the scholarly early comers who helped to give Cincinnati its tone, has left us a sprightly picture of the infant thorp. There was a swamp on the lowest bench above the river, crowded to suffocation with mosquitoes and filling the colony with malaria. Burnet and fourteen or fifteen others lay ill in a large room at the same time, "giving it the appearance of a public hospital." From a long, weedy pond on the upper level, "frogs serenaded us from Spring to Fall."

In 1799 the Fourth of July was celebrated for the first time, the first real factory, a pottery, was started, the First Presbyterian congregation completed the village's first little church, which had been seven years in the building, and a coming famous name appeared when the Territorial Legislature chose William Henry Harrison, Esq., of North Bend, late of Virginia, Symmes's son-in-law, to represent the Territory in Congress. The village was incorporated in 1802 and elected a town council and a president, the first incumbent being its first and only German citizen so far, Major David Ziegler, who had fought the Indians valiantly in its defense. Among other presidents during the ensuing thirteen years were Martin Baum, the town's first rich man. Judge Burnet recalled that for several years after his arrival in 1796, "party spirit was scarcely known in the Territory," a not uncommon phenomenon on the frontier, where the citizens were too busy at getting an economic foothold to trouble their heads with politics. The excitement of the strenuous contest of 1800 between Jefferson and Adams for the Presidency, says Burnet, "was not felt in the Territory." There were, however, enough Republicans (Democrats) in town to celebrate Jefferson's victory with a dinner at Menessier's Hotel, with "Citizen" John Cleves Symmes (a tribute to Jefferson's French Revolutionary ardor) in the chair. But on the whole, the doings of the National Government up to 1800 were not greatly important to young Cincinnati, some of whose citizens would have been willing to see the town and adjacent territory set up in business for itself.

The village grew but slowly in another decade, its population in 1805 being only 960. Thomas Ashe, an Englishman who visited it in the following year, declared that some of its merchants, making exorbitant profits, had already attained easy circumstances; but, "In general, the people of Cincinnati . . . are orderly, decent, sociable, liberal and unassuming, and were I compelled to live in the Western country, I would give them a decided preference."

A Philadelphian named Cuming who was here in 1808, saw many brick houses, generally well-built and painted with the neatness "so conspicuous in Connecticut and New Jersey." He was particularly struck with the handsome dwelling of Judge Burnet, who, at 38, had already written Ohio's first State constitution and acquired a competence in the law.

Growth continued slow until after the first crude steamboat came splashing down the river from Pittsburgh in 1811, almost simultaneously with General Harrison's crushing defeat of the Indians at Tippecanoe; a significant coincidence, for both events were stimuli to Cincinnati. They ushered in a new era for the city, during which it became the nation's greatest river port, the center of the midwestern steamboat trade, which in turn made it industrially and commercially great. Even by ark and flatboat, it had been trading with Natchez and New Orleans, sending products down at a snail's gait but with not too much difficulty, though the toil of bringing cotton and sugar and coffee back upstream by hand propulsion was strenuous and cruel beyond today's comprehension. Now, with steam, the voyage seemed comparatively easy, even though the rapids at Louisville were still a hazard and often impassable — until 1830, when a canal bypassed them. But Cincinnati did not immediately recognize the importance of steam; when in 1815, four years after the first steam voyage, Thomas H. Bosson, a commission merchant, planned to build a steamboat primarily for his own use, friends tried to dissuade him, assuring him that he would lose the shirt off his back. But the success of his boat, the *Vesta*, convinced the doubters, boatbuilding began, and the wheels of progress hummed more and more swiftly. Cincinnati's city's population was then estimated at 6,000, and it began calling itself a city, the chief executive, known as "Mayor and President," being William Corry. In 1819, with a population of 10,823, it was really incorporated as a city, the first Mayor, who served eleven years, being Isaac G. Burnet, brother of the Judge.

Morris Birkbeck, another tourist, paused here in 1817 to wonder at the miracle of growth and the driving energy behind it. Serenity had not appeared; Cincinnatians were on the make. "Every consideration of health and enjoyment yields to news of mercantile convenience," said he; "the hundreds of commodious, well-finished brick houses, the spacious and busy markets, the substantial public buildings, the thousands of well-dressed, industrious inhabitants, the numerous wagons and drays, the carriages of elegant females, the shoals of craft on the river, the busy air prevailing everywhere, houses building, boats building, paving and leveling streets, the numbers of country people coming and going, with the spacious taverns crowded with travellers from a distance.

"All this is so much more than I could comprehend from a description of a new town, just risen from the woods, that I despair of conveying an adequate idea of it to my English friends. It is enchantment, and liberty is the fair enchantress."[1]

This busy shipping and industrial town, with the odor of leaf-mold still upon it, was a precocious child, an infant Hercules, retaining much of its rustic atmosphere and innocence. In that very year 1817, when a stranger stood amazed by its tumult and dynamism, when its population must have been at least 8,000, it was just beginning to plan an inadequate waterworks, it had no daily newspaper — nor did have until long afterwards — and it was then installing its first paid — one cannot say professional — police force. During the first fifteen years of its existence, no law save that of the county protected it. All able-bodied citizens were members of the night watch, they being told off to serve in squads in their turn, to trudge about the streets, intoning mournfully at intervals, "Twelve o'clock and all's well!" "Four o'clock, and a cold, sleety morning." Why it was thought that citizens wished to be awakened from sleep to hear about the weather it is difficult to conceive. When a group met at the watch house at 8 P.M. to elect one of their number as captain for the night, the scene may at times have been faintly reminiscent of Dogberry and his sturdy fellows, back in old Messina. Not until 1817 were a marshal and six men employed at very modest wages, for night duty only; but they had no uniforms or even badges.

[1] Morris Birkbeck, *Notes on a Journey in America*, etc., (London, 1818).

We wish we knew what the town looked like in those days, but the only picture we have, a quaint woodcut entitled "Cincinnati in 1810," doesn't help us. It represents a group of sixty or seventy stiff, high-shouldered houses, as rigid and alike as a parcel of new bricks stood on end, apparently a "planned" affair created by Government or the Titanic Insurance Company and not yet ready for occupancy, for there is not a sign of life, human or animal, anywhere, save for two plug-hatted gentlemen on an "ark" headed down-river, one almost hidden in the hull, the other, half as long as the boat, standing with one hand resting casually on the steering oar. You would never suspect that about that time Cincinnati was organizing its Fire Department — one volunteer company, with a hand-pumping engine, replacing the every-man-a-fireman-with-a-leather-bucket-in-the-house regime of twenty years past.

Some handsome mansions were being erected during that era, a few of which still remain in city and suburbs. Among them are the Mount Auburn home, built in 1819, of Gorham A. Worth, who was in Cincinnati four years as director of the Branch Bank of the United States; that of Martin Baum, now one of the glories of the city as the Taft Museum, and that of David Kilgour, on a lower shoulder of Mount Adams, where Worth dined one evening and later raved, "Talk to me of the backwoods — these people live in style of princes! The costly dinner service — the splendid cut glass — the rich wines — the sumptuous dinner itself." It was gossiped that once after a dinner at Mr. Kilgour's, Governor St. Clair wandered into the river and was fished out barely in time.

At the very time when Birkbeck was awed by its bustle, Cincinnati should by all the rules have been stagnant, for it was in the midst of a financial stringency. The War of 1812 was fought too far away to disturb its peace, though some of its citizens served and even died in it, and General Harrison went on to new glory at Fort Meigs and the Thames. The young city could not manufacture ordnance yet, for there was not an iron-working shop in town. But now it got into its stride, and by 1826 there were nine small foundries, machine and engine-building plants. It went right on growing, despite an after-war depression.

Five banks had sprung up in the town within a few years. Alsatian-born Martin Baum, merchant and manufacturer, had organized the Miami Exporting Company in 1803, to do banking and down-river trading. Its transportation vehicle was a flatboat which plied between Cincinnati and New Orleans, taking six months for the round trip. It gave up the trading in 1807 and became a bank only, with Baum as president and Reverend Oliver M. Spencer—a three-year captive among the Indians in boyhood—as cashier. The other four banks included a branch of the Bank of the United States, Old Hickory's pet hate, opened here in 1817, with Judge Burnet appointed as president and Gorham Worth sent out by the home office to be cashier. Finance in general became shaky shortly afterward, and all the city's banks went through a process of liquidation. A Government replacement of the United States Bank gave the citizens the only banking facilities they had for a long time.

During this purgation period, Cincinnati had its first riot, and that a very mild one, directed against the Miami Exporting Company. A "mob" formed uptown and marched in procession down Main Street, escorting a dray on which was a coffin labeled, "Miami Bank no more," but dispersed when Mayor Isaac Burnet read the Riot Act, to which it listened respectfully.

Money troubles did not slow up the growth of the town; on the contrary, it grew faster than ever. Between 1824 and 1829 the population doubled — 12,000 to 24,000. There was a housing shortage. Hotels were becoming "elegant," as were prosperous men's new residences, but hogs and chickens still roamed the streets, as they had always done in American cities. The best in food and wines, the latest in fashions from the East was demanded, but the family cow was still driven from pasture to many elegant homes in the Basin to be milked. For men, short hair and long trousers had come in with President Jefferson, but some men such as Rev. James Kemper, Judge Burnet, Dr. Goforth and the Ganos, strode about the up-to-date city in knee breeches and braided hair for years thereafter, and the Doctor carried a tall cane to the last.

House-numbering was long delayed. You read in a directory in the 1830's such items as these, "b" standing for "between" and "h" for home:

> Groesbeck, John H., pork merchant, Canal b Main and Syc., h 4th
> b Syc and Broadway.
> Werk, Michael, tallow chandler, Vine b Court and Canal, bds at
> P. Glendinning's.
> West, George, brewer above the bridge. (what bridge?)
> Whann, Mrs. Charlotte, alley b New Market and 9th, Race and Elm

House-numbering was ordered by the Council in 1842 and a Mr. Gell authorized to attend to it, each householder to pay him 25 cents for the job. But so many rugged individualists balked at this that Mr. Gell gave up in disgust. A few years later it was decreed again, but with the same result. Finally in 1850, editors began to demand that the city do it at its own expense, and this was eventually accomplished.

A fresh impetus was given to the city when the Ohio Canal system was promoted by one of Cincinnati's own citizens, Judge and Governor Ethan Allen Brown. Another Cincinnatian, Micajah Williams, was one of the two commissioners who built the canals. Construction began at the south end of the Miami & Erie, one of the two main waterways, and by 1828-29 boats were jogging from Cincinnati up towards Middletown and Dayton, eventually entering Toledo in 1845. Coming down Mill Creek Valley, the canal's course bent slightly eastward as it entered the Basin, threaded the middle of Plum Street southward to Eleventh, turned eastward there, where it became known as "the Rhine," and finally swerved down Deer Creek, along the foot of the eastern hills, to the river, developing a new industrial area on the East Side.

William Bullock, an Englishman who came up from New Orleans in 1827, was enchanted with Cincinnati. At the Cincinnati Hotel on Front Street, "Colonel" Andrew Mack, the proprietor, after his usual custom, introduced Bullock in the lobby to all the other guests. No one was permitted to be lonely in the Colonel's hostelry. "In no part of the old Continent that I have visited," exclaimed the amazed Bullock, "are strangers treated with more attention, politeness and respect than in Cincinnati." Colonel Mack, in short, gave the whole city a pleasant reputation. And at table, "The dinner was such that an epicure from whatever part of the world. . .would have little cause to complain, as in no part of my travels have I seen a table spread with more profusion or better served." He observed that little wine was drunk at the noon dinner, there being many businessmen among the diners, who returned to their stores or offices, "with a better relish for business than is usually found after the enjoyment of the bottle."

A shrewd Frenchman, Michel Chevalier, observed in 1835 that "What makes the progress of Cincinnati more surprising is that the city is the daughter of its own works." Eastern cities had grown slowly from colonial settlements, through domestic commerce and the shipping trade, or had been built to order by capitalists of Boston and New York. Cincinnati had lifted itself by its own bootstraps, and "almost wholly without foreign aid, by its inhabitants, who have for the most part arrived on the spot poor. The founders of Cincinnati brought nothing with them but sharp-sighted, wakeful, untiring industry. . . .They seem to have chosen Franklin for their patron saint, and Poor Richard's Maxims as a fifth gospel." [2]

Here was the soundest of analyses for Cincinnati's rapid rise to eminence. As Chevalier said further, its citizens labored to make it "the great interior mart of the West"; to produce everything that a new country would need or want, and all in the plain, economical patterns which it could afford. "The prosperity of Cincinnati therefore rests upon the sure basis of the prosperity of the West"; and his "West" included the lower Mississippi Valley as well, which meant that Cincinnati was the supply depot for the whole interior of the country. The distance and transportation difficulties from Eastern industrial centers contributed to Cincinnati's domination, and aided in developing its mid-nineteenth century steamboat trade. Remote new settlements such as St. Paul, Minneapolis and Omaha were born, and steamboats from Cincinnati

[2] *Society, Manners and Politics in the United States*, Boston, 1839.

began serving them. Its boats then ran up small rivers—de Tocqueville counted 57 of them — where no steam traffic has been seen in the past sixty or eighty years. Louisiana, Arkansas and Mississippi spoke of their Cincinnati furniture, melodeons, soap and starch. Their farmers were called from their Cincinnati ploughs in the fields on week-days and everybody to church on Sundays by Cincinnati bells. That lacy ironwork on the porticos of old houses in New Orleans, Natchez, Vicksburg, even Memphis, which legend, especially on the lower river, claims all came from France — you would be surprised to hear how much of it was made in Cincinnati. Bigger things, too; in 1835 alone there were built in Cincinnati 100 steam engines, 240 cotton gins, 20 sugar mills (some even going to Cuba) and 22 steamboats. The great iron area up-river around Ironton was being developed, and Cincinnati was using much of its output. Horace Greeley thought he saw the reasons for all this; "delightful climate," unequalled transportation facilities, "enterprising and energetic population," and finally, "I doubt if there is another spot on the globe where food, fuel, cotton, iron, with everything else, can be concentrated so cheaply. . .as here."

Who first began calling Cincinnati the Queen City of the West and when, we may never know. But it was before 1834, as we learn from a tourist named Arfwedson who wrote in that year that "Cincinnati is never mentioned in America without the addition of such surnames as 'The Wonderful,' 'The Western Queen,' etc. Flattering epithets of this kind are generally exaggerated . . . but in this instance they were justified. Cincinnati is in every respect an extraordinary city."[3] Charles Fenno Hoffman, New York litterateur, remarked that on the score of beauty alone, no other mid-western city could "dispute with Cincinnati her title of 'Queen of the West.'" In 1835 Miss Martineau said, "For more reasons than one, I should prefer Cincinnati as a residence to any other large city of the United States. Of these reasons, not the least is that the 'Queen of the West' is enthroned in a region of

[3] C. D. Arfwedson, *The United States and Canada in 1832, 1833 and 1834*, (London, 1834).

wonderful and inexhaustible beauty." She was one of at least three or four Britons who admitted that if they were called upon to transfer their place of abode to the United States — "which God forbid!" hastily amended one — they would prefer this young, far inland city above all other locations.

And yet Cincinnati was not what you would call snooty with it all; she did not look down her nose at less fortunate communities. The *Gazette* in 1840 spoke quite kindly of St. Louis, "this busy, go-ahead little city with its 16,469 inhabtants." Live and let live!

CHAPTER III

Cosmopolis

An intriguing regional and ethnic blend was this callow super-town; a hybrid which, settling down to become more self-contained as the years passed, and thereafter to absorb less blood from foreign strains than most big communities, has grown into the most American of America's larger cities. The earlier city directories were quite chatty on this subject. The first one, that of 1819, remarks that, "The greater part of the population are from the middle and northern States. We have, however, many foreigners among us, and it is not uncommon to hear three or four different languages spoken in the streets at the same time.

"A society so compounded can have but few of those provincial traits of character which are so visible in older settlements. Having been bred and educated under different habits and modes of thinking, every individual is obliged to sacrifice to the general opinion many of his prejudices and local peculiarities, and to adopt a more liberal mode of acting and thinking." A slight optimism in this respect is understandable, but there were indeed, very early in the city's history, some citizens who displayed a breadth of mind not usually accredited to pioneers. In what later came to be known as Cumminsville, James C. Ludlow, son of Israel Ludlow, erected a House of Free Discussion — it still stands — for the express purpose of canvassing controversial subjects publicly. It was long used by both Old Light and New Light Presbyterians, Baptists and Disciples as a meeting house. When antislavery students seceded from Lane Theological Seminary, they fulminated here.

There was cooperation among creeds in the 1830's, when James Handasyde Perkins was city missionary and united all of them, Protestant and Catholic, in the "Relief Union," a sort of early form of community chest. Darker times for tolerance were in the decades ahead, but even when intolerance was at its worst in mid-century, it was never as virulent here as in Eastern cities. It even produced examples of what some citizens considered radical liberalism, when Spring Grove Cemetery permitted Davis B. Lawlor, a prosperous businessman and agnostic, to top his family tomb with the head of a Sphinx, expressing his conviction as to the unknowableness of the future, in sharp contrast with the implicit faith expressed on other stones.

The compilers of early directories listing only business and professional men and women and those gainfully employed, for several years asked everyone mentioned where he or she was born. Of course most women and all children were omitted, and some persons overlooked under the primitive methods then employed. Poring through the little volume for 1825, containing — as the present writer counts them — 2,411 names, the "breakdown," in modern business jargon, is astonishing. The birthplace of 40 persons is not given. Out of the 2,411, it is not surprising to find only 44 adults who were born in the new community of Ohio. The great bulk of the immigrants, 1,363 in all, were natives of the States east of Ohio; 386 from Pennsylvania, 328 from New Jersey, 225 from New York, 178 from Massachusetts, 125 from Connecticut; 44 from Vermont, 30 from New Hampshire, 29 from Maine and 18 from Rhode Island. Maryland had sent 201, Virginia 124 and Kentucky so far only 43, though it soon began to send many more, as the result of its own private depression, which came on shortly afterward. There were a few scattering contributions from other States to southward, and even two each from Michigan and Indiana.

But the remarkable thing was the foreign contingent — 533 in number, or considerably more than one-fifth of the population. There were 210 from England, 166 from Ireland, 51 from Germany, 40 from Scotland, 20 from Wales, 19 from France, 15 from Switzerland, 3 from Canada, 2 each from Prussia (then an independent kingdom) and Portugal and one each from Austria, Holland, Sweden, Denmark and Santo Domingo. The great German immigration had not yet begun. Some of Teutonic blood were already present, engaged mostly in viniculture and winemaking. Their numbers increased in crescendo until the revolutionary upheaval of 1848, when Germans crossed the ocean in great numbers and did much towards giving Cincinnati its distinctive character.

A hasty survey of those who founded and built up great industrial and mercantile concerns or rose to the top of the professions in Cincinnati in the nineteenth century seems to indicate that not one of them came from among the 44 Ohio-born citizens catalogued in the 1825 directory. The enterprises of the city which became for a time the cynosure of the continent were promoted and nurtured almost entirely by immigrants — from outside Ohio, that is, though not all from foreign countries. But as one cons the list, it seems that actually a majority of the greater businesses were the creations of men born in Europe, none of whom were well-to-do, and most of whom came with practically no assets.

Why did so many of them outstrip so many of the native-born? One theory is that they were especially favored in that they had to fight so much harder for success than the Americans. Arriving here, many of them, with little but the clothes they stood in, perhaps unable to speak, read or write the English language, they would seem to have been insurmountably handicapped. But coming from lands of restricted opportunity to middle-Western America, where the opportunities seemed limitless, the determination of these indomitable spirits was stimulated and strengthened by difficulties, even as hammering toughens iron.

Yet all this does not mean that there were not many American-born men, from one to several generations away from the immigrant, who wrought worthily and with success; such men as John Shillito, merchant prince, Charles McMicken, trader and father of Cincinnati's university, the Lytles, the Neaves, Franklin Alter, Philip Hinkle, all Pennsylvania-born; Nicholas Longworth, realty capitalist; Miles Greenwood, machinery manufacturer, Jacob Strader, steamboat and rail magnate, Dr. Daniel Drake, the Burnets and the variously active Ganos, all from New Jersey; the mercantile and professional Groesbecks, Benjamin Eggleston and Louis Van Antwerp, one of the founders of the American Book Company, these from upstate New York; from Connecticut,

Judge and Governor George Hoadly and Henry Probasco, whose fountain has forever immortalized him in Cincinnati; Thomas D. Carneal, merchant capitalist, from Kentucky; Jared A. Fay of New Hampshire, machine tool builder, John Simpkinson, millionaire shoe merchant and public benefactor; Peter Neff, born in Maryland of Swiss ancestry; Salmon P. Chase of New Hampshire, well known to history as Senator, Governor, Secretary of the Treasury and Chief Justice of the United States Supreme Court; Judge Alpohnso Taft from Vermont; Judge Bellamy Storer from Maine; Stanley Matthews, United States Supreme Court Justice, of Virginian parentage; the Virginia-Kentucky Andersons; Drausin Wulsin, born in New Orleans of French stock — the list might go on much further.

But in no city of the country was so vast a contribution made to the upbuilding of business and industry by European immigrants as in Cincinnati. None of their enterprises was a "promotion," bursting into full production upon other people's money. Nine-tenths of them began as one-man businesses, whose pinched circumstances bred a wholesome caution. Nearly all of these concerns founded before the financial tempest of 1837 weathered it; in fact, the city itself wasn't too hard hit.

One of the earliest merchants in Cincinnati was John Bartle, a Frenchman. David and John Kilgour, who had more cash than most immigrants, came from England to launch a mercantile business and a dynasty which wrought largely in street railroads, telephones and banking. Thomas Emery arrived from England to embark in candles and lard oil, and so to found one of Cincinnati's greatest fortunes. William Procter, born in England, and James Gamble, a product of the Old Sod, came to Cincinnati and started each his own little candle factory; they married sisters, amalgamated their small operations in 1837, and so bred the germ of the world's mightiest soap caldrons, with ramifications. Michael Werk of Alsace and Andrew Jergens of Germany also built big manufactories of soap and allied products.

John Brunswick of Switzerland and Julius Balke of Westphalia created here the world's biggest billiard-table factory. Germany also contributed the Marmets, who were among the nation's largest coal operators in the nineteenth century, Frederick Lunkenheimer and the Deckebachs, great copper, brass and bronze founders, the Fechheimers, the Seasongoods, Abraham Friedlander, Philip Heidelbach and others who helped to make Cincinnati in the late century the nation's greatest men's clothing producer. Of Germanic blood also were Herman Urban of Baden, safe builder, Dietrich Gruen, Swiss watchmaker, Andrew Erkenbrecher, whose starch has dignified billions of American shirts, Ferdinand Jelke in provisions, and Charles H. Duhme and Clemens Oskamp, famed jewelers and silversmiths. Bavaria sent John C. Roth, large-scale pork-packer, Balthasar Roth, who made the St. Nicholas Hotel and its cuisine world-famous, the Freibergs, whose names bulked large in distilling and tanning, and more than half of the owners of the score of big breweries which dotted the nineteenth-century landscape. One lone Scotsman was the flaw in the Teutonic monopoly of brewing.

Young Rudolph Wurlitzer, Saxon-born, descendant of a family of Viennese instrument makers, came to Cincinnati with little but a fiddle under his arm, to found a noted musical instrument house. Charles and Maximilian Fleischmann, whose distillery introduced fresh compressed yeast to America and made it big business, were from Budapest. Alexander McDonald, oil and coal baron, and Robert Laidlaw, pump manufacturer and philanthropist, were Scotchborn. Canada sent Joseph T. Carew, partner in the city's biggest clothing store and capitalist, and Levi A. Ault, of Ault & Wiborg, whose printing ink factory was long the world's biggest. From England came William Powell and William Lodge, who founded great tool, valve and machine-building businesses, and Thomas Lawson, who in 1816 started in a small way the sheet metal plant which is now the city's oldest business under the most persistent family ownership, already covering four generations.

From 1825-30 onward, the German immigration outstripped all others, with the Irish in second place, though far behind the German. Ireland produced such stalwarts as David Sinton, iron manufacturer, capitalist and philanthropist, Thomas P. Egan (wood-working machinery), James Heekin, at first in coffee and spices, then builder of one of the biggest of tin can companies;

Robert Mitchell, who established an enormous furniture factory; Thomas Sherlock, steamboat magnate; Robert J. Morgan, an ancestor of the world's biggest playing card factory, Henry and Samuel Pogue, great dry goods merchants, and many more.

Europe also gave Cincinnati some noted professional men and women — editors, publicists, teachers, musicians, scientists, jurists, divines and diplomats. There were many immigrants from across the ocean who, though they did not found great businesses or make large contributions to science or the arts, yet became decent and useful citizens; but unfortunately, there were other phases of the immigration picture of those days which tinged several decades of the city's life with distrust and bitterness. Certain European governments, finding that immigration was unrestricted here, emptied their poorhouses and jails on our shores. Naturally, our coast cities received the heaviest sediment of this unfit immigration, but some of it — and any quantity was too much — filtered through to Cincinnati, lured by its reputation as a place where you could make money just by turning your hand over. Families were found sitting at the wharfside, just off a steamboat — and the wonder was how they had gotten that far — absolutely penniless, with not the slightest idea what to do next, trusting to Providence and a humane citizenry to chart their future and then carry out the design. Many became public charges upon the moment of their arrival; the county poorhouse records during the 1840's show always more foreign-born than native-born among the inmates, sometimes twice or more than twice as many.

If the head of the family found work which paid him a pittance — and despite the rapid growth of industry, the influx of pauper labor kept wages low — he and his household had nowhere to live save in the slums which were rapidly developing, and where there were other characters, vicious ones who saw to it that Cincinnati began to have a criminal history. These latter were mostly the riffraff of the river, toughest of the tough. As the flatboat was slowly displaced by the steamboat, its professional class, including notorious bullies like the legendary Mike Fink and even worse criminals, had nowhere to go but into the service of steam, carrying their manners with them. There they became deck hands, dock laborers, stokers, gamblers, dock and warehouse thieves, though occasionally one of the abler ones rose to the dignity of mate.

There was a Negro slum, "Blacktown," it was popularly called, of most of whose inhabitants the worst that could be said was that they were freedmen and runaways, for just across the river was slave territory. But it had its delinquents, too, and it came to be pocked with the lowest of whites, men and women of all shades of color cohabiting.

There was one race of people, some of whom might be poor when they arrived, but who were almost never objects of charity and whose religion gave Cincinnatians little concern — namely, the Jews. The first of them to arrive in Cincinnati was Joseph Jonas, a watchmaker, who came from England in 1817. Their numbers increased, and the first Jewish service in the Northwest Territory was held here in 1819. Of those who came in the first half century, all were English-born until near 1830; then the German contingent began coming, with a sprinkling of Dutch Jews — LeJeunes, DeJongs, Workums and others. The first synagogue was organized by men who spoke English like Englishmen, the second by the German contingent. Descendants of these old stocks are in Cincinnati to this day, and are pillars of the community.

From the beginning, there seemed little or no prejudice; Jew and Gentile mingled harmoniously in business, benevolence and politics. Jonas, the first comer, was sometimes called the Father of Democracy in Cincinnati; for in his jewelry store, especially during the campaign of 1828, a group of Jacksonians, mostly Gentiles, met frequently to agree with each other, a sort of unorganized club which became known as "Jonas, Cist & Company." It was even celebrated in verse by a local rimester. When President William Henry Harrison died in 1841, crape was hung on Jewish doors for thirty days, resolutions of sorrow were offered in the synagogues and his name was inserted in the prayers for the dead.

Isidor Wise, asked to write the Jewish chapter in Charles Frederick Gross's *Cincinnati, the Queen City, 1788-1912,* began, "Cincinnati is the pioneer city of the West; so far as the Jews are concerned, she is the pioneer city of the world. To the long-suffering children of Israel she is indeed the 'Queen City,' and so will ever remain, though she lose her commercial preeminence ten times over. . . . How many of her children, scattered throughout the new and vast territory beyond the Mississippi, may cry with the Maccabees, 'If ever I forget thee . . . may my right hand be withered.'"

Reformed Judaism blossomed naturally in this liberal atmosphere. The first reformed congregation west of the Alleghenies, K. K. B'nai Yeshurun, was organized in 1839. In 1852 Dr. Isaac Meyer Wise, born in Bohemia — whose great ability had not prevented his being thrown out of his pastorate in orthodox Albany because of his liberal views — was elected as rabbi by B'nai Yeshurun, and here became the nation's leading representative of Judaism. B'nai Israel, the English — the orthodox — synagogue was then pastorless, and showed a breadth of view by asking Dr. Wise to serve as its rabbi also for a time, preaching in the two synagogues alternately, which he did. In '55 there came another eminent rabbi, Max Lilienthal, to B'nai Israel, which soon thereafter began to show a trend towards the Reform view.

Dr. Wise founded and edited a paper, *The Israelite*, and ably seconded by Dr. Lilienthal, made Cincinnati the center of Reformed Judaism in America. They two were the unpaid members of a faculty of five who opened Zion College in 1855 with 14 students, an opening celebrated with a banquet for 1,000 guests, at which Governor Salmon P. Chase and "the elite of Cincinnati" were present. That college expanded 20 years later into the great Hebrew Union College, the first Jewish theological seminary in the country, still flourishing under the headship of Dr. Nelson Glueck.

By 1858 there were 6,000 Jews in Cincinnati. They had wealth, synagogues, schools, a hospital, clubs, literary societies and high positions political and otherwise, all of which seemed to perturb nobody.

But Roman Catholic immigration was beginning to excite concern among the American-born masses. When the first Catholic congregation in Cincinnati was organized in 1819, it could muster only about a hundred members. But its activities soon aroused apprehension; it was doing missionary work, seeking to convert Protestants, and a school which it opened solicited pupils from Protestant parents. When Cist issued his book, *Cincinnati in 1841*, there were only two Catholic churches in the city, as against about 38 Protestant, including four which were German. On the basis of these figures, the situation would not appear menacing, but the Catholic membership was growing rapidly, not only by immigration but by local accretion. One hundred and fifty converts from Protestantism in 1829 had caused alarm and growing antagonism; the several Protestant church papers in Cincinnati — with Methodists and Presbyterians most vigorous — were attacking Catholicism before 1830, and some of the nonsectarian newspapers at times joined in the warfare, while the *Catholic Telegraph*, founded in 1831, fought back.

But there were more temperate voices raised from among the numerous prominent Protestants who favored moderation. Judge James Hall, author and editor of the *Western Monthly Magazine*, wrote a paper in 1835, asking fair play and a judicial view of the whole question of immigration, which he had some difficulty in getting printed because of opposition by the magazine's owner. But Alexander Campbell, the Baptist preacher who had founded a new sect, the Disciples, was a more dissentient type. His denunciation was so fierce that he was challenged by Bishop John Baptist Purcell — for Cincinnati had been made a diocese — to prove his charges. The final result was a debate between the two, which raged from January 13th to 21st, 1837, with two sessions daily! Some of the Protestant newspapers very fairly inclined towards the belief that the Bishop had had rather the better of the tournament, though how anyone could form a judgment after nine days of drenching under those millions of words, it is difficult to conceive.

Lyman Beecher, who came to Cincinnati in 1830 to be head of the newly founded Lane Theological Seminary, is often mentioned as a pitiless reprobater of Catholicism; but this requires closer examination. It is true that he denounced them roundly before leaving Boston; but his last philippic against them was so closely followed by the burning of a convent by a mob that the effervescent divine was roughly jolted; he had never intended that anticlerical feeling should go so far. After he reached Cincinnati, he wrote a new lecture, *A Plea for the West* (afterwards published as a book), which he delivered many times, and which was written with the studied fairness of a sobered man. He had no ecclesiastical quarrel with Catholicism, he said, simply as a religious denomination, unallied to any government. He deplored any violation of the Catholics' civil or religious rights, which should be protected as carefully as those of any other citizen. He said present-day Catholics should not be held responsible for everything that took place in the Middle Ages; and as to discussion or criticism, he held that "a declamatory, virulent, contemptuous, sarcastic, taunting, denunciatory style is as unchristian as it is in bad taste and indiscreet." But he wished that Catholics would send their children to the public schools; he objected to the church-and-state alliance, to the seeking of political power by the Church, the banning of Bible reading by the laity and other Church practices, and he claimed the right and duty to call attention to them.

Whether it was before or after the first delivery of this address we do not know, but a curious incident occurred. Dr. Beecher's daughter Harriet — later the great publicist against slavery — had joined him in Cincinnati, and had inevitably become active in a cultural way. She had started a little school and had compiled a primary geography which was published by a local concern in 1834. Perhaps by way of heaping coals of fire, or perhaps because he was moved by the moderate tone of Dr. Beecher's lecture — we shall never know why — Bishop Purcell astonished Harriet one day by dropping in unexpectedly on her school, and, as she wrote to a kinsman, "expressed himself as greatly pleased that we had opened such an one here. He spoke of my poor little geography, and thanked me for the unprejudiced way in which I had handled the Catholic question in it. I was of course flattered that he should have known anything about the book."

There were social amenities, too, which prove that the division between the faiths was ignored by most of the better type of folk in Cincinnati. For example, Miss Martineau attended "an elegant party" at the home of Nicholas Longworth in '35, at which she met a Supreme Court justice, a Congressman, numerous professional and businessmen and their families, two Catholic priests and several clergymen of other sorts. The people in such a gathering would not of course believe such fantastic rumors as the one that all the Catholic churches had great stores of gunpowder, which would presently be used to blow up the city. On the other hand, the Catholics were oversensitive. When John Quincy Adams came to speak at the dedication of the Cincinnati Observatory in 1843 and made some historical reference to Galileo and the Inquisition, they were deeply offended, and spoke of his address as "anti-Catholic."

The question, as might be expected, became ingrained in politics, which, as we have observed, was much localized before 1840. Cincinnatians casually called themselves Whigs or Democrats, which, as usual in local affairs, were just spurious labels for the Ins and the Outs, though they gave the organs of the so-called parties excuse for mock-furious denunciation of each other, the chief joy of old-fashioned journalism. The city's two dailies in the '30's, the *Advertiser* (Democrat) and the *Gazette* (Whig), led the half-dozen weekly, bi-weekly and semi-weekly sheets in name-calling — "poltroon," "calumniator," "miserable mercenary"; in lofty rejoinders — "We are honored by the abuse of the vile and worthless"; and after the *Advertiser* was bought by John and Charles Brough in 1841 and its name changed to *Enquirer*, delicate quips like this flew around, "The impudence and the low vulgar Billingsgate of the Enquirer clique is . . . only exceeded by their total disregard of truth. The vilest epithets are heaped daily upon our oldest and best citizens to gratify the *natural malignity* of these unprincipled adventurers." Very little of this had any kinship with party principles, or national or religious moot questions; it was just good, clean fun, unaccompanied by fisticuffs or shooting. But in an entertaining divertisement of 1841, the *Western Christian Advocate* (Methodist), accused John C. Wright of the *Gazette* of slurring and libelling anything that was Methodist, and boosting the Catholics. Meanwhile Catholics and evangelicals joined in excoriating the new cult of Unitarianism, which was gaining ground in Cincinnati.

What a contrast was the controversy between Rabbi Wise's *Israelite* and Editor Gordon of the *Free Presbyterian!* They couldn't resist tangling in a theological argument soon after the birth of the *Israelite,* but it was delightfully conducted on a high plane of bonhomie and kindliness. "We appreciate the courtesy and reciprocate the kind feelings expressed by our brother (if he will permit us to call him so) of the *Israelite,*" said Mr. Gordon, in delicately launching a new thrust of logic. Dr. Wise, in return, called him "Brother Gordon," and after a page of friendly polemics, he closed with, "We wish God's gracious blessings on Brother Gordon and good success to the *Free Presbyterian.*" But many Christians were concerned over the unsaved condition of the Jews, and when, at a revival meeting in '58, prayers were offered for the salvation of their souls, Dr. Wise was understandably, though not seriously, annoyed.

Immigrants were pouring in by thousands yearly in the 1840's, and Cincinnati's streets, businesses and factories were a babel of dialects — Maine to Connecticut Yankee, Southern in various shadings, the Oxford-to-cockney broad *a,* the North-and-South German guttural, the Irish brogue, the Scotch burr, with piquant dashes of French, Welsh, Cornish, Yorkshireman and others, besides thousands — with more coming daily — who could speak no English at all.

Steadily the religious dissension became political. In the election of '44 charges were made that the immigrant vote was controlled by the priests and generally thrown to the Democrats, the Whigs having come out most strongly against the Roman Church. The majority of the people who engaged in the feud were undoubtedly sincere, and some of them were terribly in earnest. It is a question whether the strongest feeling among the Protestant masses was against the Germans who made up the bulk of the immigrants, or the ebullient Irish, who stood second in numbers but were more vocal. The *Gazette* conceded that the Germans "are mostly industrious and respectable, but faithfully cherishing their nationality and religion," and "make no effort to become Americans" — which was somewhat wide of the mark. It added that there were proofs that they had been disciplined to vote as a bloc in elections.

This rumor, which revealed a curious lack of information, was fostered by the fact that the Germans had to a considerable extent segregated themselves in that elbow of the Miami Canal which we have described, made by its course through Plum and Eleventh Streets, where it became "the Rhine," because just north of it appeared a sort of little German city, the rhythmic lilt of whose nickname, "Over the Rhine," as decades passed, came to be a beloved and indelible part of the city's nomenclature and folk-lore, and eventually, only a happy memory.

If those who, in the '40's, regarded this area as a center of Papist intrigue and clergy-controlled voting had made a survey of it, they would have discovered that there were more Protestant than Catholic churches in the district, that many Germans were free-thinkers or downright unbelievers, and finally, that there were even some German Jews living quite comfortably in the quarter.

It was around 1845 that the Native Americans, organized in the East as a secret society, with oaths, ritual and passwords, appeared in Cincinnati, celebrating the Fourth of July, '47 with an address by an anti-Catholic preacher. Rapidly here, as elsewhere, they became a political party, nicknamed Know-Nothings, for the reason that they still maintained secrecy as a pose, and when asked a question about the organization, the stock reply was, "I know nothing." In 1847 another anti-Catholic society, the American Protestant Association, ostensibly social, appeared in the city, beginning a long career. During the '50's, it celebrated the "Beginning of the Reformation" — October 31st, the day when Luther nailed his "theses" on the church door at Wittenberg. There would be a parade, carrying pictures of Luther and other heroes, and oratory at the several lodge-rooms. Thereafter, it became less demonstative; but throughout the nineteenth century, you had only to say "APA" to an Irishman to arouse him to fighting pitch. In the 1890's, its fifteen lodges in Cincinnati had only 2,500 members, which, among a population of some 300,000, does not seem so many.

A letter to the *Gazette* declared that the Catholics would soon outnumber the Protestants and sweep the city elections, and that "nine-tenths of the people who are hired in the city are Catholics . . . driving out and superseding Protestant laborers and servants"; a statement difficult to prove. A result of this fear was the frequent appearance in help-wanted ads of "Protestant" or "American," "No foreigners need apply," "Irish not wanted," etc. But it must be said that this was the worst of the opposition until the Know-Nothings made their single violent gesture in 1855. Aside from that, the feeling vented itself in words only. There was no violence, no interference with anyone's worship or freedom of speech. The immigrants mentioned earlier who were developing some of the city's notable businesses or rising in the professions seem to have suffered little inconvenience; their affairs throve and expanded. In 1850 a Catholic, R. B. Warden, was appointed a judge of the Court of Common pleas — the first Catholic to hold such high office in the city. Then and thereafter, many smaller jobs were filled by Catholics. And Charles Cist said in 1851, "To the industry of foreigners, Cincinnati is indebted in a great degree for its rapid growth."

There was ample proof that great numbers of German citizens were not Catholics. In 1851 a Dr. Kinkel, an anti-Catholic professor in the University of Bonn, visited Cincinnati and was a guest of Dr. Rehfuss at his home on Sixth Street — for some Germans did not live over the Rhine. Many leading citizens called to pay their respects to him, and one evening a torchlight parade of German societies, a great concourse, marched to the Rehfuss home, cheered him uproariously and listened to a speech by him. But the most remarkable anticlerical incident of the period was not provoked by native Americans. Over the Rhine the Freemen's Society of German liberals, some 1,200 strong, mostly professing infidelity and especially antipathetic to the Catholic Church, met on Thursday evenings, and — to the distress of the pious — on Sundays at their Frei Männers Halle, at Vine and Mercer Streets, for discussion, music and recreation. Editor Hassaurek, of the *Hochwachter* later of the *Volksblatt*, was one of their leading spirits. Early in 1853, angered at finding in the city a Dr. Junghaus, who had been a spy against the Austrian revolutionaries in '48, they marched in orderly array to the Fifth Street

l burned him in effigy — a gesture which has
give partisans enormous satisfaction.

f that year Mgr. Cajetan Bedini, who stood high
erarchy, spent Christmas with Bishop Purcell.
ciety blamed him for the death of Ugo Bassi, an
had joined the revolutionaries under Garibaldi
ptured and executed. The Freemen decided to
n effigy in robe and mitre in front of Bishop
then burn the effigy. News of the project
he procession of 1,200 persons, including 200
ildren, left Frei Männers Halle late in the
four abreast towards the Bishop's residence,
ow who carried the gallows on his shoulder.
hey were halted by a force of police under
ukens. In the ensuing melee, shots were fired
nber of the marchers were wounded, one
eman was injured, also fatally. Sixty-four
d, charged with rioting, but public feeling
were discharged next day. Hassaurek then
tenants and 103 policemen arrested, on a
to do an unlawful act, but the subject was
cted on either way, and this, too, came to

, _____ were burned in several of the suburbs, with
parades and banners crying, "Down with Bedini!" "Down with
Snelbaker" (the Mayor), "Down with the Cincinnati Police";
and another crowd of several hundred from the West End and
over the Rhine burned Mgr. Bedini once more, on a lot near St.
Peter's Cathedral and squarely in front of a watch-house.

That the Germans were of many beliefs is seen in the fact that
Editor Hassaurek in that same year took part with his usual fervor
in one of those marathon debates with the Reverend Mr. Wittenberg,
a German Methodist minister, upon the subject, "The Morality
or Rationality of Christianity" — all in German, of course,
and the last time the newspapers noticed it, it had played to packed
houses for eight evenings.

The Know-Nothings — whose antipathy, remember, was rather against foreigners in general than against the Church — continued to wax in influence in the early '50's, though they made more noise than their numbers and influence justified. They had a newspaper of their own now, the *Columbian,* and it was seconded, desultorily, by the *Times* and *Gazette,* which were practically orphans, knowing not where to go, "Old Line Silver Gray Whiggery" being on its deathbed. Politically, it was a muddled era. Calvin W. Starbuck, editor of the *Times,* ran for Mayor in '53 on an anti-Catholic, though not Know-Nothing, ticket, but failed of election.

The Know-Nothings had adopted colors — red, white and blue, of course — and Know-Nothing millinery, wreaths and rosettes appeared. Children wore the wreaths — the *Gazette* editor counted 200 of them in one walk of an hour or so in '54 — and both horses and humans wore the rosettes. A small riot occurred at the railroad station at Loveland, an outlying suburb, in which "two or three Irishmen were badly used up" for knocking a Know-Nothing hat from the head of a passenger who stepped off a train. That was State and Congressional election year, and as the campaign grew hotter, it was rumored that guns in barrels and boxes were being shipped in to Catholics; but nobody tried to find them. Politicians were displaying their usual agile disregard of consistency. At the ground-breaking for the "County Lunatic Asylum" (sic) at Carthage (now the enormous Longview State Hospital), early in the year, there was a dinner, at which County Commissioner Jesse Timanus proposed a toast, "The alien vote of Hamilton County — the Irish and the Dutch." A few months later (in August), this notice appeared in the newspapers:

> "350 Men Wanted — Mechanics and laborers
> to work at the new Court House. Preference
> will be given to American Protestants.
>
> JESSE TIMANUS

In the city campaign of 1855, Slavery and Native Americanism split the Democrats into factions; the Whigs, though moribund, were still stirring feebly, a new Republican Party was being born, while the Know-Nothings, who began the year as the American Party, became the American Reform Party as the campaign warmed up. Both candidates for Mayor were journalists — Faran of the *Enquirer* on the Democratic ticket and Taylor of the *Times* for the Know-Nothings. The KN's staged a great mass meeting in the Fifth Street Market space in July, at which, oddly enough, the major subject was not Native Americanism, but the Kansas-Nebraska Act which gave those two States local option as to slavery, and which was loudly denounced, along with its proposers and supporters. However, the fundamental principle of the party must be maintained, so orators and printed manifestoes dwelt upon the arrogance and impertinence of foreigners, and decreed that "All management of National and State affairs, political, judicial and educational, should and must remain in the hands of Native Americans."

Trouble began on the day before the election of '55 when a group of Know-Nothing partisans mistreated a little German street band, bringing on a fight with other Germans, in which several were injured. On election morning, it was reported that hundreds of Know-Nothings had come over from Kentucky to "protect the polls" in wards where there seemed a likelihood of a Democratic majority. Fighting broke out early in the morning around the Eleventh Ward voting place, the Mohawk Engine House, over the Rhine. But though Germans were predominant there, Know-Nothings were not hindered from casting their votes. As news of the trouble spread over the city, hordes from elsewhere poured into the ward, charges of ballot-box stuffing were made, and in the afternoon, the mob from outside seized and destroyed the boxes. Similar attempts were made in two other wards, but the judges, forewarned, secreted the boxes.

These disorders alarmed the German citizens, who feared a general antiforeign uprising. When the Know-Nothings demanded the surrender of a cannon belonging to a German military company, they at first refused, but upon being assured that it would not be used against them, they surrendered the barrel, but kept the carriage. This enraged their opponents, who made such threats that the Germans set up barricades of vehicles in the Parisian manner north of the canal, two across Vine Street and one across Walnut. That evening a mass meeting of Know-Nothings was held in the hall of the Mechanics' Institute. After a couple of hours of aimless vaporing, most of the crowd left the hall and marched up Vine Street, yelling, singing, some carrying torches, most of them armed, with the vague notion of cleaning out Little Germany. The Germans who had for two days been gathered in Turner and Frei Männers Halls with such weapons as they could collect, were ready for them. Firing upon the mob from windows began before it reached the Fourteenth Street barricade. There many more shots were exchanged, one Know-Nothing was killed and some others wounded, one fatally. Soon the attackers fell back across the canal, milled around a while and dispersed. The Germans, feeling sure that the danger was over, removed the barricades next morning, and comparative tranquillity was restored.

This was the first, last and only bellicose act of Know-Nothingism in Cincinnati, and as riots go, it was almost inconsequential. The fact was that the Know-Nothings — who, by the way, lost the election — had passed their peak.. The better class of citizens had already moved away from them. The German language, as well as English, began to be taught in the public schools in German areas, and foreigners and Catholics were holding public offices. Some had become highly influential — Professor and Judge John B. Stallo, for example, one of the orators and leading spirits of the local Democracy.

By 1858 Cincinnati, most precariously situated of any of the nation's larger cities, was being forced to think of an issue more grave than Native Americanism. The Republic was being slowly driven apart by the quarrel which presently flamed into internecine war. As the crisis neared, the last remnants of Know-Nothingism vanished like smoke. With the outbreak of the conflict, Cincinnati's foreigners by thousands rallied to the colors, the vast majority of them, even those who had voted against Lincoln, on the Northern side. In fact, from that moment, many Germans who had never voted anything but the Democratic ticket, became

Republicans. Whole companies and regiments of Germans and Irish enlisted and marched away, many to leave their bodies on Southern battlefields, many to return maimed or ill through their remaining days.

But even after the war, some little smudges of dissent remained to mar the picture. One had been there as far back as 1842. It was then and for long afterward the custom to begin each day's school session with reading from the Bible, the King James version of course being used. Bishop Purcell objected to this, as there were many Catholic children in the public schools. After much wrangling, the school board ruled that the parents might specify whether the child should read the King James translation or the Vulgate, which the Catholics preferred. That ramshackle arrangement continued in force for thirty years.

The Catholics having opened several schools of their own, another flurry occurred in 1853, when an attempt was made to pass an ordinance through Council compelling all parents to send their children for three months each year to the public schools, but this was defeated.

The question flared up again in 1870, and in the city's spring elections that year there were Bible and anti-Bible parties. A newspaper report of the election bore the headline, "Triumph of the Bible." In 1872 the school board attempted to eliminate the long-standing nuisance to the teachers by voting to abolish the Bible-reading entirely. A legal action was quickly brought by some Protestant taxpayers, seeking to rescind this action—not altogether in a spirit of opposition to Catholicism, but quite as much because pious folk were shocked at the thought of eliminating the Word of God as a part of the children's education; though with some irritation, it is true, at the Catholics for more or less directly precipitating the contretemps. The suit reached the city's Superior Court, where a majority, Judges Storer and Hagans, granted a perpetual injunction against the board's order.

But the third member of the Court, a Vermont Yankee and a great jurist, Alphonso Taft, was in dissent. He realized more clearly than many of his contemporaries that this had become a composite nation; we had invited peoples from all other lands to come

[53]

and live with us, and we must be prepared to give them the same freedoms that we demanded for ourselves. In a powerful dissenting opinion he pointed out that the State Constitution did not recognize the Christian religion or the Protestant religion any more than it recognized the religious cults of other citizens not Christians; that to force upon these others a document contrary to their creed was a violation of freedom; that the King James translation was not accepted by the large Roman Catholic population as the true Bible, and furthermore, that our so called New Testament taught things repugnant to the rapidly-growing Jewish population, who had as yet made little complaint. There was much more to his argument, and it convinced the State Supreme Court, which reversed the Cincinnati court, sustaining Judge Taft and the school board.

The Civil War halted immigration for several years (it was never as great afterwards), and that eased the tension a bit and gave time for some fusion of the diverse elements already present. Intermarriage was taking place, though as yet mostly in the middle and lower classes. Foreign-born business and professional men and politicians had become well integrated into the life and work of the city; some were building fine homes on the hilltops. Concert halls, beer-gardens and theaters over the Rhine became more and more popular with Anglo-Saxon citizens.

There were some very substantial evidences of the passing of Know-Nothingism, which, after all, had never had any very solid footing among the more thoughtful people. Two instances will suffice. Sister Anthony, an Irish nun who had first founded an orphan asylum and then taken over St. John's Hospital, interrupted her work to serve in the Federal Army hospitals during the war. Returning to St. John's, she found it greatly in need of enlargement, but there were no funds. Some cash had been collected, but not enough, when two Protestants, Joseph C. Butler and Lewis Worthington, paid $70,000 for the Marine Hospital (which had cost $250,000 to build) and presented it to her. And when Archbishop Purcell in 1879 found himself an involuntary defaulter in a huge sum through the misdoing of his brother, to whom he had entrusted the diocesan funds, many Protestants, wealthy or well-to-do, were among those who contributed to the fund raised to help the heart-broken old prelate out of his difficulty.

When the Grand Union at Saratoga, owned by Judge Hilton — who had taken over the great A. T. Stewart store in New York after the death of its founder — began refusing admission to Jews in the 1870's, Cincinnati Jewish businessmen signed a pledge to cease all dealing with the Stewart store, and the *Cincinnati Gazette* remarked (June 27, 1877), "If Judge Hilton reads the names of the graduates of our high schools who took prizes, he will tremble for the future of our schools."

As the century entered its fourth quarter, two of the leading citizens of Cincinnati were rabbis — Isaac M. Wise and Max Lilienthal. A daughter of Dr. Wise married the eldest of three sons of a Cincinnati Jewish family named Ochs, all three of whom became noted journalists — George and Milton, the younger ones, in Chattanooga, Philadelphia and Nashville, while Effie Wise's husband, Adolph, after buying and rejuvenating the *Chattanooga Times*, took over the almost moribund *New York Times* in 1896, and made it the great, world-dominant newspaper that it is.

Dr. Wise never thought of leaving the city, having his two beloved children, the Union of American Hebrew Congregations and the Hebrew Union College — to which he donated large slices of his own salary in its infant years — to nurture. But in 1868 Dr. Lilienthal received an attractive call from New York City, and leaned toward accepting it. Thereupon a number of prominent Gentile citizens, headed by Judge Bellamy Storer, drew up a petition, pleading that Dr. Lilienthal was too valuable a citizen to be lost, and such pressure was brought upon him that the rabbi yielded and spent the remainder of his life in Cincinnati. When he died in 1882 and Dr. Wise in 1900, all Cincinnati attended their funeral services, and eminent Gentiles were among the speakers. Because of what has since taken place, a significant utterance was that of German-born Judge J. B. Stallo in a tribute at Dr. Lilienthal's bier; "His brethren were not only those to whose race he belonged; everyone who furthered the aims of humanity was his brother and friend. It is in this sense that we meet here, one great brotherhood, to mourn the loss of a dearly beloved brother."

A remarkable gathering was that dinner of a thousand guests given in the ballroom of the Hotel Gibson in honor of the Belgian Cardinal Mercier just after the close of the First World War. Manufacturer L. A. Ault was in the chair. The speakers were the Governor, the Mayor, the Catholic Archbishop. Episcopal Bishop Boyd Vincent, and Dr. David Philipson, a great figure in American Jewry, pupil of Dr. Wise and for 50 years rabbi of B'nai Israel after it removed to the suburb of Avondale. Of this occasion Dr. Philipson wrote in his memoirs "Never have I been at a civic or so-called secular function so permeated with the true religious spirit as was this tribute to this unusual man"; while the *Catholic Telegraph* called Dr. Philipson's address "a masterpiece . . . delivered with a fervor of eloquence, a sincerity of sympathy and a happiness of expression that held a large audience spellbound."

The contentment with their lot in Cincinnati, the resulting patriotism frequently voiced by Jewish leaders, undoubtedly contributed much towards making the city in later years predominantly anti-Zionist. Dr. Lilienthal, speaking at the laying of the cornerstone of the Mound Street Temple, urged his hearers to be Americans first, then Jews. "We no longer owe any allegiance to Jerusalem," said he, "save the respect all enlightened nations pay to this cradle of all civilizing religions. We cherish no longer any desire for a return to Palestine, but proudly and gratefully exclaim with the Psalmist, 'Here is my resting place. Here shall I abide; for I love this place.'" Dr. Philipson, too, often spoke against Zionism, telling his people that America is their second Promised Land. "To my mind," he said, "Zionism and true Americanism have always seemed mutually exclusive. No man can be a member of two nationalities, Jewish and American. *Aut-aut*. There is no middle way."

CHAPTER IV

Growing Pains

SOME observers believed that a prime reason for the Queen City's greatness was the fact that the Cincinnatian, like the admired Little Busy Bee, improv'd each shining hour. Birkbeck in 1817, said, "All is alive here as soon as the day breaks. The stores are open, the markets thronged, and business in full career by five o'clock in the morning; and nine o'clock is the common hour for retiring to rest." (For some people, yes.) Eighteen years later, Chevalier said, "There is no such thing in Cincinnati as a class of men of leisure, living without any regular profession on their patrimony or on the wealth acquired by their own enterprise in early life, although there are many persons of opulence having one hundred thousand dollars and upward"; which, if true, proved Cincinnati to be a real city of opportunity. A visitor of 1845 when the city may have had 75,000 inhabitants, said, "It seemed to me a city of working men. Its capitalists were master mechanics who had grown rich, but had not had time to put on their Sunday clothes or study manners. It is one of the most industrious places in the world. No trouble there about the nobility of labour. I never saw a place where there were as few idlers."

He stopped at the Broadway Hotel, which he thought the best in the city. "The weather was warm, and I think half the male guests, many of them regular boarders — solid business men of Cincinnati — dined comfortably in their shirt-sleeves." And after all, he reflected, "was it so bad a fashion?" even though it made them look like "a party of butchers."[1]

---

1 Thomas Low Nichols, *Forty Years of American Life*, (London, 1874).

But at the same time, as we shall see, Cincinnati society affairs with the ladies present was considered by other visitors to be as conventional and refined as that of the East. These men, though coatless at lunch, were living stylishly; finely furnished homes, fashionably dressed families who were now going away for the summer — farther and farther away as fortunes increased — stables full of horses and carriages and the beginnings of pet charities. The year 1832, with a serious river flood and a devastating Asiatic Cholera epidemic, caused material damage and destitution and upset business conditions for a while — besides taking one distinguished victim, Dr. Edward Fenwick, the Catholic Bishop of Cincinnati — and the panic of 1837 jarred the business structure visibly; but it is remarkable how little lasting effect these disasters had upon the growth and busyness of the young city. It had such liquid resources, such a robust fundamental virility that it just brushed aside troubles and forged ahead.

Its chief defect was that as its business tempo and volume increased, its good citizens had less and less time for local politics. A familiar American municipal melodrama was being enacted. Crooked politicians breed like maggots in a growing city where better men are too deeply engrossed in building great enterprises and making money to keep it in order, but let it run harum-scarum, like a neglected child. Even by 1830 there had come a startling decadence in public service. The small police force of some twenty men had almost ceased to function save as political tools, and the streets were poorly lighted or not at all. The latter condition continued for years thereafter. In 1837 the Briton, Charles Daubeny, going home one night from a play in "pitch darkness," found "not a single street lamp burning in any part of the town"; and yet by day he liked the place. "I must say I think Mrs. Trollope has done it a great injustice."

Fortunately, most of the best known of the touring British publicists visited Cincinnati before 1843, when politics and mushroom growth began to show too plainly upon the city's behavior and appearance. None of them mention any disorder except Captain Marryat, who saw a "row" at a theater one evening and bowie-knives drawn, which astonished him, as he thought the population were nearly all Yankees, who did not carry knives; "but as I afterwards discovered, they were worn in self-defense, because the Southerners carried them." [2]

It is a striking fact that while the rest of America seethed with indignation at the British travelers who visited parts of the United States, often hurriedly, and went home and wrote books of excoriation, Cincinnati showed little annoyance save at Mrs. Trollope and one H. B. Fearon, who didn't think it would ever amount to much. Most visitors, especially before 1840 or '45, found much to praise and far less to criticise in Cincinnati. In fact, one is puzzled sometimes by the discordance between the chorus of approval from the strangers and of self-criticism from the city's own press. An aristocratic Mr. Murray, like some other Britishers, was indignant at his fellow-countrymen who slandered Cincinnati. He was awed by the city's achievement, proud of the Briton's part in it, "and I pity from the bottom of my heart the man (and above all others, the Englishman) who can see nothing in such a scene but food for unjust comparison, sneers, raillery and ridicule!" [3]

The absence of professional beggars and of a pauper class recommended Cincinnati to Miss Martineau and others in the 1830's; but alas, those blemishes began to appear a little later. Miss Martineau, after a two or three days' stay, was so enthusiastic over the place that "I felt strongly inclined to jump to some hasty conclusions about the happiness of citizenship in Cincinnati. I made a virtuous determination to suspend every sort of judgement; but I found each day as exhilarating as the first, and when I left the city, my impressions were much like what they were after an observation of twenty-four hours."

But no one's commendation is more lovingly cherished by Cincinnatians than that of Charles Dickens, whose caustic comments on some other places and on America in general were very ill received elsewhere. Young Mr. Dickens spent only two days here in 1842, but he got around pretty strenuously. Said he:

[2] Captain Frederick Marryat, *A Diary in America*, (London, 1839).
[3] Hon. Charles Augustus Murry, *Travels in North America in the Years 1834, 1835 and 1836*, (London, 1839).

"Cincinnati is a beautiful city, cheerful, thriving, animated. I have not often seen a place that commends itself so favourably and pleasantly to a stranger at the first glance as this does, with its clean houses of red and white, its well-paved roads and footways of bright tile . . . .I was quite charmed with the appearance of the town and its neighboring suburb of Mount Auburn" — and much more to the same effect. By "paved" he meant macadamized streets.

Incidentally, the notice given by the newspapers to this famous novelist, who had already five best-sellers to his credit, is startling in its brevity. Three lines in the *Gazette* announce that "Mr. Dickens arrived in town yesterday from St. Louis, and took lodgings at the Broadway Hotel. He leaves to-day for New York via Columbus." You would never guess that his wife was with him. Fortunately, the roads were better than they had been in 1810, when a citizen who was forced to make the journey between Cincinnati and Columbus frequently, reported having been upset thirteen times in three months. He found an inside seat safest; you emerged with nothing but contusions, whereas the fellows who rode on the roof and might be thrown several yards in the turn-over, were apt to suffer broken bones or concussions.

General William Henry Harrison, who had suffered financial reverses, was "mentioned" for both governor and senator in the early '30's, but failed to get either nomination, and when suggested as a possible candidate for congressman, withdrew in favor of that rising attorney, Bellamy Storer. In 1834 he was appointed clerk of the Common Pleas Court, where foreign visitors were shocked to see the hero of Tippecanoe and the Thames serving in so comparatively humble a capacity. But when he was mentioned for the Presidency in 1836, the city began taking a wider interest in politics. Harrison's partisans were revolted by Democratic candidate Van Buren's numerous gold headed canes and silk stockings, his $3,000 coach imported from England, drawn by "four horses of the best blood, attended by servants in rich liveries and outriders," while "the plain old farmer of North Bend" habitually rode on "a pacing pony of not more than fifty dollars value, without a liveried servant."

But the time was not ripe for the General's nomination until 1840, when his log cabin home, with a coonskin nailed to the wall and a barrel of hard cider on tap became the most noted political trademark and vote-getter in our history. Some of the Democratic repartee was comic. "Log cabins!" sneered the *Detroit Free Press*, published in a village still largely of log construction. "Log cabins! What are they? Rendezvous for the depraved and dissolute — nurseries of drunkenness, idleness and dishonesty. Yes, sir, the very avenues and vestibules of Hell!" — which must have been difficult to explain to *Free Press* readers still domiciled in log houses.

At the Mechanics' Fair in Cincinnati in June of that year, a soda fountain shaped like a log cabin was installed, and two ladies exhibited silkworms housed in a miniature cabin, which the Committee thought appropriate as indicating that silk could be produced even by Western frontier folk. But the Democrats made such an aggrieved uproar over the indelicacy of dragging politics into what should be a purely nonpartisan exhibition that the Committee thought it best to remove both cabins.

The old General's election raised the city to a pinnacle of elation, and his death a month after his inauguration was a stunning blow. But Cincinnati could not mourn long. There was too much building, producing, shipping and money-changing waiting to be done to permit more than a decorous day of sorrowful tribute. For now the city, the Nation's sixth in size, was roaring into its maddest decade yet — one in which its population would multiply nearly two and a half times, reaching 115,438 in 1850 — of which more than 51,000 were foreign-born; with a continuous housing shortage — though it erected 1,228 buildings in 1844 to New York's 1,213, and Horace Greeley, dizzied by it, said that its greatness had scarcely begun; with its Miami & Erie Canal completed to Lake Erie; with its first two railroads, both of its own creation, the Little Miami to Columbus and the Cincinnati, Hamilton & Dayton, connecting those three cities; with immigrants pouring in by thousands spurred by European unrest and the lure of this new wonder city; with the narrow streets of its Basin chock-a-block with industrial vehicles, hucksters, the carriages

of the wealthy, buggies, horsemen, German parades, hand-drawn
fire engines, droves of hogs soon to be pork, casual street hogs,
peddlers; the sidewalks a babble of American regional and foreign
dialects; whilst overhead, in spring and fall — as the awed foreigners raised their eyes in wonder at the spectacle — long, massed
flocks of graceful birds, souvenirs of the frontier so rapidly passing, rippled across the sky, obscuring the sun — not in millions
as a few years ago, but at least in thousands. The *Gazette* on
September 21, 1844, said, "Clouds of these migratory birds
(pigeons) have been passing over our city all this week. During
a ramble on the hills two or three afternoons ago, we observed
some twenty flocks, each of which must have contained five to
ten thousand." There was no closed season, either for game
hunters or ward heelers; neither drought nor frost nor locust
curbed the crops of delinquency and crime springing from this
rich compost. The disorders of the following years were a natural
fruition of this tumultuous period. Already they were manifesting
themselves. The filthy city jail, where children and adults were
herded together, was a college of crime. Dorothea Dix, the prison
reformer, inspected it, and what she said was scathing, though
politicians don't scathe easily.

Street cleaning and sanitation were neglected subjects, even by
the street commissioners. A fundamental fault was the lack of
proper paving. A few streets had been "bowldered," and then
never cleaned; a few others thinly macadamized, the gravel
rapidly sinking into the mud, and the highway going back to
nature. In February, 1840, the streets around the Fifth Street
market place — where householders bought most of their food —
were said to be nearly impassable from mud, slush and filth. A
reporter daily saw "many females almost swamped in the mire"
in their efforts to cross. This market, by the way, extended thirteen blocks along Fifth Street in 1842, including the present Fountain Square and Government Square. On an August day there
were 483 hucksters' wagons there, including a hundred butchers.
In spring and fall there would be wagonloads of wild pigeons.
The town hogs dodged about between horses' and shoppers' legs,
snatching every fallen apple, potato, cabbage and bit of meat.

sometimes fighting with dogs over the bones, sometimes upsetting shoppers or causing a general melee.

When you passed the mouths of some of the alleys, you were almost felled by the stench of decaying garbage in them and of the privies, some overflowing, which bordered them. A letter to the *Atlas* in 1843 complains of sidewalks in a condition "that would disgrace Constantinople itself"; uncleaned, some so rough that persons walked on them at their peril. Many cellar doors were cut in sidewalks next to the buildings, and frequently left open even after dark, so that passersby fell into them, breaking bones or worse. One January day a "drunken Frenchman" fell into one of these and didn't get out. "The cellar being filled with water, great difficulty has been experienced in recovering the body," and at noon next day it still hadn't been found.

"The pork aristocracy of Cincinnati," wrote Sir Charles Lyell in 1842, referred to those people who had made fortunes in pork, not, as you might think, to "those innumerable pigs which walked at large about the streets as if they owned the town"; which "belong to no one in particular; any one is at liberty to take them up, fatten and kill them. When they increase too fast, the town council interferes and sells off some of them. It is a favorite amusement of the boys to ride upon the pigs, and we were shown one sagacious old hog who was in the habit of lying down as soon as a boy came in sight."[4] One of the younger sons of Dr. Lyman Beecher enjoyed this sport, as is seen in a letter of the Doctor's daughter Harriet:

"By the by, Mary, speaking of the temptations of cities, I have much solicitude on James's account, for yesterday or the day before, we saw him parading by the house with his arm over the neck of a great hog, apparently on the most intimate terms possible. The other day he actually got on the back of one and rode some distance. So much for allowing these animals to parade the streets, a particular in which Mrs. Cincinnati has imitated the domestic arrangements of some of her elder sisters. . . ."

Not all hogs were so agreeable; now and then, a child was bitten

---

[4] Sir Charles Lyell, *Travels in North America in the Years 1841-2*, (London, 1842).

by one. These lean street-loafers, most of them outright vagrants, as Lyell says, must have been of pretty tough fiber. Nevertheless, one of them disappeared from circulation now and then, most often in one of the quarters known as Dublin or Blacktown. There were even those who claimed to own some coveys of them, which came to their doors every evening to be fed, usually on distillery slops. One minor city functionary kept from a dozen to a score of them in his back yard, until one night when somebody stole all of them.

There were city scavenger carts whose chore it was to gather up the kitchen garbage, but the crooked city government didn't operate them at even fifty per cent efficiency, which gave many persons — not the decent ones, but the predominant kind — an excellent excuse to dump their garbage and trash into streets and alleys; and that being done, the hogs played their part by eating the offal, though the task was too great for their capacity, albeit they (and some assistants in the form of chickens) did their best at the job, save when some hog was tempted on a hot summer day by a gutter full of liquid to lie down and cool off in it. Which gave point to the irritation of a reporter who saw a Fifth Street market huckster washing the dust from his apples in a gutter. There faithful hogs sometimes died at their posts, perhaps struck down by a hit-and-run milk wagon, often from natural causes. *The Daily Chronicle*, on an April day in 1848 said, "A correspondent wishes to know if the Street Commissioner has made up his mind how long it will take that dead pig at the corner of Broadway and Sixth Streets to become decomposed. If three days is long enough to try the experiment, won't he please remove it?"

These "long-faced gentry whose relatives have made and lost fortunes for our citizens" were theoretically banished from the streets by Council in the winter of 1849. The great cholera epidemic of that year, with its 7,500 victims, gave the politicians a sanitary fright which as usual, proved transitory, even though the scourge was followed by another in the following year, somewhat less devastating. Though the expulsion of the hogs was far from thorough — "several large specimens being seen lounging about" months later in various parts of the city — complaints promptly arose that these "natural scavengers" having been thinned out, and the city carts, as usual, failing in their duty, the piles of garbage in the streets were becoming unendurable. As late as 1860, the *London Times* correspondent who accompanied the Prince of Wales on his tour praised Cincinnati's appearance in general, but commented on the number of hogs running at large. To which Editor Halstead of the *Commercial* retorted indignantly that he hadn't seen as many as ten hogs on the streets in a month.

'Forty-nine presents a curious picture of the absorption of young Cincinnati in its own growth, which might be likened to that of the beanstalk, were it not for its much greater hardness of fiber, nurtured by a similar hardness of purpose. There had been signs in 1848 of the corroding effects of the new age. A mob gathered about the jail one evening with intent to lynch two rapists, and the police, ordered to fire over their heads, contrived to kill at least four, perhaps seven persons (the reports varied), two of whom were mere passers-by. That was the first such incident in Cincinnati's history. About that time, the news came across the country from Sutter's Mill, and in December the *Chronicle* observed that "The California gold mania has reached our city and is producing an extraordinary excitement . . . so great that the rapid approach of the cholera is unheeded in the eagerness to embark in this seemingly rich enterprise."

But after all, fewer Argonauts went from Cincinnati than from other comparable populations. There were too few footloose young men there, too many lucratively engaged in a place where money was easy to get by intelligence and enterprise, to encourage adventuring. There were a few groups who voyaged usually by water via New Orleans and Panama, though the most important, the California Mining and Trading Company of Cincinnati, Incorporated, embracing about 50 men, with a capital of $25,000, took steamboat to St. Louis and went overland from there. Cincinnati cigar wholesalers were putting up bundles of twenty-five "pressed" cigars wrapped in sheet lead, for the use of persons California-bound, and local planing mills went in for the manufacture of ready-cut houses to be shipped to California, where there were as yet no saw mills.

The fact that the youthful city was so busily on the make was the principal reason why the imminence of cholera, which was raging elsewhere, was but little heeded. No real precautionary measures were known at the time, anyhow, save cleanliness, and the city government was too venal to attend to that. The city had had several bouts with the disease since 1830, including the bitter one of '32, but when it struck in '49, it set a record. Undertakers and grave-diggers, working around the clock, could not cope with the mortality; not only hearses but wagons, carts and drays made the hurried trips to the cemeteries more slap-dash, unfeeling, horrible. Meanwhile, all summer the great fires of tar and pitch burned uselessly in the streets, their pall of smoke intensifying the gloom; and can any reader comprehend the appointment of a man as superintendent of a hospital whose name was Absolom Death? It would be unbelievable if it were not there in the records. The cemeteries overflowed and new ones were hastily laid out. This epidemic of '49 took Harriet Beecher Stowe's youngest child and left her almost heartbroken. The city minimized the extent of the disaster; Stephen Collins Foster, a clerk in a steamboat office and already noted as a song writer, represented an extreme instance when he wrote comfortingly to his mother in Pittsburgh that she need not worry about health conditions in Cincinnati. With a touch of youthful callousness and a will to let nothing block its progress, the city, in the face of another threatened visitation of cholera in 1850, staged Ohio's first State Fair that fall, while hundreds were dying and 300 homes in the city were vacant, their occupants having fled in various directions, and while — to revert to the other hand again — the erection of new business buildings and churches went steadily on.

Another orphanage was an outgrowth of these dreadful episodes, and still survives as the General Protestant Orphans' Home. There is a super-grisly note in the annals of an old German Protestant Cemetery in Avondale where there are burials even of veterans of the Revolution and 1812. Many cholera victims of the 1830's lie here, too. When a new German cemetery was established in another place in 1843, some of the bodies were removed from this burying ground to the new one, but the cholera dead were undisturbed; there is or was a popular belief that the cholera germ never dies, and it was feared that if these graves were opened, the germs might escape and devastate the city again. Interments gradually ceased to take place in the old graveyard for the same reason — fear of releasing the dreaded microbe for another orgy of death.

The chaos engendered by these epidemics further stimulated drunkenness, disorder and crime. The temperance movement, in which the reformers, Murphy and Father Matthew, seemed to be making progress, received a severe setback. Cincinnati had no decent restaurants yet, but hundreds of so-called coffee houses, which were "no better than grog-shops." Besides these, there were the frankly-admitted saloons, of which in 1859 the Mayor reported 1,675 in the city, 1,307 of them in one police precinct. They had whimsical names, such as Broad Gauge, Narrow Gauge, Piccolomini, New York Clipper, Edwin Forrest, Atlantic Cable, Half-Temperance House, Wild Jäger and Bee Hive, which, by the way, was operated by Absolom Grapevine.

In 1858 the *Gazette*, lamenting the crime-ridden state of Cincinnati at that time, looked back through a quarter-century to a better day. It asserted that in 1833 Alexis de Tocqueville, the eminent French statesman-author, then working on his *Democracy in America*, wrote to Daniel Van Matre, then prosecuting attorney of Hamilton County, inquiring about the crime situation there; to which Van Matre was able to reply that in 1833 there was not one homicide, murderous or justifiable, in the city. One finds it difficult to accept this statment, but if true, those were among the last days of Arcadia. For only three years later, there were four public hangings in one year (there had been several before 1833, too, it must be said), and such greedy mobs gathered to see the degrading spectacles that the wiser citizens of Cincinnati induced the legislature to pass a law, confining executions to jail yards.

By 1850 the city had noisome precincts where disorder was the normal condition — Gas Alley, Charcoal Alley, Frogtown, the water front — Rat Row, Sausage Row, Spring Heel Row, where were mostly groggeries, dives and ten-cent lodgings with booze auxiliaries, the "beds" being just rectangles on the floor; though in the St. James — fancy that name! — on Sausage Row, there were tiers of bare boards rising along the walls to increase capacity and income. Many unknown murders took place in these stinking rookeries, and how many unknown — the convenient river taking care of the bodies — who can tell? The police trod gingerly here when they came at all, for the most part either carefully indulgent or allied, politically or otherwise, with the roughs. The story was told of a man's being beaten by thugs while a policeman stood by, looking on. Editors were loudly demanding some means of identifying the watch, as they were still called. They still had no uniforms (and didn't want any) and habitually wore their badges under their coats. They carried clubs, though these, too, might be concealed.

Professional beggars were earning $5 to $10 a day "by simulating various lamenesses and disabilities." Teen-age gangs fought each other savagely, and youthful pickpockets, thugs and thieves were in daily dress rehearsal. There were "kinchers" — an old English thieves' term; see *Oliver Twist* — boys who trailed and watched strangers in town or drunks with money, for the information of robbers. Pocket-picking, by the way, was practiced even on the audiences in police courts, the *chef d'oeuvre* being the lifting of the wallet of a lieutenant of police.

Some city and county officials in the '50's showed symptoms of illiteracy, and at least two city police judges, Flinn and McFall were dishonest, drunken rowdies, a disgrace to the community. Both were frequently in saloon brawls and McFall had been arrested and fined for reckless driving on both sides of the river. Flinn once attacked a German tailor in a dispute over a small bill, but the tailor felled him with his goose. Later, Flinn and McFall fought in a saloon, and Flinn was again knocked out, this time with a bottle. Trials before these two were sometimes described by the newspapers as "scenes of incredibile ribaldry and blackguardism."

Charities and missions, such as the Cincinnati Union Bethel, organized on Front Street in 1839 — primarily for the benefit of rivermen, and eventually a great power for good — were doing their best to point the way and give material assistance towards a better life, but so far the problem seemed too big for them. There was a new and uglier viciousness in the air. Hold-ups were seldom perpetrated at the pistol's muzzle. Throttling the victim from behind was the mildest method; the favorite was to assail him with clubs or slung shot and beat him into insensibility, sometimes killing or maiming him as mere incidentals to robbing him. On other occasions, men were beaten unmercifully when the motive was not always obvious. Sometimes it was because of a grudge, on other occasions mistaken identity, and there were instances which appeared to be pure sadism. Two roughnecks arrested for beating an old man nearly to death could give no other reason than that "they just wanted to try their hand." The term, "antisocial," so lightly tossed about nowadays, was, in mid-nineteenth century a hard, brutal fact; there were actual cases — men and youths who palpably held a slum-begotten grudge against their fellow men, especially those possessing property and culture. Where else are we to find the motive of those fellows who liked to stand in groups on a street corner and vent the most frightful curses and obscenity as a well-dressed woman went by? If she was accompanied by a man and the offenders were several in number, there was nothing the escort could do but set his teeth and bear it, for at the slightest sign of resentment, they were all too ready to retort with fists or weapons or both. A lady who ventured to pass certain corners, even downtown in daylight alone, ran the risk, not only of insult, but of having her skirts slashed with a knife. And as women did not carry handbags then, but had pockets in their skirts, they were prey for pickpockets, too, in a crowd. Overskirts came into fashion after the Civil War, and as they covered the pocket, they made it harder to loot. One outraged hustler grumbled, "Since the damned overskirts come inter style, I haven't made me salt."

Such was Cincinnati's reputation by 1858 that towards dusk one day a policeman saw a tall rustic with a brick in one hand almost tiptoeing along the curb on Fourth Street like a cat in a strange house, raising the brick and exclaiming "Don't come near me! Don't come near me!" every time someone approached him. The officer, by a strategic leap, succeeded in collaring him, and demanded the reason for the melodrama. The man relaxed at sight of the other's badge, and explained. He was an Indiana farmer who had just sold a drove of hogs and had the cash in his pocket. He could not get a train for home before morning, and fearing to be robbed if he went to a hotel, he had decided to walk the streets all night and apply the brick to anyone who tried to get within his line of defense.

Prostitution flourished beyond all previous records. One or two of the leading theaters had separate entrance sections of the gallery set aside for "fashionable nymphs of the pave" — as reporters liked to call them — when identifiable. Britons wondered why this wasn't done in England. Brothels appeared everywhere, decent families sometimes being driven from their homes by the noise and obscenity of one such which had begun operations near them. They liked to set up in business near a school for girls or young women, too, and the law seemed to offer no remedy. Once a beautiful, demure young woman entered a "female seminary" as a pupil, and was presently discovered to be the operator of a bagnio. Her motive was obvious.

A highly moral activity of the volunteer firemen and their friends was the "washing out" of a house of ill repute. No fire company as such ever ventured to do this alone, but their apparatus was used, and some of them always participated in the fun. Whether because of a grudge at some one of the inmates or from an impulse of pure deviltry, a mob with hand-pumping engine and hose reel would repair to some such house, smash in the front door and windows, while the occupants fled, shrieking, throw the fine furniture, including piano, into the street and make a bonfire of it, meanwhile flooding the building with the fire hose and theoretically cleansing it of its taint. One madame who suffered this vandalism had recently given $50 to the firemen's relief fund.

Cincinnati volunteer firemen were pretty hard cases, as were their kind everywhere, the good citizens who served with them for the fun of it being too few in number to be an ameliorative leaven. As was the universal fashion, companies fought over access to water-plugs and cisterns while buildings burned. When a big saw and planing mill caught fire in '51, the first two companies to arrive began fighting over a cistern, and other companies, as they appeared, joined in the fray until ten companies were at it in a battle royal. A Covington company, seeing the great billows of flame and smoke rolling heavenward, hastily assembled and ferried across the river "to help," but instead, they too waded into the melee while the mill and lumber yard burned to ashes. Among most American volunteer firemen, it was an unwritten law that nothing more lethal than fists were to be used in fights; but in Cincinnati they used anything that came handy, sometimes even to pistols, and they broke many noncombatant windows, with their brick- and stone-throwing. On the occasion of a great fireman's celebration, with companies from the three States and even one from Nashville marching in a parade five hours long, the Relief and Invincible companies of Cincinnati couldn't keep the peace, but fought with each other, almost wrecking the whole program. The firemen's motto, by the way, was "Our Only Care, the City's Good; Our Work its Own Reward."

Two of Cincinnati's notable achievements of that era were the building in 1852 of the first practical fire engine ever used, and the installation, shortly afterward, of the first salaried fire department in America. The engine, a huge, clumsy affair weighing five and a half tons and requiring four horses and its own power to draw it at a good speed, was invented by Alex B. Latta and built by him and his partner, Shawk. It brought to a climax the years-long campaign of Jacob Wykoff Piatt — one of the few good citizens who still strove against disheartening odds for better government by serving on the City Council — to bring about a salaried fire department. The volunteers were of course violently opposed to the measure, and whenever they knew that a vote was to be taken on it — as Piatt brought it up again and again — the council chamber would be cluttered with menacing rowdies. For a long time only one other councilman, Judge Timothy Walker, had the courage to vote with Piatt, though all members knew that it was a much-needed reform. Piatt's life was threatened, he was burned in effigy in front of his own home, and for some time a volunteer guard of Irish constituents accompanied him to and from Council meetings.

When Latta & Shawk's engine passed all tests, the Council still hesitated to adopt it, knowing that the volunteers would wreck it as soon as they could get their hands on it. They finally asked Miles Greenwood, foundryman and prominent citizen, to head the company that operated it. Greenwood had been a noted volunteer himself, was still the idol of the firemen, and had been in opposition to the idea of a salaried force. The suggestion that he take over the engine was regarded by some as merely putting the machine into the hands of an enemy. But Greenwood was a man of high character, and being a machinist himself, looked with favor upon the steam pumper; in fact, had put some of his own money into it. At first startled by the proposal that he command the engine company, he accepted on condition that he he allowed to select his own crew. He knew that there would be a fight, and he wanted men he could depend on.

The first alarm after the engine formally went into service came in the small hours of a night, and the legend persists that the fire was incendiary, started by the volunteers to create an opportunity to destroy the new machine. Greenwood and his men were quickly at the engine house, and he himself, a big, powerful figure in brass helmet, drove the four horses that drew the steamer. As expected, there was a fight as soon as they reached the scene of the fire, but the volunteers ran into unexpected resistance — not only the engine crew, but many intensely loyal workers in Greenwood's plant and Piatt, with a small army of 250 Irishmen from the old Thirteenth Ward, thirsting for battle. Against such opposition, the volunteers had to give in, contenting themselves with cursing and threatening Greenwood. He moved his family down from Avondale to the Basin, and for a year and a half afterward, answered every tap of the bell. The Council voted him $1,000 for his services, which he turned over to the Mechanics' Institute. Exhibiting the engine to a committee from Baltimore, he gave as two of its points of superiority the facts that it never got drunk and it never threw brickbats. Its only fault, he said, was that it couldn't vote.

On April 1st, 1853, the city's salaried fire department became a reality. Meanwhile, Latta & Shawk, rapidly designing lighter

[72]

and better machines, were building engines for Boston, Philadelphia, Columbus, St. Louis and New Orleans, followed by others. It was not long before a telegraphic fire alarm system again put Cincinnati ahead of other cities.

Mr. Latta wanted his monument in Spring Grove Cemetery to be topped by a model of his fire engine but the cemetery authorities flatly vetoed the idea. For decades Cincinnati was the chief center of fire engine manufacture, Chris Ahrens — who had been a foreman for Lane & Bodley when they made the Latta engine — becoming the leading figure of the industry.

Cincinnati inventiveness illumined many subjects other than fire engines, emphasizing the vast difference between the efficiency and honesty of the city's industry and its government. Among other things, some unknown genius built a piano in the Mohawk suburb or thereabouts around 1820, which was still in use thirty years later and said to be in good tone. Adam Hurdus,[5] New Jerusalem (Swedenborgian) minister, built an organ in 1806, and in 1843-45 two other "ingenious German mechanics," a Mr. Schmidt and John Koehnke, were each building large pipe organs on their own for churches as far away as Baltimore and New Orleans. News columns of the '50's are rich with news of inventions — agricultural and factory machinery, heating and lighting plants, new roofings, a horse drawn potato digger. Cincinnati, it was said, could supply every human need — even to counterfeit money that fooled top-ranking financiers. (Pamphlet "Counterfeit Detectors" were always among the best sellers.) The city made everything that went into a building, even the white lead and paint, all business and pleasure vehicles, the silverware, dishes and cutlery on all tables from high to low, not only many of the nation's books and magazines, but the paper, ink, plates and presses on which and with which they were printed, steamboats by the dozen, the cars and locomotives for the railroads being

---

[5] Adam Hurdus was the first Swedenborgian minister in Cincinnati, and it is a matter of record that John Chapman — known through all the Territory as "Johnny Appleseed" — a self-appointed Swedenborgian missionary and volunteer planter of thousands of apple trees for the pioneers of the middle West, was a guest at his house before 1817 and in other Cincinnati homes later.

thrown across the three States. Cist's book, *Cincinnati in 1841*, was handsomely supported by 89 pages of business and professional advertising. Cincinnati's elegant iron jail cells, made to order in sections, shipped to destination and easily assembled, "for safety, comfort and convenience," said Cist, "are not excelled in the West . . . give satisfaction to the people of the county and are a terror to evil-doers." One is slightly bemused here over the question how so comfortable a jail could be terrifying to rogues.

In iron and steel tools, Cincinnati yielded to no city in the world in excellence. She even went in for precision instruments. She competed with Sheffield in producing edged tools and fine swords, and in supplying the western Indians with scalping knives guaranteed to do a clean job. David McHardy, the British commissioner to our Centennial Exposition in 1876, said that British tools had not yet taken on improvements devised in America sixty to seventy years before. An English lady, Mrs. Bishop, saw in a store in Canada axes and spades both of British and Cincinnati manufacture, and was told by the merchant that most of his customers preferred the Cincinnati implements as being of superior quality.[6]

As early as 1845 not only furniture but window sash and doors were being made in Cincinnati by machinery which cut mouldings. A mill owner, S. Vanneman, had invented many of the machines. William Chambers, a Scotsman who came visiting in '53, was here introduced to mass production and was dizzied by it. In Great Britain, furniture was still for the most part made by hand, but in Cincinnati he saw a factory which ground out by machinery 200 dozen wooden chairs per week, "worth from five to twenty-four dollars a dozen." Among these were many rocking chairs, and the mechanical scooping out and curving of the seats and rockers seemed to the visitor clever beyond description. (Two years later 500 dozen chairs weekly was the rate.) It appeared that 1,000 bedsteads a week and 2,000 chests of drawers a year, each part ingeniously shaped on a separate machine and then assembled, were commonplaces. One manufacturer had an order to make all the furniture for a large hotel in California. The pre-

6 Mrs. Isabella Bird Bishop, *An Englishwoman in America*, (London, 1856).

cision and beauty of the turning on lathes fascinated Chambers, whose admiration extended also to the engines, machine tools, firearms, shoes, carriages made here. One shoe factory used 10,000 sides of sole leather, 40,000 sides of upper leather, 20,000 sheep-skins, 2,500 calfskins, 5,000 pounds of shoe nails and 600 bushels of shoe pegs. Clothing was one of the city's biggest industries; A. & J. Trounstine's factory alone employed 700 hands in 1857. As for Cincinnati's wines, Chambers sampled them and began to suspect that they might some day drive European wines out of the market. He was amazed to see Hamilton County strawberries shipped 1,600 miles to New Orleans, packed in ice; "but when did an American ever think of distance?"[7]

An English immigrant, a man of all work for Banker Spencer, wrote to a kinsman in 1831 that "Poor people are well paid for their work," and "My family can live for one-quarter they could in England." In 1841 William Thomson, a Scotch woolen yarn spinner, worked for a while in the mill of J. C. Geisendorff, and of course wrote a book upon his return home. "The style of living" among workingmen, said he, "is superior to anything I had hither-to seen"; and he had worked elsewhere in America, too. He could earn $7.50 a week by his toil, and he paid only $2.50 a week for good board and lodging. Women boarders were charged only $1.75 to $2. Pork-house workers earned from $1 to $2 a day, and cabinet-makers from $7 to $14 per week. "Our bed-rooms were large and airy, but crowded. In my room there were three beds, two sleeping in each; but the mistress would not venture to put two together without the consent of both parties. I observed they were cleanly in their habits, using night shirts, washing as regu-larly as they rose. . . . The morning salutations were such as are not very common in this country" (Great Britain). " 'Good morning, Miss Stone' — 'Good morning, sir' — 'Morning' — 'Morning' — 'Morning' all around. Coffee and tea, ham and eggs, roasted chickens, sallad, pickles, vinegar, pepper (black and red), hot biscuits, Jonneycake, buck-wheat cakes and butter was the

[7] William Chambers, *Things as They Are in America*, (London and Edin-burgh, 1857).

constant fare for breakfast. But the dinner was glorious — roast pig, a turkey (the very ruins of which would have dined a small family) and rounds of splendid beef." He fervently wished that British laborers might get as good beef.

"The people in this country," he noticed, "never call their employer *Master*. *Boss* is the name most generally used; and here, as elsewhere, I observed the same respectful conduct of the *Boss* to his hands. In speaking to them on the street or in the country house, he will say, 'Yes, sir' or 'No, sir.' "[8]

So here are two of the three facets of young Cincinnati — its business and its government — in startling contrast. (Its culture makes the picture still more paradoxical.) Its private business, as it firmly believed and as some visitors were disposed to concede, was the most efficiently handled in America; its public affairs, so some of its own good men and publicists declared in their rage, the very worst. Three sorts of serenity had developed in its population; first, that of the businessman, living comfortably, intent on gain, trusting government to take care of itself; second, that of the politicians, resting easily on their graft, knowing that they need give little in return; and third, the phlegmatic serenity of the 40,000 German citizens, who seldom became greatly excited over anything, and whose sound, if somewhat stodgy poise was the largest contribution to the calmness and balance which outsiders notice in the Cincinnati of today.

Mrs. Bishop, bless her heart, was so interested in the wonders of Cincinnati in 1856 that she didn't see the dirt or disorder; and as she was no fool, her picture of it reveals how easily a bustling, glittering turmoil of achievement may conceal or divert the attention of a hurried visitor from a dark, roily current of corruption slinking underneath. To her, the city was "one of the most remarkable monuments of the progress of the West . . . a second Glasgow in appearance . . . heavily laden drays rumbling along the streets — quays at which steamboats of fairy architecture are ever lying — massive warehouses and rich stores — the sidewalks a per-

[8] William Thomson, *A Tradesman's Travels in the United States and Canada in the Years* 1840, 1841, *and* 1842, (Edinburgh, 1842).

fect throng of foot-passengers — the roadways crowded with light
carriages, invariably drawn by two horses, horsemen with pal-
metto hats and high-peaked saddles, galloping about on the magnificent horses of Kentucky — an air of life, wealth, bustle and
progress . . . Germans smoking chibouks . . . German ladies in the
evening, driving among the hundreds if not thousands of carriages,
light wagons and trotting baskets driven to the cemetery and
along the roads. As everybody who has a hundred yards to go
drives or rides, rings are fastened to all the sidewalks in town to
tether the horses to." In the shops, she found "the richest and most
elegant manufactures of Paris and London. A bookseller's store,
an aggregate of two or three of our largest, indicated that the
culture of the mind was not neglected." She considered the church
singing and chanting "of a very superior order"; and she greatly
admired the church interiors as being more pleasing than "the
hallowed but comfortless antiquity of our village churches."

Evidently, by rare good fortune, there were no dead animals
lying on the streets through which she passed; she didn't visit the
slums or dens like the Blazing Stump on the Public Landing; she
heard nothing of the chicanery of councilmen or police, the lack
of law enforcement, the left-handed alliances with crime. She
didn't hear of the dozen street-cleaning machines owned by the
city which wouldn't work when it was too dry or too wet. She
missed seeing things like that tumulus of dirt and trash in Vine
Street described by the newspapers of '58 as being fifty feet long
and four feet high, with a foul tarn beside it deep enough to drown
a horse in. Probably during her stay there were no newspaper
items like that bitterly satirical one in the *Gazette;* "Several men
were yesterday engaged in making excavations in the piles of dirt
and filth in Fourth Street. At a reasonable depth they came upon
a very good bowlder pavement in a fair state of preservation."

CHAPTER V
Porkopolis

I⊤ ɪs difficult to discover when the first pork was packed in Cincinnati for other than local use. The business was being pretty rigidly regulated in 1809, as proven by notices inserted in the papers by Peter Mills, "Inspector of Hamilton County," who warned that the packing of Beef, Pork or Lard for shipment must be done under the eye of city supervisors or not at all.

There being no form of transportation in early days for hogs unless the grower lived near a river, pioneer porkers walked to market on their own four feet. Ohio hogs crossed the Alleghenies thus to New York and Baltimore, with great loss in weight, despite many rest periods, and from eastern Ohio they continued to do so, even after Cincinnati became a market. But western and southern Ohio, as well as Indiana and Kentucky farmers found a new and welcome outlet in the Queen City.

In the earlier years, even on good land, some razorbacks were produced, and these were harder to drive to market than the doltish fatbacks; they were rugged individualists, bolting in all directions at times, and it is related that the eyelids of some of the wilder ones were sewn shut to keep them from straying. The city razorbacks, by the way, were smart; they took care never to become entangled in any of the droves en route to the abattoirs. The packers soon began refusing such animals; they wanted a hog which, when cut up, would make a barrel or more of pork. Droves often ranged in weight from 350 to 500 pounds each. The loss from fatigue of the heavier animals was enormous. One hog which weighed 1,100 pounds when it left its home in Kentucky was down to 975 pounds when it reached the killing pen in Cincinnati. One drover had a very large specimen which could not keep up with the rest of the herd, and as he entered the city, he entrusted it to a passing stranger, who agreed for a price to bring it along more slowly to the abattoir. The owner never saw hog or stranger again. Droves from Kentucky had to be ferried across the river save in very cold weather when the river froze hard enough to enable them to cross on the ice, as thousands did during the great packing period. Here the venerable wisecrack about a hog on ice was exemplified, to the entertainment of idlers who gathered to watch the transcursion. We have not discovered an instance when the ice broke beneath a drove, as it occasionally did under a too-venturesome wagon and team, with almost inevitably fatal results.

Both of Cincinnati's famous nicknames were of early origin. In the 1820's, George W. Jones, president of the local branch of the Bank of the United States, and popularly known as "Bank" Jones, was so proud of the city's pork industry that he boosted it far and wide. In his letters to the bank's Liverpool correspondent, he seldom failed to mention the fact that from 25,000 to 30,000 hogs were being processed annually, and to predict Cincinnati's future supremacy as a provision market. At length the Liverpool man had two little papier-machè hogs made, branded, "George W. Jones, as the Worthy Representative of Porkopolis," and sent them to the Cincinnatian. Jones was delighted with them, and the city's new pseudonym was soon known to all the world.

At first salt pork — mess pork, it was called by the trade; the principal and staple ingredient of the sailor's diet, and which made scurvy the curse of the seven seas — was the packer's only product. The British Government began buying Cincinnati mess pork for its Navy, and presently transferred nearly all its business from Dublin, then the world's greatest pork-packing center, to the Queen City, to become its biggest customer. In the meantime the industry had ramified rapidly — smokehouses to cure hams and bacon; then renderers of lard, and then factors of candles, lard oil, soap, chemical and other by-products. In 1840, two of the nation's greatest soap manufactories were being developed — that of Michel Werk and what all Cincinnati now calls P & G. It was told with awe in '59 that the latter had 80 employees and sold a million dollars' worth of soap and candles annually. Wholesalers and brokers of pork products became big business.

The industry soon localized itself. Slaughtering would not have been permitted, of course, in the downtown area, so two arenas of immolation were developed. Tinkling among moss-covered rocks down a wooded ravine from springs near the top of the plateau as you went to Walnut Hills came a pretty little stream called Deer Creek. One of Cincinnati's pioneer beer gardens was up that vale, centering around a fine spring, with much "ornamental" rock-work and an aviary of woodland birds. But now the pork-butchers chose this as one of their fields of operation because of the creek, which would carry away their sewage. The beer garden vanished and the once beautiful glen became a place of horror, the creek nicknamed Bloody Run or Bloody River — it literally ran red — and citizens weren't any too happy at seeing it entering the Ohio so close below the water-works intake. The glen became the "Valley of the Shadow of Death," and as various odorous by-product plants were erected in it, "Valley of Desolation" was one of the least offensive of its sobriquets.

The other place of execution was Brighton, a suburb at the northwest corner of the Basin, as it were, where Mill Creek entered it. Down that stream's valley from up-country came great droves of hogs and herds of cattle and sheep, as the city's needs and the meat industry expanded. In the smokehouse and wholesale area, where the canal turned down along Deer Creek towards the river, two- and four-horse wagons, some loaded with barreled pork, some stacked high with whole or half-carcasses, singed and drawn, threaded thoroughfares almost blocked by the barrels of pork which overflowed the sidewalks, into the streets. Mrs. Houstoun, a British visitor of the late '40's, was nauseated by it all. Cincinnati, she said, "is, literally speaking, a *city of pigs* . . . a monster piggery. . . . Alive and dead, whole and divided into portions, their outsides and their insides, their grunts and their squeals, meet you at every moment."

When she and some friends went for a drive in the suburbs, they encountered a great multitude of "the unclean beasts, grunting along under the very wheels of our carriage" — on their way to their deaths, of course. "Those horrible Cincinnati pigs! . . . We could not look into a warehouse in the street without being agonized by the sight of thousands of dead corpses, heaped and piled upon one another, up to the ceiling, all singed and white and cold-looking, huddled together without any regard to decency, or any consideration for the feelings of the survivors. . . .

"The universal announcement over every third house that 'tripe and pigs' feet' were to be had within, and the confirmed fact that every third person you meet is unquestionably a pig merchant, who can wonder that the impression made upon the mind of a foreigner by the general aspect of Cincinnati is of a most material and far from romantic nature?" [1]

"The killing season is now fairly commenced," said the *Daily Atlas*, early in December, 1844. "On all the avenues leading to the city, droves of hogs may be seen, greater or less in number. There is scarcely an hour in the day in which Broadway is not alive with them" — these coming from Kentucky, we surmise; and as lower Broadway was one of the swankiest of society thoroughfares, hogs just couldn't have been tolerated there were it not for the fact that they were helping to support lower Broadway. It was annoying to have one's carriage halted in its tracks, perhaps when hurrying to a wedding, by an oink-oinking army filling the street from building to building; but upon reflection, it might have been pork that paid for the carriage and horses, so there was nothing for the ladies to do but smile and be patient. And if the progress of drays and wagons serving other businesses was hindered — well, after all, pork was king in Cincinnati.

In 1835 Dr. Drake pointed out to Miss Martineau an Englishman who had once been his servant, but who had turned "pork butcher" and was now worth $10,000 and still accumulating. That would have been mere pin-money ten years later. In the middle '30's, with pork at peak prices in the East; new packing houses and new mansions were springing up in Cincinnati, new carriages, horses, diamonds, pianos were everywhere. A satirical Eastern preacher said that the difference between the Upper and the Lower Ten in Cincinnati was that the latter killed the hogs with their own hands, the former did it vicariously.

[1] Mrs. Houstoun, *Hesperos; or Travels in the West*, (London, 1850).

Steadily, expansion went on, new abattoirs and packing houses appeared, with a higher speed of output. William Neff's pork house installed gaslights in 1848 and began working around the clock, and it was followed by others. Half a million hogs were killed in Cincinnati that year, and by 1850 the city had surpassed Dublin in volume of business. Tourists who could endure the sights visited the abattoirs to marvel at the speed of what might be called the disassembly line. Here, in the rapid mechanical forwarding of the hog from killing through cleaning to cutting up, is the real origin of the assembly line so often credited to Henry Ford, the better part of a century later — it having meanwhile risen through the Chicago packing houses. There is no telling how early the process began, but Dr. Drake described it in 1835 to Miss Martineau, who couldn't endure the thought of seeing it herself. From the time when the hog was smitten on the brow with a hammer — "which deprives him of consciousness," explained Mrs. Bishop — only three and a half minutes had elapsed since he was, in Captain Marryat's words, "grunting in his obesity," until he was, save for cooling and salting, ready for the barrel.

The clogging of roads and streets by porcine hordes seemed to be little affected by the building of the canal and the first two railroads into the city, though both forms of transportation brought thousands of them. As the industry came under still higher pressure, animals began coming to the killing pens even in late summer. A large drove which arrived by the Little Miami Railroad one August day in '54 were overcome by heat as they were being driven towards Brighton and lay down, squealing, in Fourth Street, putting that thoroughfare completely out of business. A Humane Society agent procured a fire hose, attached it to a plug and gave them a cooling shower, after which they were able to proceed.

Scandals, real or alleged, had of course begun to appear. Some bankers as early as the mid-forties were accused of speculating in pork, some of refusing to lend money to operators in pork unless the latter would agree to manipulate the market for the benefit of the lenders. And in '56 it was found that at least one packer was cheating the hog-growers. The Chamber of Commerce learned that one Shaw was weighing the hogs he bought with a "false pea" (weight),which was too heavy.A member of the Chamber strolled into Shaw's place and weighed himself on the scale, which represented him as balancing the beam at 220 pounds, whereas his real weight was 235. This meant a considerable loss to a farmer on a drove of hogs. An agent of the Chamber seized the weight, and after a hearing, Shaw was expelled from membership in that body, then was arrested and fined.

Other fauna, too, were cluttering the roads into Cincinnati. In December, '48 a flock of 300 turkeys walked ninety miles from a farm in Indiana to furnish forth the Christmas tables of the burghers — the first of a long series of such marches. Turkeys were among the greatest enemies to piety because of their intransigence, their tendency to leave the road and fly up into trees or elsewhere. A dealer in Cincinnati had a yard full of them one December when they all decided to take flight, and in a twinkling the roofs all over that part of the city were dotted with them. The scrambles after them went on for days afterward, and many a poor family dined on turkey that Christmas without cost. They could not have afforded to pay the twenty-five cents or more demanded in the markets for such a bird, for turkeys were much higher than they had been in 1805, when H. M. Brackenridge found that you could buy one for 16 cents in Cincinnati, and if you demurred to that figure, the dealer would offer to throw in a goose for good measure.

The butchers of the city staged a great meat publicity stunt each December, a parade with bands and the finest live animals that could be procured, scrubbed, wreathed and decorated with colored paper and bunting. In the Fifth Street market in '51 were suspended the whole carcasses of "66 bullocks, of which probably three-quarters were raised and fed in Kentucky and the residue in our own State, 125 sheep, hung up whole, 350 pigs displayed in rows on the platforms, ten of the finest and fattest bears that Missouri could produce, and a buffalo calf, weighing 500 pounds, caught at Santa Fe."

Or near the Santa Fe Trail, perhaps was meant. Which reminds us that as the Pacific Railroad lines were pushed across Kansas and

Nebraska in the 1860's, Cincinnatians had opportunity to discover the excellence of buffalo steaks when carcasses were shipped east by freight in midwinter weather, which kept them frozen or nearly so.

At the first Ohio State Fair, held in Cincinnati in October, 1850, the agricultural as well as the mechanical achievements of Hamilton County were made much of; for it had been supplying not only manufactured goods, but vegetables and vegetable products, including barreled sauerkraut, to many parts of the West and South, even as far away as New Orleans. One day in 1844, a steamer left for New Orleans with 1,500 heads of cabbage piled on the hurricane deck, all space below being crowded. The reckless lading of steamboats was appalling to the British traveler, Captain Oldmixon. Boarding the *Paul Anderson* in midwinter, 1854, with the river dotted with floating ice, he found the boat already overloaded, yet it took on 70 horses, 800 turkeys and chickens in coops and other cargo. The boat was so low in the water that icy waves slopped over the horses' hoofs as they stood on the boiler deck, while the fowls, their coops stacked on the hurricane deck, rapidly froze to death and were tossed overboard in batches.

Situated in a great grain-producing area, Cincinnati turned corn and wheat, on a big scale, into three major products — pork, flour and whisky. *De Bow's Statistical Review* for 1850 asserted that Cincinnati was the world's greatest whisky-producing center. The distillers were in the meat business, too, though in a dubious way; they all built stock pens as adjuncts to their distilleries, in which cattle and hogs were fed on the still slops. When a big distillery burned in 1879, nearly a thousand head of cattle were roasted to death. The hog-pens of another such plant, built on stilts over the Mill Creek flats, once collapsed under the weight of 2,400 animals. Increasing concern was felt over the numerous dairies within the city limits which fed their milch cows on the refuse of the stills. Many of the cows never left their stalls, and the effect upon their bodies was too deplorable for polite reading. Editors raged against this, but more than half a century passed before the better influences in Cincinnati succeeded in curbing the evil. That so many nineteenth-century citizens weathered it through to middle age is a tribute to ancestral toughness.

A pioneer habit of pouring sorghum molasses on pork and greens, still to be seen in Cincinnati's public dining places in the 1830's, and still common in certain hill areas of the South in recent years, was looked upon tolerantly by at least one stranger, Captain Marryat. "We laugh at the notion of pork and molasses," said he. "In the first place, the American pork is far superior to any that we have salted down; and in the next, it eats uncommonly well with molasses. I have tasted it, and *it is a fact*. After all, why should we eat currant jelly with venison, and not allow the Americans the humble imitation of pork and molasses?"

Cincinnati acquired an international reputation for ham, too. Thomas H. James was one of several Englishmen who liked it. "The only ham that I ever saw in the States that could be pronounced eatable was in Cincinnati,"[2] said he; but he couldn't recommend its bacon. The *Philadelphia American* praised Cincinnati ham as being as good as Philadelphia's best, and superior to Westphalian ham, which was high praise indeed. Warren Stagg, a Cincinnati packer, sent a dozen hams, nicely canvassed (only recently they were being wrapped in paper) to Queen Victoria in '52, and presently received a letter from Windsor, acknowledging the gift and saying further;

> "I have the satisfaction to inform you that these Hams have been so much approved of that you are requested to forward, on the receipt of this letter, 24 hams of precisely the same description, addressed to The Queen, Buckingham Palace, London.
>
> "I will at the same time beg you to forward me the bill for the same.
>
> THO: BIDDULPH
Master of the Household."

Said the *Gazette*, "We trust that Mr. Stagg will allow his children to play with his neighbors' children as heretofore, notwithstanding his sudden elevation in the world of trade."

[2] *Rambles in the United States and Canada during the Year 1845*, by Rubio. (London, 1846).

In the early days of the industry there was much waste, and parts of the hog that couldn't be used were given away. An immigrant English workman wrote enthusiastically to a friend back home of the cheapness of living in Cincinnati. Said he, "We can take a basket and go to the slaughter house and get as many pig hearts and lights as we please for nothing." Later, much better portions were given away or thrown away; spare-ribs, for example, not to mention the feet and some other parts. Cist said in 1845 that he remembered seeing cartloads of spare-ribs dumped into the river because they could not be barreled as salt pork. "Even today," he added, "a man may get a market-basket filled with tenderloins and spare-ribs for a dime." Poor folk, it would seem, had little reason to go hungry in those days, if they didn't tire of fresh pork.

But steadily the by-products increased in number and volume. The tallow from sheep killed for the local market went into candles. The hog and cattle parts formerly given away or discarded were now turned into lard, lard oil, soap and greases, while the hides built up great tanning, saddlery, leather goods and shoe manufacturing businesses. Weird effluvia increased in number and strength, and the oil, candle and soap factories exhibited an unpleasant tendency to blow up their boilers or burst into flames and spread new fumes over the town. A portion of the boiler of a soap and candle plant which exploded in 1872 was hurled nearly half a mile, to kill two little girls playing on the sidewalk.

When the candle makers began discarding tallow to make candles with stearic acid as a major ingredient, and glycerine and oleic acid for the making of soap and lubrication of yarn as by-products, the result was a sourish-rancid odor which was described as terrible. A plant at the foot of Vine Street, when the wind was southerly, spread woe and gnashing of teeth all over the lower Basin residence area, as far as Eighth and Broadway. Yet other and smellier yet profitable uses continued to be found for the hog's *disjecta membra*. As the Englishman, Charles Mackay, wrote in 1859, "Palaces and villas are built, and vineyards and orchards cultivated, out of the proceeds of their flesh, their bones, their lard, their bristles and their feet." He overlooked the hides and the

blood, which went into black puddings and chemicals. So, add tan-
yards, bone-fertilizer factories, glue factories, chemical plants,
the depots and caldrons of men who transmuted into useful elements animals that had died more or less naturally, supplement
these with odors of the foul streets and the back yards, and it is no
wonder that Basin residents who could afford it began fleeing to
Yellow Springs or farther as summer came on. Coleridge, in the
misnamed city of Cologne,

> "counted two-and-seventy stenches,
> All well defined, and several stinks;"

but had he visited Cincinnati in mid-century, his highly selective
nose might have isolated an even greater number, though he probably couldn't have named them. The city was fortunate, in that
few of its book-writing visitors seem to have been assailed by the
worst of the odors — or was it because they were accustomed to
such things in European cities? The direction of the wind was
anxiously noted when distinguished guests visited the Queen City,
and care was taken to keep them, if possible in untainted
atmosphere.

The only drawback to a residence in Walnut Hills was that the
main road to it led up the "Valley of Hinnom," another of the ran-
corous names of Deer Creek, which had not only abattoirs but
by-product laboratories. Operatives who spent ten or twelve
hours daily in that glen must have had strong stomachs. In 1849,
before Walnut Hills and Mount Auburn commuters had developed the exemplary forbearance which they later displayed, two
men whose "prussiate of potash factory" up the hollow must have
dispensed odors beyond our conception, were haled into court on
the charge of maintaining a nuisance. Witnesses tried in vain to
describe the fetor. The defendants retorted that they were burning only the most innocent materials, such as "cracklings," iron
filings, potash and charcoal and that their fumes were a powerful
disinfectant, having "the effect of correcting other stenches in the
neighborhood." Verdict: not guilty. Legitimate business must not
be throttled because of a few sensitive olfactory nerves.

But there was a time when the worm turned, and another nuisance was more summarily dealt with. Halfway up the valley a dead animal collector built a shack to serve as his private morgue, but it disintegrated in flame and smoke one night, leaving only the chimney. After a time another hut was built around the chimney, and became the headquarters of a ghoul catering to the medical colleges. That, too, was mysteriously incinerated between dusk and cock-crow on a moonless night.

A reporter visited the hollow — he called it Golgotha — one day in '56, and found the assignment "not as pleasant as might be desired. The roads, the houses, offices, nooks and corners are coated with mud, blood, grease and other filthy ingredients. The atmosphere is full of the odors that arise from these deposits, and at times, the wind and weather favoring, it supplies a portion of the city with a mixed vapor for breathing purposes ... decidedly more dense than is encountered in other localities. This, however, is endured by our citizens with a degree of patience that is somewhat remarkable. It is regarded as one of the necessary evils connected with the business of the city."

One cannot canvass the subject of odors without paying tribute to Cincinnati's most famous (or notorious) producer of them — a useful citizen named Josiah Keck, who appeared around Civil War times and flourished for many years thereafter. What was known to all Cincinnatians as Si Keck's Stink Factory was located at Anderson's Ferry, a down-river suburb, where the carcasses gathered by his men all over the city were resolved into valuable elements. Neighboring suburbs, Sedamsville, Riverside and Delhi, complained bitterly, and when the rich purple fumes from his plant rolled up the slope of adjacent Price's Hill to the pretty suburb on its summit and to the park maintained by Mr. Price on the brow, there were roars of protest from up there. There were murmurs, too, from the dwellers around Sixth and Front Streets, regarding the near-by wharf where Mr. Keck assembled his *reliquiae* for forwarding down to the factory by boat. He spent no little time in fighting off injunctions and summonses for maintaining a nuisance, which he did with a lively combativeness, occasionally losing his temper, as when he assaulted one of the most vigorous speakers at a mass meeting of protest.

His very name lent itself to jocosity. When a revival of the old-fashioned spelling bee flared up in 1875, and business and society folk were having a merry evening of it at Pike's Opera House, L. C. Hopkins, a prominent dry goods merchant, was ordered to spell the word "psychic."

"S, i, Si, K, e, c, k, Keck," was his answer.

"Wrong!" thundered the interlocutor.

"That's the way the *Commercial* spells it," defended Mr. Hopkins.

A Letter to the Editor on a Wednesday in 1878, said "The attention of Si Keck is called to a dead dog which has been lying in the gutter on Plum Street between Third and Fourth since last Friday." The writer was satirically unsure that Mr. Keck was the proper person to notify, but "If the sanitary officer should happen that way, he might take a look at it."

The moral relapse following the Civil War brought about some shocking revelations — hogs dying of cholera in the distillers' pens and even in the abattoirs, where afflicted animals had actually been killed and made into pork; inspectors bribed to pass unfit animals, in turn holding up packers, making them pay for the approval of sound hogs, and even speculating in pork themselves.

Meanwhile, the complaints about Deer Creek swelled in volume. In '71 Attorney Drausin Wulsin was leading a citizens' fight in Council to have its industries removed to Brighton or still farther, the valley cleaned up and taken by the city for park and reservoir purposes. "The eloquent councilman from the First Ward" (name not given) agreed with them. "Deer Creek," said he, "is an infernal stink-hole. Sodom and Gomorrah was a pandemonium of purity compared to it." Council did nothing, and some of the members of the Park Board were plainly under the influence of industrialists up the hollow. As a sub-headline over a description of a Board-meeting broil on the subject, the learned and witty Richard Smith, editor of the *Gazette*, inquired, "Tantæne Animis Cælestibus Iræ?" (Can such wrath dwell in celestial minds?). "Why this hurry about Deer Creek?" demanded Commissioner

Carson. "Has that Gehenna, that Golgotha become so much worse, so much more offensive within the past ten days that it becomes important to the city of Cincinnati that it be filled up? No, sir, there is no change. It has been there since the city was organized, since your ancestors came here. The miasma arising from it may be very offensive, but it didn't kill our early ancestors. Why, they flourished and got fat on it. It didn't kill them any more than Mill Creek did my ancestors."

But by this time the creek's useful but objectionable businesses were yielding to the need for railroad facilities, and moving away. Now the gulch became a bare, ugly wilderness of scrub growth, dotted here and there in tributary ravines by flimsy shacks inhabited by low forms of animal life, who murdered each other occasionally without disturbing the delicate balance of society. For several years around 1880 a band of thugs, the Nuttle gang, harbored in an old railway tunnel, running from Deer Creek under Avondale, which had been years in building and was finally abandoned. A policeman chased one of the ruffians to the mouth of the tunnel one day, but dared not enter it. Not until some of them were caught outside their lair was the band broken up.

The handwriting on the wall for Porkopolis, faintly seen during the war, was now plainly visible. In 1859 Cist had counted thirty-three large-scale pork-packing houses in the city, and several smaller ones, not to mention a few devoted to beef. But it was an ominous sign when, in the early '60's, the column of pork-market news in the Cincinnati papers began to have dispatches of increasing length from Chicago and Milwaukee, and then from Peoria and St. Louis. Pork, like other things, was following, or rather moving ahead of the center of population westward.

But Cincinnati had not yet yielded the crown, and did not for years afterward. In one number of the *Cincinnati Price Current* in 1873, thirty-eight local packers advertised their brands of ham, and these were not all. The industry employed the artist, Henry F. Farny, to make three huge paintings, each five feet high and thirty feet long, depicting the whole process of pork-producing in Cincinnati, and sent them to the Vienna exposition of 1874. But the whole picture was changing now, including that of some of the by-products. After 1859 American kerosene (not to mention gas) rapidly displaced candles and lard oil as illuminants. Candles for certain purposes persist even unto this day, however, and they are made in quantity in Cincinnati. But the Great Plains, now being threaded by steel rails, became a vast empire of grass and corn and wheat, and thereby a nursery for food animals, and packing plants naturally moved nearer to the source of supply. As Chicago became the nation's and the world's greatest railroad center, it currently became the chief producer of America's fresh and cured meats — ably seconded, as we have noticed, by other plains cities, eventually including Kansas City and Omaha. Gradually, the packing houses of Cincinnati liquidated or moved away. A few are left — some very good ones, too; but the old predominance is gone. There was an ephemeral quality in it. As you bowl along either of those two busy streets, Gilbert Avenue or the Reading Road, traversing the two sides of what was once the Deer Creek hollow — a depression where there is no longer a creek, but a park and some railroad yards and factories, and up towards the hilltop, some homes — it is impossible to conceive of it as the place of horror, yet profitable horror, that we have sketched but lightly in words. It gives the whole story a sort of unreality, especially when you try to find one great Cincinnati fortune of today that was built wholly or even mostly on pork. It eludes you; it makes Porkopolis seem like one of those cities of legend which suddenly and miraculously appear from under the earth or somewhere, full-peopled and busy with men and women in the garb of another age, bustling about affairs of seeming pith and moment for a few hours, then quite as suddenly and mysteriously vanishing again into some unearthly nothingness for another destined span of years.

CHAPTER VI
Home and Fireside

THAT eminent citizen, Dr. Daniel Drake, in his *Notices Concerning Cincinnati*, sketched the Cincinnatian of 1810 for us. His diet was "similar to that of the Eastern States," so probably he was eating less wild game and pumpkin bread than previously. The dress was "similar to that of the other inhabitants of the middle States. The females injure their health by dressing too thin" (it seems to be an eternal habit) "and both sexes by not accomodating the quantity of clothing to the changes of the weather. The amusements of balls and other evening parties so destructive to female health in all parts of the United States are engaged in here, but not to remarkable success." He didn't think there was much card-playing, either, both being amusements which he regarded as unnecessary. Most of the inhabitants, he said, were temperate. "There are not a few, however, who daily but quietly become intoxicated, and no very inconsiderable number have been known to fall victims of the habit.

"Bathing in the river is practiced by some, but is less regular and general than it ought to be."

In 1815 the Doctor elaborated his picture. "During the winter, select parties are frequently assembled, at which the current amusements are social converse, singing and recitation. . . . . Sleigh riding and skaiting are rarely enjoyed, on account of the lightness and instability of the snow and ice. Sailing for pleasure on the Ohio is but seldom practised, and riding out of town for recreation, on horseback or in carriages, is rather uncommon, for want of better roads. Evening walks are more habitual, in which the river bank and the adjacent hills — the *Columbian Garden* and the *mound* at the *west end*, are the principal resorts."

After this rather dreary picture of the state of social diversion, we are scarcely surprised when he informs us that "Hysteria, hypochondria and insanity are not uncommon." A strait-laced puritanism did for a number of years hold society in a certain limited thraldom, though other evidence indicates that there was a great deal going on of which Dr. Drake, engrossed in his science and his medical controversies, was not aware. As much as nine years before this, Thomas Ashe, a visiting Englishman, found the balls and amateur theatricals a subject of remark.

Benjamin Drake and Edward D. Mansfield, writing on *Cincinnati in 1826*, believed that "An entire freedom from political restraint" was responsible for a more rapid amalgamation of feeling and manners than would be expected from so many dissimilar elements of population. In the matter of behavior, "As our city has hitherto had scarcely any other police than public opinion, we must of course attribute the good order and morality which prevail among us to the correct feelings and sentiments of the inhabitants." Drinking was less common, they declared, than in the East, one possible reason being that the Cincinnati climate was "unfavorable to the longevity of drunkards." We had had the impression that this was true of any climate.

Gorham Worth's testimony, already quoted, about the splendor of David Kilgour's mansion and way of life proves that luxury was creeping up on the Cincinnatian as early as 1820. As the new captains of industry and commerce — who had usually begun by living in rented cottages or lodgings, some even in a single room — rose rapidly in fortune, they wanted homes of their own. In the earlier years, there were some handsome homes on Front Street, but when the flood of '32 rippled impudently through their upper floors and steamboats paddled through the street back of them, Front was ruined as a place of residence. Within a few years the steamboat offices and warehouses were competing for space there with saloons, flophouses and dives.

So society moved up the slope. But the market prices of property rose so rapidly, and there were so many of the newrich who wanted to live in the Basin that the centuries-old European practice of packing houses together like wasps' nests — which still exerted an influence on early America — caused the erection of those elbow-to-elbow rows of handsome dwellings, some of which still remain in Cincinnati's cross-streets. Some wealthy citizens demanded a bit of grass and a few trees, but there were not a great many of these in the Basin. The most notable concentration of such splendor was on the lower East Side. Martin Baum's mansion — now the Taft Museum — on Pike Street, as old as David Kilgour's or older, set the tone for that small area of elegance which has not yet quite lost all its older residents, its greenery and its stateliness. East Third and Fourth, as they crossed Broadway and approached Pike, passing such places as the Lytle mansion, with its big yard (now Lytle Park) and the home of Jacob Strader, steamboat and railroad magnate, were very select. But around these enclaves of *ton*, business and the human entities classified by modern survey bureaus as Cs and Ds were apt to nudge up closely, as did the industrial odors.

Take lower Broadway, for example — for a couple of blocks as impeccable a thoroughfare as you might find anywhere. On a corner of Fourth Street was the magnificent Dexter mansion, with a wondrous mahogany and marble interior. But only a few doors up Broadway from it, and you ran into business; while around the corner in Fifth Street were sales stables which carried on horse auctions, trotting and galloping horses to and fro in the street, while the auctioneers bawled and crowds gaped and made bids. Over one stable was the Red Jacket Saloon, and near by were Monkey John's grocery and the William Tell Coffeehouse. "Families cannot reside in that part of town," said the *Gazette*, "with any degree of comfort or quiet." But we take it that the disturbance was not too obnoxious as far down as Fourth Street.

Going down Broadway from Fourth, refinement prevailed for a block and more. There was the mansion of Thomas D. Carneal, Kentucky-born capitalist, a restless, whimsical builder of some seventeen or eighteen such manors on both sides of the river, in each of which he lived briefly; this one presently passed to George K. Schoenberger, ironmaster, who lived in it until he moved to the hills. Other important families who lived in that block and a half at one time and another were Lee, Pomeroy, Latham, Mayor

Samuel W. Davies, Judge Bellamy Storer, Professor Ormsby M. Mitchell the astronomer, Captain John Good, Dr. John Moorhead, pugnacious medical college professor, Alfred Gaither, Adams Express official and others, practically all figures in society. But halfway to Second Street the block began to deteriorate, and at the corner of Second, Bob Riley had his grocery store, selling liquor, as most grocers did then, making a bargain price of two drinks of whiskey for a picayune (6¼ cents), with a "common cigar" (very common, we surmise) thrown in, and plates of herring and crackers on the counter to nibble at and increase your thirst for another drink; one of the earliest instances of the free lunch which became so great a factor in the retail liquor business in later years.

After the decline of Front Street, the stylish regions of abode moved rapidly northward, and presently Fourth Street, mostly residences, but with just a touch of high-class business, was being called Cincinnati's Fifth Avenue. An item of 1851 said that one of the most beautiful dwellings in the city was that of Dr. Wood, on Fourth Street — three stories high, with cut-stone front, "displaying a pleasing originality of design, with a high degree of architectural elegance and chastity." But already the rapidly growing phalanx of moneyed folk were finding new homes to northward, passing over Fifth and Sixth Streets as too commercial, to light on Seventh, which in '51, was "rapidly becoming a pleasant fashionable portion of the city," where "costly and tasteful residences" were appearing, as well as the largest concentration of houses of worship in the city. Several residences were named in the newspapers as being "chaste and beautiful in architecture, three stories high, with stone fronts." Promotion was under way; a builder was razing some old houses farther west, to be replaced by three-story, stone-fronted dwellings, all no doubt of chaste design and probably rental property, which had come to be a considerable business, for we find a Cincinnati Landlords' Association functioning as early as 1862. Eighth Street was next invaded by fashion, but an irritated dweller there wrote to the papers in 1858 that it was being turned into a racecourse by swagger young sports in buggies, *"especially on Sunday,* and has this special excellence, that no arrests by our municipal *gens d'armes* need be feared."

James Silk Buckingham as early as 1840 found the private dwellings in general as large and commodious as those in the Atlantic coast cities, but more of them built of stone and fewer of wood than in the East. "A greater number of them have pretty gardens, rich grass-plots and ornamental shrubberies and flowers around them than in any of the Eastern cities . . . every comfort and convenience, mixed with a sufficient degree of elegance, is found in all the residences of the middle and upper classes; and it may be doubted whether there is any city in the Union in which there is a more general diffusion of competency in means and comfort in enjoyments, than in Cincinnati."[1]

Home heating in early days was all by fireplaces burning wood. Even the cooking was done in, or with a "reflector" in front of a fireplace. Then stoves came in, and the sawing of cordwood into parlor and kitchen lengths became Opportunity for the casual laborer. When a load of it was delivered at a home, either by alley in the rear or in the street in front, the wood-sawyer, who might have been following the wagon, appeared with saw and sawbuck hooked over one shoulder and an axe over the other, and asked for the job of working it up. In '53 two young genii, whose names history failed to record, created a sensation by going about town with a portable sawing rig operated by a small steam engine. It did the work in quick time, though some fastidious folk disliked the industrial atmosphere and the crowd of children and idlers that gathered to watch it work.

In the 1840's, Kanawha and Hocking Valley Coal was coming down the river in increasing volume, but many householders were reluctant to use the smutty stuff, though new homes began to be constructed with grates instead of fireplaces. It may surprise some to learn that both steam and hot air furnaces for central heating were in use that early. The House of Refuge, completed in 1850, had 250 rooms all heated by steam.

[1] J. S. Buckingham, *The Eastern and Western States of America*, (London, 1842).

Mr. Philip Hinkle — who had arrived in Cincinnati a poor carpenter bereft of his kit of tools stolen from him en route, and who became a prosperous builder and manufacturer of ready-cut houses, which were shipped all over the Great Plains and even to Texas and California — decided to sell his home at Fourth and Smith Streets in 1857; perhaps the fumes of that candle factory down Vine Street drifted his way too often. His advertising of the property in the newspapers gives us a good idea of a prosperous dwelling house of the period. A small woodcut in the notices pictures it as simple in design — chaste, let us say — three stories high, and we hear that it, too, had a stone front. The text describes it as "heated by furnace, also supplied with grates and ash flues, hot and cold plunge and shower baths, speaking trumpets (tubes), bells, gas in all the rooms" — possibly including a gas cooking-range in the kitchen, though he doesn't say so. There were even coal gas generators procurable for public and private houses, schools and churches. There were "benzole" (benzene, not benzine) gas-lighting plants for country residences, some of which were in use in Cincinnati's suburbs.

The house lacked only electricity, a telephone and sewer connection to have been quite modern. Only a couple of small and more or less ineffective sewers had been built at that time. The waste water from Mr. Hinkle's and other kitchen sinks and bathrooms therefore ran out through a drain pipe into the street gutter, and so made its way towards the river. For his and thousands of other families, the outdoor, back-yard latrine was a necessity. In the business district, these were tucked away behind stores and in all sorts of nooks within the block, sometimes several concerns using one. Their wooden floors were often neglected for years, until now and then one of them gave way and precipitated a user into the vault. One collapsed under the weight of a man, his wife and two children, causing the death of the wife, though the other three escaped. Even as late as 1872, when William P. Tyrrell, a "fashionable boot and shoe maker," moved into a store at the corner of Fourth and Walnut Streets, he was annoyed for several days by a bad odor which he thought might indicate a dead rat under the floor. At last, one evening, he pried up a plank and discovered a black chasm underneath — an abandoned vault. By way of research, he twisted a piece of paper, lighted it and dropped it into the hole. Immediately there was a muffled explosion which bulged the floor upward, hurling him backward and jarring stock off the shelves. Fortunately, no fire ensued.

In the earlier years, householders paid the operators of "night carts" to have their vaults cleaned, and through poverty or parsimony, some neglected this until the vaults overflowed. Editors at times threatened to publish the names of these offenders against the public, and when on rare occasions they did so, the quality of some of the names on the list was surprising. The city took over this task in the 1850's, but did not perform it adequately. The sullage was hauled to a wharf, loaded on scows, taken to the middle of the river and dumped. A dreadful incident took place in later years when a passenger train ran into a string of night carts on their way to the wharf about 1:00 A.M. and wrecked three of them.

Henry L. Mencken's famous canard of a few years ago, naming Cincinnati as the place where the bathtub originated in 1842, has even gotten into reference books. The truth is that it is impossible to say when or where the modern bathtub originated. They had hip or sitz baths in the eighteenth century, and they might have had some full-length ones, too; though, truth to tell, there wasn't a great deal of bathing done. There were public bathhouses in Cincinnati in the 1820's, and maybe earlier; we read during the summer of '29 that "an old bathhouse on Sycamore Street" had been remodelled into a theater. J. Walter, "plumber and lead pipe manufacturer," advertised about the same time that he would sell and install bathtubs.

When a man in the summer of 1842 proposed to establish a floating bathhouse in the river at the foot of Vine Street, the *Gazette* thought the idea a good one. "The water is always pure, because these baths are so constructed as to pass through them in a constant stream." He must have forgotten about that Deer Creek sewer, or else he relied strongly on the river's ability to purify itself in the course of a few hundred yards.

In 1843 the Arcade Bath House was advertising warm, cold,

shower and salt baths every day and at any hour. "To the ladies' apartments the entrance is on the South side of the building, where a respectable female will attend them. Spare Bathing Tubs for the accomodation of invalids sent to any part of the city."

Alack, there is no means of discovering now whether ladies of high degree ever patronized a public bathhouse or not; whether the clientele of the Arcade consisted of respectable ladies not wealthy enough to have bathrooms of their own, or whether it included "fashionable nymphs of the pave," we do not know. Charles Cist, an enthusiastic advocate of bathing, wrote editorials in his *Advertiser*, urging his readers to use the public bathhouse, and reciting the benefits of bathing. In one such article in 1845 he remarks, "Many of our late improvements have bathing apparatus introduced within their walls" — meaning homes, of course, and possibly even some new hotels. The city water supply was inadequate, and he urged that it be amplified, not only because of fire danger, but because of the increase in the popularity of bathing. But a few months later, he declared that there are "thousands in our country whose bodies have not had a regular washing since last summer"; he advised such to hie to the bathhouse "and divest themselves of the unnatural covering of filth which six or nine months have accumulated." Of course he couldn't have been speaking of the better type of citizens. By that time, good toilet and shaving soaps, made of palm and vegetable oils and richly perfumed, were being made in Cincinnati.

The *Gazette* in 1866 staged a vain crusade in favor of a public bathhouse to be owned and operated by the city. It may be taken for granted, however, that Cincinnati society folk have not, for a century past, had to use perfumes to conceal bodily uncleanliness, except when the city hydrant water was too muddy to bathe in. Yet as late as 1872 one finds the *Evening Star* deprecating too frequent ablutions as uncalled for. If one wore light underclothing, said the editor, or none at all, and took plenty of exercise, the perspiration would throw off impurities from the body, and an occasional bath was all that was necessary.

There were other comforts and home conveniences even before mid-century; a washing machine, Cincinnati-invented in 1828, which you had to rock back and forth by hand, it is true, but which, it was claimed, eliminated the washboard; wringers, refrigerators, ice cream freezers, and many other devices, even aids to gracious living which we of today do not have — perfumed matches, for instance, a great advance on the old suffocating brimstone article, "in fancy boxes selling at $1.25 per gross of 10,000," which, emitting a delicate fragrance when struck, were delightful for lighting the hall and parlor gas. The same local match company also made "the Young America Taper, elegantly painted, which, when going off, produces the same report as the Chinese Crackers. They will be got up for the fast, fancy and progressive class of the rising generation." Not for parlor use, of course.

Artificial ice was being made as early as 1850, but perhaps not very successfully, or else it was too expensive, for ice cut from lakes and ponds was used for decades afterward. But in antebellum days it was advisable to get your ice from a reputable dealer such as Peter Gandolfo of the Farther North Ice House. If you bought from the first rickety wagon that came along, you might get a murky article cut within the city from that dubious duct, the canal, which was the common midden for all the dwellers along its banks. Brewers cut ice from the canal, too, but they used it only to refrigerate warehouses for keg-beer.

Of course a home must be protected by lightning rods, especially after they began to be manufactured in Cincinnati in 1847. Within five years this grew to be an extensive business, with several factories, and orders coming in from every State in the Union, as well as from Canada and Mexico.

The last item in Mr. Hinkle's ad revealed that his home had both hydrant and cistern water. The city water from the river was apt to be muddy, especially in wet weather, and the sooty taste of the cistern water, drained from the home roof, grew more pronounced as the years passed. Soot also peppered down on the family wash in the back yard (which, incidentally, if you did not live in an irreproachable neighborhood, might be stolen from the line) and crept into the parlor and the bedroom. A three-column news article appeared in 1857 about a newly-invented smoke-consumer, in which the smoke elimination "is completely under the control of the fireman." Wonder whatever became of that invention?

There were other killjoys, too; rats, among them, one of the downtown curses before the Civil War; big, vicious fellows against which households fought unending warfare with cats, dogs, poison and even guns. The *Gazette* in an editorial in 1852 said some families had even been driven from their homes by rats. The editor dwelt upon the enormous cost to the community of the rat pest, and urged that measures be taken for their extermination; but a century later the rats are still with us, though in diminished numbers.

Captain Oldmixon, a traveler of 1854, stopped at the Broadway Hotel, "one of the best here and second only to Burnet's, which is an immense pile, but in an out of the way street" (Third and Vine), "while this is the center of the stir and fashion of the town, and pretty close to the river." But what particularly intrigues us is the Captain's interest in a backyard melodrama viewed from his bedroom window. A flock of chickens had their home in the yard, while rats denned under a woodpile in the corner. At intervals during the day a servant would come out and throw food to the fowls, and then the rats would poke their heads forth and make sallies, trying to snatch some of the eatables. But they didn't get much, for a big red rooster who was boss of the flock kept his eye on them, and when one approached, he made a dash at it and drove it in disorder to its lair, then strutted back to the dining-table, quawk-quawking a few modest remarks to the hens about his own prowess.[2]

Another of the great crosses of a woman's life then was the nation-wide tobacco-chewing habit; and with Kentucky, the greatest tobacco-producing State, just across the river, Cincinnati was seemingly a little worse off in this respect than most other large cities. Every home must, in self-defense, be equipped, especially in the parlor, with spittoons, often of tastefully painted china and elegantly designated as cuspidors. If the head of the family didn't chew, there were always plenty of guests who did,

[2] Captain Oldmixon, *Transatlantic Wanderings*, (London, 1855).

and some attempt was made to have such guests seated within easy range of a cuspidor, for marksmen who could kill a fly at nine feet were comparatively few, and all were inclined to be careless. Visiting publicists shuddered audibly at seeing beautiful Brussels carpets with inwoven roses as big as cabbage heads befouled by what came to be Southern-rurally known as "ambeer." Quite as bad or worse was the fact that the finest ladies' dresses, sweeping floor and sidewalk, had to take some of the punishment, too.

Of course carpeted hotel bedrooms suffered from the vandalism of men who felt free of all restraint in such places, and the hotel lobbies, with their wooden or marble floors, were, despite the big brass receptacles all about, fairly inundated. A traveler who stopped at the comparatively new and magnificent Burnet House in '54 wrote, "The handsome hall and steps were seas of filth; numerous spittoons . . . were unheeded; groups seated around the columns preferred filling the concavities of the flutings, which they did with great dexterity, or hitting more distant objects." Every morning there was a "lavatory process," effected by a hose, "which caused a brown cataract to rush down the hotel steps." [3]

A curiously delicate distinction was drawn between smoking and chewing tobacco. No gentleman would think of smoking in a friend's parlor, or anywhere in the presence of ladies without asking their permission; a request, by the way, seldom voiced. A man might even be forbidden to smoke in his own parlor; but no permission was necessary for tobacco chewing and spitting. Smoking, however, was freely permitted on street cars and buses for many years before being banished; and now it has come back again in many places. Incidentally, in 1858, "smoking tubes" (cigar holders) were introduced, by which "smoking is rendered not only not injurious, but to have a delightful medicinal effect." Sounds like present-day cigarette advertising.

Most housewives did a majority of the shopping for food, though not a few rapidly grew too proud for such chores. The

[3] Charles Richard Weld, *A Vacation Tour in the United States and Canada*, (London, 1855).

cost of food was no problem for folk from the middle class upward in those halcyon days. In 1826 beef and veal were quoted at from 3 to 4 cents a pound, ham 4 to 6 cents, mutton 2 to 4 cents, bacon 3 to 5 cents; turkeys 25 to 37 cents each, geese 18 to 25 cents, ducks 8 to 12 cents, chickens 6¼ cents each. Potatoes were high — Irish 25 to 50 cents a bushel, sweet 37 to 62 cents. Three decades later, prices had risen greatly; steak to 10 or 12 cents; fresh pork and sausage 10 cents, ham 12 cents, mutton 5 to 6 cents, eggs 12 cents, a chicken 20 cents, green corn 5 cents a dozen ears, Irish potatoes 10 cents a peck, sweet potatoes and tomatoes 15 cents a peck, cabbage 2 cents a head. The most astonishing item in the Family Marketing Column on an April day, right between eggs and chickens, is "Puppies, 4 to 6 weeks old, 25 cents." They were, of course, not catalogued as food.

The turkey was a Christmas necessity then, but had not yet become a concomitant of Thanksgiving, which holiday, by the way, was not then the important affair that it has now become. An item of 1850 says that Thanksgiving that year — on the last Thursday in November as now — was "but slightly observed." Most business houses remained open. The churches had services, but they were poorly attended. Christmas, however, was the great eating orgy of the year, climaxing the all-year heavy, unbalanced diet which accounts for one of Drake and Mansfield's notes on the city's health, "Of chronic diseases, indigestion or dyspepsia merits a special designation."

By December 1st you began to hear that "John Hunt, the prince of apple-buttermen, is boiling over 2,000 pounds of mincemeat for the holidays." And about that time — after the railroads were built — carts began going about the streets with cries of "Fresh oysters! Shell oysters! Fresh from New York yesterday." An editor grew lyrical upon seeing a cartload of them, "with the mud and sand of Perth Amboy still sticking to them, and the salt and fragrant water still oozing from the delicious bivalves." But he was less enthusiastic upon passing a butcher's wagon doing house-to-house sales in July, 1850, "which had enough cholera seed in it to plant a square" — meaning that it stank abominably. With the city's worst cholera epidemic just past and another imminent, the editor, though he knew nothing of germs, rightly feared dirt and decay as admirable breeding places for disease.

Fastidious buyers always tested meat and butter by smell before accepting it. Milk was another suspicious article, too; many dairymen watered it unconscionably, and the rising criticism of milk from still-slop-fed cows narrowed the list of dairymen who could be trusted, and caused some families — middle-class folk, that is, towards the outer rim of the Basin — to cling to their cows long after any good pasturage had faded into the distance. But the Council, in a burst of civic righteousness, rose up in 1855, declaring that city life had fallen into most admired disorder, and warned citizens not to let the authorities see any cows standing, lying or feeding on the sidewalks. Apparently they were still tolerated outside the curb. Pools of stagnant water or putridity would not be tolerated on any premises. No garbage or ashes to be thrown into the street; the scavenger wagons would perambulate daily, on a regular schedule, ringing a bell. There were other rigid provisions.

But was this fine program carried out? The *Gazette*, in a scathing editorial a year later, said conditions were nearly or quite as bad as ever. Dishonest councilmen nullified their own ordinance, failing to enforce it save upon a few unfortunates who had no influence, and fattened their own pockets by collecting for services unperformed. "Something has been done, but the Hoosac Tunnel could be completed by hand-drilling before the filth that has accumulated in our streets and alleys would be removed under the present inactive administration. . . . Even fashionable Fourth Street — where silks and laces are daily aired by their fair proprietors . . . Fourth Street, which is first shown the visitor — this street is neglected by the cleaners, and the filth is carefully stuck down by frequent waterings.

"For two days a dead dog has been lying in front of Mr. Fletcher's, on this same Fourth Street, between Walnut and Vine, and if some benevolently minded private man does not interfere, will probably continue to lie there till decay has resolved him to dust and he is swept away by ladies' dresses or blown into the public's face.

"The streets are made the general sinks of the houses upon them, and decaying vegetables, filthy slops, putrid meats and the miscellaneous refuse of the kitchen is thrown into them. . . ."

A citizen thereupon took pen in hand and wrote to the editor that if he walked up Broadway, no matter how hot the evening, he would find all houses shut up as tight as drums because of bad odors. "At the corner of Fifth and Culvert is the soap and candle factory, some 20 feet below the street, the stench of which, on warm nights, compels persons residing within a thousand feet of it to close their doors and windows. On the east side of Culvert street there is a small pond in which dead hogs and dogs are always to be found." For three years, he said, Council had been petitioned in vain by citizens to force a clean-up and ground-fill of this place.

Of course there were decent, civic-minded folk who did not join in this befouling of the city, and even succeeded in keeping short sections of their streets passably clean; but their efforts were vain as against the swinishness of others and the flying dust from unsprinkled, generally untended streets. In the fashionable West End, dust was said to be inches deep in the summer of '48, forcing the closing of all doors and windows, no matter how hot it was, and even then, creeping into elegant parlors, into the whole house, ruining carpets and furniture, making food gritty — and think of the meat hung or stacked in the open markets! "They say a person eats a peck of dirt before he dies," remarked a matron. "I've had mine this summer." Germs? No one had ever heard of them, and they couldn't have been as deadly as we've been told they are, else there wouldn't have been a Cincinnatian left. And again it should be emphasized that in this respect, Cincinnati wasn't unique.

It was amazing how many middle-and lower-class children wandered from home and were lost, and how many, when picked up, not only didn't know where they lived, but couldn't even remember their names. There were criers who searched for lost children in the latter '50's, riding about the streets on horseback, ringing a bell and describing the youngster. The fee for finding the child or for information leading to its recovery was five dollars. On one occasion the lost one was found and restored by friends of the family, and while an impromptu celebration was in progress at the home, the bellman who had been sent out appeared and demanded his fee. The father demurred because he had had nothing to do with the recovery. One word led to another, and presently the crier bounced from his horse and he and the father fell to, hammer and tongs. When the neighbors had separated them, the father had a black eye and a bloody nose, but he saved his five dollars.

From the troubles we have listed, the ladies of the city did not demand "emancipation," other than what could be gained by having more means and perhaps a home on the hills — to which a slow movement of people of means was under way in mid-century. Women were of course interested, and packed the halls when early Woman's Rights missionaries, such as Lucy Stone and Lydia Jenkins, came around in the early '50's, especially in the former, for she was a sort of connection of Cincinnati; it was her husband, Henry Blackwell, a local businessman whose name — by agreement — she did not assume when she married him; and he, in turn, became the first male protagonist of woman's suffrage.

When Amelia Bloomer — whose heart would have ceased beating at sight of a modern woman's beach outfit — "reformed" women's dress in 1851, there was immediate though very limited response in Cincinnati. It was reported early in June that the wife of J. L. Michner, a merchant, had adopted the "bifurcated togs," as the journalists liked to call them. And in July, "A lady resident of Hopkins Street made her appearance on Fourth Street in the new costume. The dress was made of blue silk and reached slightly below the first joint above the ankle." (And just where is that?) "The pants were of white satin. Very little excitement was caused by the novelty of the spectacle." She appeared frequently thereafter, and was spoken of in the papers as "the mysterious woman"; though why mysterious when they knew exactly where she lived, it is not for the twentieth-century mind to fathom.

In the following January, '52, the *Gazette* noticed "ladies navigating the streets yesterday, a la bloomer." And even two years later, "A Bloomer in plum-colored silk dress and pants" attracted much notice on the streets. But by that time the fad was subsiding. Its most prominent adherent in the city had been that popular and philanthropic society matron, Mrs. Edward King, daughter of Governor Worthington, who wore them briefly. But in general, they caused scarcely a ripple among Cincinnati women.

But hoopskirts! Ah, there was a garment which, being the most maddeningly inconvenient thing imaginable, naturally held their unswerving loyalty for years. Impracticality meant nothing as against fashion; the problem of getting the hoops through crowds, on and off buses and street cars was faced with iron determination. The papers record an instance of two women passing each other on Fourth Street, when the foot of one became entangled in the hoops of the other and she fell, breaking an arm and a leg. One of the street car companies decided to build special cars, roomy and elegant, for ladies only. The first one was brought out around a midnight in '62, just after Second Bull Run, and the wrong sort of ladies must have boarded it on the first trip, for the *Commercial* says that it "created so much uproar at the corner of Vine and Fourth, between the crowd on board and the crowd in the street that it was thought by persons some distance off that news of a great victory in the East was about to herald the Fourth of July." The experiment went no further.

A noted episode of the hoopskirt era was that of one day in '57 when a lady, "dressed in the extreme of the mode," descending the steps of the Post Office at Forth and Vine, slipped and fell, breaking some of her hoops, which so entangled her feet that she could not get up. As she vainly struggled to regain her feet, with hair becoming dishevelled and clothing disarranged, man after man offered to assist her, but she waved them all away with increasing vehemence, and finally burst into tears. The more she struggled, the more she displayed her legs and underwear and the more waspish and hysterical she became. She even kicked and screamed whenever a man approached her, offering aid, which several did, sincerely pitying her situation. Now weeping copiously and a picture of disarray from head to foot, her case demanded a hero, "some dauntless fellow like Swedish Charles, who would storm a fort alone or contend with a host single-handed." And he appeared; rushed in and seized her in his arms despite kicks and screams. She struck him in the face, tried to claw him with her gloved hands, and as he bore her down the steps, one of her feet kicked the breath out of a portly banker, the other whacked a prominent attorney on the knee and brought him down. The hero drove through the crowd, tossed the lady into a for-hire carriage, slammed the door and told the driver to take her where she belonged. The young man himself was somewhat dishevelled. A few bits of whalebone, a feminine shoe-heel, a bracelet and some scraps and tatters of cloth left on the sidewalk were gathered up as souvenirs.

Cincinnati women were not yet in politics, but they were not the satin-bowered spirituelles that women of that period in general are supposed to have been. They were stepping out — driving and riding horsback, skating on the Canal and Mill Creek, taking physical culture in gymnasiums such as that of Mr. and Mrs. Samuel Barrett, founded in 1838, which had male and female departments, both reputed to be of the highest respectability. "Two females of our acquaintance," said an editor, wanting to see the construction progress of that railroad tunnel under Avondale which took longer than the Hoosac to build, "descended two hundred feet" into the broken rock and muck, to explore and ask questions.

True, it had already begun to be said that Cincinnati's only leisure class was feminine — a logical development — but not all the grande dames were idle. Both they and middle-class women were going in for several sorts of good works. It was a group of twelve women, by no means wealthy, who, in the winter following the cholera scourge of 1832, founded the Cincinnati Orphan Asylum, still in existence, to take care of the children left parentless by the epidemic. They started with only eight dollars in their treasury and no other source of revenue assured; but butchers, hearing that they were having difficulty in finding food for the orphans, donated left-overs of meat, country hucksters on their way home in the evening, dropped baskets of unsold vegetables at the gate of the dwelling house which was their first asylum. General public sympathy was quickly aroused; lodges, churches, fire companies, police, theaters, business groups and individuals made donations, even down to a poor woman who gave all she could, a half bit, 6¼ cents.

Rapidly increasing wealth in the precocious young city gave rise to stores — dry goods, jewelry, silverware, millinery, furs, books, everything — which, for size, for variety and value of stocks, were the wonder of foreign travelers, male and female, "many of them as elegant in appearance and as well supplied with the best English and French goods as in the largest cities in the East"; even, "as in London and Paris," said another. Such Ali Baba caves inevitably meant more of the housewife's time spent in "shopping," whether one bought anything or not, and making the fatiguing rounds downtown called for refreshment. Soda fountains flourished. As early as 1815 D. Drake & Company, the Doctor's drug store, announced in the columns of *Liberty Hall* that they were preparing "Acidulous or Seltzer, Soda, Saline and Chalybiate Waters, all medicinal," while the Acidulous Soda Water was "much esteemed as a beverage in hot weather." In 1840 there were "upwards of 200" soda stands in the city, and some hopeful drys thought they could see "a thinning of the crowds around the dram shops"; just wishful thinking, of course. But even soda was corrupted; when General Harrison was clerk of the circuit court in the '30's, he liked to drop into Pulaski Smith's drug store on Main Street and ask for a glass of soda "with a stick in it," which didn't mean vanilla syrup. The ladies' restaurant, equivalent of the modern tearoom, appeared in the '50's; "elegant" places such as that of Mrs. A. J. Higgins & Company, which "The ladies will find a convenient place after shopping to step in and get a glass of ice cream or a cup of coffee." And there were modern diversions offered to strollers on the streets. In the latter '50's a man with a telescope on the sidewalk on Fourth Street would let you look at the heavens through it for a nickel. (Donati's comet was paying us a visit then). Or you might sit in a chair suspended from a steel spring and get weighed for three cents.

Housewives, thought some, were showing signs of being spoiled. There was less home baking done; the sales of "baker's bread" was increasing enormously. The Mechanical Bakery, at

Elm and Canal, boasting of its cleanliness, was always open to visitors. Ladies and gentlemen were particularly urged to visit it about eight in the evening, when baking was at its height. The invitation was accepted, and the place was crowded every evening.

Believe it or not, the growing practice of living in hotels was being deplored a hundred years ago. In fact, as early as 1811 there were ladies who so disliked housekeeping that they were the chief supports of Mrs. Willis's Columbian Inn, "a sort of fashionable hotel," says Mansfield, "where many of the gay people of the town boarded." The great tremor of December 16th, which began the series of earthquakes of 1811-12, set chimneys swaying and houses bouncing in Cincinnati and was particularly effective on this inn. "I remember," said Mansfield, "to have heard a good deal of laughter at the odd and curious appearance and grouping of maids and madames, bachelors and husbands, as they rushed into the street, tumultuous in midnight drapery."

From time to time, as decades passed, editors and others criticised the drift away from the home, and towards the irresponsible artificiality of hotel life. "The beautiful structure of the family," said the *Gazette* in 1854, was being impaired, not only by the hotel but by perversion in family arrangements. "Families do not possess that wholeness which they once had, but are broken into as many fragments as there are persons in them." The parlor, once the genial gathering place of the whole family, was more and more deserted. "The various members of a family are convoked together . . . scarcely more than once or twice a day; at dinner generally, and sometimes perhaps at tea. Breakfast is a scattering affair, at which every one arrives, as he does at church, at any time during the morning.

"The propensity to spend the evenings away from home is growing general. Need we look for an explanation beyond the fact that there is so little intercourse and social pleasure and amusement in the domestic circle? . . . The home is consequently deserted nightly, first for the theatre and ball-room, then for the taproom and debauch. . . ."

Among the hotels specially favored for residence then were two old favorites, the Broadway and Dennison; the Gibson — in

'54 the only one in the city entirely heated by steam — the new Walnut Street, with a two-story observatory on the roof which boasted a "magnificent view." The first story of this penthouse affair was a "refectory"; had you been thinking that the rooftop restaurant was a recent idea? Above that was a dome with a railed observation gallery around it. Even the magnificent new Burnet, opened in 1850, was home for some of the *nouveaux riches*, though many foreigners were awed by its size and splendor, its wilderness of corridors and four grand staircases. One of them, William Hancock, said that "Cincinnati is not inferior to any city in the Union in the number and magnificence of its hotels, and one of them, the Burnet House, is more like a royal palace than anything else." Every one of the Burnet's 340 rooms was reached by J. D. Jackson's Annunciator or Hotel Telegraph, "dispensing with the hundred of jangling bells so generally in use in large Hotels, and which keep the house in continual clamor." Hundreds of tons of ice were especially cut and packed for the Burnet in winter around Sandusky and Dayton; its ice bill was $25 a day! Its gas bill was $3,000 a year! The quantities of food it consumed were listed in awe-stricken sentences.

But the guest at the Burnet occasionally got a dash of old-fashioned homeliness. Weld, early on the morning after his arrival, was awakened in his back room by a loud squawking of chickens. Rising and peering from the window, he saw in the yard below two large wagons loaded with cooped chickens, which a man was dextrously hooking forth by the leg, one by one, with a sort of little shepherd's crook. He handed them to another man, who decapitated them in the old, rustic fashion; seizing the head, he swung the body violently in a circle, wrenching it from the head after four or five revolutions, then tossed it into a barrel of hot water. Learning that this was the regular morning immolation of the day's table fowl, Weld asked that he be moved to a front room.

CHAPTER VII

Grove of the Muses

ONE finds a certain striking parallel between Cincinnati and the Renaissance, in that each developed a remarkable culture amidst dirt, disorder and public corruption. Cincinnati's achievement was in some respects the more praiseworthy. Europe took nearly three centuries to bring about her great awakening, whilst Cincinnati, starting from the primeval forest, had done wonders in half a century. Lowell, in a *Biglow Papers* preface, remarked something to the effect that modern Europeans had an advantage over us, for they could just sit and absorb culture through their pores from the atmosphere around them, which reeked with it, while it required "weary years" for America to acquire such improvement from books and art galleries; and if this were true in Lowell's Boston, how much more difficult the task of Cincinnati, a century and a half younger, where, if you sat on a log in the wilderness awaiting inspiration, all you might absorb would be chiggers and malaria. Yet the time came when Cincinnati challenged the East in culture, and musically, when it was only three-quarters of a century old, was said by some Eastern critics to be a step in advance of Boston.

To be sure, Cincinnati did not have to start with nothing but its bare hands. A pioneer settlement which could produce so many learned judges, statesmen and intellectuals, so many books and magazines as this in its first four or five decades must have received no little culture with its first settlers. This soon began to express itself in the founding of schools, in urges for expression and print, as well as in debating and cultural societies. "We are a scribbling and forth-putting people," said editor-author Timothy Flint. True, its early violent infant epidemic of writers' itch produced some feeble tenuities, but as the amateurs were gradually weeded out or turned professional, the quality improved.

The log settlement was not yet quite five years old when William Maxwell began issuing its first newspaper, the *Centinel of the North-Western Territory*, in 1793. A tiny, four-page sheet, it was printed, one side at a time, on a little hand press made all of wood. The type and all other equipment of the shop would not have overloaded a wheelbarrow. Maxwell married Nancy Robins and taught her bookbinding, whence we infer that she may have bound the *Code of Laws of the Northwest Territory*, the first book printed in that vast area.

Through the next two or three decades, little newspapers were born and died like mayflies, with colorful, usually double-jointed names like *Liberty Hall and Cincinnati Mercury*, *Western Spy and Hamilton Gazette*, *Cincinnati Chronicle and Literary Gazette*, *Spirit of the West*, *Inquisitor and General Advertiser* and the like. They were apt to change owners, editors and names every year or so. The hand presses on which they were worked off also took on the job of printing Cincinnati's first books and magazines. Paper at first came from Pennsylvania, then from Kentucky, but by 1815 mills on the Little Miami River were supplying it.

The Reverend Timothy Flint, the New England parson who came down the river with his family in 1815 found the local writing in general poor and in bad taste, because of the "forwardness" of inferior writers and the "unwarranted disdain" which kept really refined and educated persons from competing with them. However, this condition was corrected shortly thereafter when magazines appeared; the refined and educated persons seized their goosequills, and with plenty of culture but no skill as authors, began grinding out stuff that was as dull as ditchwater.

The craving for reading in pioneer Cincinnati was not easily satisfied, because the village was so far from the publishing centers in the East; yet early circulating libraries were as puny infants as early newspapers and magazines, and for now obvious reasons; they were not *public* libraries. One was organized on a winter day in 1802 at Griffin Yeatman's tavern by a group of gentlemen who took enough shares at $10 each to provide a capital of $340. Governor St. Clair, John Reilly (Cincinnati's first schoolmaster), promoter Martin Baum, Judge Burnet and other well-known names — Sedam, Kilgour, Wade, Findlay, Yeatman, Vance — were on the subscription list.

But this project languished, and a second library "society," with Dr. Daniel Drake as president was organized in 1814. Beginning with 300 volumes, it accumulated 1,400, but did not flourish, possibly because only shareholders might read the books, and most of the shareholders were too busy accumulating money to have time for reading. As years passed, the books descended to the basement of Cincinnati College, and then to the basement of a book store, where mould and insects wrought upon them disastrously. But though limited-circulation libraries were neglected, the bookselling business flourished. The public library was as yet a thing unknown, but Cincinnatians craved books — the intelligentsia because they wanted to read, and the fortune-builders, those who were not bookworms, needed books as home furnishings, to prove that they were more than mere money-grubbers; in short, to keep up with the highbrow Joneses in a cultured community.

Polemics was a favorite intellectual pastime of our forebears, and was an important factor in the production of those now extinct American statesmen who could rise at a moment's notice and talk intelligently and forcefully without manuscript or notes. Young Daniel Drake "ventilated his intellectual fires" in various debating societies, including one known magnificently as the School of Literature and the Arts. In a lengthy anniversary address, which was "published by order," the president reported twenty-three essays and addresses given during the year, plentifully seasoned with poetry. To the doers of this scrivening, President Drake frankly admitted that "New countries, it is true, cannot afford the elegancies and refinements of learning, but they are not so unpropitious to the growth of intellect as we generally suppose." Here the Doctor failed in justice to Lexington, 80 miles to southward, which was admittedly saturated and dripping with *litterae humaniores*. A traveler of 1815 remarked, "If its only rival, Lexington, be, as she contends, the 'Athens of the West,' this place is struggling to become its Corinth"; which, we think, entitled Cincinnati to demand an explanation, for Corinth had, as we recall it, a pretty purple reputation morally. But such was Cincinnati's growing commercial prowess that some of its citizens who knew their ancient history saw it as neither a modern Athens nor Corinth, but Tyre. A local poet of the 1820's, in the course of one of those "Come, pass 'round the bowl!" staves, carolled,

> "For we boast, do we not, of our city's success,
> And hail in full bumpers, 'The Tyre of the West.'"

Even later, Dr. Drake was deprecatory as to Western culture, accusing many writers of lacking polish and being too little concerned with "classic propriety"; in fact, some of them openly defied it, relying entirely on "inspiration." They write, he said, for an audience "whose taste is for the strong rather than the elegant." But as we see it, the major defect of most of Cincinnati's early writers was a verbosity and dryness from which Drake himself was not entirely free. Yet it must be admitted that in those years he was Cincinnati's leading author and best publicity man, not even excepting Nicholas Longworth. His handbook, *Notices Concerning Cincinnati*, issued in 1810, was followed in 1815 by his *Picture of Cincinnati*, a well-written compilation of 250 pages, all gathered from first-hand observation, which was read even in Europe, and is said to have brought many new citizens to his home town. In 1807 he wedded a wife, and then of evenings, he was frequently "found sitting with an infant in one hand and writing with the other, by the dim light of a dipped candle," indicating a power of concentration which has been denied to most of us.

The pioneer soul's efforts to rise and soar above the common circumscription were like a nestling's first essays at flight. Aims were high — and turgidly stated in christening the ventures — but infant wings were weak, and the brief flights usually ended in flutterings to earth; a school organization of 1806, for example, ambitiously baptized as Cincinnati University. Dr. Drake, with elegant restraint, tells us that "Its endowments were not exactly correspondent to its elevated title, consisting only of moderate contributions." It obtained a lottery privilege from the Legislature, "a scheme was formed and a great part of the tickets sold; they have, however, not been drawn, and but little of the money which they brought refunded. On Sunday, the 28th of May, 1809, the school house erected by the corporation was blown down, since which time it has become extinct."

But reverses did not discourage the Parnassan pilgrims; they kept trying. After an "academy" had been organized and died, a Lancastrian school — a widely heralded type in which elder pupils acted as monitors or assistant teachers — was launched in 1814, with Judge Burnet as president, with considerable (though not predominant) Methodist influence among its backers, and quickly sold $12,000 worth of stock. A Presbyterian congregation gave it a lot on which to build. There were seven directors, who — and here is the almost incredible thing — who might be of any or of *no* religion. Here we have an early gesture of liberalism in Cincinnati; a word which in those days did not mean socialism, as it is apt to do now, but rather tolerance, breadth of thinking. A pioneer community of the early nineteenth century, when and where religion exercised a powerful influence on all public and private activities, yet where a school for the instruction of young children could be organized, largely under church sponsorship, with the concession that none of the directors need be adherents of any religion, if the stockholders thought best, is probably unique in our history.

Another notable instance in that same year was the organization by a group of high-minded citizens belonging to "all religions in town," so we are told, of the Cincinnati Miami Bible Society, whose object was to distribute Bibles free among the poor of the Miami country, especially those in the backwoods, far from churches. True, the liberalism in these cases was mostly among the intellectuals. The bigotries which permeated the masses spread and intensified as new and alien elements came into the population, and ugly issues such as slavery arose, eventually tainting the minds even of the more thoughtful and well-disposed folk.

Twenty years later, Catherine Beecher observed of Cincinnati that there was "in the general tone of life a breadth of ideas, a liberality and freedom which come from the consorting together of persons of different habits of living." Admitting the condition, one questions the full validity of her explanation. Captain Mar-

[116]

ryat, too, found Cincinnati broad and intrepidly tolerant. In his
Diary in America, First Series, he had said some things about
America as scathing as any of Mrs. Trollope's — which brought
furious rejoinders from several quarters, though none from Cincinnati. An effigy of him was even carried in a parade in St. Louis
and treated with indignity. In the second series of his diary, he
said that there were few instances of moral courage in America,
but "The most decided specimen I met with . . . was at Cincinnati,
when a large portion of the principal inhabitants ventured to
express their opinion contrary to the will of the majority in my
defence, and boldly proclaimed their opinions by inviting me to a
public dinner. . . . I have an idea that Cincinnati will one day take
an important lead, as much from the spirit and courage of her
citizens, as from her fortunate position."

The new Lancaster Academy soon packed its building with 420
children of both sexes, at fees of eight dollars per year. A second
building, for girls only, was begun, and the directors ordered
another building for children of color. But even this institution
had its ups and downs. It was chartered with university privileges
in 1819 as Cincinnati College, and from that point the present
University of Cincinnati traces its life story. The indefatigable
Dr. Drake had lobbied at Columbus for both its charter and that
of the Medical College of Ohio, which also still lives, and is now
a unit of the University. A law department was added to Cincinnati College, and for several years, permanency seemed assured.
Then the depression following the British war settled like a cloud
of poison gas upon the city, and as has been remarked, somewhat
hyperbolically, "A large part of Cincinnati passed in title to the
Bank of the United States." The college closed its doors in 1825
(though the medical college continued) and its rooms were rented
to private teachers. After ten discouraging years, it was revived
and placed under the headship of a young clergyman-professor
whose name was destined to bulk large in the annals of education,
William Holmes McGuffey.

To Timothy Flint, upon his first visit to Cincinnati in 1815, the
town seemed strongly New Englandish. The people "have the
same desire for keeping up schools, for cultivating psalmody, for

... attending upon religious worship; and unfortunately, the same disposition to dogmatize, to settle not only their faith but that of their neighbor, and to stand resolutely and dispute fiercely for the slightest shade of difference in religious opinion"; which explains why there were, as we hear, thirty-seven varieties of Presbyterians in early Cincinnati. The Presbyterians were the dominant sect for years after the first settlement, and lacking effective opposition from other denominations, they squabbled with each other and founded new congregations.

Early Cincinnati preachers were the most versatile fellows in the world. Their favorite avocation was that of editing a magazine or newspaper, secular or religious, the latter with some such title as *Christian Apologist, Western Christian Advocate, Star in the West* (Universalist), *Western Midnight Cry* (Millerite) or *Watchman of the Valley* (Rev. Epaphras Goodman, editor and proprietor). As Mr. Flint remarked, they were happiest when swapping punches with some other sheet over minor doctrinal points or just in a sort of general belligerency. That indefatigable Irishman, the Reverend Alexander Campbell, who would rather wrangle than eat, had an eight-day debate in the spring of 1829 with Robert Owen, the eminent socialist, Owen attacking religion in general and Campbell upholding Christianity. Twice a day for eight days, audiences packed the Methodist Church, which would seat only 1,200; many standing and hundreds turned away from every session. Believe it or not, people came from as far away as New York, Pennsylvania, Virginia, Tennessee and Mississippi to hear that controversy. Mrs. Trollope attended the first session, and when Owen opened fire by flatly denouncing Christianity as a fraud, she was amazed that he was permitted to continue. She was shocked again when Campbell, discussing one of the most serious of subjects, peppered his opening speech with such wisecracking and witticism at the expense of his opponent that he kept the audience in a roar, Mr. Owen himself joining in the laughter as heartily as anybody. At the conclusion of the final session, the audience, by a rising vote, overwhelmingly declared Mr. Campbell the winner. Only "a few gentlemen and one lady" arose in support of Mr. Owen.

Six of Mr. Campbell's numerous debates were eventually published, for he had stenographers present on almost every occasion.
After his oral battle with Bishop Purcell in '37, he took on Parson
Skinner of the Universalists, with whom he waged war for two
years through the columns of the *Millennial Harbinger*.

And as for versatility, there was the Reverend John W.
Browne, an English divine who, in a log hut in 1804 founded
Liberty Hall and Cincinnati Mercury, which in 1815 merged with
another to form the *Cincinnati Gazette*, the city's best newspaper
through several decades; there was the Reverend Oliver M.
Spencer, the boy captive of the Indians, who took on banking as a
side-line and then as a principal business, and who appears several
times as one of the managers of the Buckeye Balls, an unusual
instance of liberalism for an early clergyman; there was the Reverend and Doctor (not D. D. but M. D.) Peter Smith, preaching
the Gospel and practicing medicine in Cincinnati from 1794 to
1804; Parson Gano running a sawmill; Christopher B. Cranch,
pastor of the First Congregational (Unitarian) church, also poet
and painter. Reverend William Burke was the city's postmaster
for 28 years, from 1814 to 1842. Reverend John Smith was one of
Ohio's first two United States Senators, also an extensive trader to
New Orleans, and thereby became allegedly involved in Aaron
Burr's adventure and ruined — with the connivance, so it has been
charged, of the Jefferson Administration. Early city directories
reveal others — "Oliver Lovel, house and sign painter and New
Jerusalem minister," and "Daniel Roe, attorney at law and New
Jerusalem minister."

Starting a newspaper in those days was as easy as turning your
hand over, but keeping it going was quite another matter. No small
part of the space in early newspapers was given over to pleadings
from journalists — and other businessmen, too, for that matter —
to debtors for a little cash on account. One angry Cincinnati credi-
tor originated, as far as 1800, a modern popular truncation when
he called upon those who owed him for "immediate payment or
else —" No newspaper or magazine subscription was ever paid for
in advance; to ask for it would have been an affront, and you
wouldn't have got any subscriptions.

Sol Smith, the old "ham" actor who wrote delightful reminiscences, was also a printer and musician of sorts. When the little barnstorming companies with which he played in his younger days went broke, as they usually did sooner or later, he would odd-job his way back to Cincinnati, where his two brothers were businessmen. He spent the winter of 1818-19 in that city, and sketches a pleasant picture of its cultural urge at that time, not on the topmost level, but that of the general public. "The evenings were delightful," said he; "Singing meetings, debating societies, religious gatherings, oratories, family parties and politics ... added to which I attended a series of law lectures, performed the duties of clerk in one of my brother's stores at a salary of $8.00 a month and played the organ in the New Jerusalem Church three times every Sunday and every Thursday evening, besides teaching a whole lot of young New Jerusalemites the art of psalmody two evenings each week." Towards spring, "finding I had a little time to spare," (!) he joined a Thespian society.

Smith testifies — and he was not a bad critic — that the Columbia Street Theatre was seeing some good acting around that time, too. Its particular star at the moment was Mrs. Groshon, a young English actress of whom Smith says, "I have never seen her superior as Lady Macbeth," and more eminent critics agreed with him. She died there rather suddenly in 1822, and her simple monument in Spring Grove Cemetery bears lines by an unknown hand, in the favorite meter of Alexander Pope, and which Pope himself would not have been ashamed to acknowledge.

In that same year, while doing part-time acting at the theatre and conducting a singing class in Newport, over the river, Smith heard someone remark that Cincinnati needed a new newspaper. A hint was as good as a command to this versatile chap; he went directly to a printing shop, and by permission, picked up a composing stick and set a ten-line announcement that he was establishing a new paper called the *Independent Press*. The shop ran off a hundred copies for him, he went up Main Street with them in hand, and in a short time had ninety subscribers. He then went to John P. Foote's type foundry, which had just begun operations, selected $200 worth of type, and displaying his subscriptions, asked whether he might have it on credit. The answer being a ready Yes, he borrowed a wheelbarrow and trucked the type over to Farnsworth's printing shop, where he made a deal for presswork and space in which to do composition for his paper. He then doffed his coat and went to work on his first issue, writing his editorials directly in type, and no doubt lifting quantities of foreign news and hack material from other papers, as was everybody's custom. Tattle about prominent citizens, which kept him in hot water, nevertheless increased his circulation to 300 almost immediately, and within a few weeks, to 700. The more subscriptions he got, however, the more money he lost, for almost nobody paid up; and he soon had to sell out to a man under whose direction the sheet peacefully expired fifteen months later.

It was the better sort of newspaper that attracted subscribers who really paid. Such was the Whiggish *Gazette*, already mentioned, which in 1827 became the first daily in the West — one attempted the year before had died at the age of four months — under the editorship of Charles Hammond, lawyer, legislator, historian and poet, whom Daniel Webster considered "the greatest genius that ever wielded an editorial pen." His favorite antagonist was big, rough Moses Dawson, of the Democratic *Advertiser and Journal*, with whom he would exchange banter over drinks at a Front Street coffee-house. In 1841 Dawson and his partner sold their paper to John and Charles Brough, who changed its name to *Enquirer;* and as such it flourishes today, the city's one morning daily. These two, with the *Commercial*, founded later, were Cincinnati's three leading morning newspapers of the nineteenth century. The *Gazette* installed the first power press west of the mountains, but do not be misled; the power was that of two stalwarts toiling at a big crank and fly-wheel.

As for magazines, they bred in the atmosphere of Cincinnati like cholera germs, but didn't thrive as well. The earlier ones were all insistently literary, reminding us of Alexander Woollcott's comment on the literary magazine which he edited in college; "It wasn't much of a magazine, but it was as literary as all get-out." A leaflet called the *Literary Cadet* appeared in Cincinnati in 1819, but within six months was taken over by the *Western Spy* newspaper, though with what advantage to the *Spy* we cannot imagine. Then the *Olio* rose and quickly fell, though some of the best people in town wrote for it.

John P. Foote, Connecticut Yankee and versatile genius, did the publishing business of Cincinnati a great service by launching a type foundry in 1820. He then opened a bookstore and began to have editorial symptoms. At his store one evening in 1823, Peyton Symmes, Benjamin Drake, John H. James and other cognoscenti met and projected a new magazine, the *Literary Gazette*, whose first number appeared on the following New Year's Day, with Foote as editor.

> This is the age of magazines;
> Even sceptics must confess it.
> Where is the town of much renown
> That has not one to bless it?

wrote Thomas Peirce, a local bard, in an early number of the magazine. Its object, presented as a motto, was "Not to display learning, but to excite a taste for it." But no magazine so dry and heavily written could have titillated the uncultured palate. The local intellectuals were erudite but pedestrian; their work was a desert of verbosity and stuffiness. Also, they tended to pad their writing and display their learning by much quotation from the classics, a common fault of the time. Some of the best of them wrote for the *Gazette*, but they wrote with the prevailing heavy hand. Laudable attempts were made to lighten the pages with sprightly, even humorous pieces, but as W. H. Venable, a later commentator, remarks, "The fun is invariably serious, and the serious writing never funny." In his valedictory, a year after the founding, Foote mourned "the futility of hopes founded on the anticipated encouragement of . . . a people whose highest ambition would seem to be exhausted in acquiring the means of support." Two other optimists now strove to lift the fainting ephemeris, giving it a shot of pecuniary adrenalin, which kept it going for another few months, and then it really died.

Up the river from New Orleans early in 1828 came the lady who was destined to be better remembered by Cincinnati down to this moment than many a more famous person, even among its own eminences — Mrs. Frances Trollope. With intent to mend the family's fortunes and establish her son Henry — who had shown no sign of doing it for himself — in a lucrative business, she left her husband in England, and with Henry and two daughters came to the great Western wonder-city, to "fix our son there," and to remain until he "felt himself sufficiently established." After she had written her scathing *Domestic Manners of the Americans*, the *Philadelphia Sun*, in a sort of "you're another" retort, described her as "a *Bas Bleu*, a learned lady, short, thick and vulgar-looking . . . much given to being slovenly and slipshod. She might be seen ever and anon in a green calash and long plaid cloak dragging at her heels, and walking with those colossian strides unattainable by any but English women."

She erected for Henry's commercial venture what she called a Bazaar, a weird creation, predominantly Moorish-Arabesque, as one critic described it, with touches of Gothic and God-knows-what. Miss Martineau considered it "the great deformity of the city." In its semi-basement was an elegant coffee-house and bar, the floor above was the store, with an ice cream and oyster parlor, also elegant, back of it, while the whole top floor was a ballroom, where many a gay and brilliant affair took place in the years that followed. Ceilings and panels everywhere were frescoed in classic designs by the French artist, Auguste Hervieu, a friend of Mrs. Trollope's.

In the store, she stocked jewelry, pictures, laces, bric-a-brac and articles of virtu, which she bought mostly at retail prices and marked up, naively supposing that in so colorful a setting and from a cultured Englishwoman, the dazzled bourgeoisie would buy at any price. But they did not, and after two unpleasant years — during which time easygoing Henry (who sometimes drank too much) manifested not the slightest taste for business, the embittered woman gave up the experiment with a loss estimated at $30,000, and after visiting the Eastern United States, returned to England. There she vented her disappointment and pique in a book which, though often spiteful and distorted by her grievance, told — with no merciful consideration for America's youthfulness — more unpleasant truths about the young, raw country than it liked to hear.

In Cincinnati she found no culture whatsoever save in the home of the Reverend Timothy Flint, with whom somehow she became a fast friend, and whom she greatly admired, calling him "one of the most talented men I ever met," with conversational, satirical and critical powers "of the highest order," yet "great kindness of nature and of manner." Only in his family circle could she find good, intellectual conversation, "an exception to everything else I met at Cincinnati." By contrast, one evening at Mr. Flint's home, she met one locally known as "a scholar and a man of reading," who pontifically told her that Shakespeare and Byron were obscene, Pope, Dryden and Gray outmoded, Chaucer and Spenser obsolete because of their archaic language. He had never heard of most of the seventeenth-century dramatists.

She must have given offense at the start by some superciliousness, for she had little opportunity to see the best that the city had to offer, either culturally or socially. Joseph Tosso, Cincinnati's pet musician for many years, tells of a party which she herself gave "to about a hundred guests," he thinks, though it is hard to believe that she could muster that many acquaintances in the city. But she knew some prominent men, such as Dr. Price and Morgan Neville, for they took part in some dramatics given that evening, with Henry Trollope playing Falstaff; and as he was moderately drunk, he was considered very funny. He played a part, too, at Dorfeuille's Western Museum, a project which Mrs. Trollope found interesting. This museum, founded as a joint-stock company, with the ubiquitous Dr. Drake as promoter, opened in 1820, after two years of specimen-gathering, with a middle-aged, impecunious wanderer named John James Audubon as taxidermist. He claimed in after years that he could never collect all his salary; he had to paint cheap portraits to maintain his wife and himself. The building where he lived, at 414 East Third Street, was still standing only the other day. In October, 1820, he boarded a flatboat for Louisiana, and Cincinnati knew him no more.

The museum, at first housed in the Cincinnati College building, began as a strictly scientific affair, containing mounted fauna, fossils and geological specimens. But it was not well sustained, and in a few years the collection was removed to another building and passed under the management of a Monsieur Dorfeuille, who was said to be a French nobleman. Whether or not this was true, he was a born showman, and he proceeded to enliven the museum, not only with paintings, Indian relics and gadgetry, but with things calculated to strike a popular chord; a chamber of horrors, for example, wherein knives and hatchets (still bloody) used by celebrated murderers and the ropes that hung them were displayed, as well as the head of one celebrated assassin, hideously swollen and distorted, in alcohol. To these were added wax groups representing some of the actual crimes, modelled by a young fellow named Hiram Powers, then unknown, but destined for fame as a sculptor.

But the *chef d'oeuvre* was the exhibit announced in the papers in 1828, the "view of the Infernal Regions, after the model of Dante, and also a distant view of Elysium." The figure of Minos, the judge of the underworld, "is colossal, great and imposing; and the other figures, as well as the plan of the scenery in general, are well calculated to excite in the mind the most horrific sensations. The whole is shown by a light which renders darkness visible. . . .

"The view of Elysium is beautiful and imposing, executed with great taste and accuracy." (!) Some theologians, so it was said, believed that the whole would be "apt to inculcate a great moral lesson." A rhyming ad in the *Mirror* exhorted the public to

> Come hither, come hither, by night or by day.
> There's plenty to look at and little to pay;
> You may stroll through the rooms and at every turn
> There's something to please you and something to learn.

> *　　*　　*　　*　　*　　*

> And further, a secret I still have to tell,
> You may ramble upstairs, and on earth be in ——.

It was in —— that the genius of young Hiram Powers came

into play again, for he modelled the figures, devised the clock-work which moved them and created lighting effects — "dwarfs that by machinery grow into giants before the eyes of the specta-tor," said Mrs. Trollope; "imps of ebony with eyes of flame; mon-strous reptiles devouring youth and beauty; lakes of fire and mountains of ice"; all seen through a massive iron grating lightly charged with electricity, a rare novelty at the time; and the cries and jumps of those who touched it greatly entertained the others who had had the experience.

Cincinnati was now nearing the 1830's, the first decade of its Golden Age. Increased catering to literary and artistic cravings, increased activities in the arts, proved that the Renaissance was just around the corner. An art school had been launched and painters were opening studios. There was another natural history museum; there were three circulating libraries, of 1,300 to 1,500 volumes; there was the Ohio Mechanics' Institute — organized "to promote a more general knowledge among that portion of society who labor with their hands" — with its library of 1,600 volumes; a Gallery of Paintings (which Mrs. Trollope considered pretty bad); two public reading rooms, of which the better one, the Atheneum, spent $400 a year on newspapers and magazines, and was open from 8:00 A.M. to 9:30 P.M. Bookshops and printeries — the two often combined — were multiplying rapidly. Fine bind-ings and old prints were being collected. Mrs. Trollope found a cobbler named Madison Franklin Harris whose poems were being printed in the newspapers. Professor Francis Glass wrote a life of Washington in Latin, *Washingtonii Vita*. Even children were alive to the value of erudition, said two visiting divines, reporting a colloquy overheard on the street between two little girls of nine and thirteen respectively. "Do you know," quoth the younger, "Caroline says she will no longer go to school."

"Foolish girl!" commented the elder. "She will live to repent of that." And if we know the parents of those days as well as we think we do, it didn't take long.

The strongly pietistic flavor of the literary culture of early America, though not quite so dominant in Cincinnati's writing, was nevertheless noticeable, by reason of the many clergymen who were also editors and authors. Yet some of these were broad-minded and humorous, too. The Reverend Timothy Flint completed his fine book, *Recollections of the Last Ten Years in the Valley of the Mississippi,* and launched the *Western Monthly Review* in 1827. Yet Flint, a gifted author, whose factual books as well as his novels were bright and entertaining, whose life of Daniel Boone delighted generations of boys, now endeavored to show the East that Cincinnati could produce a really highbrow magazine, and only succeeded in making the *Review* heavy and dull. It was suspended after three years.

The new era may be said to have dawned in 1830, when Fanny Wright, the radical reformer, first lectured in Cincinnati, when the First Congregational (Unitarian) Church was incorporated there — though a little group had gathered in 1824, with Adam Bancroft, father of the historian, as their leader — and when Dr. Lyman Beecher was called to the presidency of the newly organized Lane Theological Seminary. In the following year, almost simultaneously, came that eminent Unitarian, James Handasyde Perkins of Boston, and Dr. Beecher with his friendly grin, trailing some of his numerous talented children with and after him.

The Unitarians, a Yankee-nurtured cult, shocked Christians by rejecting the Trinity, the deity of Jesus, original sin and eternal punishment, yet they found, so their leaders said, more tolerance, more freedom of thought in Cincinnati than in Boston, where mass opinion "rules with a rod of iron," said William Ellery Channing, their high priest, "often crushing individuality of judgment and action." After Perkins came others of their ministers and leaders — James Freeman Clarke, Horace Mann, Abiel A. Livermore, William Henry Channing, Samuel Longfellow, Thomas Vickers, Robert Collyer, Christopher B. Cranch, Samuel Osgood, the younger William Ellery Channing, who here met and married a sister of Margaret Fuller — for later comers had brought with them that peculiar development of New England revolt, Transcendentalism, of which Ralph Waldo Emerson was the avatar, and which he tried to explain to Cincinnatians, along with some other matters, in two series of lectures. So raptly was he admired locally that when he stopped at the Burnet House in '52, they put him into the bridal suite. "It is beautiful," complained the sage, "but how can one think in it?"

Van Wyck Brooks says that Ohio in 1837 was "beginning to rival Connecticut in its interest in things of the mind." One modern student sees Cincinnati as "an outpost of Boston liberalism."[1] Among other Unitarian activities, they sponsored a magazine, *The Western Messenger,* which, though always edited by ministers, was more literary than religious, and during its lifetime, 1835 to 1841, was one of the best of its period. Reverend Ephraim Peabody was its first editor, followed in turn by Clark, Perkins and W. H. Channing. All the literati of Cincinnati, whether Unitarian or not, wrote for it — Foote, Cranch, Osgood, Albert Pike (later General), Timothy Walker, Joseph Longworth, the talented son of old Nicholas, Thomas Shreve, who, said a critic, "has a Bulwerian control over language and a Byronic grandeur of imagination and gloom of thought"; William D. Gallagher and Otway Curry, the poet, true Arcadian shepherds, of whom one hears as reclining on the river bank — in a field of asphodel, no doubt — Curry wooing Calliope and soothing his friend's troubled breast with a pastoral air on his flute. (Shouldn't it have been an oaten pipe?) Editors and authors were all young, few of them more than thirty.

But there were even more noted contributors. Emerson's first four poems appeared in the *Messenger,* as did work by Oliver Wendell Holmes, Elizabeth Peabody and Margaret Fuller. Through John Keats's brother, who was in business in Louisville, the magazine acquired a short, unpublished poem (of mediocre quality, sad to say) by the author of "Endymion," as well as portions of a diary which he had kept in Scotland in 1818. The final achievement of the *Messenger,* shortly before it ceased publication, was the launching in 1840 of the famous *Dial,* of Boston, almost entirely by Transcendentalist editors of and contributors to the *Western Messenger.* In fact, the *Messenger* considered the *Dial* its own child — an offspring, by the way, which evidently

[1] Avis Baker, *Cincinnati as a Western Outpost of Boston Liberalism.* Thesis for the degree of M.A., University of Chicago, 1918. Typed MS, New York Public Library.

sapped the strength of the parent and caused its death less than a year later.

In 1831 Cincinnati first saw stocky, florid Dr. Lyman Beecher, an eccentric who, to combat his dyspepsia, was wont to caper on parallel bars, to saw his own firewood and his neighbors', too, if they would let him, and on rainy days, to shovel a pile of sand back and forth across his cellar, who relaxed from lectures and heresy trials by scraping jigs on a fiddle and dancing to them — to the delight of his children — with his shoes off, if his wife were absent, for she deplored the wear and tear on his socks. When he took over the presidency of Lane Seminary, then just two gaunt, ugly buildings in hilltop forest, whence a so-called road, alternately dusty and muddy, wriggled down to the city where hogs wallowed in the streets, the Doctor saw everything through rosy spectacles. Cincinnati he considered already as notable a literary emporium as Boston. "The West is a young empire of mind and power and wealth and free institutions," he proclaimed. "All at the West is on a great scale, and the minds and the views of the people correspond with these relative proportions."

With him came his eldest daughter Catherine, then 31, tall and homely, her piety impaired by the death of her fiance, though her father seems to have taken her skepticism in his stride, wisely trusting to time to allay it. She wrote to her sister Harriet, then still in the East, "I have became somewhat acquainted with those ladies we shall have most to do with, and find them intelligent, New England sort of folks. Indeed, this is a New England city in all its habits." She was soon entreated by townsmen to start a school in Cincinnati similar to the one she had operated in Hartford, and which gave her nation-wide fame. She wrote that "pious people" in Cincinnati felt the need of a good school, "and yet for want of a better, they send to a lady who writes tragedies for the theatre, and takes her pupils to see them acted." Mrs. Caroline Lee Hentz was the *bas bleu* thus delicately ticked off. Catherine began in a small way, calling her school the Western Female Seminary, but to do a proper job, she needed some thousands of capital. She could not solicit this herself; moneyed men would have been alienated by such unladylike behavior, and the male friends who undertook the task were not very successful. Anyhow, the project was abandoned, and oddly enough, was taken over by the Catholics for a nun's school.

When Sister Harriet came out to Cincinnati a little later, she was enchanted with Lane and its surrounding hills and vales, where "the straight, beautiful shafts" of the beech forests might have been "columns for a Dryad temple" — supposing the devil-may-care Dryads had had any use for a temple. Her father had a large, comfortable brick dwelling by this time, set in a pretty lawn, and as Henry Ward and other sons came to attend the seminary, and Aunt Esther to supervise the menage, the house seemed full, and yet frequent visitors were always squeezed in somehow. Harriet loved it with the girlish enthusiasm of nineteen and twenty. "It was an exuberant and glorious life while it lasted. The atmosphere of the house was replete with moral oxygen. Nowhere else have I felt anything resembling or equalling it."

Her spirit soared, not only because of the "purity, vivacity and inspiration" of the home atmosphere, but because of the literary oxygen which she found downtown. There she was admitted to the Semi-Colon Club, which met alternately at the homes of William Greene, Charles Stetson and Samuel E. Foote, brother of John P. Foote — "Uncle Samuel" and "Uncle John" to the Beecher girls, their sister, Roxana Foote having been Dr. Beecher's first wife. Uncle Samuel lived at Third and Vine streets, hard by the home of Dr. Drake, who also had a salon of his own. The club meetings, like all such, were given over to the reading of papers and discussion, interspersed with music. The most brilliant array of talent in Cincinnati might be seen there — the Footes, the Drakes, Judge James and Rev. E. B. Hall, Judge Timothy Walker, E. P. Cranch, General Edward King, James H. Perkins, Edward D. Mansfield, Salmon P. Chase, Ormsby M. Mitchell the astronomer, pudgy Professor Calvin E. Stowe of Lane, who soon took over the chore of escorting Harriet to and from club meetings, Professor and Mrs. Hentz (the noted bluestocking), the Beecher sisters and the three brilliant Blackwell girls, sisters of Henry Blackwell husband of Lucy Stone, and notable because two of them later became physicians, in a day when almost no medical college would admit a woman; in fact, Elizabeth was the first licensed woman doctor of medicine in modern history, and had a distinguished career in America, France and England. Messrs. Chase and Perkins met their future wives at Semi-Colon meetings.

Harriet Beecher soon tried her hand at fiction, and her first published work, a "New England Sketch," appeared — when she was 22 — in Judge James Hall's *Western Monthly Review*, where it won a prize of $50. Hall, a Semi-Colon brother, member of a literary family of Philadelphia, soldier of 1812, frontier lawyer, judge and journalist and a State official of Illinois, had started a magazine there and removed it to Cincinnati in 1832. All the literary talent of the city, now more extensive and of increasingly higher quality, was enlisted for its pages. Hall wrote copiously himself; among his numerous books, his *Legends of the West* was long a best-seller, and his *History of the Indian Tribes* challenged Audubon for magnificance, being published in three huge folio volumes, lavishly illustrated and selling for $120 a set. Marryat considered him one of the best of American authors, and Allibone declared that "few men have done so much for the cause of Western civilization and the intellectual improvement of the country at large."

Harriet Beecher married Professor Stowe in 1836 and began producing babies so rapidly that she had little or no time to write the short stories which magazines were requesting from her. She dedicated her first book, *The Mayflower*, to the Semi-Colon Club in 1849. She returned to New England that year and soon began work on *Uncle Tom's Cabin*, the material for which she had gathered in Cincinnati and in a short visit into near-by Kentucky. Thus the famous parable may be said to be largely a Cincinnati product.

Daniel Drake's private gatherings of the intellectual elite were called to order with a bell — you might know that there would be a certain *lucidus ordo* — and the program would begin. Sometimes there were prepared papers, perhaps with a bit of poetry or a story for diversion, sometimes the evening was passed in an open discussion of some suggested topics — literary, social, educational, religious. The refreshment was apt to be lemonade, served from a large bowl of buckeye wood—a popular utensil for punches and egg-nog — though we hear also of coffee and wines upon occasion.

Dr. Drake took a leading part in the establishment of the Western Literary Institute and College of Professional Teachers in 1833. On December 26th of that year the forty-fifth anniversary of the founding of the city was celebrated with a "Buckeye banquet" of 160 guests, with Major Daniel Gano, his hair still in an unruly pigtail, in the chair. A pioneer dinner, with entrees from forest, air, and river, was topped with raccoon meat. Four huge buckeye bowls were filled with sangaree, and Nicholas Longworth's famous Catawba wines flowed freely, 51 toasts being drunk. There were addresses by General Harrison, Joseph Longworth (son of Nicholas), Peyton S. Symmes, Charles D. Drake (the Doctor's son), and Edward King, while Dr. Drake delivered a panegyric on the buckeye tree; whence local legend, always inclined to give credit to local heroes for everything, has claimed for him the honor of nicknaming Ohio the Buckeye State.

Drake and others kept a watchful eye on the movements of foreign literary luminaries, and were ready to welcome them. When Miss Martineau arrived at the Broadway Hotel on her visit in 1835, she found there the cards of several persons who had called the day before. Some of them came again that day — Dr. Drake, Rev. Ephraim Peabody, Miss Beecher (possibly Catherine), and several merchants with their ladies. "The impression their visits left on our minds was one of high respect for the society of Cincinnati, if these were, in manners, dress and conversation, fair specimens."

Dr. Drake and his daughter (his wife had died some time before) took her for a drive on the hills, during which he showed her "two handsome dwellings with gardens, built by artisans from Birmingham." who were evidently making their fortunes. She went home with the Drakes to tea, which was served in the Doctor's garden in the gloaming, with the tiny lamps of fire-flies flashing all about them, and "I doubted that I had ever heard more sense and eloquence at any Old World tea-table than we were entertained with as the twilight drew on."

Charles Fenno Hoffman, poet and author from New York, and founder of the *Knickerbocker Magazine*, professed himself daunted by the pansophical culture he found in Cincinnati. At a "literary soiree," he wrote a friend, "I opened my lips but once in a learned discussion, and was so frightened at the sound of my own voice that I took the earliest opportunity to escape from the premises."

Magazines continued to rise and fall. Among the ephemera which breathed floridly for a brief moment was the *Western Lady's Book*, founded in 1840 by "An Association of Ladies and Gentlemen," with the motto, "The Stability of our Republic and the Virtue of her Institutions is with the Ladies." It appears to have died after one 26-page issue, in which one of the stories was "The Village Graveyard," by "Jane," telling the sad love story of Charles Anson and Caroline Lee, who succumbed to tuberculosis soon after their marriage and were buried in the same grave. Much of the lesser fiction of the day was pitched in this doleful minor key, especially in the religious press, inculcating the clerical theory that life and religion are or ought to be pretty gloomy experiences; an inheritance not entirely from the Puritans, as alleged, but from English dissenters in general (See Dickens's Mr. Stiggins of Emanuel Chapel; he wasn't a Puritan). A well-balanced parson, Timothy Flint, describes an American Stiggins, "sitting at a camp preaching among the ministers, and ever and anon uttering a dismal groan, as if seized with a colic pang, and a face of the more elongated and rueful sanctity." The lugubrious color given to religion by its leaders, especially of the evangelical denominations, burdened it with a handicap which it has never quite been able to shake off.

This weepy fiction was nowhere in stronger evidence than in the *Ladies Repository and Gatherings of the West*, which had a career of 36 years, largely because it was published by the powerful Western Methodist Book Concern, founded in Cincinnati in 1820. Its first editor, L. L. Hamline, was in rapid succession lawyer, preacher, editor and bishop. Among articles on such subjects as "Self-Cultivation," "Female Influence," "Zoology" and "Conchology," one finds others entitled, "The Graveyard," "Solitude," "The Mourners" and "Man and the Grave." The poems fairly wallowed in dolor; "A Mother's Shade," "Hours of Gloom," "The Consumptive," "She Hath Gone," "The Lament," "Resignation," "The Last Wish of Pocahontas," "Be Happy Today" — for tomorrow will be terrible, was probably the implication. One story began thus: "It was the twilight hour. Within a room, whose heavy satin draperies and costly furniture told of wealth and luxury, knelt a fair young girl in deep and earnest prayer. With hands slightly clasped and tears glistening on her pale cheek, she seemed more like the inhabitant of some brighter (!) world than a child of earth; and though time had traced no lines of grief or care upon her pale brow, yet the expression *now* was one almost of agony."

William Davis Gallagher and Lucius A. Hine were two unterrified youths who set magazines afloat in air as one would blow soap bubbles, and though some of them survived but little longer than the bubbles, others endured long enough to make an impress; and these two youngsters, Gallagher in particular, are still honored as having contributed much to the development of Western culture. In childhood, Gallagher lived on a farm near a family of distant kinsmen, named Cary, whose daughters, Alice and Phoebe, were ardent readers — though their only light at night was a twisted rag in a saucer of lard — and who were scribbling for the local magazines and newspapers in their teens.

Billy Gallagher's mother was a widow, and he was a wage-earner before he was old enough to go to school. His schooling was brief; omnivorous reading supplied most of his education. At 10 or 12 he was learning to set type; at 16 he wrote verse for the *Literary Gazette;* at 18 he was assistant editor on an agricultural paper, and he and an elder brother launched a magazine, the *Western Minerva*, which died within the year. After four years of newspaper work be became editor, at 24, of the *Cincinnati Mirror*, a semi-monthly literary opuscule. Two years later he and Thomas H. Shreve bought the magazine and made it a weekly, adding a little to its name. In the following April, Rev. James H. Perkins's *Chronicle* merged with it — changing the name again — with Perkins becoming a third editor. But in October they all sold out to another man (name changed again) who in January sold to Flash & Ryder, booksellers, who resumed the name, *Cincinnati Mirror* and reengaged Gallagher and Shreve as editors. But in less than no time, Gallagher and Ryder quarrelled, Gallagher and Shreve resigned, and the magazine folded up. With life so uncertain in those days, it must have been difficult to get annual subscriptions. But such was magazining in Cincinnati, and it came near getting the better of Gallagher. With cash as scarce as angels' feathers and new babies accumulating at home alarmingly, he once wrote to Otway Curry, "I must do something to raise a little money, for I am almost too badly clad to appear on the street." Even his best magazine, *The Hesperian*, which paraded a fine array of talent across its pages and is spoken of with admiration by scholars today, lived only three years. At last he was taken into the *Cincinnati Gazette* fold by that great editor, Charles Hammond, and spent many years there, his genius contributing to the high quality for which that journal was so long noted.

Religion and the classics; those were the two bright guiding stars of literature in early Cincinnati, as elsewhere. Editors and authors spouted Greek and Latin, and invoked the Muses, the Graces, and the colossi of ancient poetry. James G. Percival, a Cincinnati poet, issued two thin volumes of verse under the titles, *Clio No. I* and *Clio No. II*, which strikes us as making the Muse of heroic poetry and history sound like Sears-Roebuck catalogue items. But Gallagher followed his example with slim emanations between boards entitled *Erato No. I, Erato No. II* and *Erato No. III*. Even business caught the infection and wooed the public in verse. A shoe dealer with a fine taste for history and the age of chivalry, who modestly called his ads, "Eshelby's Poetical Gems," promulgated his brightest bit of lyric advertising in 1845:

> "Said a lady fair to a gallant knight,
> 'Sir Rupert, pray mount thy gray, strong steed,
> And to Palestine hasten to join the fight,
> For thy aid now the Christians have full need;
> And when thou returnest to my rose-clad bower
> Thy wife I will be from that very hour.'

*   *   *   *   *   *

"But the sigh is started, the tear-drop fell
    As he mounted his dapper gray;
To his feet he looked down as he said farewell,
    He was loath still to haste away.
'Ah, why dost thou linger, such delay is not meet!'
'Ah, love, I've no handsome boots on my feet.'

"In his ear, then, she whispered a magic word,
    And delight thro' his dark eyes shone.
He right gallantly girded on his sword,
    One kiss — mounts his steed and is gone.
    Oh! why at one word did his griefs depart?
    One word which was breathed by the love of his heart?

" 'JAS. ESHELBY,' that was the magic name
    She breathed in her true lover's ear,
'No. 10 Sixth Street,' and that store full of fame,
    Why, then, should he longer fear?
    To that store he hastened his boots to buy,
    And spread Eshelby's fame beneath Palestine's sky."

The issue of Dr. Wise's paper, *The Israelite*, for September 25th. 1857, was notable for the appearance therein of the first poem, "Sinai," signed by "Mrs. A. Isaacs Menken, New Orleans, La." Thereafter, her work appeared frequently in that paper for several years. But when she came through Cincinnati, playing the lead in *Mazeppa*, in which she, as the Cossack hero, was bound, supposedly naked, but really in fleshings, on the back of a wild horse and sent into the steppes, her contributions to *The Israelite* ceased, e'en though her fame burgeoned and she crossed the ocean, to hobnob with the great literati of England and the Continent.

Never was a city so eager to hear literature, the arts, philosophy, religion and economics expounded by lecturers. There were lecture courses every winter in the three decades preceding the Civil War, the Young Men's Mercantile Library Association and the Mechanics' Institute's "Lyceum" leading the way, with the best speakers the country had to offer, and sometimes a foreign celebrity such as Thackeray, with his famous "The Four Georges." (The *Gazette* critic didn't think much of it.) When

Donald G. Mitchell, "Ik Marvel," — author of those exquisitely saccharine pencillings, *Dream Life* and *Reveries of a Bachelor*, beloved by the ladies for decades thereafter — appeared, delivering one of his only two lectures, the *Commercial*, which had no reporter present, reviewed and criticised (from manuscript) the one he didn't deliver, with chatty little touches aimed to show that the writer had been there.

There were whole courses on science, progress, good citizenship, constitutional history, great authors and orators, debates of such questions as whether Christianity and philosophy can be reconciled. From the East came the most eminent men to be seen on the platform in the '50's, at rates of $40 to $75 per lecture, and they were greeted by packed houses; while the best of Western celebrities could command no more than $15 to $25. With all its boasting, the West was still awed by the East.

Devotedly, relentlessly, culture was sought by organization. The literary and debating clubs and groups were numbered by dozens, and there were undoubtedly many of which we know not. Gallagher belonged to so many of them that one wonders how he found time to do any editing or lucrative writing. One was the Franklin Society, which met in a corner of an old church, huddled, shivering, around a small stove on winter evenings, often debating and orating in overcoats. Another was the "Inquisition," which was "attended by the beauty and fashion of Cincinnati." Another was a select group of eight, the "Tags," named from the initials of the four organizers, Thomas, Atlee, Gallagher, and Shreve. And a little later there were the "Forty-twos" — so named because at its founding, all its members were between 41 and 43 years old — which met at the law offices of Salmon P. Chase on Third Street.

Finally, most famous and most enduring of all, the Literary Club was organized at the rooms of Ainsworth R. Spofford, later Librarian of Congress, on October 29th, 1849, and has now just passed its hundredth birthday. Among the first-year members were Henry B. Blackwell — destined always to be remembered as the husband of Lucy Stone — Judge Manning F. Force, Rutherford B. Hayes, Stanley Matthews, John W. Herron (father-in-law of President Taft), Lucius A. Hine, John H. McDowell and a dozen others. Its membership limit, at first 25, is now 100. On its roster through the years may be found many high-ranking names in the professions, business and industry, regardless of creed. Among them have been those of two Presidents of the United States (Hayes and Taft), one Chief Justice of the United States Supreme Court (Chase), one Associate Justice of the same court (Stanley Matthews), as well as ambassadors, ministers, senators, representatives, judges, generals, scholars, eminent workers in the arts and even in big business. One of its members, Dr. Lawrence Carr, so loved the club that he made it his legatee, and requested that his funeral service be conducted in the clubrooms, with the sermon preached by (although Carr himself was a Gentile) Rabbi David Philipson, another club member.

In its present home, a gift from Charles P. Taft, a mellow, old, old mansion on East Fourth Street — much older than the club — whose interior has been slightly remodelled to provide a small auditorium, its members assemble faithfully every Monday evening, to listen to one paper (or more), then to clot in groups, to canvass and squabble happily over beer and sandwiches for another hour or two about Cincinnati history and all else under the sun. It isn't quite as literary as it used to be, but who or what is? The thousands of papers read at its lectern have glanced at well-nigh the entire field of human knowledge and speculation. Dr. Philipson said of it that it "is in all truth an aristo-democracy, to use Plato's term — a democracy of the best. Its meetings have been high intellectual and social feasts to me."

CHAPTER VIII

Reading, Writing and Radicals

THERE was a passion for education in the Mississippi Valley which in the course of time lifted it to a plateau of literacy higher than that of the East. For decades, Cincinnati was the great book-publishing center of that area, and its product — after the subsidence of an early fad for almanacs — was largely schoolbooks; at times as much as 75 to 90 per cent of the total output. Some of the most famous and most influential school texts in the history of American education were not only published but written in Cincinnati. Local authors at times had to ask New York and Boston to publish some of their fiction and collected poems because Cincinnati presses were too busy with school texts and religious books to handle them — though they did occasionally pause to pirate a bit of foreign fiction, on which they would have to pay no royalty.

After Maxwell and his Nancy had turned out that volume of *Laws of the Northwest Territory* in 1796, eight years elapsed before even a pamphlet was printed. Several almanacs, each a single-shot venture, were published before 1820. A curious volume of 1813 was *The Indian Doctor's Dispensatory; being Father Smith's Advice respecting Diseases and their Cure";* with some fifty words more of subtitle. The author, "Peter Smith of the Miami Country," in his preface just comes right out and lays it on the line; "The author would notify the purchaser that he puts the price of one dollar on his book, well knowing that 75 cents would be enough for the common price of a book of this size; but those who do not chuse to allow him 25 cents for his advice, may desist from the purchase. He claims this 25 cents as a small compensation for the labor and observation of fifty years. . . ."

Dr. Drake in 1815 remarked that since 1811 twelve books and many pamphlets had been printed in Cincinnati; the books of moderate size, it is true, but they were bound and had more than 200 pages each. Now look forward a mere eleven years; in 1826, there were published in Cincinnati 61,000 almanacs, 55,000 spelling books, 30,000 primers, 3,000 copies of the Bible and 14,000 of the New Testament, 50,000 table arithmetics, 6,000 readers of two different grades, 3,000 of *Kirkman's Grammar* and 6,000 or more copies of other books, not to mention music and hymn books. And this was only the beginning of the city's eminence as the great midcontinent publishing center.

Books were sold alongside drugs or dry goods or from a printing shop until John P. Foote, type founder and author, opened the first all-bookstore in the city in 1820. John T. Drake presently opened another one which, in the latter 1830's, had a business of $80,000 to $100,000 annually. A famous name among bibliopoles was that of Uriah P. James, who came with his brother Joseph from rural New York to Cincinnati in 1831 when he was 20 and built a publishing, printing, typefounding and bookselling business so large that some called the brothers the Harpers of the West. After their passing, the publishing was dropped, the famous bookshop was continued by younger generations, and eventually passed to others.

Among the many book marts, that of Alexander Flash (for some time Flash & Ryder) was usually seen by visiting celebrities. Marryat met some of the local literati there. Miss Martineau saw some good and handsome books there at reasonable prices, and learned that there were book clubs in the city. "We heard good accounts of the improved and improving literary taste of the place, shown in the increasing number of book societies, and the superior character of works supplied to them."

In 1830 the biggest book and general printing concern in Cincinnati was Morgan, Lodge & Fisher. It owned and printed the *Daily Gazette*, and had five presses, "propelled by water-power, each of which could throw off 5,000 impressions daily." This shop did the printing for Truman & Smith, just organized but destined for fame as the publishers for McGuffey and Ray and ancestors of the world's biggest publishing house. Ephraim Morgan, a young Quaker, head of the printing company, was the first in Cincinnati to obtain the publishing rights for Noah Webster's *Spelling Book*, the famous little blue-backed brochure from which the majority of nineteenth-century Americans learned to spell more expertly than their descendants. A memorandum in Webster's own hand,[1] written in 1843, says that 19,000,000 copies had then been sold, and it was going at the rate of half a million yearly. The sales figures on educational books in those days make a modern author faint with envy.

No one publisher in a city, it seems, obtained the sole right to issue his books, which included the dictionary and other volumes. William G. Webster, his son, went to Cincinnati in 1835 to start a publishing business, including rights to his father's books, and found "The expenses of living, in comparison to those of New Haven, enormous." There was a housing shortage in the fast-growing city and he had difficulty in finding a place of abode. But his sales figures presently began to suggest that the cost of living didn't greatly matter. On October 10th after his arrival, he wrote his "Dear and Honored Father" — who always kept a keen eye on the accounts — that since July 1st, his concern had published and sold 7,250 Elementary Readers, 6,000 Western Readers, 5,500 Primary Readers, 1,000 of the old man's now forgotten *History of the United States*, 50,000 spellers and 6,500 copies of a hymn book. On November 5th, he casually adds in a postscript, "Am just sending 200 dozen spellers to New Orleans. Last month we sold 17,000." Again our mouths water as we wistfully contemplate life in young Cincinnati, a city where books were Big Business, just like iron and pork.

Webster's Spelling Book was an Eastern product which was a "must" in the West, but Cincinnati educators brought forth others which were if possible more famous. In all the story of American schools, there is no other series of texts which have not only exerted so much influence but so won the love of those who used them — a thing quite unique, by the way — as the readers compiled

[1] Noah Webster papers, New York Public Library.

by William H. McGuffey, who spent some of his best years in Cincinnati and there published the books whose memory elderly men and women — especially the men — cherish with deep affection to this day.

McGuffey, working on a backwoods farm in childhood, had no early opportunity for formal education. But like other indomitable souls of those days, he took destiny into his own hands, and untutored, packed all his grammar school and academy education into evenings by the light of an open fire or tallow dip; then hammered his way through college, making such a record that even before he graduated (though he was 26) he was appointed as professor of ancient languages at Miami University at Oxford, a few miles from Cincinnati.

A prominent figure in Ohio education during his seven years at Miami, he was also surveying all the world's great literature, from which — but principally from the British and American — he was compiling a series of readers. It was in 1836 that he was called to the presidency of Cincinnati College, which Dr. Drake and others had revived, though with insufficient endowment. And in that same year, a milestone in American history, Truman & Smith of Cincinnati brought out the first two McGuffey readers. The others followed at short intervals until the series of six had been completed. They were a small library of interesting stories, poetry, historical episodes, travel, biography and great oratory, most of it inculcating moral lessons, yet without engendering boredom and hatred of it in the minds of such pupils as had minds, as did so many textbooks. It is true that some pupils obviously didn't know what they were reading about — one recalls an oversized, lubberly blank-faced girl intoning:

> We are lost thee cap-tain shoo-ted
> As he stayjered down the stars ——

But many others cherished and some still cherish the memory of McGuffey as long as memory survives. Clubs and societies of McGuffey alumni attest their popularity, and there are elderly folk today who can still recite lines from them, though they may not have opened the books in half a century or more.

Cincinnati College collapsed again, and after four years as president of Ohio State University, another poverty-stricken institution, McGuffey took a position with Woodward College, as Cincinnati's Woodward High School was called for a time, but two years later joined the University of Virginia faculty, and there spent the rest of his life. Back in Cincinnati the presses were vomiting his readers by the hundreds of thousands, which eventually became millions, as Truman & Smith, through various metmorphoses, at length emerged in 1877 as Van Antwerp, Bragg & Company; and they, in 1882, when they were publishing 4,000,000 schoolbooks yearly, were already claiming to be the biggest in the world. A decade later, when they had become the American Book Company and nearly doubled that output, their claim could hardly be questioned.

They had another asset which has not been given sufficient recognition. Joseph Ray, Virginian and mostly self-educated, had struggled part-way through college by intervals of teaching when he came to Cincinnati. He was a professor in and then president of Woodward College, where he remained until his death in 1856 at the age of 49. A prominent figure in education, he was President of the State Teachers' Association for a time. But his chief claim to fame — a fame, alas, transitory — is his compilation of Ray's arithmetics, First, Second and Third Parts — in board covers of something like a light clay color, with an undertone of brickish red — from which millions of nineteenth-century American learned all that the average citizen needed to know about figures in the days before hegemonic mathematical necromancers devised modern income taxes and demonstrated that a huge national debt is a national blessing. For practical purposes one need never mention billions then, but school children memorized the names of them all, up to decillions. Ray also compiled higher mathematical works, of minor importance, by comparison with his arithmetics. But mathematics is not a widely beloved subject, which may explain why Joseph Ray and the details of his life are today but little known, even in Cincinnati.

As the city's press capacity increased, its output broadened, and included much locally-written fiction — both novels and volumes of short stories — poetry, essays, history and biography. There were Cincinnati best-sellers — Emerson Bennett, for example, who came West poor when scarcely grown and first peddled a device for marking linen, then sold subscriptions for a magazine. Infected by the virus in the air, he began to write for the magazine, and then to grind out thriller novels — "Yaller Kivers," as they were called by their favorite audience. Famous before he was 30, Bennett's *Leni Leoti* and *The Passion Flower* are said to have sold 100,000 copies each. Others did nearly as well.

Bookshops, with or without printeries, swarmed downtown in the 1840's and '50's; you might hear of thirty or forty functioning at once. They were as thick on lower Main Street as on lower Fourth Avenue in New York today. When a new book appeared, from the East or abroad or from a local press, there was often a race between dealers to be first to lay copies on the editors' desks, hoping for mention in the review. Editors complained, however, that there was at times unseemly wrangling over who had arrived first, and petty jealousy over good reviews given to competitors.

There was a New Jerusalem bookstore on the scene very early, and later there came to be Catholic and Jewish bookstores. There was a bookshop on far West Sixth Street in 1857 kept by a woman whose name we do not know, for the newspapers, in accordance with the custom of the time, delicately withheld it. She lived alone in a room back of the store. One night a burglar had just effected an entrance when she heard him, and in nightgown and bare feet gave chase along the street, her cries attracting the attention of a watchman, who joined in the pursuit; but the news item does not even inform us whether or not they caught the marauder!

In 1850, at the age of 21, appeared one of the greatest of Cincinnati booksellers, Scottish-born Robert Clarke, whose first venture was in second-hand and rare books — for there were already many collectors in the city and thereabouts. In later years, as the head of Robert Clarke & Company, Cincinnati's major bookstore after most of the others had passed from the scene (and still functioning as John G. Kidd's), he continued handling old books along with the new, and his catalogues became famous. Historians, such as John Fiske and Justin Winsor praised them, Winsor calling them "the most important Americana lists" then being issued.

In the latter 1850's some private collections began coming upon the market in auction sales which were eagerly attended by other bibliophiles. Reprints of rare books began to appear in Cincinnati, too, and under the strangest of sponsorships. A former Governor of Vermont, a well-known book collector with a particular interest in New England and Indian history, visiting Cincinnati, asked a book dealer how to reach the office of a publisher named William Dodge. He was directed, but at the given address, a frowsy building on Ninth Street, he saw nothing but a shoe repair shop, a man inside with a boot between his knees, and a woman in a farther corner, toiling over a washtub. To his breathless amazement, the Governor learned that the cobbler was the William Dodge who had reprinted Penhallow's *Indian Wars*, the Sketch of Captain Cresap, Lion Gardiner's *History of the Pequot War* and other rare items of early Americana. They sat down, Dodge on his bench and the visitor on a chair, and for hours they talked books, the Governor forgetting his surroundings, despite Dodge's loud, rough voice, his ungrammatical speech and occasional profanity; all in such violent contrast to his bookishness that he was a fascinating, an incredible character.

Born in Massachusetts, orphaned in childhood and apprenticed to a cobbler, he delighted in reading Colonial Indian history. He settled in Cincinnati in his thirties and began trading in books, keeping his small stock on shelves over his bench. In 1859 he made his first reprint venture, following this with others. Then came the Civil War and he served as fife major in the Union army. After the war, he gave up shoemaking and tried to live by the book business. Because of his lack of education, he had to have help in writing notes on his reprints, in making out catalogues and invoices. Notwithstanding the fact that he had some noted bibliophiles and historians among his customers, he could not support his family by bookselling, and was driven to work for the city at superintending street jobs. He died in 1875.

In the cultured atmosphere of Cincinnati, shoemakers seemed to take to literature as men to the manor born. Mrs. Trollope, we recall, found one whose verse was published in the newspapers. And there was another, a mere youth named Howard Durham, who came from New Jersey in 1847, laid down his hammer and awl and began to promote and edit magazines. His first two were not greatly consequential, but his *Genius of the West*, born in 1853, made a considerable name for itself. For a time he had Coates Kinney, a noted poet, as his partner, but the two could not agree; Durham sold out to Kinney, started a rival but unsuccessful magazine, and within two years was dead of cholera at 27. Kinney engaged another famous local litterateur, William T. Coggeshall, as editor of the *Genius*, and under him it engaged the services of all the best talent of the Ohio Valley, and published much valuable historical and other matter. But when Coggeshall left it to become State Librarian in 1856, it soon died.

Of this magazine's writers, fully one-third are known to have been women. One cannot of course know who wrote the unsigned pieces or those coyly credited to "Laura," "Titania" or "Lilly Lute." But the women were tireless scriveners. Think you that they were all unimportant because you never heard of ninety-nine out of a hundred of them? Importance is relative, temporal. Later in the century J. C. Derby, a prominent publisher, declared that a novel, *The Dead Letter*, one of several written by a Cincinnatian, Mrs. M. V. Victor, had been second in sales only to *Uncle Tom's Cabin*. Both author and novel are now as completely forgotten as most of today's best sellers will be a century hence.

Among the leading nineteenth-century bluestockings found in the pages of the *Genius of the West* were Alice and Phoebe Cary, who were no longer of the local colony. They had gone to New York in 1850-51, where for years their home near Washington Square was a salon, the haunt of the great and near-great writers of the East. Alice returned to Cincinnati for a few months in 1853 to edit the *Parlor Magazine*, whose life-span was not greatly longer than her editorial incumbency. Inclined to regard the death of her mother and two or three sisters as bereavements greater than anyone else had ever been called upon to bear, Alice was — though one

(Cincinnati) reviewer declared her "emphatically the first poetess of the New World" — rather too much given to the dismals to suit modern tastes. Even *Putnam's Monthly*, when her first volume of poems appeared, called it "a sob in 399 parts. Such terrific mortality never raged in a volume of the same size before. It is a parish register of funerals rendered into doleful rhyme."

One of Cincinnati's most noted magazines lived exactly one year. Moncure D. Conway, born and reared a Methodist in Virginia, fell under Massachusetts influence and turned Unitarian and anti-slavery. Entering the Unitarian ministry, he was called to the Cincinnati Congregationalist Church in '56, and in 1860 — the Boston *Dial* having long since risen and fallen — he founded Cincinnati's *Dial*, an untrammeled journal of "Literature, Philosophy and Religion." Its brilliance began with its chief contributor, Conway himself, and was heightened by Emerson, Charles Eliot Norton and other Eastern luminaries. William Dean Howells, then a young journalist in Columbus — he had tried police reporting in Cincinnati and was completely repelled by one night's experience — scribbled some poems for the *Dial* and was rapturous in his approval of it as a forum for free thinking, "nobler than pork, sublimer than Catawba, more magnificent than Pike's Opera House." But though rich in its promise, the Cincinnati *Dial* was short-lived.

The brain reels at contemplation of the spate of specialized periodicals which poured from the presses in those ante-bellum years— religious, denominational, sunday school, dental, medical, pedagogical, agricultural, horticultural, industrial, general scientific, fraternal, philosophical, often several of each kind; counterfeit detectors, and at one time and another, three price currents. The itch for print extended to Covington, where the young ladies briefly — until the creditors began to glower, we assume — published the *School Girl's Experiment*. Two type foundries labored overtime, supplying the dozens of printeries on each side of the river. And incidentally, Cist in 1859 counted thirty bookbinderies in the city.

Experiment; that word was significant and characteristic of Cincinnati, as the many firsts that it accumulated bear witness.

New, independent and radical ideas were constantly buzzing in the bonnets of Cincinnatians. The young city took them all in its stride, as it had taken the Unitarians, with their virtual junking of the New Testament. If anything, the Unitarians were a stimulus to Cincinnati's individualism and independent thinking. The splitting of old sects, the questioning and liberalizing of established creeds, seem elementary now; but they were often daring and radical then, and provoked bitter controversy with the conservatives. As the New Lights, who aimed to "reform" religion, especially the Presbyterian, used to sing;

> "Though by the world we are disdained
> And have our names cast out by men,
> Yet Christ our captain for us fights;
> Nor death nor hell can hurt New Lights."

Have you been thinking that Volapuk, proposed in 1879 and followed by Esperanto and other systems, were the earliest suggestions for a universal language? By no means. James Ruggles published an original scheme for one in Cincinnati in 1829, fifty years before Volapuk. Simplified spelling was another Cincinnati innovation. Socialism and communism were budding here when Karl Marx was still a schoolboy in Treves, though they were of comparatively harmless types, with no Russian dressing, no hints of overthrowing our Government. All that the left-wingers of those days tried to do was gently to convert others to their beliefs.

Among the radicalisms for which Cincinnati was a breeding ground was women's suffrage; women's rights, it was called then. There was Lucy Stone, of course, though she spent most of her time lecturing elsewhere. And there was Mrs. E. A. Aldrich, who for some time edited a suffrage paper known as *The Genius of Liberty*. She and Mrs. Moore of the *Western Lady's Book*, also local, joined in a mass attack upon Horace Mann, then president of near-by Antioch College, who had coincided in the theory that woman's mental powers are not equal to man's, because her brain is lighter.

In this they were at odds, curiously enough, with a woman — a tall, handsome Scot named Frances Wright, who in general preferred the society of men to women, because, she said, of their superior intelligence. Miss Wright was one of a number of radical innovators — Rapp and Owen of New Harmony, Warren, Longley and others in Ohio — who did their experimenting in the Middle West. There was even a short-lived free love colony, Memnona, near Cincinnati. Fanny Wright's endeavor was the education and rehabilitation, at a colony in Tennessee, of some thirty Negroes whom she, with ample means, had purchased from slavery. But finding the problem beyond her physical powers, she gave it up.

As might be expected, Miss Wright drew enormous crowds when she first appeared in Cincinnati in 1830, not only because of her views, but because of the fundamental novelty of a woman's appearing in public on the platform, and with intent to defy almost all established beliefs and systems, at that. Mrs. Trollope heard her first lecture and was enthralled by "the brilliance, the overwhelming eloquence," the "almost unequalled command of words the wonderful power of her rich and thrilling voice." She spoke that evening upon "The Nature of True Knowledge," which was a sort of introduction to her more startling addresses later, when she denounced religion, the influence of the church in politics, the existing system of education based on authority, the legal obligations of marriage and other established ideas. There is a story that a few missiles were thrown at her on one occasion, but they did not halt her speech, and for the most part, Cincinnati listened to her with its accustomed tolerance. She liked the city and spent her latter years there, continually writing and propagandizing, adding to her former theses a demand for the abolition of the banking system, maintaining that capital of all kinds should be held by the State, by which all citizens should be employed. One of her books was in advocacy of Epicureanism. She died in Cincinnati in 1852.

As slums, poverty and crime increased in the larger American cities, young men like George Lippard and Lucius A. Hine of Cincinnati began to feel such things as a burden on their consciences. Lippard wrote sensational fiction reeking with crime, murder and political intrigue, always interwoven with denunciation of the causes of such woes. He founded a semisocialist Brotherhood of the Union, whose aim was the elimination of the sources of poverty and crime. His novel, *New York; Its Upper Ten and Lower Millions*, published in Cincinnati in 1859, was blood-and-thunder, seasoned with romantic socialistic preaching. Lucius Hine, a serious, talented young man whose remedies for the correction of society's ails were prophetic of those long afterward propounded by Henry George and Edward Bellamy, proposed to administer them in homeopathic doses in a publication to be called the *Western Literary Journal and Monthly Magazine*. To handle the literary side, he took on the most impossible of partners, Edward Z. C. Judson, a breezy youth who blew in from somewhere, who wrote sea stories signed "Ned Buntline," and who was supposed to supply a part of the capital, but never did. But Judson thoughtlessly killed a man at Nashville, fled with a mob at his heels, and than ended the magazine in the spring of '45, after six numbers had been issued, to which the best of Western authors had contributed some good material.

Hine promptly launched another magazine, the *Quarterly Journal and Review*, in which he gave more space to his political and social propaganda. This ran for more than a year. In the meantime, communistic communities had appeared in the vicinity of Cincinnati. The Clermont Phalanx, organized in 1844 on the plan of Fourier, was located on the banks of the Ohio, not a great way above the city. It wanted Hine as editor of its organ, the *Herald of Truth*, so his *Quarterly* was merged with that paper. But the Phalanx failed in '47, and with it, Hine's magazine. The community buildings were bought by a brotherhood of similar aim, but scarcely had it gotten under way when a great flood in the river undermined the village's principal building, a brick structure, and it collapsed, killing 17 people. And that ended *that* experiment.

Hine was next taken on by a Mr. Hitchcock to edit the *Western Quarterly Review*, an ambitious affair of 200 pages per number, in which socialistic propaganda began to dominate the literary element. But the publisher disappeared and the *Quarterly* expired after two numbers had been issued. After another editorial billet,

Hine turned to lecturing on his cherished reforms. In 1869, when he had grown sterner, he struck harder and boldly through the title of a new, all-reform magazine, *Hine's Quarterly, or The Revolutionist*, but it could endure through no more than three numbers.

The man whom some people considered the most notorious of all was Josiah Warren, a gentle intellectual who opened his "time store" in Cincinnati in 1827 to vindicate his theory of "labor for labor." He sold merchandise at cost plus 7 percent for handling, plus a labor charge for the clerk's wage. His venture did not last long, but he was to be heard of again. Twenty years later he founded another Fourierian community near the Clermont Phalanx, calling it "Utopia," again with his favorite motto, "Cost is the limit of price." But it proved little more substantial than Sir Thomas More's dream, and Warren returned to New England, where he continued to write pamphlets which brought upon him the charge of being the first anarchist or the father of anarchy; for he didn't believe in government, insisting that its functions could be handled by private persons.

Foster's Crossing, 32 miles northeast of Cincinnati, was long a hotbed of independent opinion. There in his latter years, in a congenial atmosphere, lived Orson S. Murray, antislavery and anti-religion agitator, who regarded prayer as a crime and who wrote his own funeral sermon, declaring that death ends all, which was dutifully read at his interment. There lived the Longley brothers, Elias, Septimius, Servetus, Cyrenius and Alcander, who were originals. They seem to have had the first playing-card factory in the country, outside of New York. They presently removed it to Cincinnati, where they printed not only playing cards and fancy paper linings for trunks, but magazines carrying their favorite messages. Elias, the eldest, a devotee of simplified spelling, started the *Wecli Fonetik Advocet* in 1850. Its title soon began to be spelled in the conventional way, but it ran for eleven years. Meanwhile the brothers compiled a *Manual of Phonography* and a primer, first and second readers in phonetic spelling, which had large sales all over the country. It really looked as if they were about to put Webster to rout, but their vogue eventually waned.

Alcander, the strongest Fourierian faddist in the family, spent two years in a phalanx in New Jersey, then rejoined his brothers, whereupon they began publishing a radical magazine, *The Type of the Times*, which was partly in phonetic spelling. On his own account, Alcander launched in 1857 the monthly *Phalansterian Record*, but he was too restless to stay in an office long. He tried living in two or three other phalanxes, then came out flat-footed for communism, and in '68 he launched *The Communist*, which soon died. War and its tinsel prosperity had put an end to the radical age in Cincinnati.

So erudite a community — such enclaves as Blacktown, Rat Row, Sausage Row, the Canahl, Brighton and Cumminsville (then known as "Helltown," and notorious for brawls and feuds, dogfights, drunken revelry and horse-racing; it reformed long ago) must always be understood as exceptions to such a generalization — would of course have a plentiful supply of schools. Nathan Guilford of Cincinnati is credited with being one of three men (the other two being non-Cincinnatians) who did most to establish Ohio's public school system. He and his colleagues worked tirelessly for years to overcome opposition to tax support for schools, and in the election of 1824 they won. Guilford was rewarded for his efforts, for he was an extensive publisher of school books, even a compiler. He infuriated an elderly gentleman in New Haven by putting forth a speller which he entitled, *The Western Spelling Book; Being an Improvement on the American Spelling Book by Noah Webster.*

City teachers, public and private, organized an association in '29, and this promoted a teachers' convention in the city two years later, where a Mid-Western association was formed. The so-called College of Professional Teachers, which was merely a group intended to stir public interest in favor of the free school system, the city having been slow to put it in motion, had some distinguished members during the ensuing years — Stowe, Beecher, McGuffey, Ray, Williams, Alexander Campbell, and among others, a singular Scot, Alexander Kinmont, whose lectures on *The Natural History of Man* caused Henry James, the novelist, to declare long afterward that Kinmont was a man of genius, born too soon. Kinmont's schoolboy classrooms had a twentieth-century free-and-easy look — "liberty subject to self-control" was his motto, and he let no one tell him what to do. When offered a place on the Cincinnati College faculty at $2,000, a large salary for the time, he refused to surrender his liberty; he wouldn't be "told how to teach by a set of professional donkeys."

And there was George Graham, school principal, who, to promote public support for the building of schools, paraded his children through the streets to band music, and fired teachers who refused to march. When the Council failed to provide money to build a needed school in the Second Ward, he raised the cash elsewise, built it with an eye-catching cupola atop, and then demanded that the Council pay for it. They did so — for all but the cupola. Within a few years, eight other buildings of four rooms each were erected. Male principals drew $700 annual salary, female principals (probably because of the lighter brain) only $250. Assistant male teachers were paid $300, females $200. Instruction in German was begun in 1840, and the first public high school was created in 1847, but in a few years it was merged with two high schools privately endowed. Thomas Hughes, an eccentric English-born shoemaker — another of those enlightened cobblers! — whose only real friends were a pony, a dog and a pet hen, founded one; the other was fathered by William Woodward, whose fortune had come, like Longworth's, by the increase in land values. Hughes and Woodward are still two of the city's proudest high schools, and their alumni were long the city's most persistent reunionists. Woodward lays claim to Professor Green, who wrote, "Old Grimes is dead, that good old man," a folk song of our fathers.

William Chambers, the Scotch tourist of 1853, was deeply impressed by Cincinnati's public schools, which were then a step in advance of those of other cities. "Where free education exists in England," said he, "it is a charity; here it is a right. The natural fruit of a system so exceedingly bounteous is an educated population possessing tastes and aspirations which seek a solace in literature from the materialities of every-day life. I do not know that I ever saw a town of its size so well provided as Cincinnati with publishers, libraries and reading rooms." He looked with amazement at the 14,000 volumes on the shelves of the Young Men's Mercantile Library Association, and its reading room tables, where nearly a hundred newspapers from nearly as many cities, were on the tables. This association has a 10,000-year lease on any building on the northeast corner of Fourth and Walnut Streets. The brevity of the leasehold gives no concern, for it is renewable.

The City Directory remarked in 1829 that "There are 47 ordinary schools in the city, in which are 963 boys and 725 girls, receiving the rudiments of an education." Of course most of these were private schools, of which there were scores in Cincinnati before the Civil War, but whose number slowly decreased as the public school system grew, though many parents, for one reason and another, continued to patronize them for decades afterward. They were not all small affairs. Joseph Herron's seminary for boys had 200 to 300 pupils annually. When Mr. Herron died, his alumni placed a monument over his grave in Spring Grove — as did the old boys of the school of D. S. Brooks, another wellbeloved master.

Colleges were appearing, too — St. John's College, a transient on lower Broadway, the Farmers' College at College Hill, female colleges at Glendale and Mount Healthy, and Cincinnati Wesleyan. Cincinnati College was on its feet again and progressing shakily. The Cary Academy, founded at College Hill in 1832 by Freeman Cary, a cousin of Alice and Phoebe, has become Ohio Military Institute. And there was the Ohio Mechanics' Institute, the first technical school west of the mountains, founded in 1829 and in mid-century occupying a home built for it by Miles Greenwood, where a boyish telegraph operator named Thomas A. Edison went nightly to devour every scientific book he had time for. The Catholics, beginning with the Atheneum in 1831, developed it into today's Xavier University, whose beautiful home between Avondale and Evanston, is one of the city's comely sights. It long ago took over the name of the theological Seminary of St. Francis Xavier, then temporarily inert, but now thriving as Mount St. Mary's Seminary of the West. In the 1840's this was one of three theological schools claimed by Cincinnati, the others being Lane and a Baptist seminary in Covington. In 1875 a fourth, the now great Hebrew Union College, was added. The Mount Auburn Female Seminary, which, under the long presidency of H. Thane Miller, was a noted institution, was situated, said the *Gazette* in '57, "amid scenery that needs only to be located in Switzerland or Italy to have its praises on every tongue."

Cincinnati even claims to have had in 1849 the first real college of business; not teaching merely bookkeeping, stenography, spelling and penmanship, but giving instruction also in business law, management and banking. Which reminds us that in that same year a midtown dry goods merchant named John M. Bradstreet, who had for two years been gathering credit information for a growing list of business subscribers, set up one of the nation's two great mercantile credit agencies, long since amalgamated into one. Ten years later he moved to New York and Cincinnati well-nigh forgot him.

The so-called College of Professional Teachers threw out rami with names sometimes longer than they could live up to — the Cincinnati Society for the Promotion of Useful Knowledge, for example, and the Great Western Academy of the Sciences and Literature — the latter the brain-child of that little Kentucky pepperpot, Ormsby McKnight Mitchel, whose design in this case was overambitious, but who was destined to bring glory to Cincinnati. A West Point graduate, he came to Cincinnati to practice law with E. D. Mansfield; but neither of them cared a hoot about law, so Mansfield went on with his writing, whilst Mitchel, at 27, became a scientific professor in the reborn Cincinnati College in 1836. Helping to promote and surveying the Little Miami Railroad in his off moments, his love of astronomy led him to ponder the building of an observatory in Cincinnati, something which neither New York nor Boston yet possessed.

Cincinnati already claimed the distinction of having the first little observatory in the United States — a three-foot telescope, a transit and an astronomical clock, the only instruments of the kind then in the country, bought by the Jefferson Administration for United States Surveyor-General Jared Mansfield (father of E.D.) to enable him to establish meridian lines as bases for public surveys,

and housed in his home, formerly Israel Ludlow's, near Cumminsville. They now repose in the military museum at West Point.

The story of how Mitchel, a five-foot-six-inch dynamo, cam-
paigned for that observatory — delivering impassioned lectures,
with only sixteen auditors at the first one, but packing the hall at
the third and having to move to a larger hall to accommodate 2,000
for the fourth — canvassing furiously to sell $7,500 worth of stock
which he naively thought would be enough to build and equip the
plant — going to Europe to buy the telescope and falling in love
with a $10,000 uncompleted job, the second largest in the world,
at Munich — dashing back to high-pressure Cincinnatians for
enough additional money to buy the instrument — all this is only
the beginning. That Old Reliable, Nicholas Longworth, donated
the land on top of a high hill overlooking the Basin, as a site for
the building; but there was still little money in sight for erection
when the cornerstone was laid, November 2, 1843 — a day of great
celebration, with the 76-year-old ex-President John Quincy
Adams, making the long, wearisome journey by train and canal
boat to spread the first mortar and to make the chief address, and
as a graceful afterthought, the christening of the observatory's hill
Mount Adams in his honor.

When work began on the site in the spring, money was so scarce
that only three laborers could be employed, but Mitchel made a
fourth, swinging a pick and shovelling earth with his accustomed
feverish zeal. He persuaded the laborers to take some of their pay
in shares, the building slowly rose, the equipment — including a
sidereal clock and transit donated by the Coast Survey — was installed, and within another year Cincinnati had another "first" —
the first observatory west of the mountains.

Mitchel had impulsively promised his service to it for ten years
without pay, expecting to earn his living by his college professor-
ship; but that unlucky college burned to the ground in '45 and he
was out of a job, so he turned to lecturing on astronomy to support himself, and indirectly, the observatory. As usual, he was an
enormous success. At New York, said a newspaper account "The
hall is thronged night after night to hear his impassioned eloquence
poured in an unbroken flow of thoughts that breathe and words

that burn on the excited thousands." And this about astronomy, mind you! We wish we could have heard one of those lectures.

With the outbreak of the Civil War, Mitchel entered the Union Army and died of yellow fever at Beaufort, S. C. After the war came another great director to the observatory, Cleveland Abbe, to shed more luster on Cincinnati with ideas which have become so integral a part of human procedure that no one now even wonders when or how they originated. In 1869 he began issuing storm warnings, based on telegraphic reports; very limited at first, of course, for lack of means. When he appealed to the Chamber of Commerce for aid, it agreed to pay for telegrams from not more than sixteen places at not more than 25 cents each — four dollars a day! Slowly the service widened, and he began drawing the first weather maps. His activities spurred Washington to the organization of the United States Weather Bureau, and in natural sequence, it took Abbe away from Cincinnati. It was after leaving that he propounded his other great idea, that of time zones and the standardization of time which is now so essential to the conduct of all human affairs.

Finding that frequently one couldn't see stars, moon or even the sun through the telescope because of smoke, another location was sought for the observatory. John Kilgour donated the cash to erect a new building on Mount Lookout, an eastern suburb, in 1873, where a bigger telescope was installed, though the old one, for which Ormsby Mitchel worked so hard, is still there beside it. It rests on the old cornerstone, too. That's Cincinnati.

Another institution reared in those days still graces the city, though lacking the support it deserves. The Historical and Philosophical Society of Ohio was organized in Columbus in 1831, the three charter members from Cincinnati bearing the familiar names of Longworth, Foote and Flint. Never prosperous, the society had, fifteen years later, reached the point of omitting two annual meetings when it was proposed that it be joined with the Cincinnati Historical Society, organized in 1844. This was done in '49, the name of the State society being retained, and the library and headquarters were removed to Cincinnati, where the centenary anniversary has just been celebrated. It is an honored institution, with a distinguished membership, but twentieth-century Cincinnati, which let its Public Library become a public reproach before taking steps to give it an adequate home, has also, notwithstanding its wealth and culture, failed to give its Historical Society the support it deserves.

CHAPTER IX

Elegance and Eclat

To PRODUCE the state of coagmented activity known as Society in a city, three fundamental ingredients are necessary — money, and in diminishing degrees, manners and beauty. A dash of culture does no harm, though some cities have got along very nicely without it.

Cincinnati had the three. Its Eastern pioneers, followed by its Virginians and Kentuckians, brought good manners with them. As we have seen, its accumulation of money made the rolling snowball look sluggish and inefficient. And according to foreign observers — who, if prejudiced at all, were usually prejudiced against America — Cincinnati had beauty from very early days. In 1805-6, when the town was still one-third log construction, the Englishman Thomas Ashe asserted that the ladies of Cincinnati had everything — comeliness, distinction, taste, tall, slender figures, with "much animation and expression." Those women must have had good manners, else he would not have called them ladies, and would not have hesitated to mention their crudeness.

The favorite amusements, he said, even at that early date, were balls and amateur plays. The building of the Baum and Kilgour mansions in the frontier village indicates a rapid improvement in housing conditions. Elias Pym Fordham, another Britisher, in 1817, when the Midwest was still largely wilderness, found in Cincinnati "some dwellings with their proud porticos that look too aristocratic by half for the State of Ohio." Charles Fenno Hoffman, the popular New York author and editor, visiting in 1834, added more testimony as to local beauty. "What would most strike you in the streets of Cincinnati," said he, "would be the number of pretty faces and stylish figures one meets in a morning. A walk through Broadway here rewards one hardly less than to promenade its New-York namesake. I have had more than one opportunity of seeing these western beauties by candle-light, and the evening display brought no disappointment to the morning promise." Captain Marryat was so struck by this fact that he thought the climate of the West must be especially favorable to beauty. "I think I saw more handsome women at Cincinnati than in any other city of the Union," he said. Other visitors spoke of Cincinnati women as "considered very handsome," "simple and unassuming," evincing "a high taste for literary and mental accomplishments."

Among the "noble private dwellings of cut stone and of stucco" that Hoffman saw, "there are several with greater pretensions to architectural beauty than any I remember in New York." As for the people, "Nothing can be more agreeable than the society which one meets with in the gay and elegantly furnished drawing-rooms." The only possible criticism, he said, would be that of a slight lack of repose — which, however, was inevitable in a young, vivacious, growing city. He quoted a common saying in the Midwest, "We all come from some place or other," and commented, "It is therefore in the highest degree absurd to speak of the Cincinnatians as a provincial people in their manners, when the most agreeable persons that figure here hail originally from New York or Philadelphia, Boston or Baltimore, and are very tenacious of the style of living in which they have been educated. . . .

"I have been here now nearly ten days, and scarcely an hour has passed without some gay and agreeable entertainment. . . . My table was covered with cards on the morning after my arrival, and I could see no end to the polite hospitalities of the place, should I prolong my stay."

On the other hand, Mrs. Trollope in 1828-29, found here "a total and universal want of manners, both in males and females," none of "the little elegancies and refinements" enjoyed by the middle classes in Europe, little worth-while conversation at evening gatherings, tobacco-chewing and spitting in public — which was painfully true — and an exaggerated religiosity and puritanism, carried sometimes to farcical lengths, in which there was too much truth for comfort.

But Cincinnati had its rejoinder. A lady told Captain Marryat that they were not angry with Mrs. Trollope for describing the *"society that she saw,"* but for pretending that it was representative, the best society. The gossip was that she was able to get into only three homes of any consequence, including Mr. Flint's. Captain Marryat, ten years later, said, "Whatever the Society of Cincinnati may have been at the time that Mrs. Trollope visited there, I cannot pretend to say; probably some change may have taken place in it; but at present, it is as good as any in the Union, and infinitely more agreeable than in some cities." He thought it possible that there might be some unpleasant truths in her screed, but "that it would be a libel on the Cincinnatians of the present day is certain."

Portraying what she believed to be a society too pious to enjoy itself, Mrs. Trollope revealed that some spoofer had told her (and she believed it) that in Ohio you were liable to a fine of $50 just for having a pack of playing cards in your possession. But Drake and Mansfield had said, in their *Cincinnati in 1826*, that at the private parties so "frequently and elegantly given . . . cards, music, dancing and conversation constitute the principal sources of amusement." Society played cribbage, piquet, Pope Joan, spoil-five or whist, all without betting, whilst humbler folk got along with casino or all-fours, and gentlemen who gathered in a hotel room or somebody's downtown lodging to risk money on the cards, played the new game, poker, which had recently come up from New Orleans. In short, it was a fairly normal society. Dickens in 1842 found "the society with which I mingled intelligent, courteous and agreeable," though he couldn't have seen very much of it in his brief stay.

One of the social highlights of the 1820's was the visit of General Marie Jean Paul Roch Yves Gilbert Motier, the Marquis de Lafayette, who was making a farewell tour of the United States and having a typical American experience, including shipwreck on the Ohio River. At Cincinnati, as may be imagined, vast preparations had been made for his coming. As he stepped ashore from the boat, he confronted a long strip of crimson velvet, leading up the slope of the landing for him to walk on. But smart politician that he was, he detoured it, remarking audibly that good

American earth was fine enough for him; which of course made a terrific hit with everybody save the committee who had provided the velvet. Major Daniel Gano, whose grandfather the General had known as a chaplain in Washington's army, had the honor of providing the carriage and six fine bay horses, the only outfit of the sort in the city, which carried the distinguished guest uptown. For days on end he was dined and feted, shown all the sights, including the city market and the Pearl Street Theatre, sung at by 600 schoolchildren, toasted by spellbinders, and exposed to the charms of these Cincinnati beauties — not without danger, for at 77, the Marquis was still highly susceptible. There was also a fete in Major Gano's "brilliantly illuminated" orchard, at his home near Cumminsville.

Society was dancing, too, Mrs. Trollope; balls, cotillions and even an assembly, a series of balls supported by subscription each winter. Philadelphia and Charleston were not to imagine they were the only ones that could achieve such gentilities. True, their assemblies were more genealogically exclusive than Cincinnati's; they would have looked down their noses at the shopkeepers, manufacturers, lawyers and doctors on the Cincinnati guest list, with not one man of leisure, not one young man who wasn't holding down a job somewhere, not one family that had been in town more than one generation — and many not that long — and some who probably didn't know who their grandparents were! This genial democracy accounts for a delicate distinction drawn by Drake and Mansfield; "The general features of the fashionable portion of our community are similar to those of the same class in the Eastern cities, with an equal amount of refinement, if not a like degree of useless etiquette."

In an assembly invitation of 1826 in the Historical and Philosophical Society's collection, "The honor of Miss Jane Morris's company is requested for the season" by a representative list of managers — Morgan Neville, David Kilgour, Bellamy Storer, William Greene, Archibald Irwin, Alfred Hayden, William R. Foster and Thomas M. Carman. There were also the Bachelor's Balls, which persisted even into the twentieth century, the Buckeye Balls, which commemorated the settlement of the Miami country, the Military Balls, all of which were annual festivities, not to mention casual and private affairs.

The town had always danced, as was proven by the fact that even Andrew Burt's tavern, which was built in the village when Fort Washington was still garrisoned, had a ballroom of sorts. But this was soon outgrown, as were the various halls that followed, and the town had never had a satisfactory ballroom until Mrs. Trollope built her Bazaar. On the third floor of this building, said the City Directory of 1829, there was "a magnificent Ballroom, the front of which, looking upon the street, will receive the rays of the sun, or emit rival splendors of its gas-illumined walls, by three ample arabesque windows, which give an unrivalled lightness and grace to the festive hall." The room was supposed to remind the beholder of the Alhambra. In the back was "an orchestral gallery whence dulcet music will guide the light fantastic toe in the mazes of the giddy dance." Here for years some of the best of the balls were given.

These affairs were unnoticed by the newspapers, there being neither society page nor society column in those days. Personal items were also lacking, especially as to the ladies. It was axiomatic that a lady's name appeared in the newspapers only twice in her lifetime — and tersely, at that — when she was married and when she died. But a poem written in advance of the first assembly ball of 1830 got into print, gayly though unmetrically tossing about the names of some of the prominent participants — with how much heartburning among those *not* mentioned, God alone knew — and with such a glow of happy expectancy that one longs to have been there, too:

> Wend ye with the world to-night?
> Brown and fair and wise and witty,
> Eyes that float in seas of light,
> Laughing mouths and dimples pretty.
> Matrons, beaux and belles and all
> Tonight are going to the ball.
> There the mist of the future and gloom of the past
> Will all be forgot in those moments of pleasure,
> And the old and the young and the first and the last
> May join the glad throng in treading a measure.

THE SERENE CINCINNATIANS

Wend ye with the world tonight?
Sixty gray and giddy twenty,
Flirts that court and prudes that slight,
Stale coquettes and spinsters plenty.
Mrs. Lytle will be there
With all the charms that nature gave her,
Miss Slocum, too, with city air,
The Misses Bartow and Mrs. Taylor.
Longworth with her group of graces,
Both the Sellmans kind and true,
The Riskes with their charming faces
And winning Foote with eyes of blue,
Matrons, beaux and belles and all
Tonight are going to the ball.

Wend ye with the world tonight?
Owen, Stannard, Drake, we know
And Worthington, and Jones and Wright
All — to a man, intend to go.
See the tide of fashion flowing,
'Tis the noon of beauty's reign,
Misses Greene and Brooke a going,
Werth and Walker and McLean.
Mrs. Guilford gaily smiling,
Miller — Nature's protege,
Miss Phillips — all hearts beguiling,
Cassilly, Currie and Miss Lee.
Matrons, beaux and belles and all
Tonight are going to the ball.

Wend ye with the world tonight?
Where dark eyes are brightly glancing,
While the measures of delight,
Set feet and eyes alike to dancing.
There Mrs. Garard will be seen,
Hamilton and Neff and Lawlor,
Conover, Thomas, Yorke and Greene,
And Mr. Perry — a little taller.
Many a maid of pleasing mirth,
Benbridge, Reillys and Miss Turner,

Guilford, a man of modest worth,
Benson, Storer, Rives and Urner;
Symmes and Benham will be there,
Bowler, Somerby and Bellows,
Ludlow and Southgate, I declare,
And many other clever fellows,
Matrons, beaux and belles and all
Tonight are going to the ball. . . .

As the bard's name was known, one questions his judgment in babbling of flirts, prudes, spinsters, and worst of all, of "stale coquettes"; but as folk were saying as far back as 1855, that was his funeral. They did not have to wait as late in the evening for their gayety to begin as do later generations. The clop-clop of hoofs and the clatter of wheels on the rough streets began to be heard by eight o'clock, and dancing might be in progress within the hour. And though dancing in those earlier years was gay and some of it quite athletic, there was a decorum about it, too; the waltz, though popular in Europe, was not yet seen in Cincinnati; it was too palpably "hugging set to music," as the Methodists later charged that it was. Quadrilles were still much in favor, especially the new one, the lancers, recently introduced from England. The gavotte, though a little out of fashion, was still seen on an occasional program; and Poland was contributing no end of sprightly ideas — mazurka, polonaise, polka — Gad, those Polacks must spend most of their time dancing! — frequently to the lovely music of a young chap named Fred Chopin, who was quite the rage in Paris. The Polka came along in the middle 1830's, and as it was not too easy to learn, a frequent question of a gallant to a lady in asking for a dance was "do you polk?" Some of that Polish dancing called for no little leaping and hopping about, *solo*, which was embarrassing to self-conscious persons, especially if they were not too expert in the figures.

There had been dancing teachers ever since the town was a hamlet, but none who became so popular, in fact, so necessary to society as Monsieur Charles Ernst — often miscalled Ernest — who appeared at least as early as 1843. He hadn't a sou when he arrived, so it was said — nothing but a magnificent military bearing, floridly exquisite manners (including feminine-hand-kissing) and a knack for turning occasions to his profit. He set up a dancing school downtown, and quickly made an impression. His rooms were thronged with pupils, and he lived in accordingly elegant style. But after a year and a half, he vanished one day — the story was that he had gone to New York to look over the latest foreign Terpsichorean importations. But he did not return, and it was noised about that he had left many unpaid bills behind him. Society was doleful without him, however, and when it was learned that he had gone no farther than Pittsburgh, ladies of *ton* petitioned fathers and husbands to advance the cash for his debts and bring him back. Society, they said, just couldn't get along without him.

This was done and he returned, to be welcomed, figuratively, with open arms. Whether he repaid all the money he owed, we do not know, but thereafter he prospered and did not get so deeply into debt as before, perhaps because tradesmen were more cautious and his earnings larger. He married a Cincinnati woman of good family, but in 1854 there was a divorce, with the details carefully omitted from the public prints. Soon afterward, on a vacation trip to Paris, M. Ernst married a Frenchwoman, who was a faithful spouse and became indispensable to him. As time went on, she did more and more of the hard drilling, while her husband played the fiddle and collected the cash. All this, however, was merely gossiped behind fans, and did not appear in print until twenty years after. Within a few years, the *maitre* was believed to be worth between $40,000 and $50,000. Claiming to have been a French army captain of distinguished record, he was made captain of the Rover Guards, one of the military marching companies which were so popular in all cities in those days. But when the Civil War broke out and the Rover Guards were taken into the Federal Army, M. Ernst, it appeared, had certain disabilities which made it impracticable for him to enlist. Nevertheless, inexplicably enough, M. Ernst somehow came to be popularly known as "Colonel," and his noncombatant attitude was no deterrent to his popularity or his income.

As wealth rapidly accumulated, so did its inevitable concomitants, leisure, summer vacations, costly dress and suburban mansions. Even by 1850 there seem to have grown up a few young near-faineants who were not chained to a desk all day, for a news item of that year said, " 'Matinees' is the title given to parties which are now made at midday. The shutters are closed, gas is lighted, the company assembles, and cotillions, waltzes, polkas and flirtations become the order of the day, as they have heretofore been the order of the night at fashionable assemblies. As far as these matters relate to the health of the parties concerned, we entertain no doubt but that it will be found a material progressive reform." But this fad did not last long. It was a pointless striving for novelty by a few too-idle women, and there just weren't enough young men available for such doings.

Bal masques were a rage in the winter of 1850-51. Society had just been given a great lift by the opening of the magnificent new Burnet House. When the Burnet casually ordered 500 tons of lake ice from Sandusky and 300 tons from Dayton for the ensuing season, its fame flashed from coast to coast. In its ballroom, 78 feet square, it began giving weekly hops in '51, with supper, wines and music by Joseph Tosso's orchestra. Residence there became a desideratum for those who could afford it and who couldn't be bothered with the care of a home.

With the accretion of wealth, dress became a matter of prime consideration, and Cincinnati did not propose to let the latest modes of New York, London or Paris age noticeably on their way West. Birkbeck, as early as 1817, was impressed by the number of "gay carriages and elegant females" seen on the streets. A year before that, Platt Evans had come from Albany, New York and opened a tailoring salon, carrying his own cloths in stock, instead of merely showing samples; in short, he was the first merchant tailor; and in a suit of his cut, you might walk down Pall Mall or Piccadilly without embarrassment, conscious only of admiring and envious glances from other elegants.

Fine stores for ladies were multiplying rapidly, and some of them are still functioning, though the ownership of most of them has changed. In the 1840's, ladies' conversations and letters were laced with references to strange garments such as bustles, cardinales (a short cloak with hood), tunics, etcetera; in the '50's they were still more exotic — gilets, canzenous, pelerines, mantles and mantillas, a nice distinction; costumes made *en marquise*, with such appurtenances as ruchings, quillings, puffings, spotted blondes, berthes and guipure flounces, and using not only the ordinary fabrics, such as silk, satin, organdy and so on, but Frenchy-sounding textiles such as jaconet,solitaire,*moir d' antique*, *mousseline de bagé*. If you heard them mention half-gipseys or cottages, they were talking about hats.

According to a prominent hairdresser, writing in 1859, "There are two fashionable dress-makers in Cincinnati at present, where almost all the fashionables are to be met with. They go there more to display their elegance and to see those who are a step or two higher than themselves, than to have their dresses made. I know a number of ladies who have private dress-makers and plain seamstresses in their own houses; but once in a while they take a dress to these dress-makers, so as to keep up their acquaintance."

The wasp waist, an objective in mid-century, was attacked by Catherine Beecher in her *Letters on Health and Happiness*, and by John P. Foote, who told women sternly that "Altering their complexions by cosmetics and their shapes by corsets will never make them more lovely or more beloved." All with the usual water-off-a-duck result. Tight lacing clashed with the advocates of exercise, of which there were schools, such as Mrs. Barrett's Kalosthenium, or Academy of Exercise for Young Ladies. Kalosthenics was "intended to impart symmetry to the form, grace, activity and elegance to the movements, animation to the countenance, and a happy serenity and firmness to the mind." Kalosthenics was being taught in the Cincinnati public schools, too. There were even exercising machines for women, as you may see by perusing *Godey's Lady's Book* for 1852.

New Year in early times was a working day, just like any other. Gradually the conviviality in the taverns began to be reflected in social circles; the custom of calling to offer good wishes grew until by 1850 New Year was an established holiday. The *Gazette* of January 3d said, "Throughout the city, business of all kinds was suspended on Tuesday, and citizens of all classes went about, congratulating each other on the advent of the new year."

The custom of keeping open house had begun then, and the *Gazette* gave instructions on New Year's calling; "All that is *fashionable* and necessary to say on entering a parlor is 'Good morning (or evening), Mrs. ———— or Miss ————,' as the case may be. . . . 'I wish you a very happy year.' She, or all together, will reply, 'Thank ye. May you have a countless number of them. Will you take a glass of wine, Mr. ————?' You will then sip the wine, and gently placing your finger on the cake, retire, bowing yourself out, saying, 'Bless me ———— I have a great many calls to make to-day.'

"Now, as each of these *highly complimentary* visits can be accomplished in about one minute and three-quarters, any person can make before midnight from 150 to 200, and even if his list of acquaintance outnumbers that, he has no excuse for not calling upon all, provided he can engage a first-rate Virginia race horse, that will stand without hitching."

Here the writer was assuming that rigid restraint would be used in eating and drinking. It was notorious, however, that many men, especially the younger ones, liked the wine not restrainedly, but too well. By dusk or before, some of them were past locomotion from house to house, unless they were traveling by carriage, into and out of which their progress was uncertain. Gate-crashing was appearing even that early, too. One hostess saw so many visitors who were total strangers to her that she wished she had engaged a police officer to watch the silver.

Notwithstanding the touting of Cincinnati as a pleasant summer resort for Southern planters, its own citizens had long since begun seeking some cooler spot in the dog days. This began very modestly. Drake and Mansfield remarked in 1826 that "In the summer season, excursions to Big Bone and the Yellow Springs serve to assure those who have leisure and inclination to seek for pleasure, health and rural scenery." The Big Bone Lick, a deposit of mastodon fossils, was in Kentucky, a few miles from the city, and Yellow Springs was two counties to northward. In the '30's, the Springs was as high as society aspired; in fact, in midsummer, it was considered a *beau monde* quite *distingué*. But as bank accounts grew more portly, it began to appear that Yellow Springs just wouldn't do. After all, it was little, if any, cooler than the city, and the society there — well, one had sort of grown away from it. One began to see some rather queer people there, too. Put-in-Bay on Lake Erie was much cooler, and a few even braved the long, jolting carriage or stage ride to White Sulphur, where one might meet some of the most armorial of Southern aristocrats.

But in 1841 the editor of the *Gazette* excoriated the inhabitants of American cities for having "a villanous way of spending the summer." Instead of wasting their money in going to high-toned resorts, why didn't they build up resorts in the country immediately surrounding their cities, where people of not so great means could enjoy country air and relaxation? *"There are good pike roads in all directions from Cincinnati,"* he italicised, whereby such places could be easily reached. Of course the people who patronized the plushy resorts did not much desire the company of persons of small means, so his protest lacked plausibility. But as if in answer to it — or probably the editorial was written to induce the advertising — the Cheviot Hotel, L. Frink, Proprietor, on the Cincinnati and Harrison Pike, "six miles from, and on the most elevated ground in the vicinity of Cincinnati," announced a thorough renovation and readiness to receive families or single guests, amid the cooling breezes that blew over the hilltops. Joe Harrison's was another cool hilltop hostelry, and the omnibus, *Lady of the Lake*, left Broadway and Front Street every day for that place, the fare each way being 25 cents. Across the river, William Dollens advertised his Eight-Mile House on the Lexington and Covington Turnpike, one mile from Florence, where he had "one of the best and strongest *Sulphur and Mineral Wells* in Kentucky."

But these houses had to be content with guests of comparatively modest means, for the wealthier ladies were looking elsewhere. That journey to White Sulphur had proven too arduous to endure, and besides, my dear, one can meet so much wealthier and more fashionable people at the Eastern resorts, even some titled foreigners.

So Cincinnati ladies began to be seen at Saratoga and Long Branch, some even at Newport and the Massachusetts beaches. Husbands and fathers for the most part — though not always — remained at home on the job. It was a long and strenuous journey at first, by river or canal, stagecoach and perhaps a bit of rail. In 1845, five days and eighteen hours were required to travel from Cincinnati to Boston; by 1857, with good luck, you could cover it all by rail. But no matter how tough the job of getting there, the ladies considered that the reward was worth it all.

Plateau suburbs which became famous and are still beautiful were in process of creation. Four miles of rough pike led to East Walnut Hills in the 1840's, and an omnibus known to the commuters as "The Beast" carried them to and fro. Conditions steadily improved; there was better bus service, but mansions were now being built on the hills by men who had their own carriages or saddle horses to convey them to their businesses. But even Mount Auburn, Avondale and Walnut Hills had their plague spots, their disorderly elements which it took a long time to clean out. Other suburbs were being created in the 1850's; Corryville (middle class) between Walnut Hills and Mount Auburn, and Clifton, most imperatorial of them all, a miscellany of millionaires, where lawns were measured by acres and rooms by dozens in the pinnacled chateaux. Yet many well-to-do families still clung to their well-appointed homes on Broadway, Pike and the cross-streets in the Basin, within easy walking distances of their businesses, shaking their heads pityingly over those long, rough, muddy drives that must be endured by the pioneers on the hilltops.

In 1859 society was startled by the publication of *A Hair-Dresser's Experiences in High Life* — anonymously, but generally known to have been, in the words of a reviewer, the work of "the bold, if not very polished pen of Mrs. *Potter* (formerly Mrs. Johnson)," who had dressed ladies' hair in several cities, but who, in her book, paid particular attention to the social cosmos of Cincinnati, her home town. Naturally, it was a best-seller. How else, where else on earth could so much succulent gossip be procured as from the babbling tongues of women when loosened by the soothing ministrations of a hairdresser? Who else than she could have such opportunities of collecting scandal? Mrs. Potter of course mentions no names; she frequently uses an initial, though we can never be sure that it is a true one. In the words of the *Gazette* critic, "Before her graphic narrative, as before the spear of Ithuriel, the illusions that becloud the common fancy disappear like dew before the orb of day; the aroma of divinity with which, aided by imagination, art, French fabrics and perfumery, we are in the habit of investing the lovely creatures in whose sweet faces all the virtues seem to be reflected, is dissipated, to return no more forever."

Mrs. Potter was writing of a society in a state of flux. Population and wealth were growing with such dizzying rapidity that standards and class lines were only blurred approximations. New figures were constantly appearing, and already, a few of the oldest families were beginning to show signs of withering. Hordes of new climbers were toiling upward, as factories, stores, steamboats and railroads wrought for husbands and fathers like modern genii for their Aladdins. True, the old aristocracy had begun as impecuniously and commercially as the parvenus, but memories of such things grow dim after a couple of generations. They had a valid thesis, however — that their founders in the West were by training and behavior ladies and gentlemen, and society should still be like that. And so, as new wealth took on polish, new names were added to the golden scroll of society, and those families, as the years wore away, were added to the list of Old Families.

Mrs. Potter tells of several ruses for improving one's position when accumulating dollars at length made it feasible for one to nourish aspirations. One was to take up residence at the Burnet House. There you identified the regular boarders with means and some social standing; you scraped acquaintance with them in parlor or dining room, then visited in their rooms, adroitly learned which of them had the best social connections and cultivated those women most assiduously. "I have known ladies," said the chronicler, "who, having wealth and a reasonable position in society, were so anxious to get into a circle they considered a little higher that they would crouch and bend, wire in and out to get in, and often would go to people they had no acquaintance or business

with, and tell them something they had heard, for the purpose
of speaking to them."

With not only interlopers and *soi-disants*, but positive adventurers lurking in every covert, the chastity of society would seem
to have been in a parlous state. Mrs. Potter tells of being summoned (she did most of her work in her clients' homes) to a certain
house to "comb" — her categorical term for her service — a woman,
and upon arriving there, saw two or three other young women.
She asked her client whether this was a dressmaking establishment or a boarding house. Neither, was the reply; it was a private
home. But when some other rather brassy-looking young women
were seen moving about, the hairdresser began to have her sus-
picions. When "a tall lady I had often seen in some of our most
fashionable stores came in and asked me if I would comb her,"
Mrs. Potter agreed and went to her room, hoping to learn the truth
about the place. She asked the tall lady whether this was a boarding house, to which the latter replied, "Yes, it's a fancy boarding
house"; and the word "fancy" had dreadful implications then. The
informant told Mrs. Potter that one of the inmates of the place
was entirely too bold; she "went to public places, concerts and
even to the Burnet House hops, and took a pride in boasting of it,"
which the tall lady evidently considered pretty indecent conduct.

The hazard of making acquaintance at hotel hops is here all too
plainly revealed; which makes us wonder about those balls at the
Mechanics' Institute in the 1850's, which a journalist called "brilliant and recherche gatherings" of "fashion and female loveliness."
One fancies they were pretty democratic.

A person into whose ears so much gossip was poured, quite
naturally passed some of it on to others. Mrs. Potter says that the
first remark of some clients when she appeared would be, "What's
the news?" "What have you heard?" or "What about so-and-so?"
though she does not admit ever having told anything. She must
have kept the secrets of her more valued clients rather judiciously.
Continuously backstage in the social melodrama, she seems to have
become a sort of social arbiter and fixer — which is entirely possible. When Mrs. Parvenu had prepared her invitation list for a
big affair, she might submit it to her hairdresser confidante, say-

ing, "Iangy, is there anyone I have forgotten?" and then Iangy
would usually suggest a few more names. "The hostess at these
large parties," she reveals, "receives many ladies that are not on
visiting terms with her, or that she would not even know were
she to meet them on the street"; and she adds modestly, "Many
ladies would be entirely forgotten but for me."

Mrs. Potter's best stories are of the climbers. She was supposed
to know who would be invited to the imminent social functions
of her clients. When it became known that "Mrs. Colonel H."
was soon to give a party, dozens of women hastily had dresses
made or remade in the hope of receiving invitations; for Mrs.
Colonel H.'s affairs were always extremely elegant. "Before the
invitations were issued, those who were doubtful of getting invitations, when they would meet me on the street, would ask, "Oh,
Iangy, am I invited?' 'Do you know whether I will have an invitation?' or, 'Oh, how I wish I was going — I would so like to be
there,' and such like. . . . They did not like to ask me to try and
get them invitations, but by repeating, 'I wish I were going; I
would give anything to go,' they, as plainly as they could, hinted
it to me. I have obtained many invitations for ladies to large parties,
where they would not for one instant think of asking them had it
not been for my request. I work for a great many of those who
give large parties, and they know I would not ask for any one
unless I knew them to be ladies, both in manners and principle."

Climbers just leaving the lower slopes often provoked feelings
of resentment among acquaintances who observed that they were
beginning to be "stuck up," and there was a remarkable method,
occasionally practiced, of making their faces red. Mrs. Potter, one
day passing a house whose front door was evidently close to the
sidewalk, saw hanging on the doorknob an old dress, some spools
of thread and a thimble. She learned that this was the device of
a neighbor to remind the woman of the house, who nourished
social ambitions and was showing symptoms of snobbery, that
everybody remembered that her mother had been a dressmaker.
Similarly, old shoes, old hats, tin pans, rags and horseshoes were
hung on the doors of people beginning to be purse-proud to
remind them of the humble occupations of their fathers.

The two instances which Mrs. Potter cites of pretentious parties at which some of the hostess's jewelry and guests' furs disappeared illustrate the dangers of promiscuous invitation and not even knowing all your guests. It is not at all improbable that there were gate-crashers in those days who took advantage of such situations. These incidents were ignored by the papers, which, however, had a delightful way of telling bits of scandal with names of the prominent folk involved omitted: "A cowhiding case came off yesterday at the corner of Sixth and Lodge Streets" (1848); "A well-known and respectably dressed individual was caught on Saturday afternoon stealing spoons from the William Tell Tavern" (1856); during a drunken melee in Court Street after the laying of the cornerstone of the new Court House in 1852, a reporter saw "at least one City Father (councilman) with a black eye," and "a portly judge in dangerous proximity to the scene"; "A row occurred at a drinking saloon under Woods Theatre yesterday afternoon, in which bottles, tumblers and fists were pretty freely used. One of the parties is a member of the School Board" (1859); "A woman attempted suicide at a house on Eighth Street near Linn, occupied by two or three females, partly at the expense of a Water Street merchant" (1865). On more than one occasion a building is mentioned, "owned by a Fourth (Third, Main, etc.) Street merchant and occupied by a brothel." Crime's eternal fascination was proved when "several society ladies", more or less disguised by veils, were seen at the trial of a servant, for killing his employer, a prominent citizen.

One of the best stories that have come down to us was told in the newspapers in '57 of "a wealthy citizen living on Broadway," who had various eccentricities, the most pronounced being that of antipathy to social gatherings of any kind, especially in his own home, where they were flatly forbidden, much to the embarrassment of his daughters, who pleaded vainly that they could not or should not accept hospitality without returning it. "He would take the girls to Europe or Saratoga or Newport or Nahant, get them new sets of jewelry, anything but that." On one occasion some cousins came to visit the daughters, and the latter decided to have a party by stealth. Their father always retired early and slept soundly, so their invitations specified an hour of assemblage late enough to see the old man safely in bed and snoring. They engaged an orchestra, and ordered fine refreshments from a caterer, in short, prepared for "one of the most recherche affairs of the season." Their idea was that even if Father awoke during the festivity, he would find himself confronted by a *fait accompli*, and would just have to grin and bear it. They had steeled themselves to endure the storm that would burst over them next morning.

The evening came, "the beautiful and brilliant, the gay and fashionable, the witty and elegant" assembled in such numbers that there was not much room for dancing; but they were doing the best they could at it, amidst great merriment, when a woman's scream electrified the assemblage, and "an apparition as if from the tomb" appeared, striding from the stairway towards the drawing room — the head of the house with grim face and dishevelled hair, clad only in night shirt and slippers, with bare legs and clutching his cane. He was "swearing like a Templar" and shaking the cane as if about to break up the party by violence. The ladies shrieked and covered their eyes. As he advanced into the drawing room, "a general stampede took place. Ottomans and chairs were overturned, and in twenty seconds the late crowded rooms were deserted." Carriages, hastily summoned, rolled away with the guests, the weeping daughters of the house went upstairs and the rooms were darkened. The cousins departed next day.

According to the code, the name of a well-behaved woman was rigidly excluded from the newspapers unless she wrote a book or went on the platform — in which case there might be doubts of her being well-behaved — or was married or died, when she might get three or four lines of type. Social events, too, were considered entirely too private affairs to be spread vulgarly upon the pages of a newspaper. It is only through letters and reminiscence that we know of the dramatic happening on that evening in 1834 when the solemn, pious young attorney, Salmon P. Chase, was wedded to beautiful Katherine Garniss. No more humorless man than Chase ever lived and attained prominence. He could not repeat a joke without wrecking it. He faithfully kept a diary, in which he chided himself on his sinfulness and unworthiness (though he was really a conceited person). He repeated Scripture while bathing and dressing; card-playing and wasting time were sins. He had once known a young woman whom he could have loved, had she not been "fond of the gay world" and "disinclined to religion," which he prized "more than any other earthly possession." Evidently Miss Garniss passed the test, for they were married. But during the reception after the wedding, the bridegroom was stricken by illness which for a time seemed mortal; and the comely bride, settling at once into her position as devoted wife, sat by his bedside in her wedding gown, ministering, holding his hand, smoothing his pillow, until the danger was past. Strangely enough beautiful Kate herself lived less than two years thereafter.

When the golden wedding of Nicholas Longworth and his wife was celebrated with pomp and circumstance on Christmas Eve, 1857, the *Commercial* carried an account of it, the editor apologizing for thus "intruding into private life"; but he thought "such a rare occasion might be viewed by readers as possessing serious *historical* interest, and might therefore perhaps be forgiven."

Society was still highly moral, and when Dumas the Younger's *La Dame aux Camélias* was translated in 1848 and became a bestseller in Europe and the East, it sold well in Cincinnati, too, though oddly enough, few ladies could be found who would admit having read it. It was one of those books which, like Byron's Poems, was hidden under the mattress by young women readers, lest Mother catch them with it; though, truth to tell, Mother herself probably would have read it if she had the chance. But when the sweetly sinning Marguerite Gautier was dramatized as *Camille* in '52, she became a real international hit. When the play appeared in Cincinnati, there were some ladies who blushed at uttering its title in their own parlors, and in many homes it was not mentioned at all. No well-behaved young man would have thought of taking a girl to see it. The ladies who boldly went to the performances, always with male moral support, were looked upon as very advanced, even reckless — just didn't care what they did. And there were greater numbers of heavily veiled women, usually two or three of them together, at those performances than ever seen in Cincinnati before or since; some of them, declared Mrs. Potter, ladies who had been the loudest in denouncing the play and saying that they would never be seen at such an immoral exhibition. The multiple veils were much in the way of the eye-wiping and nose-blowing necessary in the last act, as the tubercular Marguerite gracefully sank towards the tomb, but at least one could see, though dimly, what took place and hear the lines.

But as Pope remarked about vice, there are only two steps from enduring to embracing. Verdi promptly put the frail heroine into an opera, *La Traviata*, and within three or four years, ladies who had abhorred *Camille* went to hear *Traviata*, because "the music is so elegant." Opera was only occasional in Cincinnati, however, until the winter of 1857-58, when Pike's big opera house was nearing completion, and he announced a long season of opera, to be presented by a distinguished Italian company. This precipitated a crisis. The panic of '57 had given a boost to morality, for war and depression are great promoters of piety. Any opera was bad enough, said the opponents, but the Italian brand was the most risque of all; the plots were sordid and immoral, and the ballet frequently an indelicate feature. Many ladies announced flatly that they would not be among those present.

It was here that Mrs. Potter appeared in her strongest role, that of a liberal crusader. "I had made a vow that I would not comb anyone for the concert" (some weeks before the opera opening) "who was too sanctimonious to go to the opera. . . . On reaching home, I found various orders for next day for the concert. On going to the places, I would always ask if they were going to the opera; if they said no, I just walked out." This created a hullaballoo among her patrons. Some of them demanded, Was she irreligious? Had she no respect for Christianity? "I said I was actually afraid to comb anyone who was so good that the sight of a green curtain frightened them." Surely, liberal heroism could go no farther than this!

Again, some of those ladies who had so piously repudiated opera, nevertheless attended under veils — "disguised," Mrs. Potter called it. But the opposition was weakening. The opening of the opera house was preceded by a grand ball, a milestone in social history. On the day of the ball, Mrs. Potter worked continuously from 7 in the morning until 11:30 P.M., dressing hair for 24 ladies, and having to refuse 38 others for lack of time. She had done the same for the Burnet House opening in 1850, and she commented upon the great increase in affluence and prodigality since that time. At the Burnet House function, she said, there was not a gown in the ballroom that cost more than $500, and one lady who wore $10,000 worth of diamonds was tops in that respect. At the opera ball, eight years later, the cost of dresses was incalculably higher and one lady in garnet velvet glittered with $20,000 worth of gems.

The opera took the city by storm. It played a two month's engagement at Pike's, and thereafter, opera was never an important subject of moral controversy.

Visiting heroes were given due — and on one or two occasions, more than due — recognition by society. When General Zachary Taylor, victorious over Democratic skulduggery, both in the Mexican War and the national election, visited Cincinnati just before his inauguration, he was kissed, we are told, by fully a hundred beautiful young ladies, presumably all Whigs; which proves that the Hobson osculatory madness after that hero's naval exploit in 1898 was nothing new. And so many locks of hair were snipped by the ladies from the old General's thinning supply that he was in danger of resembling a delinquent under sentence.

When Louis Kossuth, the Hungarian patriot, came on his American tour in '52, collecting money and bonds everywhere for his "cause," Cincinnati suffered a sort of antimonarchist brainstorm over the guest. We do not hear of any kissing, but he was lauded, dined, feted, given resolutions, scrolls and what was more to the point, thousands in cash; and for sixteen days the newspapers devoted from one to three and a half columns of small type daily to him, always reporting his numerous speeches in full. But social homage was never manifested on any other occasion quite so fervently as when the city which eight years ago had gone slightly mad over an antimonarchist, now welcomed with even greater adoration a future king — the handsome, nineteen-year-old son and heir of Queen Victoria, who, in the solemnly farcical fashion of the time, was going about the country theoretically disguised as a mere noble named Baron Renfrew. He didn't give Cincinnati much time, and they had to pack the entertainment in rather tightly. He and his retinue were domiciled at the Burnet House. (Heenan the pugilist had stopped there the year before and drawn quite as big a crowd into and around the building, though of somewhat different character.)

On the first evening of his stay, the Prince and his noble companions were given a banquet, which ravaged all the seas and continents for its viands and wines, at the great mansion of Robert B. Bowler (wholesale dry goods) in Clifton. On Saturday night there was a grand ball at Pike's Opera House. The Prince opened it with Mrs. Pike herself, and later danced with — all this is a matter of careful record — Miss Rebecca Groesbeck, Miss Alice Hilton, Miss Edith Burnet, Miss Hattie McGregor of Mount Auburn, and by way of recognition of the Kentucky shore, Miss Mattie Taylor of Newport. Whatever untoward circumstance Fate might have in store for those girls in after life, they were sustained through it all by an aura of enchanted glory whose complacent rapture no ordinary mortal could ever know.

And so ended an era. The muttering nimbus of war was already darkening the Southern sky; this was the last great social fling before the storm.

CHAPTER X

Over the Rhine

"Shall I begin with the usual jokes, such as the audience always laugh at?" asked Aristophanes's clown of his master in *The Frogs*. We were reminded of him by Hans Wagner — not Honus, the immortal shortstop, but the Cincinnati brewer in an operetta, *The Prince of Pilsen*, around the turn of the century. He was for most Americans an avatar of Cincinnati; and his query to the beautiful young ladies who greeted him at Monte Carlo, "Vas you efer in Zinzinnati?" was a line which became deep-rooted in American consciousness, even to this day.

Cincinnati acquired a kindly feeling for the Germans very early in her history. As already mentioned, her very first German citizen, David Ziegler, who had fought Indians in her behalf, was elected as the first village president in 1802. Martin Baum, the first banker and industrialist, was of German stock, and others were coming in those early days and performing public service. Colonel Harry Zumalt commanded a Cincinnati regiment that went to the front in 1813. Baum promoted selected immigration; he had an agent at Philadelphia, a favorite port for immigrants, to persuade the best appearing of the newcomers to locate in Cincinnati, where Mr. Baum found jobs or business openings for them. Some of the earliest German and German-Swiss immigrants to Cincinnati engaged in viniculture on hillsides which may have reminded them of the valleys of the Rhine and Moselle. They preceded Nicholas Longworth in that activity, though he went into it on the largest scale, and was so great a publiciser for it that most people believed he was Cincinnati's original viniculturist. He loved to write, and the pamphlets into which he wrote his new-found knowledge with amateurish enthusiasm and sent to Europe, lauding Cincinnati's advantages for such pursuits, brought many more Germans to that city and vicinity.

In 1817 Jacob Gulich, an early German immigrant, was working in Martin Baum's sugar refinery when a steamboat came down the river, on which were 23 German immigrants from Baden. They had not been able to pay all their passage money across the ocean and so, in accordance with a rather common custom of the time, they bound themselves to the captain or his assigns, to work out the balance after reaching America; they became indentured servants. Upon landing at Philadelphia, the captain sold their indentures for $50 each to another man who thus became in effect their owner. He brought them down-river to Cincinnati, and offered them for sale at $450 each, but found no buyers, so he decided to try New Orleans. But Jacob Gulich had heard of their plight, and resolved to spend everything he had, if necessary, to rescue them. He rushed to an attorney, who attached the boat and began suit to test the contract. It was declared illegal, the men were set free and became Cincinnati citizens. Some of their descendants may be there today.

Cist reported in 1840 that 3,440 citizens of Cincinnati had been born in the Germanic states. Realtors that year were offering "To German Emigrants" superior garden plots of one to six acres. The Germans were more apt to bring a little money with them and launch small businesses than some other immigrants. But as we have seen, this was not true of all of them. Nor were they all hard-headed, practical fellows, either. In one Cincinnati family the story has come down of an ancestor and his chum, two young chaps who had been reading Byron, and who were divided in mind whether to emigrate to America or to storied Greece. It was only by a hair's weight that they finally decided upon the United States.

When the brig *Louise* from Bremen reached Philadelphia on a day in April, 1840, a correspondent of the *Baltimore Patriot* said nearly all the passengers were German immigrants, and that he had "never seen a finer looking collection of men on shipboard from any foreign country." It may be presumed that the women and children, if there were any aboard, rated equally well. Cincinnati having become a favorite Promised Land for these people, it received more than its share of such contingents. Its public landing was cluttered with their big, clumsy bags and bundles of belongings tied up in cloth, while the owners, some still in wooden shoes, stared about them at the unfamiliar scene with somewhat bewildered blue eyes. They were 28 per cent of the population in 1840, and city ordinances soon began to be printed in German as well as English. German became a part of the public school curriculum. All the German states, even the free city of Lubeck, had consuls in Cincinnati.

Quite early in their Cincinnati story, they began clustering in the northern part of the Basin, near the foot of the hills, and in the elbow of the canal, which promptly became the "Rhine." With its jumble of short, narrow streets, its plain, sturdy, well-painted red brick houses abutting directly on the swept sidewalks, their front steps whitewashed every Saturday morning, the potted plants in the windows, the tiny garden plots in the rear, the women knitting on the sidewalk in the shade on warm days, the old men with long pipes, watching babies or trundling their perambulators, the stocky, red brick or stone churches resounding with Bach chorals and nearly all topped with clock-towers, the signs everywhere in German — "Backerei" (Bakery), "Spezerei-handlung" (Grocery store), "Apotheke" (Drug store), Wein und Bier Halle" — it might have been a city in the Fatherland. Wooden shoes were still being made and worn. The quarter was celebrated in the "Over the Rhine Waltz," published by John Church, on Fourth Street. You might go about for hours there and not hear a word of English spoken; the residents didn't need it in their affairs. Some of them, especially the women, became quite static; some never did learn to speak English. In a later decade a Mrs. Ritter, a woman 55 years old, was mentioned as not having been half a mile from her home near Thirteenth and Vine Streets, in 35 years.

Filling the bight of the canal, the community began lapping across it in places, and climbing the hills to northward. There were some Germans who prospered and who chose to live in more fashionable sections of the Basin, and some even on the hilltops, Colonel Leopold Markbreit, for example — editor and publisher and at various times water works commissioner, Mayor of the city and Minister to Bolivia — and his wife, a former Austrian actress, had a handsome home on Mount Auburn, where they were popular among their neighbors. But such people did not dissociate themselves from their fellow countrymen in the Trans-Rhenish area, as downtown newspapers liked to call it; they returned there to the beer halls and restaurants, the numerous clubs and societies — political, literary, musical, athletic — for their relaxation and intellectual exercise.

Here, too, they began to labor strenuously, at publishing newspapers, sending forth the first one, the *Ohio Chronik*, in 1826, and the second, *Der Weltburger* in '34. With the development of American political leanings, the *Volksblatt*, Democratic in tone, appeared under a famous editor, Stephen Molitor, and continued for a century. Friedrich Hassaurek, Viennese and perhaps the most noted of Cincinnati German editors, a fiery radical at the start, who eventually swung over to the Republicans and was one of the Republican delegates who nominated Lincoln in 1860, at first ran the *Hochwachter* — "Socialistic and infidel of the deepest dye," said Cist; and there were also the *Volksfreund*, *Republikaner*, *Democratische Tageblatt*, some religious papers, an agricultural paper and Karl Klaupprecht's *Fliegende Blätter*, launched in 1843, the first German illustrated paper in America.

Newspaper reporting was in its infancy in mid-century, and the few overworked reporters and their informants didn't always try to cope with German names, with the result that there were many items like these: "A German was badly beaten by two soldiers on Seventh Street last evening"; "A German had his pockets picked on Vine Stree last night, losing six dollars"; "A German wood-sawyer, an old man, was run over by a furniture car on Race Street yesterday and probably fatally injured"; "The body of a German named Peter —— was found in the river yesterday." In some cases the journalist wasn't sure of the person's nationality: "A foreigner was robbed last night in New Street of $17 by a person whom he had met in a house of ill-fame."

The Germans did not all prosper. They had their poor — and a few delinquents, too — who drifted into slum sections and were in trouble now and then. But let it not be thought that they were not respected. Lady Emeline Stuart Wortley wrote in 1850 that at Cincinnati, Pittsburgh and other places she asked people how well the Germans were liked, and "You almost invariably received the same reply: 'Very much. They are the best immigrants possible; industrious, generally sober and quiet.' "

There were three subjects upon which an occasional German might work up controversial heat — religion, philosophy and politics. Most of them were calmly pious folk, about equally divided, in the earlier years, between Catholic and Lutheran, and usually unshakable. They were apt to have pretty clear-cut, sturdy ideas about religion. They were either for it or against it; and Protestant and Catholic were in strenuous opposition. An oddity, as it seems to us now, were those few German Jews living over the Rhine, where they could speak the language in which they had been brought up; still faithful to their religion, but accepted by their neighbors as a bit eccentric, yet pleasantly symbolical of free America, where there were no ghettos. When William Nast, a native of Wurttemberg, came to this country as a Methodist preacher and missionary and organized in Cincinnati the first German Methodist church in the United States, one of his most influential converts was Ludwig Sigmund Jacoby, a German Jew who had previously joined the Lutherans. He and his Roman Catholic wife now turned Methodist, Jacoby became a missionary and carried Wesleyanism down the Mississippi River and thence to Germany and Switzerland.

The many agnostics and unbelievers — "free thinkers," as they were more delicately called — among the Germans aided in giving Cincinnati the philosophical or "liberal" tone which distinguished it. Theological, latitudinarian and metaphysical quibbles supplied material for much of the endless debating that went on in beer-halls, clubs and societies. And yet where else will you find an area so thickly peppered with churches as Over the Rhine? For the observing stranger, they identify the quarter instantly, for nearly all of them, with Teutonic persistence, are still there; most of them as sturdy in build as Herr Wagner's torso, the naves almost as tall as they are long, either of red-painted brick or stone, and with German inscriptions on their fronts; such as the big church of "St. Johannes Baptist," which was "Errichtet AD 1845, Renovirt

AD 1867." Not all are Lutheran or Catholic; there is even a "Baptisten Kirche." The "Deutsche Evangelische St. Paulus Kirche, 1850" presents a sort of motto in another line, "Wahrheit — Tugend — Freiheit." "Truth — Virtue — Liberty"; here is no emotional religion, but something of the savor of a system of ethic.

St. John's, a union of German Lutherans and Swiss followers of Zwingli going back to 1820 (it lost many members years later when it turned Unitarian), erected its present edifice in 1868. Sixteen years later it still owed $30,000 on it, and casting about for means of raising money, decided to wall off one corner of the church and install a drug store there (where it is yet), with which aid they finally paid off the debt.

The symbols on the spires of the churches are among the pleasant sights of the old quarter. St. Phillippus spire is topped with a gilded fist, the index finger pointing sternly to Heaven. St. Peter's (organize'd in 1832), with true German logic, did not shrink from allusion to the one appalling sin of its patron saint, crowning its spire with a gilded image of the cock which crew thrice when Peter denied his Lord. Most elaborate and impressive of all is that on the "Deutsche Evangelisch Reformirt, Salem's Kirche" at Sycamore and Orchard Streets — a large, gilded Angel Gabriel in full flight, sounding the warning of the Day of Judgment. Its story is delightful. The congregation wanted a Gabriel to serve as a weathervane. The image was made, but when delivered, qualms arose in the breasts of many of the members. The trumpet was pointed straight before him, and when placed as the manufacturer intended, the dissidents objected that Gabriel appeared to be lying flat on his stomach, which they considered an undignified position for the one of the chief angels in Heaven. Their idea was that angels ought to fly standing up, which of course is contrary to nature; nothing flies like that. They tried standing Gabriel on his feet, with his horn towards the zenith, but in that position, it was impossible to use him as a weather vane. After long argument, the opposition was still so strong that the figure was finally stowed in the basement of the church, and as years passed, almost forgotten.

But with the passing of time, new members grew up into the congregation, some of the older ones mellowed a bit and confided to each other that they still wanted a Gabriel, so it was decided to take the image out of the basement and have another look at it. But search the place as they would, it could not be found, and its disappearance has remained a mystery to this day. Now, however, the congregation yearned for a Gabriel as strongly as before, and by a strange coincidence, someone heard of a second-hand one that could be procured, in the queerest imaginable place. The church records show that the angel which now soars above the roofs of old Germantown once topped the steeple of the deserted Mormon Church in Nauvoo, Illinois. To the practical German mind, no taint adhered to it because of that association. This Gabriel is in precisely the same position as was the original one which caused so much debate (a thought; perhaps it's the same one, sneaked out and sold by a janitor!), evidently flying at top speed — as one must who is announcing the end of the world — for his body is horizontal, with robe fluttering behind, tooting the trumpet pointed straight before him — which two exertions simultaneously must call for considerable lung power.

It is said that after 1840 most pharmacists were German. The English did the first brewing in Cincinnati, but the business was on a small scale until the Germans developed it, some of their breweries becoming enormous affairs. In fact, the brewers became so wealthy that they were regarded by their fellow-nationals as financial Rocks of Gibraltar; and in the crash of '57, when banks began failing, many Germans took their savings to one brewer or another and begged him to keep it in his safe until the danger was past. Some brewers accepted the trust, though reluctantly. One of them was awakened just before dawn one morning by an insistent ringing and pounding on his front door. Coming down in nightshirt and slippers, he was confronted by a man who had left some $200 with him, but who had become fearful as to the brewer's solvency, and had been unable to sleep all night for worrying. The informal banker was furious. Fortunately, he had that much money in the house. He brought it, slapped it into the "depositor's" hand and roared in a wrathful discord of German and English,

"Heraus-get von mein haus! Put your Gott-verdammt gelt die bank into, und neffer again ask me!"

Dr. Louis Rehfuss, a native of Wurttemberg, came to Cincinnati in 1835 and established a wholesale and retail drug business, later going in for grape-growing and wine-making. It was the Germans who introduced the Christmas tree, now so beloved and so indispensable, into America, and Dr. Rehfuss is said to have set up the first one that Cincinnati ever saw.

Nathaniel S. Shaler, great geologist, paleontologist and long professor at Harvard, born in Newport, was in his fifteenth year given a German-Swiss tutor named Escher. This man, as was the custom of those days, "when literature was taken more seriously than it is today," says Shaler, caused the boy to memorize, by the time he was 18, "not less than 50,000 lines of English, Latin and German verse, a larger part of which stays with me to this day, and has been a helpful store.

"With Escher," he continues, "I found my way to the society of Germans in Cincinnati, a most interesting group of men, from whom I had much enlargement. Some of the ablest of these men were accustomed to meet at a beer hall in the part of the town north of the canal. There were many of these men of quality, the best of the exiles of 1848. Of these I recall Stallo — afterwards minister to Italy — a newspaper editor and a rabbi whose name has not abided with me, though his admirable shape is still plain. These were strong men; their talk made a great impression on me, and their personal quality did much to lift me to a higher level of ideals than any our people supplied."

The appreciation of education extended to all classes. A district school building, the Heberle School, and an impressive monument in Spring Grove Cemetery both commemorate the faith and devotion of a poor German horse-car driver and teamster, Joseph Heberle, who himself had never had opportunity for any but rudimentary schooling, but who was shocked to find that in a country of free education the children of many poor families could not go to school because their parents could not buy textbooks, and so, were often put to work. A vehement opponent of child labor and advocate of vocational training, Heberle devoted his spare time

— which was little enough, God knows! — and some of his sleeping
time to a house-to-house propaganda campaign in favor of free
textbooks in public schools. Eventually this came about; and then,
long after his death, a school and a monument expressed the community's belated appreciation.

Charles Richard Weld opined in 1855 that "The entire want of
rest and peace" in America, including Cincinnati, "must be fatal to
longevity." He suspected that even the Germans were infected by
it; but if so, it is not apparent in the chronicles of the time. They
still took time to live, to develop themselves, not only physically
but culturally, and so instilled into Cincinnati a tincture of their
own unruffled, serene philosophy, which it has never quite lost.
Despite their supposedly phlegmatic temperament, nobody else
seemed to have quite as much fun — what with social clubs, literary
and debating clubs, military companies, jäger or rifle clubs, singing
societies, small bands and orchestras.

In Cincinnati the Germans promoted effectively their own two
favorite forms of recreation, or rather of art — for those early
comers would have called physical culture an art, and as honorary
doctors' degrees are now given in the subject, perhaps they were
right — music and athletics. Here for the first time in the United
States, they organized these two activities, and in a large and permanent way.

They came singing to America, and they never ceased. Their
first singing society in Cincinnati was formed in 1838 by a group
of young men who met every Thursday evening in a room at the
Rising Sun Tavern, at Thirteenth and Main Streets. Among them
were Frederick Gerstaecker, a noted traveler and author. They sat
around a table with music books before them, and alongside each
book was a quart pot of beer whose price paid for the lard oil used
in the two hanging lamps.

A few years later the members of the choirs of a German Protestant and a German Catholic church combined in a society —
fancy that! Could it happen today? — which met in the home of
a watchmaker named Fritz Tappe, on Clay Street. The Gesang
und Bildungsverein Deutsche Arbeiter, an ambitious organization
of 1846, produced Haydn's *Creation*, under its conductor Xavier

Vincent. The Schweizerverein, a German Swiss group, and two or three others organized in the 1840's later united as the big Cincinnati Männerchor. The great musical event of the era was the meeting of the German singing societies of the three river towns, Cincinnati, Louisville and Madison, at Cincinnati on June 1st, 2d and 3d, 1849 in the first Sängerfest in our history. Then and there, too, the German Sängerbund of North America was organized.

The other notable event was the organization of the Turn Verein (Athletic Club) on November 20, 1848, the beginning of the Turners in America. Our Government issued a stamp commemorating the centenary of the founding in 1948. Few inanimate things in this old city tell a story more plainly than the representation of a lyre topping the front of Turner Hall, on Walnut Street, an athletic headquarters for the better part of a century. Music in a gymnastic playhouse? Certainly; if it be German, there is no incompatibility. Rehearsals and concerts of singing societies and orchestras have shared time in the Hall with acrobatics and inverted pyramids; and a third tenant has been politics. Many important political rallies, caucuses and city conventions were held in Turner Hall in the latter part of the century. From his official table in near-by Wielert's Garden, George B. Cox, the Republican boss of the 1880's and '90s, always kept an ear cocked towards the Hall, for what went on there might be vital to him.

In addition to their winter activities, nearly all organizations must have at least one picnic every summer, and as many individuals were members of several of them, there was no lack of opportunity for recreation. Ross's Hill and Jackson Hill, adjoining Rhineland on the north, were favorite outing spots, because most of the crowd could reach them in parade fashion behind a band. There were parades with bands, by the way, on the very slightest provocation. The *Daily Chronicle* was mystified one November day in '48 when "Several of the German military companies paraded through the city, but for what purpose we know not — unless it was their regular monthly parade day." That this proclivity is still strong is proven by a news item of almost precisely a century later — early December, 1948: "Rain snuffed out the torches of the Flamm Social Club's annual Over-the-Rhine parade

Tuesday night, gagged the big horn of Smitty's Band, and sent the red-and-blue top-hatted marchers scurrying. Returning to the headquarters over Flamm's Tavern, McMicken Avenue and Elder Street, the clubmen elected the entire slate of blue ticket officers with one exception." And listen to the names of the blue ticket candidates — August Ohm, Anthony Flamm, Ollie Grimm, Fred Jaeger, Carl Markley, Joseph Wagner and Matt Bedel, who became sergeant at arms. The Rhine may be gone, but the spirit and some of the Rhinelanders are still there.

A typical musical and athletic event — note the conjunction — took place on June 9, 1851, in "the Vine Street hills, about half a mile west of Mount Auburn." The downtown newspapers were not clear as to the sponsorship of the affair, though they said "some out of town societies" were also present. They marched up the hill with bands playing, enjoyed vocal and instrumental music, acrobatics by the Turners (who, in their white jackets and trousers, were well-nigh omnipresent) and "the exchange of those kindly civilities which so justly distinguish our German fellow-citizens." The *Gazette* once remarked that German picnics were "always orderly except when invaded by Irish or Anglo-Saxon roughs." But Anglo-Saxons found it hard to accustom themselves to the Teutonic propensity for having their outings on Sunday. "A strange sight," said an editor when on a summer Sunday morning, just as the bells were ringing for church services, a double line of boys of 16 and under, marshalled by men and carrying footballs, fencing foils, etc., marched through the city to the Newport ferry, to spend the day in physical culture on the Kentucky hills.

On a June day in '56, when the annual "fest" of the Sängerbund took place at Ross Hill — gymnastics and rifle practice as usual sharing attention with the singing — from 3,000 to 6,000 were present during the day. But perhaps the biggest outpouring was in '59, when 10,000 marched or otherwise surged up the hill in celebration of the tenth anniversary of the Protestant Orphan Asylum which the Germans had been largely instrumental in founding in 1849. "The usual decorum," said the *Gazette* of the Sängerbund affair, "observed at all such German festivals was noticeable on this occasion. In the afternoon we noticed a few cases of exhilaration, but none of that brutal intoxication which is too common in large gatherings of the Anglo-Saxon race. The comparatively unstimulating beverages in which they indulge has something to do with this, but the practice of taking all ages and sexes to these meetings has more." It should be said that nothing stronger than beer might be sold at German outings. Once when an outsider tried stealthily to purvey hard liquor, his bottles were seized and broken by the managers.

A party given in 1869 by the German Workmen's Society in honor of General August Willich and attended by many prominent business and professional men, German and non-German, again excited a reporter's admiration. "The fellowship was contagious; everybody was affected by it," he said. "We must not omit the children, from babies up to the man in second childhood. Little girls, as many as wanted to dance among the elders, looked for all the world like grown people seen through a spy-glass with the big end to the eye. Everybody seemed as happy as everybody else, and everybody was intent upon making everybody else as happy as could be. We commend this example to other people, not better, but more pretentious."

The same *gemütlichkeit* was noticeable at indoor affairs. At German theatres, waiters traversed the aisles between acts, carrying beer, Rhine wine and substantials to the order of purchasers. There were racks for empty glasses on the backs of the seats. For some time in the '50's, good music, orchestral and vocal, was served at Turner Hall on Sunday evenings for a ten-cent admission. Upon protests from some church folk, they were finally banned by the Mayor as a violation of the Sabbath; and then the Germans spluttered indignantly when he permitted a concert for charity on Sunday evening at the Catholic Cathedral, with tickets at fifty cents.

New organizations, such as the Gambrinus Society and the German Pioneer Society, meant more meetings and feasts. May Day and Whitsuntide called for volksfests, and the Fourth of July was eagerly seized upon as occasion for another. Visiting celebrities, such as Johann Gottfried Kinkel, poet and revolutionist, and Louis Kossuth, the Hungarian patriot, were serenaded, and Kossuth had to address them twice, once to the North Germans, once to the South Germans. They loved anniversaries. Humboldt's birthday was a favorite; parade and dinner, of course. In '69 they began the day with a 100-gun salute from Jackson Hill at dawn, which must have delighted the Mount Auburn neighbors. Schiller's birthday was another "must," sometimes celebrated by presenting one of his plays. They eagerly seized upon Washington's Birthday, too; in '72 a downtown newspaper asserted that there were masques and full-dress balls in almost every Trans-Rhenish hall that evening. They joined with the Italians in 1858 in a memorial demonstration in honor of Orsini, the Italian who had been executed for trying to assassinate Napoleon III, the parade being a funeral procession with hearse and coffin, but also with many banners and transparencies.

With the outbreak of the Civil War, the Germans' hatred of slavery, a measure of gratitude on the part of some for what America had done for them, and for the majority a strong infusion of that martial ardor which is an unfortunate legacy from their centuries of existence in the central battleground of Europe,[1] sent them flocking in great numbers to the Union colors. A thousand Turners promptly became the Ninth Ohio or Turner Regiment; in fact, 1,500 volunteers within three days after the call for troops kept Turner Hall busy around the clock. The 28th and the 106th Ohio were also recruited there.

The only non-German in the Ninth was the Colonel assigned to it, Robert L. McCook, of a famous Ohio fighting family, and as he was a law partner of Judge J. B. Stallo, he might be said to have had a German connection. McCook had had comparatively little military training, and the drilling of the regiment fell almost entirely upon the adjutant, Lieutenant August Willich (veteran of '48, editor of the *Republikaner* and later a general of division), while McCook gave his time to the equipping of his regiment and its records; as he humorously remarked, he was "only a clerk for a thousand Dutchmen." When the regiment's first test came, upon

---

[1] Yet oddly enough, there was a large antiwar element among them, who even favored the abolition of West Point!

the small but important battlefield of Mill Springs, it made one of the first bayonet charges of the war, precipitating the rout of the Confederates. It was then under the command of Major Gustave Kammerling, McCook having been elevated to the command of a two-regiment brigade. "McCook's regiments," said an historian, "were admirably drilled and disciplined, and moved to the attack with the order and steadiness of veterans."

Despite much volunteering *überm Rhein*, many prominent Germans were dissatisfied, because there were some slackers among them. They called a mass meeting in Turner Hall in August, 1862 "to take into special consideration the unworthy conduct displayed by persons who, having enjoyed the benefits of a residence in this country and prospered in its peaceful period, now that a war is upon it and a duty may be required of them, so far forget themselves as to seek to escape from this duty on the ground that they are not citizens of the United States." The considerable pressure which they brought resulted in more applications for citizenship and more enlistments.

During the war their soldiers acquitted themselves honorably and well, and produced many officers, all the way up to generals; as for example, General August V. Kautz, prominent in the Army of the Potomac, and General August Willich in the West, taken prisoner at Stone's River, exchanged and serving thereafter with the Army of the Cumberland to the end. General Gottfried Weitzel had the honor of leading the army into Richmond as Lee retired. General Andrew Hickenlooper became a prominent figure in Cincinnati business after the war as head of the Gas Company and long a sturdy opponent of electric lighting.

The return of peace found the Rhineland settling into its old routine, as though it had never been out of it. There were many armless and legless men now, men scarred, blinded, bowed and crippled by wounds and disease, but most of them still able to sing. The Turners and other German organizations were thereafter top-ranking celebrants of the Fourth of July. Turner acrobatics were introduced into the public schools by Louis Graeser, who had been appointed professor of gymnastics. A German Veteran's Society and several more singing societies were organ-

ized, and in July, '66 the Cincinnati Männerchor, the Young
Männerchor, the Druiden Gesang, the Sängerbund and the Harmonic Society, about 400 in all, marched to the wharf with silken
banners flying — the Sängerbund's huge, richly embroidered flag
was insured for $800 — to embark on the steamboat *Wild Wagon-
er* — shouldn't it have been *Wild Huntsman?* — for the annual
Sängerfest at Louisville. Presumably the St.Cecilias, the Harugari,
the Orpheus and other singing societies, some dozen in all, went
by other boats. The St. Cecilia was noted for its balls, "of the most
recherche character," to which on rare occasions, "a few Americans who are so fortunate as to have friends at court" were invited.
All of these gave bal masques sooner or later, and the Orpheus in
1869 scored a great hit with a locally-written operetta, *The Kingdom of Frogs.* And there was the Schützenfest in October, 1870,
with bands, banners, parades, all Rhineland swathed in decora-
tions, cannon booming on the Schützenplatz, followed by a whole
week of bang-banging, adding many medals to those already tinkling on marksmen's bosoms for this and that.

Some of the participants may have added zest to their work by
fancying themselves shooting at Frenchmen, for the Franco-
Prussian War had begun late in July, and the nearly 50,000 Germans in Cincinnati were much wrought up over it. "Die Wacht
am Rhein" was probably never sung as often per diem at any other
time in history. Mass meetings passed resolutions, declaring that
although deeply loyal to America, they could not forget the
Fatherland — an attitude which, overemphasized by some of them
many years later, brought their nationality into discredit. An aid
society was organized, concerts and other affairs were given to
raise money for German widows and orphans and to send German soldiers home, for there were still many unnaturalized Prus-
sians and others who owed their native States army service. News
of the French debacle at Sedan threw Rhineland into a delirium
and swathed it in the German and American colors. A parade
hastily organized at Turner Hall, followed a band to the various
German and English newspaper offices to cheer, but paused in
front of the *Enquirer,* the only one which had favored France, to
utter three mighty groans.

So much nationalism was aroused, some expressions of loyalty to the Fatherland were so fervent that thoughtful Germans were made uneasy by them. On August 16, 1871, just as the war was drawing to a close, a German-American Society which had for some time been in contemplation, was organized, with pledges of loyalty to our Government, and of appreciation of the freedom and opportunity afforded the immigrant in America. The objects of the Society, briefly expressed, were: to procure a better mutual understanding and closer contacts between the German and English-speaking populations, to smooth away misconceptions and national prejudices; to disprove slanders on American society and American institutions then so prevalent in Germany, and to give the German public a true picture; to render operative for the practical benefit of American life, German science, art and the treasures of the German language and literature, to bring to the attention of German-Americans the special excellences of the American character and to promote appreciation of them.

Anti-French feeling among the Germans seemed destined never to die. When Clara Longworth, of the eminent Cincinnati family, became engaged to a French nobleman, the Count de Chambrun, she had become a Catholic. She relates[2] how she went to the Bishop of Cincinnati, who "possessed a German name, German classical education and spoke with a strong German accent," and requested permission to employ a Catholic priest to perform the ceremony. But she was met with a flat refusal. Why? she inquired. He replied that he was opposed to all "mixed" marriages, and particularly to this one.

Music remained supreme in Trans-Rhenish culture. For the Sängerfest of 1870 a great auditorium 110 by 250 feet was constructed on Elm Street, opposite Washington Park (which had long been a neglected burying ground of pioneers). As the event drew nearer, some of the singing societies which had been quarrelling, buried the hatchet. Bands and singers came from all over the Middle West. There were more than thirty out-of-town reporters

---

[2] De Chambrun, Clara (Longworth), *Cincinnati: Story of the Queen City*, (New York, 1939).

in attendance, including some from New York and Baltimore, and one who represented papers in Leipzig and St. Petersburg. Great arches spanned Fourth and Vine Streets, through which an hour-long procession passed. On the first evening, fully 12,000 persons, sitting and standing, packed the hall, and an estimated 2,000 more stood listening outside the building.

In 1870, Cincinnati was a bi-lingual city. Of its 216,000 population, 49,000, more than one-fifth, were German. They were described as "frugal, personally honest, trustful and slow to anger" — this by a Jewish fellow-citizen, A. Julius Freiberg, as quoted in the *Proceedings of the Atlantic City Conference for Good City Government*, etc. (1908). Most of them were still packed into that Over-the-Rhine area, long since overflowing. Wealthy German brewers and pork-packers had made Dayton Street, west of the Plum Street stretch of the canal, their Fifth Avenue; no large yards, just sturdy brick and stone-front mansions, close-set, and within easy walking distance of several of the breweries. The buildings are there yet, melancholy mementoes of a vanished world.

Just north of the hills, a generation before the Civil War, Germans had founded the hamlet of St. Bernard. Andrew Erkenbrecher, starch maker, planted a factory there in 1859, gave the place an industrial lift, and more Germans came. Today the immediate vicinity is the world's greatest concentration of factories of soap, cleansers, shortening, candles, stearic and oleic acids, glycerine, oils and chemicals — Procter & Gamble, Emery, Werk, and Harkness & Cowing, covering hundreds of acres with their operations and queer odors, while in old St. Bernard, on Corpus Christi and other holy days one may see long processions of the pious around the church, as *im Mittelalter*.

In 1868-69 it was remarked that a "building fever" was raging amongst the Germans. This was coincidental with their promotion of building and loan associations in the city. As in the case of the chicken and the egg, it is difficult to tell which came first, the "bauverein," as the Germans call it, or their building boom. The date of origin of the building and loan asociation idea is disputable, but it was in the latter '60's that it had its great early development in Cincinnati, with German citizens as the principal promoters. In the bauverein the thrifty German mind saw the ideal opportunity for savings and home-owning; and their tremendous promotion of them has put Cincinnati in the front rank of home-owning cities, and contributed much to that shock-proof placidity which impresses visiting observers. True, Anglo-Saxons and others have joined in the movement extensively, but the Germans were the first and largest contributors. A visitor to Cincinnati is struck by the relatively few large apartment buildings — fewer than in any other city of its size. That helps to explain why Cincinnati was less affected by the recent depression than cities whose population work mostly for the support of landlords, and where a slump in income may mean a loss of shelter.

Organized by small neighborhood groups of amateur financiers, simple and even primitive in machinery and method, seemingly piddling in transactions and volume, the bauvereins were in mass effect powerful agencies. In those early B. & L.'s in Cincinnati, one might pay only 25 or 50 cents a week towards the acquisition of a modest cottage, though he might soon borrow the few hundred dollars necessary to build one. The man who paid a dollar a week was a plutocrat. On a designated evening in each week, the treasurer would be at his "office" in somebody's store, or far more often, in the back room of a *wein und bier halle*, with his book, to receive payments. If it was not convenient for the stockholder to be there on meeting night, he would leave his money with the saloonkeeper, to be handed to the treasurer. Thus, many saloon-keepers became bauverein treasurers, a logical development. They were usually reliable, and though amateurish in their bookkeeping at first, they learned. It has been remarked that the bauvereins have given thousands of people experience in handling other people's money, and failures among them or embezzlements have been well-nigh as scarce as hens' teeth.

In 1870 there were 26 B. & L.'s in Cincinnati. Before 1900 they had increased to 170. In 1949 there were 260 in Hamilton County and 34 more in the two counties across the river. Every hilltop suburb and township is sprinkled thickly with them. Some of them in the city are now huge affairs, owning their buildings or having large office suites and staffs, really savings bank operations. The criticism is made nowadays that not a few of the smaller ones have a political cast; little folk go in to pay their assessments and receive gratis partisan political advice.

German citizens also began to protest — though for years without apparent effect — against the high taxes and graft of the George B. Cox regime. They organized the first Taxpayers' League in 1880, and Fred Tuke, its president, published a paper, the *Citizen and Taxpayer*, later succeeded by another and more elaborate one, which doubtless played its part in the great reform that finally came about.

The new German home-building began to be noticed in 1868 on the steep climb of Sycamore Street up the hill, where lots were cheap, and the new houses clung to the slope like cliff-swallows' nests, so that it began to be remindful of a hillside town in Bavaria or Baden. They dispersed widely elsewhere, too. More were added to St. Bernard; the building of five inclined planes in the '70's helped to scatter them on the hilltops — Corryville and Price's Hill and elsewhere — and the completion of the Suspension Bridge in 1867 sent many more to Covington, some areas of which became almost as Germanic as the Rhineland. A clutch of them plumped themselves down in what had been called O'Bryonville, in East Walnut Hills, to the annoyance of Irish neighbors. Descendants of both are on the spot yet; Cincinnati is the least nomadic of large cities.

Vine Street, which bisected the heart of Rhineland, was becoming a street of amusements, many of them non-German-operated, many more rowdy and brassy than the average German liked. That helped to crowd out many of the old settlers, though some clung to their homes there, and do yet; and there and elsewhere there were those who stubbornly maintained the ancestral language and more, doing business in German, writing checks in German — "Ein hundert u. Achtzehn Thaler" — some of them knowing little English even well past the turn of the century. A certain prosperous businessman, to preserve the knowledge of the German language in his family, decreed that only German might be spoken at home, and banished one of his children from the table if it uttered a word of English during a meal. The duty to music was quite as strongly emphasized by many. In the family of the Geiers, of the great milling machine works, there were ten children, and every one was required to become proficient on some musical instrument. And they were not unique.

The WCTU temperance crusade of 1874 was particularly irksome to the German citizens. For weeks on end, mass meetings, with adjunctive prayer meetings of businessmen and church groups, went on. Saloonkeepers were warned that if they did not close their doors and go out of business immediately, they would be visited by committees of ladies, to try whether "psalms and prayers will not have the desired effect." Sure enough they came, sometimes kneeling on the sidewalks, sometimes striding past the "No Crusaders Allowed" signs into the saloon, to kneel on the sawdusty floor to pray and sing some gospel hymn. German saloonkeepers could only stare and grumble helplessly; some of other blood blustered or tried to take it with a laugh and made motions of pouring some liquor into the gutter. The Germans were particularly infuriated, because so many of their bars did not, as a rule, vend hard liquors, and did not tolerate drunkeness and disorder. Some places sold nothing but beer and wines, some only beer.

The crusade did not put anybody out of business, but it gave the Germans such a fright that, among other things, a number of them formed an antitreating society, pledging not to treat anyone to a drink or to accept a treat. *Gemütlichkeit* suffered, but it seemed that something must be done.

Beer being one of the city's chief products during the latter quarter of the century, the German brewers were large supporters of art and music and charity, and were prominent in civic affairs — one or two of them unpleasantly prominent as the Cox gang rose to power. As you strolled through the north and west portions of the Basin, you were frequently aware of the pleasant, sweetish-barmy aroma of processing malt and the rich, mellow clunk of hub on axle of the brightly-painted brewery wagons, two-tiered with kegs fresh from the icehouse and glistening with sweat, a team of ponderous, beautifully groomed horses and a similarly powerful aproned driver with massive arms and sometimes a golden-brown beard — arms capable of lifting one of those full kegs by the chines higher than his head.

Some old-timers will tell you that John Hauck brewed the best beer in Cincinnati in the long ago, and he was as particular as any vintner of Rheims or Epernay as to his processes and handling. Along with many other connoisseurs, he shook his head when beer began to be bottled in the '70's; beer should always be kept in wood. He demanded that saloonkeepers who handled his beer should keep it in cellar coolness and handle it gently. His drivers were not permitted to drag a keg off the wagon and let it thump down on a pad on the sidewalk; it must be lifted down carefully and lowered into the cellar with equal care.

Only two of the old German drinking places still survive — Mecklenberg's Garden, up on the hill in Corryville, and Grammer's Cafe, on Walnut Street in the ancient Rhineland. Frank Grammer himself, the last of the old *Schenkwirten*, carries on the Hauck tradition at his place, which is something lifted right out of the past — leaded, colored glass in windows and doors, a quiet dining room where you can get good German food, with beer or wine only. There are no raised voices here, and drunkenness would be a shocking indecorum. At a long table in a rear room. where special group dinners are served, a German literary club met for many years. Mr. Grammer himself, a slender, gentle little wisp of a man, born over his father's beer hall when it was on Vine Street in 1872, loves to tell you about the making of beer and ale — the proper sort of hops and Moravian barley, the *kreusin*, or crossing of beer of two ages to produce the right fermentation. He deplores metal kegs and tells you that if a keg of beer is so much as rolled across an ordinary room, it isn't fit to drink for two days.

"Hertzlich Wilkommen!" was the *Gazette* headline when seven descendants of that Baron von Steuben who had come over and reorganized the Continental army during our Revolution, came to Cincinnati for a visit in October, 1881. They were a Colonel-Count, a Baron-Major, two captains and three lieutenants. Bands, Turners, the Landwehr, military companies, the Mayor and many citizens, German and non-German, met them at the railroad station. In the ensuing parade, each von Steuben rode in a separate open carriage with a group of local dignitaries.

Their visit was productive of important results. Talking with Baron Richard, the Royal Chief Forester of the German Empire, some citizens became interested in the idea of tree-planting in the city's neglected parks, especially Eden Park, once covered by Longworth's vineyard, but never reforested and mostly bare. A committee of Anglo-Saxon, German and Jewish citizens labored through the winter, producing the first American Forestry Congress at Cincinnati in April, 1882, with most of the distinguished foresters of the United States and Canada in attendance. April 27th was named as Arbor Day, Ohio's first. Schools were dismissed, and a parade led the way to Eden Park, where thousands of citizens, old and young, dug holes and planted a Presidents' Grove of 21 trees named for the Presidents, a Pioneers' Grove, Centennial Grove and others. The next step was the organization of the Ohio State Forestry Association.

As an instance of the persistence of the German language, the *Times-Star* on January 19, 1898 described a trial in a Cincinnati court which was unique. A German wife was suing her husband for divorce. Tafel & Schott were her attorneys, Schwab & Schultz appeared for the defendant, and Judge Spiegel was on the bench. The first witness was a German woman who spoke little English. It was then discovered that the court interpreter was at home, ill. Someone remarked that the witnesses were all German.

"Your Honor," suggested one of the attorneys, "suppose we conduct the case in German."

"I am perfectly willing," said Judge Spiegel.

"It's all right with us," said the opposing attorneys.

Turning to the clerk of the court, the Judge said, "How about you, Mr. Clerk?"

"Go ahead," replied the clerk; he was German, too.

Not only he, but the bailiff, the messenger, and even the janitor were German. So the trial proceeded, the counsel arguing and squabbling in German and the Judge taking notes in German.

As late as 1903, when a picture book of Cincinnati was published, it was thought desirable to print German translations of the captions; as, "City Hall — Rathhaus." The Tyler Davidson Fountain was named in English, but the German caption called attention to its German manufacture, "Entworfen und Ausgeführt von Ferd von Müller, München, Deutschland."

The terrible explosion of war in Europe in July, 1914, so wholly unexpected by most of the world, was a tragic milestone in the history of Cincinnati Germans, as in that of all humanity. The eighty or ninety years past had been an era — broken only briefly by the Civil War — of peace and advancement; of rising standards of living, of music and philosophy and debate and physical culture. Many did not grasp the fact that in such a war, the sympathies of a majority of Americans must inevitably be on the side of the British and French democracies. This blind spot was personified in Archbishop Moeller, who had so disapproved of the Longworth-Chambrun wedding, and who, speaking unconsciously only to his German parishioners now said that "we" must inevitably be on the side of the Fatherland. The time came when he practically retracted that statement. The nearly three years of American neutrality, 1914-17, gave American Germans full opportunity for presenting their theory of the European trouble, and unfortunately for themselves, many of them lacked restraint. Add to this the raising of funds for German relief, large subscriptions to German bonds, public demonstrations in behalf of Germany, the sinking of American ships and the loss of American lives on the *Lusitania* and other foreign vessels, all these alienated many who had been friends. Even before our entrance into the war, ugly stories were afloat.

On the forenoon of April 6th, 1917, two prominent citizens, one Anglo-Saxon the other of German blood, both commissioners for the construction of the new Courthouse, were walking from that unfinished structure down Walnut Street. Presently they heard a newsboy crying an extra; he approached, and they saw the headlines, telling of President Wilson's "God helping her, she can do no other" speech and Congress's prompt declaration of war. Tears sprang to the eyes of the German, an excellent citizen, and coursed down his cheeks. "Now the language is dead in Cincinnati," he said. "All German influence is lost."

At the moment, it seemed that he might be right; that the work of nearly a century was undone. Foolish remarks such as that of Dr. Ernest Kunwald, conductor of the Cincinnati Symphony Orchestra — who, after playing the "Star-Spangled Banner" to open a concert, turned to the audience and admitted, "But my heart is on the other side" bolstered the belief that all Germans were disloyal, and presently put Kunwald into Federal prison as an enemy alien. Professor Emil Heerman, concertmeister of the orchestra, was also arrested, but released in custody of the faculty of the Conservatory of Music, and eventually regained good standing by investing most of his income in Liberty Bonds. There were horrific rumors of plots — of German meat-packers mixing ground glass in sausages and frankfurters. Even today, there are old-timers who will tell you that Cincinnati narrowly escaped big trouble of some sort. Undoubtedly there were persons of ill-intent among the Teutonic population; but there is little evidence of overt acts against American neutrality or plots or sabotage in Ohio. Secretary of State Robert Lansing ventured the opinion that nine-tenths of the stories of German plotting in the United States were exaggerated.

On the German language, the effects of the war were far-reaching. It was quickly banished from the schools; German churches began holding services in English, and all Germans took pains to speak English in public to the best of their ability. Not a few German family names were changed or shortened to English form, as for example, Holtzinger to Holt, Schultz to Stratford, Sternberger to Stevenson. The bauvereins hastened to anglicise their names; the Sonne became the Sun, Mond turned to moon, Stern to Star, Adler to Eagle. Erkenbrecher Avenue was renamed Albany, but the old name, honoring the Zoo's founder, was restored to it when sanity returned in later years. The loyal services of many German-Americans in our armed forces, the deaths of many in action, exorcised a part of the curse; but the Second World War dealt another blow to Cincinnati's Germanism, though nothing can eliminate its cultural and spiritual contributions, which will be felt long after we who now write and read are dead. But to this day, if someone in Cincinnati does not catch your last remark, he or she is apt to say, "Please?" — the "Bitte?" which a German would say, politely requesting repetition. And Dr. Martin Fischer who should know, says that a German accent may be heard from some Cincinnatians today whose British roots in American soil go back to our Revolution and beyond.

The Canal having been abolished, it was replaced along the line of old Eleventh Street by a broad, tree-laced street with the appallingly unimaginative and bromidic name of Central Parkway — the sort of thing that the ordinary city council may usually be depended upon to supply. Why the word Rhine was not preserved in its name, or why, as has been suggested, it was not called "The Towpath," are inept questions in view of the fact that the colorful and memorial name of Bloody Run Road, scene of an Indian massacre of 1789, was gradually prettified through Bloody Run Boulevard (that word "Boulevard" must be dragged in by the ears whenever possible) into Victory Parkway. It is to be hoped that some day, intelligence may prevail and the original name be restored.

The home-owning urge and the rowdy, Bowery invasion of upper Vine Street, drove most of the former inhabitants of the old *Stadt* beyond the Rhine away years ago, as we have said. Quieter tenants have moved in since, but some descendants of the old burghers are still there; one may mention a prominent attorney who was born in the house at 9 Mercer Street — a thoroughfare probably thirty feet wide from curb to curb — and in middle life, still lives there. Whenever you pass one of those ancient brick dwellings flush with the sidewalk, a plain, stocky house that looks as if it had been painted yesterday, the stone step scrubbed, the sidewalk swept and potted geraniums and coleus on the windowsill inside, you may be reasonably certain that one of the old families of Over-the-Rhine still inhabits the place and may have been there for three or four generations.

CHAPTER XI

Cold War on the Border

HARRIET MARTINEAU — whose keen eye and longer stay in Cincinnati made her a compendious commentator on the city as it was in 1835 — reports a breakfast scene at the Broadway Hotel which startles us. "I saw at the table," she says, "a better thing than I saw at any other table in the United States; a lady of colour breakfasting in the midst of us!" One wonders whether she could have mistaken some swarthy West Indian Latin for a person of color; Negroes were not welcome at the tables of the better Cincinnati hotels at that time. The race problem had begun causing unpleasant incidents years before.

The Ordinance of 1787, which created the Northwest Territory, forbade slavery or involuntary servitude therein save as a punishment for crime. The early settlers in Ohio being predominantly Northern, there was little proslavery sentiment there for a long time, and several attempts before 1800 to repeal or modify the antislavery clause failed. By the census of 1800, there were only 337 Negroes, all free, of course, in Ohio. But increasing immigration of Southern whites into Ohio finally brought about the passage through that state's Legislature, beginning in 1807, of the series of Acts known as the Black Laws. Henceforth, a Negro of any degree of colored blood was forbidden to settle in the State unless he could prove by documents that he was a free man; this because of complaints of planters across the river that Ohio was becoming a haven for their runaway slaves. There were heavy fines for hindering the recapture of a runaway slave, or promoting the escape of a slave across the State — for Canada was the goal of most of them. Every Negro was required to give bond of $1,500, with two good sureties, as a guaranty of good behavior. Next, a Negro was prohibited from testifying in court against a white man — which made any outrage on a Negro by whites, even to murder, possible with impunity, unless another white man saw the act and would tell the truth about it. The final law forbade admission of Negro children to the public schools and barred Negroes of all ages from asylum, poorhouse or other institutions.

Until abolitionists became active in Ohio, these laws were practically inactive in Cincinnati. But now the picture changed; abolitionism, despite its laudable purpose, appeared to many as a curse and an evil, because its only effect for many years was to darken counsel and to intensify the bitterness of feeling between North and South. It also brought the first violence to Cincinnati. In 1829 many of the local Negroes had signed their names to a petition to the Legislature to repeal the Black Laws. But already the divisive effects of the problem were so alarming that colored churches split upon the question whether it was wise to petition the Legislature.

Very shortly, the city authorities called upon the local Negroes to comply within thirty days with the law requiring them to post a bond for good behavior, which had never been enforced, as it was a practical impossibility for most Negroes to comply with it. The Negroes, seeing no alternative but exodus, asked for a thirty-day stay of action, and sent a committee to Canada to seek a place of refuge. The month passed, the committee had not returned, and another thirty days was asked for and granted. When that, too, had expired with no action, certain self-brevetted reformers of the rugged sort decided to drive the "naygers" from the city. Mobs carried on desultory turmoil for three days, most Negroes barricading their homes and fighting, though some fled. Soon after order was restored, the committee returned from its long stay in Canada with the news that a town named Wilberforce would receive colored settlers. It is said that 1,200 emigrated from Cincinnati, and the Black Laws were not too rigidly enforced on those who remained.

The American Anti-Slavery Society, organized in Philadelphia, entered Ohio in 1835, and within a year, had 120 local branches, with a membership of at least 10,000 and probably more. This startling growth of the great abolitionist organization was disquieting proof that the Northern element in Ohio's population were deeply concerned over the intrusion of slavery. Thereafter it was not safe for a Southerner to bring his slaves into the State.

Arthur Tappan, wealthy New York merchant and abolitionist, had promised a large donation to the new Lane Theological Seminary if it would make Lyman Beecher of Boston its president. As a Bostonian, Dr. Beecher was congenitally opposed to slavery, though he had been much more alarmed over other menaces, such as Roman Catholicism and the Princeton type of Presbyterian. But he found at Lane a firebrand, Theodore Weld, professor of sacred rhetoric and oratory, who demanded quick and total abolition and elevation of the colored population of Cincinnati through "social intercourse according to character, irrespective of color." His activities so alarmed the Lane trustees that they forbade public meetings of any sort on the campus or participation of students in meetings elsewhere without permission. Finally, they ordered the disbanding of the students' Anti-Slavery Society, organized by Weld. Beecher, though deploring Weld's trouble-making, wrote angrily to the board that he would never consent to the abridgement of the students' right to discuss public questions. With the students be pleaded for patience, but in vain. Weld took all of them away from the Seminary save three or four — two of whom were young Beechers — and led them to Oberlin College, then trying to get under way, giving that infant institution just the lift that it needed.

The seminary was almost empty. The South, from which many students might have been expected, was now alienated, and the panic of 1837 ruined Arthur Tappan and crippled the financial support of the institution. President Beecher could not even draw his own salary; his drafts were dishonored in New York, and Calvin Stowe and others thought the whole project might as well be given up as hopeless. But Beecher was unconquerable. Skittering around Ohio in search of students, he ran across a dozen young men, most of whom had intended going to another school, unblushingly talked them into coming to Lane, and so started the Seminary on an upward trend again.

Lane's Gethsemane was a prelude and a prophecy of the long purgatory into which Cincinnati was entering, which split religious denominations in twain and which would end only with war. Up to the latter '30's, in the words of the city's great lawyer, Rufus

King, "there had been a certain tacit tolerance of slavery by the people of the State, so that Southern slaveholders visiting Ohio or traveling through, were accompanied by their servants, without question and by a sort of common concession of right." By deep Southerners, Cincinnati's hilltops were then regarded as a summer resort. Drake and Mansfield remarked in 1826 that "It may be supposed that the period is not remote, when many of the wealthy planters and professional gentlemen of the south, will have their summer villas within the environs of Cincinnati, and those who may feel unwilling to be deprived of the services of their slaves, can still have the advantages of a city life, by locating on the Kentucky shore, in the villages of Newport and Covington, both of which are healthy, and delightfully situated opposite to Cincinnati."

In this last sentence they were overcautious; as King remarks, in those early days slaves could and did accompany their white folks into Ohio without question. But in the latter 1830's, the picture was changing. Slaves brought into Cincinnati might abscond, with a certainty of abolitionist effort to protect them and spirit them off to Canada; they might be enticed away or discharged by writs of habeas corpus procured in their names. The "Underground Railroad," a series of abolitionist homes and hideouts, with a large percentage of Quaker personnel manning it, was in operation nightly by several routes northward across Ohio and Indiana to Canada. It had stations even in Kentucky; fleeing slaves might spend the daylight hours, for example, in the basement of one of the several mansions of Cincinnati capitalist Thomas D. Carneal, one still standing on East Second Street in Covington.

As King saw it, "The abolitionists had become fanatical and lawless in their delirium of conscience, while rioters and mobs took equal pleasure in affording them opportunities for martyrdom." [1] King here represents, even in his latter years, the ante-bellum opinion of most of the leading business and professional men of Cincinnati, including many of Yankee birth or extraction, that the abolitionists were just as great a menace as the slaveholders,

[1] Rufus King, *Ohio; First Fruits of the Ordinance of 1787*. Boston, 1888.

perhaps worse, in that they insisted upon upsetting the status quo. Great numbers of Cincinnatians who disapproved of or abhorred slavery were so conscious of the city's great dependence upon the South for its prosperity that they were furious over abolitionist activity. The attitude even of Lyman Beecher, an antislavery man, was in effect, "A plague o' both your houses." Said he, "I regard the whole abolition movement . . . and action of the South in the justification of slavery as signal instance of infatuation permitted by Heaven for purposes of national retribution."

Nowhere else in our history has there been a city situated quite as was Cincinnati in those years; a city on free soil, yet just across a narrow river from slavery and deriving most of its essential trade from that area; a city where idealism, humanitarianism and the New England conscience were forced into a bitter battle with self-interest; a city where Northern blood predominated in the greater concerns of business and industry, but whose very life seemed to depend upon maintenance of friendship with the slave-holding South by tacit condonation of its chief sin.

In 1836 hostility between the opposing schools of opinion flamed into violence. James G. Birney, a Kentucky-born attorney, who had grown up on a farm operated by slaves, and had turned abolitionist, had issued only four numbers of an antislavery paper, *The Philanthropist*, in Cincinnati when, on January 22, a meeting was held at which were present the highly respected Mayor, Samuel W. Davis, Judge William Burke, clergyman and city post-master, Judge Jacob Burnet, former United States Senator as well as member of the Supreme Court of Ohio, Morgan Neville, Re-ceiver of the Land Office in the District, and Reverend Oliver M. Spencer, wealthy preacher-banker. Resolutions were passed de-ploring abolitionist agitation which were intended to convince the South that the best thought in Cincinnati respected its rights. Abolitionist manifestoes could never muster so eminent a list of signatures.

It was no contribution to harmony when, in April, the Ohio Anti-Slavery Society voted to place its Executive Committee offices in Cincinnati and to assume sponsorship of *The Philan-thropist*, Birney continuing as editor. Some weeks later a handbill appeared, mockingly offering a reward for Birney as a fugitive from justice in Kentucky. He was described as white in external appearance, but black "in all his associations and feelings." There was no real violence until July 12. Then, one midnight, a band of 30 or 40 men with ladders scaled a wall around the home and printing shop of Achilles Pugh, who was producing *The Philanthropist*, tore up the week's supply of paper, destroyed the ink and carried away some essential parts of the press, without ever awakening Pugh. The names of the party were not publicly known, but it was darkly hinted that some prominent citizens were present.

As soon as repairs could be made, publication was resumed, with a blast at "this outrage on the property and peace of a quiet and law-abiding citizen." This brought on a mass meeting at the Fifth Street Market, with the Reverend Postmaster Burke presiding. Declaring that they drew their inspiration from the Boston Tea Party, those present formally warned Birney through a committee — which included many of the most eminent and respected citizens — that he was forbidden to publish *The Philanthropist* in Cincinnati. Several testified at the meeting that abolitionism was injuring business, menacing Cincinnati and would soon destroy the liberties of the country. Judge Burnet professed himself alarmed at the excitement prevailing in the city and vicinity. When asked how Cincinnati was being hurt by the agitation, he said that a few years ago they might expect at least thirty or forty Southern families, each bringing some indispensable slaves, to spend most of the summer in Cincinnati; now they were afraid to come. The abolitionists retorted with a clipping from a recent issue of the *Commercial*, remarking that all hotels and boarding houses were so crowded — with many Southerners among the rest — that other Southerners who wanted to come couldn't find accommodations. The campaign was carried on in the newspapers, with only the *Gazette*, edited by W. D. Gallagher, refusing to attack the abolitionists.

Birney ignored the warning, and nine days after the market meeting, when he was out of town, a mob assembled at midnight broke into Pugh's shop, threw the type into the street, broke up the press and other equipment, invaded Pugh's home for some obscure reason, and tossed the remains of the press into the river. They then went to Blacktown to wreck some houses from which the inmates had fled. During the entire duration of these two episodes, we hear nothing of any police officers appearing on the scene.

Louisville, a strong slavery center, held up her hands in righteous indignation at Cincinnati for "persecuting men of independent opinions for mercenary reasons." Salmon P. Chase, a youthful but deadly serious Yankee-born lawyer, aged 28, who had come to Cincinnati a few years before, declared that he would "sooner give ten thousand dollars than see the free press destroyed." Mr. Chase didn't yet have $10,000, but his meaning was clear. Eastern publicists then and later were severe in their denunciation. James Parton called Cincinnati "the Old Hunkers' paradise." He said there was no city, not even Baltimore, "more saturated with the spirit of Hunkerism — that horrid blending of vanity and avarice which made the Northern people equal sharers in the guilt of slavery while taking the lion's share of the profit." And years later, Professor Albert Bushnell Hart called Cincinnati "a Southern city on free soil; the Southern buyer gladdened the heart of the merchant; the Southern traveler and his family took the best rooms in the hotels; and in times of crisis, Southern sympathy to slavery was visible in the newspapers." In most newspapers, yes; the proslavery *Evening Post* actually threatened violence to Birney and his paper in an editorial.

Birney, after fighting off the charge of harboring an escaped slave in his home, took up his abode in New York, where he continued his work, while *The Philanthropist*, a little restrained in its utterances, resumed publication under another editor. Achilles Pugh went right on printing what and when he pleased until he died, and then his posterity carried on; and the big Pugh printing plant of today is not so very far from where young Achilles pulled the lever of his little hand press more than a century ago.

Around this time young Henry Ward Beecher, then a student at Lane, was briefly acting editor of the *Cincinnati Journal*, and wrote scathing editorials against slavery as well as putting a pistol in his pocket and going out with other volunteers to protect

Negroes. His sister Harriet also wrote for his paper, "satirizing the anti-abolition mode of thought." The Beechers were thankful now for the long, muddy roads leading from the city up to Lane; they discouraged city hoodlums from attacking the Seminary where it was more than once rumored that runaway slaves were hidden. Dr. Beecher told Henry Howe years later of advising his students to "arm themselves, and if the mob came, they could shoot." Then grinning, "But I told them not to kill 'em; aim low — hit 'em in the legs! Hit 'em in the legs!"

There was reason for concern, for partisanship was apt to be rough. Wendell Phillips, the Massachusetts abolitionist, was driven from the stage of Pike's Opera House and escaped by a rear entrance, while a mob waited in the street, hoping to hang him; yet the same city, complained a Whig editor, permitted William L. Yancey, the Alabama firebrand, "to utter the most bitter, disloyal tirade, with threats against the North, without a whisper of dissent from an audience of 3,000."

In the spring of 1841 a familiar figure, a relic of more peaceful days, passed from the Cincinnati scene when Solomon Scott, known to everyone as Old Solomon, died, reputedly aged 120. For many years the old Negro had tottered about the streets with palsied hand outstretched, quavering, "One cent, Massa; only one cent!" He left behind him a venue which was steadily growing more difficult for his people. The signs had been ominous since January, when a destructive riot was precipitated in Dayton — which had a large Southern population — by the coming to town of a prominent abolitionist who was scheduled to speak in the evening, but who, because of the disturbance, departed without doing so. In June, a Kentuckian named McCalla came to Cincinnati in search of a runaway slave, and traced him to a cake shop kept by an Englishman. McCalla and an officer went to the house — this was nine years before the passage of the Fugitive Slave Law, which authorized such official action — where they were resisted by the shopkeeper and his family, but seized the Negro. Meanwhile, a crowd gathered and broke the shop windows. The Englishman and all his family were fined and given jail sentences.

On the 31st of August there was a quarrel on the border between "Blacktown" and "Dublin," in which several were hurt with clubs and stones. There were other skirmishes in the next four days, and finally, on the evening of the 3rd a mob — alleged by Whig editors to have been organized by Kentuckians and recruited on the wharves and steamboats — assembled openly in the Fifth Street Market and began attacking Negro stores on the outskirts of Blacktown. From using clubs and stones, both sides proceeded to use firearms; many were wounded, and there were rumors of some deaths. Before dawn some militiamen appeared and the mob retired.

That forenoon a large group of prominent citizens assembled at the Court House, and solemnly resolved to "uphold the law." They assured "our Southern brethren" that the laws would be carried out, and "every Negro who escapes from his master and comes within our borders" would be returned. They requested the Mayor, Sheriff and police to go at once to the dwellings of blacks and disarm them of all weapons, but to protect colored persons until they gave the bond required by law or left town. Finally, they "Resolved, that we view with abhorrence the proceedings of the Abolitionists in our city, and that we repudiate their doctrines and believe it to be the duty of every good citizen by all lawful means to discountenance every man who lends them his assistance."

On that same day a large group of Negroes met in a church and issued an abject, even pathetic address to the Mayor and citizens, deploring the fighting and arms-carrying, promising to do all in their power to keep the peace, promising compliance with the law of 1807. They even tendered thanks to the Mayor, police and military for their efforts to protect them. Sympathetic citizens gave bond for some of the Negroes, and some left the city, but the authorities decided, by what process of reasoning we know not, to put others in jail for "protection." Some 250 or 300 men were rounded up and marched to jail with difficulty, a yelling mob pressing around the regular police and eighty volunteers in the escort, sometimes throwing stones. In prison the Negroes remained, separated from their families, over the week end and then were released. That Saturday night a troop of cavalry and some companies of infantry were supposed to be on duty, yet a mob junked the abolitionist printing plant again, broke into Negro homes and stores in various parts of the city and wrecked a Negro church.

Because of the troublesome matter of slavery in the District of Columbia, there was talk again in January, 1849, of abolishing the District, giving its acres back to Maryland and Virginia, and removing the Capital to Cincinnati or somewhere else in the Middle West. This had been first suggested in 1838 by Senator Thomas Morris of Ohio. Among several eastern newspaper backers, the *New York Herald* strongly favored the idea and rather expected to see it carried out within ten years. That Cincinnati was a border city with its society and politics poisoned by the slavery problem, that state and national laws regarding slavery were being violated there daily, that it was therefore quite as unsuited to being the nation's capital as was Washington did not seem to occur to the proponents.

Year by year the Underground Railroad was offering better facilities and increasing its traffic. With the coming to town of Levi Coffin and his wife, North Carolina Quakers and implacable enemies of slavery, it took on still greater efficiency. The Coffins had for several years lived in that solidly Quaker village, Richmond, Indiana, an important stop on the Underground. In 1847 they removed to Cincinnati, where Mr. Coffin ran a store at Sixth and Elm Streets, which sold no goods not made by free labor. Mr. Coffin was variously and humorously known as the president or the dispatcher of the Underground; the basement and two upper floors of his store might be called waiting rooms. When the old building was razed in 1936, in its west foundation wall and in the foundations of buildings for three blocks westward, it is said that there were indications of a walled passage five feet high and four feet wide, extending to John Street, and connecting with another that ran north and south under that street. The Coffins for a time lived near the Beecher home on Walnut Hills, and Mrs. Stowe pictured them and their Richmond home in *Uncle Tom's Cabin*.

The passage of the Fugitive Slave Law in 1850, which facilitated the recapture of runaways in the North, touched off a long series of kidnappings of colored men and women in Cincinnati and elsewhere, often without any court action whatsoever, and in many cases of legally freed persons by miscreants who purposed selling the victims after they had gotten them into slave territory. One of the first, a Negro named George Jackson, was seized in daylight on a Cincinnati business street by two men, one of whom brandished a pistol, the other a knife. Jackson cried to the bystanders for help, but received none, and the men hustled him towards the river, with a crowd following, though not interfering, and the police, as usual, invisible. A block or more from the river, some in the crowd began to throw stones, but the men reached the wharf with their prisoner just as the Covington ferryboat was beginning to move. "Hold up, or you're no true Kentuckian!" the men shouted to the boat's master, and he waited for them. Beyond some more futile stone-throwing, the crowd did nothing, and Jackson was taken away. Whether he was a legal freedman we do not know, but he was known to have been in Cincinnati for several years, being for some time bartender at the National Theatre. So far as Cincinnati knew, he now disappeared into oblivion.

There were cases in which Negroes were seized, tried before United States courts and returned to their owners in legal fashion. But the arrests sometimes failed in their purpose. George Brown, a Negro barber of long residence, was arrested, charged with being a fugitive slave, but proved his right to freedom, and promptly sued the United States Marshal for $10,000 for false imprisonment. Even documentary proof of freedom, however, did not always avail. A freedman coming from Illinois on the steamer *Jacob Strader*, was imprisoned by the boat's officers just before reaching Cincinnati, and though he had a certificate of his freedom from a court in Illinois, he was turned over to the law in Covington on suspicion of being a runaway slave. And there was a bondman who stowed away on a steamboat at New Orleans, reached Cincinnati before he was discovered — and promptly returned to Louisiana.

One of the most pitiful cases was that of a Negro who was

seized near the wharves, manacled and thrown into a yawl to be taken to Covington, but leaped out before they were half way over and was drowned. Another man named Benjamin Chelsom, of Estill County, Kentucky, who was set free by his master in his will, made his way to Cincinnati, where he lived as a laborer. Meanwhile, some of his former master's heirs brought suit to break the will and were successful. Thereupon, they began plotting to recapture Benjamin. He was finally caught by kidnappers at a spot near the wharves and after a fight in which he was felled several times, he was overpowered and carried away to Kentucky.

There were curious instances of another sort, too. In the summer of '53 two Southern gentlemen, Major Choutard and Judge Picney, registered at the Burnet House, with four slaves in attendance. Two of the Negroes promptly absconded, and the owners made no effort to apprehend them. Next morning, just as the gentlemen were about to continue their journey, writs were served upon them, requiring them to appear before Judge Stallo on a charge of detaining two Negro men — the two who had not run away — as slaves. But when brought into court, the two Negroes professed themselves satisfied to remain in bondage, and the case was dismissed. A few days later a Mr. Orville Thomas of Louisiana arrived in the city with two slaves, whom he offered to set free on the spot by legal manumission, but they too preferred to stay with their master rather than risk the economic hazards of freedom, and so returned with him to Louisiana; which seems to prove that there *were* St. Clairs in the Deep South.

In 1852 the book counters of the city were stacked with copies of a first novel by the recent well-known bluestocking sojourner in the city, Mrs. Harriet Beecher Stowe, now back in New England. As might be expected, *Uncle Tom's Cabin* stirred hot controversy in Cincinnati, but the city did more than its share in bringing about the enormous sale of the book. And when, in the following year, the play concocted from it came around, it "gave great satisfaction to the audience," said a critic, whence we infer that antiabolitionists didn't attend. That was an eventful year. Lucy Stone addressed a meeting of Negroes and told them that they ought to seek admission for their children into the public schools. Shortly afterward, her husband, Henry Blackwell, Cincinnati merchant, was instrumental in having a slave girl taken from her master in upstate Ohio, whereupon Memphis, home of the owner, threatened to boycott Cincinnati, while Louisville and St. Louis berated the Queen City for harboring predatory abolitionists.

An odd circumstance is that during quiet periods through all these years, certain slaves of Colonel Taylor of Newport, owner of the Newport ferry, crossed to Cincinnati daily to shop for foodstuffs at the Lower Market, near the river, without molestation or objection by anyone.

Never had parties been so riven by dissension among leaders, never the rank and file so befuddled. The Whig party, cloven to the chine by slavery, was on its deathbed. The American (Know-Nothing) Party was also slowly fading. The Free Soilers began coagulating with some antislavery Whigs and Democrats to form the Republican Party, and the *Gazette* and *Commercial*, orphaned by the demise of the Whigs and for some time flirting vaguely with the Know-Nothings, espoused its cause in 1856. The Democrats were rent by divergent views on the dominant question. At a Tenth Ward (Over-the-Rhine) Democratic meeting in the Fall of '54, where George S. Pendleton, W. S. Groesbeck and Judge Stallo spoke, the Judge denounced Democratic President Pierce as "kneeling to the Free Soilers of the North and the disunionists of the South"; his administration had been "miserable, sneaking, skulking, cowardly"; neither he nor Stephen A. Douglas deserved respect. Strong words these, from a Democrat about two Democratic leaders. The fact is that any politician who ventured into high office in those years had to do so much truckling to the two infuriate factions that he himself got more kicks than ha'pence. The Democratic National Convention met in Cincinnati in June, '56, with the Soft-Shells — opposing the extension of slavery — and the Hard-Shells or Southern faction with many adherents in the North, ready to slug each other at the drop of an innuendo, though they finally managed to nominate a Presidential candidate, doddering old Jeemes Buchanan, who did his best to be on everybody's side.

There were many indications of abolitionist sentiment in Cincinnati in the '50's. The Ladies' Anti-Slavery Sewing Circle, for example, staged bazaars and other money-raising functions now and then for the relief of the colored people of the city; though some of them didn't seem to need relief, according to J. Richard Beste, an English traveler, who on a Sunday was astonished by the sight of "the free negresses, with their white muslin dresses, white satin shoes and green silk parasols, to preserve their complexions." We wonder, too, as we turn the pages of the years, whether the abolitionists were not acquiring a certain influence. The steady operation of the Underground Railroad, year after year, forwarding hundreds, and finally thousands of refugees through the city, with very rarely a slip-up, seems to point to something more than mere police ineptitude. With any real vigilance, the Underground's operations could have been badly upset. The Law thereabouts had somewhat the aspect of a man trying to carry water on both shoulders. True, it had to make an arrest now and then, but when it did, the punishment was often ludicrously like a slap on the wrist. In '57 a party of United States marshals captured two Negroes in an upper floor of a downtown business building — the property of Attorney Alphonso Taft — after a scuffle in which a deputy and a Negro were slightly injured. This was said to be an Underground station, but whether Mr. Taft knew what was going on there was not discussed by the newspapers. One William M. Connelly and his wife were arrested in the affair, bailed, and nearly a year later, after a long-drawn-out trial, Connelly was sentenced to twenty days in jail and a fine of ten dollars! Mrs. Connelly likewise received a light sentence, and upon her emergence lectured upon the Underground Railroad.

This occurred some time after, and probably was influenced by a tragedy which gave Cincinnati a shock from which it did not recover. In January, 1856 a party of Negroes from farms southwest of Covington escaped to the river and crossed it on the ice. Among them were an elderly couple, their son and his wife and four young children, the property of one Henry Gaines. This group was given shelter by a freedman's family living near the mouth of Mill Creek. Lacking the protection of the Underground, their presence became known to officers, who went to the cabin, and when they were not immediately admitted, broke open the door. The young father shot off two of a deputy's fingers with a pistol, but was overpowered. The youngest child, a mere baby, was found dying with its throat cut, and two other children were injured about the head. It came out that the parents had tried to kill all their children when the officers began smashing in the door. They freely admitted this, and Margaret, the mother, said that she next intended killing herself. They added that they would "go singing to the gallows," rather than return to bondage under Gaines, by whom they said they had been brutally treated.

This dreadful instance of desperation was like a blow in the face to Cincinnati, and little else was talked about in the city during the hearings that followed. Attorney John Jolliffe, who donated his services in a number of such cases, took up the defense of the family. He had already suffered for his championship of fugitive slaves. Just after the trial of a previous case, three years ago, he was on his way to market with basket on arm and his wife and niece with him when the notorious City Judge Flinn, standing with some pals at a street corner, knocked him down and beat him until police rescued him. The assailant escaped with a fine of $30 and costs.

Jolliffe's objective was to have the family tried for murder, with the idea of keeping them on Ohio soil and getting them off with a light sentence or perhaps a pardon by Governor Salmon P. Chase, who had just taken office, and who could be depended on to be sympathetic. The hearing on Gaines's ownership was held first, and soon disposed of. The informalities of justice in those days and in such cases are confounding both to present-day legal and lay minds. After this hearing, decision was reserved until the trial of Margaret for murder could be held. That occupied five days. During one session, one of the attorneys made a jeering reference to Lucy Stone, and that lady — who was in the city between speaking tours, visiting her husband, Mr. Blackwell — strode into the next session, whereupon everybody, the judge included, remained after adjournment to hear her make an antislavery speech.

The trial for murder — without a jury — was ended, but there was no verdict. The judge took nearly a month to think it over. In the end, the murder indictment was sidestepped, and all the Negroes, Margaret included, were returned to Mr. Gaines. There was quite a celebration among proslavery partisans when the verdict was announced, and an interesting demonstration of the marvelous dexterity of the human mind in discovering flatly contradictory meanings in any given event. As the cheering procession wended down Broadway, the *Gazette* gloomily saw it as "the funeral of the sovereignty of the State of Ohio"; and some of the Kentuckians, as they went aboard the ferry with Gaines, exulted, "We've got this damned abolition State under foot now, and by God, we're going to keep it there!" But during the celebration by United States Marshal H. H. Robinson and others at the Magnolia House, a crowd in the street called for Robinson, and in a balcony speech, he said, "We in Ohio may well be proud this day that our sovereignty as a State has been maintained by vindicating the sovereignty of the State of Kentucky."

Jolliffe now asked Governor Chase to reopen the case, and the latter issued a requisition to Kentucky, asking for the return of Margaret, so that she might be tried for murder. Governor Morehead promptly granted the favor, hoping to establish a precedent which would influence Ohio to act similarly in Negro cases. Owner Gaines announced that he had placed Margaret in the Covington jail to await the warrant, but when two Ohio officers went there, they were told that she had been taken away the night before on an order from Gaines. Where she went, the jailer didn't know. A few days later it was reported in Cincinnati that Margaret had been taken to Louisville, en route to New Orleans to be sold. The Cincinnati sheriff wired the Sheriff at Louisville, asking him to hold the woman there until she could be sent for, but there was no reply; and so Margaret disappears from history.

This affair gave Cincinnati's complacency a violent jolt. It lay uncomfortably on the city's conscience. The ugly implications of the national problem had been made stern realities in its midst. For the first time, in the secret souls of some folk who had been trying to push away the inevitabilities leering in their faces, the seed of a conviction was planted that in this matter there would or could be no compromise. Something must break. A majority still refused to face it; but it is noticeable that the operations of the Underground Railroad became a matter of casual comment. "Three fugitives from slavery," said a news item of October, '56, "passed through this city on Thursday on their way to Canada by the aid of the Underground Railroad."

But Attorney Jolliffe was not yet done with the affair. The trial was a year in the past when one day he and Mrs. Jolliffe were invited to dine with a Covington friend. She went over in the morning, and he followed shortly after noon. Proceeding uptown from the ferry, as the Devil would have it, he came face to face with Henry Gaines. The irascible Kentuckian's temper flamed instantly. "You damned rascal, you damned nigger thief!" he snarled. "Come over here to steal our niggers, eh?" A crowd began to gather as Gaines thrust his fist into Jolliffe's face, trying to provoke him to violence. The crowd grew threatening, and Jolliffe went into a store for protection. Outside, Gaines harangued the gathering mob, telling them that Jolliffe had come over there to steal more Negroes.

Jolliffe went to the door and told them that if they were determined not to let him go to his friend's house, he would return to Cincinnati. The crowd cursed, derided and threatened him; but the city marshal and another officer, attracted to the scene by the tumult, placed themselves on each side of him and escorted him towards the ferry. Gaines, following them, ran into house after house along the way, trying to borrow a whip. At length he found one and began to belabor Jolliffe with it; whereupon the marshal arrested him, and next day he paid a small fine.

That year '57 was remarkable for the number of men from the far South, mostly from Mississippi and Louisiana, who brought Negroes — usually mulattoes or lighter — to Cincinnati and freed them by legal manumission. Freedmen in those later years showed a tendency to settle farther away from the river than Cincinnati, from which it was too easy to snatch one across to Kentucky. Xenia, a county seat with a population of 5,000 in 1860, was one-fifth Negro, and white people complained of being shouldered off the sidewalks by them. Young Whitelaw Reid, who had just bought and was editing the *Xenia News* found that he must be very guarded in his comment, and was relieved when he could sell out and go to work for the *Cincinnati Gazette*.

The political chaos prevailing in the by-election year of 1858 is significant. There were two factions in Democratic ranks known as Dead Rabbits and Live Rabbits, and in party caucuses the two came to blows in several places. But there was a bipartisan, antiDemocratic, antislavery fusion known merely as "the Opposition," which swept the election, nearly all its candidates carrying city and county by large majorities. Slavery and disunion were losing ground in Cincinnati. And "Almost everybody," said the *Gazette*, "seems pleased with the election of Mr. R. B. Hayes to the City Solicitorship." Mr. Hayes was soon to be called to another field of action more vigorous than law.

CHAPTER XII

The Storm

CINCINNATI heard the Southern threats of secession with a peculiar concern. The thought of a division of the Union horrified it no more than did the threat of the loss of all Southern trade. It had perhaps a larger stake in the South than any other Northern city; the very life of many of its enterprises seemed to depend on their Southern connections. If a break must come, commercial Cincinnati was selfish enough at that time to hope that it might be accomplished peacefully and with no disturbance of business or good will. Murat Halstead, editor of the *Commercial*, even favored the assembling of a national convention to devise an orderly end to the seventy-one-year-old partnership.

A little-known lawyer named Abraham Lincoln who was employed in a patent case in Cincinnati in 1855 and who was roughly snubbed by his superior counsel, Edwin M. Stanton, went unnoticed locally. But when, as President-elect, he arrived on February 12th, 1861, his own birthday, on his way to Washington, never to return, the city was swathed in bunting and flags, crowds packed the streets, windows and house-tops, and cannon boomed as the open carriage, drawn by six white horses, moved slowly from the station to the Burnet House, the tall, grave-looking guest doffing his high hat and managing faint smiles for the cheering multitudes. At the Burnet House, hundreds jostled in to shake the new President's hand, children from the Orphan Asylum shrilled "Hail, Columbia!" and a little girl handed him a bouquet.

One evening, just three months later, electrifying news flashed about the streets. An orchestra concert was in progress with a packed house when a whisper ran through the audience. Singly and in groups, people began to tiptoe out, and before the program was over, the hall was almost empty. On the streets, newsboys were crying extras, with the first dispatches about the firing on Fort Sumter. Overnight, the city stiffened from a half-uncertain, half-indifferent state of mind to one of strong partisanship, with

Union sentiment predominating. Democrats who had declaimed and voted against Lincoln were now confronted with a new situation; no longer a question of parties, but one of loyalty or disloyalty. Many of them still with partisan reservations, took their stand on the side of the Government. Others, especially if of Southern birth or ancestry, were more or less vehemently in opposition. Fist fights or worse on the streets were of frequent occurrence. Superficially, the city would appear to be solidly for the Union; the flag flew everywhere and thousands voiced their willingness to bear arms against the rebellion. Yet Cincinnati supplied not a few soldiers to the Confederate army. Here, as in Kentucky, close friends and even families were divided, one member taking a stand with the North, one with the South. Recruiting for the Confederate army was at first carried on with little or no attempt at secrecy. One man engaged in this work was arrested, but not until a year later — which illustrates the curious slowness with which the serious meaning of war penetrated the public mind, and how delicately some portentous situations and essentially treasonable acts were handled. Just one week before the attack on Sumter, three cannon shipped from Baltimore and addressed to the "Southern Confederacy" at Jackson, Mississippi, were permitted to pass through Cincinnati with no hindrance. On the day before that (although seven States had already seceded), a slave was remanded into the custody of his master by a United States Commissioner in Cincinnati.

Ohio, like Indiana and Illinois, with a large Southern-born population in its Southern half, was destined to suffer much travail. On Jackson's Day in January, '61, at a State Democratic celebration, a resolution was adopted, pledging the aid of "the 200,000 Democrats of Ohio" in blocking any attempt to coerce the South unless its demands were satisfied. When Jacob D. Cox, a legislator, later a Federal general, expressed surprise at this to David Tod, a Democratic member of the Legislature, Tod retorted, passionately, "You Republicans will find 200,000 Ohio Democrats in front of you if you try to cross the Ohio River." But when the test came, when Ohio filled its quota of volunteers within sixteen days after President Lincoln's call, the fire-eating Tod and thousands of other Democrats reversed their stand, proclaimed their loyalty, many even volunteering as soldiers. Tod was elected Governor during the war and served faithfully.

Most Cincinnatians were determinedly optimistic, insisting that the war would be just a brief, skirmishing affair; it was unthinkable that Americans would seriously fight Americans. But there were horrid fears on the part of many; Cincinnati, squarely on the border, with a slave State across the river, which, they gloomed, would undoubtedly secede, would be a battleground, if there was any real war. There was immediate talk of fortifying the hilltops.

The city rallied heartily to the President's call for troops. Patriotic citizens solicited recruits personally and by advertising, and contributed money towards the equipping of units. Some soldiers bought their own arms and uniforms, while some companies were equipped by their commanding officers or by public subscription. At a patriotic rally, Judge Storer made a stirring appeal for young recruits, concluding with, "I'm an old man of sixty years" (he was really sixty-five), and then, with flashing eyes and outspread arms, "and I now volunteer!" This touched off the organization of the Storer Rifles, who soon appeared on the street, the Judge himself among them, marching awkwardly to drum and fife but wearing handsome uniforms and equipment, all at their own expense; mostly wealthy men, gray-haired, white-haired, some much overweight. They were accepted as home guards, and had opportunity to see service of a sort before the war was over.

The various military companies — Guthrie Grays, Rover Guards, Highland Guards, Continentals, Zouaves and others, which had hitherto been just good fun, now turned from jest to earnest and were enlisted into service. The Tenth Ohio, an Irish regiment — they were but little less zealous for service than the Germans — was commanded by William Haines Lytle, youthful veteran of the Mexican war, a lawyer more interested in poetry and the military than law. He was a major-general in the State militia, but modestly accepted a colonelcy to begin the war. The Turners, as already mentioned, became the famous Ninth Ohio, or Turner regiment. In their drilling — of which they stood in no great need — they wore the Turner costume, white roundabout jackets and trousers. Colonel McCook, their commander, was a curious figure on horseback, with sword girt at his side, but in civilian garb and a plug hat.

Among the remarkable instances of volunteering was that of the Literary Club. Fifty-one of its members — a majority, really, and most of them young lawyers — offered themselves, and turned their clubrooms into drill halls. Robert W. Burnet, a graduate of West Point, having volunteered to drill them, they called themselves the Burnet Rifles. But Burnet found himself, after years of civilian life, rusty in the manual, so a rough-and-tough sergeant from Newport Barracks was called in to give the instruction. Aware of the quality of his pupils, he held them in high respect; but at times, carried away by artistic emotion, he would yell something like, "Damn you there on the left, hold up yer heads!" and then, remembering his company, would bow and say, "I ask your pardon, gentlemen." Courtesy would thenceforth prevail until another slip provoked another vitriolic rebuke, to be followed by another apology.

From those Literary Club recruits emerged, before the war was over, one Major-General — none other than Rutherford B. Hayes — five Brigadier-Generals, eight Colonels, four Lieutenant-Colonels, eleven Majors, fourteen Captains, five First Lieutenants, two Second Lieutenants, and one unfortunate fellow whose name is mercifully withheld, and who never rose above the rank of private. The meetings of the Club were suspended from April, 1861 to April, 1864. By that time a few members had come home wounded or invalided; and regular meetings were resumed.

Captain George B. McClellan, a retired army engineer who had for several years been president of the Ohio & Mississippi Railroad — connecting Cincinnati and St. Louis — was called upon by the Governor ten days after Sumter to take command of all Ohio troops, with the rank of Major-General. Another engineer officer, Captain William S. Rosecrans, who had retired from the Army some years ago to set up as an architect and engineer in Cincinnati, also investing in coal mines and a kerosene oil refinery, now re-enlisted and built Camp Dennison, on the Little Miami River, for the Ohio troops.

Lacking Government uniforms, McClellan's men wore the so-called, mostly homemade Garibaldi garb — red flannel shirts, blue trousers and slouch hats — giving the enemy no trouble as to visibility — when they were thrown over into western Virginia after four or five weeks of training, to protect the loyal mountain folk and make it possible to set up a new State government. In the difficult mountain fighting of that summer, the Cincinnati men bore themselves well, and there Lytle received the first of his several wounds. By autumn, McClellan had gone higher, and Rosecrans, now a brigadier-general, was in command in Virginia. He later commanded the Army of the Cumberland.

The Cincinnati Chamber of Commerce, painfully aware of the divided sentiment in the city, voted to demand of its members an oath of allegiance to the National Government. Some bitterness was aroused by this, and it was easy to identify those who were lukewarm or quite lacking in their allegiance. Many members took the oath readily, but some demurred on one excuse or another, and those who resisted beyond a certain date were expelled.

Trading with the enemy was also frowned upon. As the chief supplier of the South, Cincinnati was faced with the loss of an enormous volume of business and of great sums of money owed to its manufacturers and wholesalers for goods already delivered. To some of these men this was or appeared to be a vital matter. The Chamber of Commerce, two months after Sumter, laid a charge against one of its members, J. A. Skiff, of "Furnishing the enemies of our Government with provisions, contrary to law." He had been arrested, charged with smuggling butter southward in barrels, masquerading as "ale" — though why the South must buy butter from Cincinnati, and why butter was contraband when ale was not, are dark mysteries. Skiff pleaded, as many another wholesaler might have done, that so many of his customers lived in the South that he couldn't afford to lose the business. A clipping from the *Vicksburg Whig,* quoting a letter from Skiff to a Vicksburg customer somehow made its way back to Cincinnati. In it he said that he was kept in jail eight days before he was permitted bail, and that his office papers and letters were seized. "I thought it best to let you know what a mob spirit rules here. . . . In this city our business is ruined, rents have fallen one-half and many of the stores closed"; which, if true, gives us another sidelight on the city in the spring of '61.

In the following winter, the Chamber of Commerce found that some members "have left our City and gone south and are engaged in business in the rebel army, giving aid and comfort to our enemies." They too were expelled.

There were others who found it easier than did Mr. Skiff to ship products to the enemy — or perhaps they knew better how to rig the machinery. There were foundries and factories in Cincinnati which even for some time after the beginning of the war, manu- factured arms and supplies for the enemy. Cincinnati-made bombs are said to have destroyed Federal gunboats on the Mississippi, and muskets were made here for the Knights of the Golden Circle and other "Copperhead" groups who planned armed uprisings in Indiana. It was seemingly easy to smuggle these things out of the city. Those intended for the South went by river — until Federal armed craft succeeded in shutting off that traffic — or by rail through Kentucky under Southern sponsorship. Both these avenues were pretty effectively closed within a year or two.

There was a far greater production of necessities for the Union. The Chamber of Commerce made strong representations to Washington, which were eventually successful in getting many orders for Cincinnati. Samuel Ashcroft made thousands of tons of shells for the Army and Navy. James Hollenshade made Army wagons and pontoon bridges. On one contract for 80 boats and 160 wagons, to be delivered in 20 days, he standardized parts and devised assembly-line methods which resulted in the production of the order in 12 days. The local shipyards built many new boats and turned others into gunboats, cutting down their upper struc- tures and sheathing them with iron.

As for Miles Greenwood's Eagle Iron Works, it kept 400 to 700 men busy. The United States Arsenal at Springfield could make only 200 muskets a day, but the Eagle Works, when handed 60,000 old flint-lock muskets, rifled them and changed them to percussion-lock guns at the rate of 800 a day. Greenwood also turned out some 200 cannon, many gun-carriages, caissons, tools and implements. More than one attempt was made to burn his plant, but though considerable damage was done, its work was scarcely halted. Mr. Greenwood — now president of the Covington & Cincinnati Bridge Company, which was beginning to build Roebling's suspension span across the river — also found time in '62 to give a dinner for his employees and their families, about 1,000 persons in all, at the Walnut Street House on his 55th birthday and his 30th anniversary in business. After the dinner, there was a dance — all quite in the manner of Scrooge's old employer, Mr. Fezziwig.

The freedom of the press was never more thoroughly put to the test than in those years. Some Democratic editors, in an unbridled indulgence of partisanship, outdid all previous vilifications of the Chief Executive. Certain small-town newspapers, even in the northern half of the State, denounced "the Thief Lincoln," "this damned Abolition war," "hired Hessians going to the sunny Southern soil to butcher by wholesale, not foreigners, but good men, exemplary Christians," and an Administration which "has put arms in the hands of outlaws, thieves, murderers and traitors." But there were fewer arrests of editors than one would expect. Cincinnati journalism was more circumspect. The Democratic *Enquirer* called President Lincoln a "King," but indulged in no such billingsgate as that we have quoted; in fact, it was far outdone by the Republican *Commercial*. Editor Halstead of that sheet was a badly-balanced, pugnacious firebrand, who enjoyed beating up critics who came to his office to complain of some extravagant statement. He won a reputation as a great editor, but as Charles B. Murray, already quoted, said, "He was a forceful journalist, governed more by an impulse to rip things open and to have credit for such work than by scrupulous and considerate treatment of questions and measures. . . ." Halstead, furious at the Administration after Bull Run, raved, "There could not be a more inefficient man President of the United States than Abraham Lincoln. . . . The poor, silly President sucks flattery as a pig sucks milk." (Later, his opinion underwent a change.)

Some of the most vicious of all editorial writing was done by Clement Vallandigham, of the *Dayton Empire*, the "King of the

Copperheads" in the Middle West. As a result of a half century of immigration from the South, the southwestern corner of Ohio, with Cincinnati as its metropolis, became the leading secessionist center north of the Ohio River. Southern agents, some of them well known, swarmed in the city, being especially numerous at two hotels. One of these, the Spencer House, an excellent hostelry on the Public Landing, had an inside, windowless, sound-proof but ventilated room designed for gambling (some of the leading river gamblers made their headquarters there between trips), but which proved useful for secret meetings, too. Vallandigham was once arrested at the Spencer. The Clifton House, on a hilltop — oddly enough operated by a dignified old New Hampshire Yankee, John W. Dunklee — was another favorite resort for Vallandigham and other Southern sympathizers.

There were mixed sentiments on both sides of the river. The home of a disloyalist in Newport who expressed the hope of seeing Jefferson Davis President of the whole United States, was bespatted with rotten eggs one night. On the Cincinnati side, the Reverend Sabin Hough, a Copperhead who made no bones of it, was arrested in the fall of '61 for publishing a secessionist sheet, but escaped on a technicality. In the following spring he was caught selling treasonable books at Wheeling and jailed, but released on condition that he would go south and stay there.

The softening effect of three-quarters of a century of freedom of speech and of the press is seen in this case as in that of Vallandigham and many others who, in Europe, would probably have been executed. By contrast, however, in some communities there were long imprisonments and brutalities meted out by zealots, often to mild offenders or perfectly innocent persons. There was a tendency to regard every Democrat with suspicion. To the Cincinnati Republican editors, the entire staff of the *Enquirer* and of all other Democratic newspapers were Copperheads. Even after the close of the war, when a Turner picnic was invaded by roughs, the *Gazette* spoke of them as Copperheads. Any turmoil in the North, such as the Sioux Indian uprising and massacres in Minnesota in 1862, was believed to have been instigated by Southern agents.

When Vallandigham became too much of a nuisance in '63, a detachment of troops went by special train from Cincinnati to Dayton by night to arrest him — the size of the posse indicating the official fear of mass intervention in that secessionist town. They succeeded in getting him away to Cincinnati, but next day an infuriated mob wrecked and burned in reprisal the loyalist *Dayton Journal* building.

So loath was the Administration to present the appearance of persecuting mere political partisans that the only punishment dealt to Vallandigham was banishment to the Southern States. Meanwhile, he had been nominated by the Democrats for the Ohio Governorship. He presently went to Canada, and in the following year was back in the North as a delegate to the Democratic convention which nominated General McClellan for the Presidency.

It was in the autumn of '62 that Cincinnati had its first taste of war's alarums. General Bragg's Confederate army invaded Kentucky in September, mildly threatening Louisville and Cincinnati. General Kirby Smith made some gestures towards Cincinnati, though he never approached in force as near to that city as it has always believed. But City and State were enormously excited. Governor Tod urged all loyal men to arm themselves, form companies and proceed to Cincinnati, to place themselves under the orders of General Lew Wallace, then in command there. And soon they began to pour in, a heterogeneous lot, including many from the back country, in homemade jeans clothing, some in coonskin caps and carrying long squirrel rifles. Martial law was proclaimed. Many business houses closed; hordes of people crowded the sidewalks to watch the recruits drilling in the streets. A thousand Negroes were under arms, with Judge Timothy C. Day as their colonel. The shipyards were busy, clapping more or less flimsy sheathings of iron on steamboats and supplying them with light guns. General Basil Duke saw two small steamboats that were bulwarked only with baled hay, and carrying two small howitzers each.

A pontoon bridge of coal barges had been thrown across the river at the first alarm — for there were as yet no other bridges —

and across it marched the enlisted men headed for the twenty-mile-distant "front," and the home guards, including the elderly Storer Rifles, to take post on the crescent of hills back of Covington and Newport, now seen as a natural defense. Thousands of others — merchants, manufacturers, doctors, lawyers, preachers — also crossed, with all the picks and shovels that could be found, to raise more blisters than were ever suffered in a like space of time anywhere, digging entrenchments on those hills. On the Ohio side, Mount Adams and Price's Hill were also fortified.

That episode was also notable for the invasion of Kentucky by Billy Glass, Democratic boss of the river wards and captain of No. 1 Fire Company, who had made an imperishable name for himself in '54 when, with pistol in hand, he protected a ballot-box from the onslaughts of Know-Nothings. Billy now hitched four of No. 1's best horses to one of the available cannon in the city, and in company with some other irregulars, started for the front. But somehow, out in the knobs, his plan of campaign went wrong, Billy and his cannon were captured, and with them the Fire Department lost four horses so fine that General Morgan sent word to the city that he would like to have some more of the same quality.

After the Battle of Perryville on October 8th, the whole Confederate army retired from Kentucky. All the cash in Cincinnati's banks had been removed and was on its way to Columbus under cavalry escort when news came that the danger was over.

Colonel William H. Lytle, making a heroic defense against odds at Perryville, was wounded and taken prisoner. Upon being exchanged, he was made a brigadier-general, and at Chickamauga, nearly a year later, he was near the spot where Rosecrans's mistaken order opened a gap in the Federal line and let the enemy pour through. Fighting desperately to hold them back, he received the fatal bullet which ended his career at 37. A lieutenant in the Mexican War at 20 and a captain soon afterward, Lytle had also served in the Ohio Legislature in the '50's. He was possessed of an old-fashioned punctilio that would have fitted him into the picture at Fontenoy. He did not give orders to his subordinates; instead, "General Lytle sends his compliments to Colonel Beatty,

[233]

with the request to send a company to the rear, to guard against
guerillas." His funeral was the occasion of one of Cincinnati's
greatest demonstrations of sorrow.

This knightly soldier was the author of one of the finest poems
written in America, in which the dying Mark Antony, a suicide
by his own sword, apostrophizes Cleopatra. Lytle's friend, another
poet, William W. Fosdick, found it lying on the General's writing table one day in the summer of 1858, and with the author's
consent, handed it to the *Commercial*, calling it "One of the most
masterly lyrics that ever adorned American poetry." Its majesty
of thought and organ-toned melody are a little out of fashion in an
age when earthiness and atonality are often perforce substituted
for such qualities in the arts; but it will survive.

Lytle was a native-born hero, though Cincinnati supplied a
number of other Union generals, and claimed more. Among these,
ten major-generals and twenty-one brigadiers — with some
brevets in each rank — may be legitimately granted; for to tell the
truth, Cincinnati was apt to claim as a citizen any general who so
much as stopped overnight at the Burnet House. McClellan and
Rosecrans, who were there in business for a few years before the
war, may be included. Some add Pope, who was stationed there
more briefly, Grant, because his father lived in Covington, and
Sherman, on a still more shadowy synthesis.

Cincinnati supplied war correspondents, too, notably Whitelaw
Reid, who, as the decades passed, became the millionaire owner of
the *New York Tribune* and then Ambassador to Great Britain. In
'61 he was on the *Gazette* staff, "a tall, graceful youth with an envi-
able black mustache and imperial," wrote William Dean Howells,
"wearing his hair long in the Southern fashion, and carrying himself with the native ease which availed him in a worldly progress
uninterrupted to the end." He went to the front for the *Gazette*,
and on his dispatches in vivid and coruscant prose laid the foundation of his career.

When the blockade of Southern ports shut off the supply of
raw cotton to England, when great English cotton-mill cities lay
idle and near famine in the fall of '62, President Lincoln appealed
to America to help the operatives, and Cincinnati quickly

responded. Judge Alphonso Taft, William Procter and William Heidelbach called a citizens' meeting, with the slogan, "Let your Christmas gifts be to the starving millhands of England," and the response was generous. The city sent 5,000 boxes of bacon and large quantities of pork, flour and hams in one of the three shiploads that crossed the ocean.

Street cars had been introduced in 1859, and Negroes now discovered that although the war was being fought in their behalf, they were still up against certain social barriers. The street car companies — or at least, one of them — had a rule that while colored women might sit inside a car, colored men must stand on the front platform with the driver. A negro named Isaac Young hailed a Fourth Street car and boarded it with his wife. There were eight persons and a dog — "riding without objection," said an item — in the car. The wife passed inside and sat down, and Young refused to obey the conductor's order that he go to the front platform. The conductor called on the driver to aid him in ejecting Young, but the driver refused. The conductor stopped the car, tried vainly to find a policeman, and finally sighted "some sporting men" standing on a corner, who, at his request dragged Young violently from the car. He brought suit against the company, and upon Judge Storer's charge that he was entitled to compensatory damages, the jury awarded him $800. That brought about a liberalization of street car rules.

General Morgan's madcap cavalry raid through southern Indiana and Ohio in '63, which was intended to incite secessionist uprisings in those areas but did not, found Cincinnati ungarrisoned. A serio-comic home guard, headed by one Gus Copt, a deserter from the German army, but currently Mrs. J. Handasyde Perkins's gardener, hastily assembled and prepared for action, but was not needed. Some of the troopers dashed through Glendale, upsetting that swanky suburb terribly for a moment, but they were too hard-pressed to pause long. When Morgan, captured and immured in the Ohio Penitentiary at Columbus, escaped with some of his comrades, the theory in the South was that they had tunneled their way out. But there was a counter-story in Ohio that the prison guards, bribed by Copperheads, had manipulated the escape. A mysterious woman, never identified, sometimes from Cincinnati, sometimes from Covington, was said to have carried $30,000 in cash to Columbus for the purpose. When the General escaped, he boldly came — unrecognized because minus those sweeping mustaches and imperial — through Cincinnati, and loyalists were fit to be tied when they heard a few days later that he had crossed at the Fifth Street ferry and enjoyed a leisurely dinner with "a prominent Rebel friend in Covington" before being driven southward in a buggy.

During one of these raid scares, butter rose to 70 cents a pound and eggs to a dollar a dozen. But for the most part, prices were not far from normal; butter 18 to 23 cents a pound, eggs 12½ cents a dozen, beef, steak or roast, 8 to 10 cents a pound, pork 6 to 7 cents, live chickens 15 to 25 cents each, potatoes and onions a dollar a bushel. Life, however, was much more austere for most folk. In society, parties were reduced to a minimum; ladies served on committees, promoted patriotic meetings, scraped lint; and now, for the first, young women were seen — in front of Woodward High School and elsewhere — serving coffee and sandwiches to passing soldiers. Women did much of the work of the Cincinnati Aid Association, and all for the Daughters of Temperance, both aiding soldiers' families in need. They were active in the United States Christian Commission, which dispensed not only religious literature, but cash. Some ladies served by day as voluntary nurses, though at night, appeals were made for young men to "sit up" with serious cases. In mid-December, 1863, General Rosecrans opened the Great Western Sanitary Fair at Mozart Hall, with exhibits, lectures and money-luring stunts, continuing through the New Year, to raise $250,000 for soldiers' relief.

The veteran tragedian, James E. Murdoch, had retired to a home a few miles north of the city, but came in occasionally for a lecture or a reading. During the war, he was always available for patriotic meetings and rallies, and his recitations in his big, mellow voice were the real hits of the programs. One day late in 1864, Grafton the artist and Judge Alphonso Taft met that versatile genius, Thomas Buchanan Read, painter and poet in front of a bookstore, in whose window a new painting grandiosely envisioned General Sheridan's recent dash from Winchester to the field of Cedar Creek, to rally his retreating army.

"There's a fine subject, Read," said Grafton. "Write a poem on it."

"Yes, and read it at our soldiers' benefit next Thursday evening," added the Judge.

Obviously, Read, only about five feet tall and usually weighing less than a hundred pounds, was scarcely the man to read an heroic poem effectively, so it was presently announced that Mr. Murdoch would recite it, if Read got it ready. He didn't succeed in completing it until the day of the benefit, and Murdoch didn't have time to memorize it; but skilled performer that he was, he read it with gestures and fine effect, to tremendous applause. From that moment, "Sheridan's Ride" was a favorite American poem and schoolboy recitation.

A mighty effort was made to win the vote of Cincinnati for its "own" General McClellan when he ran against Lincoln for the Presidency in 1864, but it was vain. A significant epilogue a year and a half later was the sale of 600 pounds of campaign posters bearing McClellan's portrait to a confectioner, to be used in wrapping candy.

For some on the fringe of society, life seemed to go on normally — too normally. There were gangs, such as the Mohawk Boys and the Brighton Boys, who were not boys at all, but tough young men, who fought intermittently; and Cumminsville was sporty, quarrelsome and riotous, as it had been for years. One day in '63, "some two-legged brutes," said the *Gazette*, had arranged a fight out there between "the Red Dog" and "the Brindle Dog." "The animals were wrapped in blankets and carefully placed on the seats of a street car, while the fifty brutes accommodated themselves as best they could, no smoking being allowed, lest the health of their betters should be injured."

Fellows like this showed no disposition to rally to the colors, but nemesis was close behind them. In the summer of '63 a draft was ordered, with no one of service age exempted save upon payment of $300. Early in the war, local business men had offered and paid from $30 to $40 each to young men who would volunteer, but that was pin money now. National, State and local governments were offering bounties of $100 and up for voluntary enlistment. This brought on a new type of racketeer, the bounty-jumper. The substitute broker, too, appeared almost overnight, with a roster of fellows who were willing, for a price — which rose within a few months from $300 to $500 — to take the place of well-to-do drafted men who didn't want to serve. Before the surrender, some rich young men were paying $1,000 to $1,500 for substitutes. Early in '65 the city's wards were appealing through the news-papers for contributions from their citizens to free them of the draft. Some wards raised the cash, and were out from under. On March 9th the Sixteenth Ward announced that "having made every effort to clear the ward of draft," it was notifying eligibles that all who would pay $40 by Saturday, the 11th, "will be pro-tected by having recruits put to their credit if drafted." The war was becoming very tiresome to most folk. Fortunately, the end was only a month away.

The news of Appomattox set the fuse to days of wild rejoicing which had only begun to calm when the awful backlash came, the murder of the President. Junius Brutus Booth, Jr., was in the midst of a two-weeks' engagement at Pike's Opera House, and the pre-vailing holiday spirit was making it greatly successful. Now in a flash, all was changed. He was a Booth, and whether the Booths were all in the plot or not, mob spirit, as might be expected, flared against him. Threatening demonstrations were made at his hotel, and the manager posted a strong guard in the hall leading to his room while the actor stole out through a rear door and made his escape from the city. Laura Keene and her company, whose per-formance of *Our American Cousin* Mr. Lincoln was enjoying when he was shot, went directly from Washington to Cincinnati. Four days after the assassination, when the Cincinnati newspapers were still full of the crime and its after-events, they were also carrying notices of Miss Keene's coming appearance in *She Stoops To Conquer*. Of course, everyone wanted to see the players who were there on the stage at Ford's, going through their routine when the crack-brained murderer ran right though their midst to escape, so the company played to packed houses.

Less than a month after Appomattox, Cincinnati was startled by the first railroad train hold up in history. Shortly after dawn on May 5, '65, an Ohio & Mississippi train en route from St. Louis to Cincinnati was derailed by an obstruction at North Bend, fourteen miles from the city, the engine and the baggage-and-express car being overturned. A gang of roughs promptly took over the train, some robbing the passengers — gallantly sparing the ladies — while others looted the express safes, making off with a large amount in cash and bonds. They were said to have escaped across the river in skiffs, which seemed to confirm the belief that they were guerrillas, the irregulars who had been ravaging parts of Kentucky for years and continued to do so for several months more.

CHAPTER XIII

Capital, Culture and Celebrity

As THE Moving Finger turned a leaf at the close of the Civil War and began tracing another page in Cincinnati's history, it appears to us now that Unborn Tomorrow differed from Dead Yesterday only in intensity. Wealth was greater, education, music and art richer, entertainment and vice gayer and wilder, shady politics rising in crescendo to new heights of power. The two halves of the city's soul, the better and worse, seemed to draw farther apart.

As it always does, war had left the entire country with a lowered moral tone, a lowered respect for human life and property, a lowered political ethic, too much folding money in unaccustomed hands, and a preoccupation with business and play which gave politicians unlimited opportunities. The post-bellum period in Cincinnati was destined to develop into one of the darker pages in American municipal history. There were ugly holdovers from the past — still-filthy streets, slums and dives. Crime was still too common; law enforcement was at one of those numerous new lows. There were roughneck police judges and evidences of collaboration between the police and crime. A batch of stolen goods was found in a patrolman's home. Tom Snelbaker, chief of police, after a bloody brawl on a street car in 1874 with two men, one of whom was a special policeman, later encountered the latter in a police station and shot him dead; in "self-defense," of course, so there was no interruption of Snelbaker's career as a promoter of flashy theatres and risque shows.

So many prisoners were escaping from the County Jail in 1870 that it was nicknamed "The Sieve." Headlines read, "County Sieve Drops Two More Offerings," and "County Sieve Passes Two More"; while an item revealed that "Franklin W. Prince and Thomas Smith were the only two who escaped from the County

Jail yesterday." There were 3,500 drinking places in the city in the early '70's, many of them open all night and known to be hangouts for crooks and prostitutes. In the small hours of Sunday morning when they were boldly violating a closing ordinance, they were particularly noisome and dangerous.

Cholera reappeared in the East in '65, and editors suspected that it was in Cincinnati already "In an undeveloped state," in "those heaps of loathsome rubbish" in gutters, alleys, tenements and "plastered thick on our most fashionable promenades." Sure enough, it struck near the end of the following July. On August 5th, 24 died, and the daily rate rose rapidly through 40, 50 and 60 to 70 — 1,133 dying in that month. Some people fled from the city, but editors sneered that they would be no addition to the communities where they took refuge. There were 457 deaths in September, 441 in October and 167 in November. Then the plague quickly died out, never to return again so devastatingly, though it reappeared in a smaller way as late as 1873.

Cincinnati had not stood still, but her days of phenomenal growth were past; others had inherited them. With the spread of railroads, her river traffic, ice-locked in winter and sometimes mud-blocked in summer, no longer had its supreme importance. Many individual fortunes had been greatly increased and new ones created by war contracts, and the city itself was prosperous, but the fact could no longer be concealed that strategic advantages had now moved to Chicago on the Lakes and St. Louis on the Mississippi, both with growing railroad networks; and that Chicago was becoming — becoming? — nay, it was already, the metropolis, the chief railroad center of the Middle West, that it was rapidly stealing Cincinnati's pork-packing industry, and that even St. Louis must be considered a dangerous rival.

The almost fatal frights given to Congressmen and top officials on those occasions when the muttering of Confederate cannon could be heard in Washington, now again stirred the suggestion that the nation's capital, for safety's sake, be moved to the Middle West. Thereupon, nearly every municipality in the Mississippi Valley, including Junction City, Kansas, set forth reasons why itself was the only logical location. The *Chicago Tribune* named four possibilities — Chicago, Cincinnati, St. Louis and Memphis. The *Cincinnati Gazette*, in an editorial in '69 maintained a calm objectivity that was little short of Olympian. The *Tribune's* editorial had remarked in its beginning that the center of population had moved as far west as Columbus; but later on in the same editorial it said that Cincinnati was unsuitable because the center of population had moved west of her.

"This scatter-brained style of editorial," said the *Gazette*, "is not noticed in Chicago, for the scatter-brained style is universal there." If Chicago were a permanency, the editor continued, he would not object to its being made the capital, "though it is not the best location. But is Chicago a permanency? We must judge this by inquiring whether the conditions that created Chicago are permanent."

Lake transportation, the editor pointed out, had created Chicago, but now railroads were outmoding waterways. Tyre, Sidon, Sodom, Gomorrah and Babylon were cited as commercial cities that had risen and fallen. Chicago papers were now — of all things! — trying to boost that town as a summer resort. This was among the "symptoms that the Chicago people are impressed that the condition which made that place are not permanent. These appear in the temporary character of their buildings, the transient feeling of their citizens, the general recklessness as to business reputation, the gambling character of their trade and the general looseness of their morals. . . . Obviously, it would be improper to locate the national capital at Chicago. As to the features of the site, without the business and what the business has made, it is the most forlorn that can be imagined, both in its topographical features and in its climate. Cincinnati offers all the beauties of site, climate and civilization, but Cincinnati does not need the capital. If the country desires to put it here because, as the *New York Times* argues, this is the best place and with the most metropolitan character of any place but New York, we shall acquiesce as a patriotic duty. . . . Cincinnati, the Queen City of the West, does not seek the National Capital, but is in a position to be sought by it."

A Convention on the Removal of the National Capital, with

delegates from many sections, met in Cincinnati in the following year, but as every delegation favored its own city, the meeting accomplished nothing. And the capital is still where it was.

The great Chicago fire, in October, 1871, seemed a stroke of fate. That was a weird autumn, when vast fires ravaged thousands of square miles of forest in Wisconsin and Michigan, their smoke hanging like a pall over the whole Ohio Valley, and you could actually smell burning pine trees 300 miles and more away. And then, in two awful days in early October, the heart of Chicago, one-third of the city was reduced to ashes, and 200 persons died. There were those in Cincinnati and St. Louis who rubbed their hands and said privately to each other, "Well, this ends Chicago. She'll never recover from it. It'll kill her, dead as a herring." But Cincinnati promptly forgot rivalry, and rushed to the aid of the stricken community. A detachment of the city's police were sent immediately to aid in keeping order. A citizen's committee, headed by Mayor S. S. Davis and Si Keck, quickly followed, taking $2,600 in cash, with which they set up a soup house. Carloads of food, clothing and blankets were soon en route; the City Council voted $100,000 for relief. The theatres and local orchestras gave benefits. Some saw condescension in all this, a note of triumph over a fallen and forever beaten rival. But the chief motive was undoubtedly that great-hearted American sympathy which always overflows at times of disaster and suffering, no matter where.

Hundreds of those made homeless by the fire were sent to Cincinnati for temporary shelter, the Union Bethel alone housing 100. And every bum and panhandler on Cincinnati streets promptly became a Chicago fire sufferer.

Cincinnati found it difficult to believe that the Phoenix of Arabic legend arose from its ashes as nimbly as Chicago did from hers. The fire seemed actually to have given her a boost; almost before you could say O'Leary, she was in the lead again. But the older town was not licked; objectively pondering its own eminence as a commercial and cultural center, it could not feel overboastful in claiming still the sobriquet, Queen City of the West. As late as 1875 it mentioned as "satellite cities," Covington, Lexington, Dayton, Springfield, Indianapolis, Terre Haute, Evansville and Memphis! For a wonder, it did not include Louisville, whose *Courier-Journal* not unreasonably referred to Cincinnati as "our clever but rather vain sister up the river." Wealthy and with businesses that seemed to defy competition, she was solid and sure. The numerous new chateaux of her plutocrats were not only a paean of triumph, but a defiance. She was still striving for bigness in various ways. A prosperous citizen named Joseph Buddeke wanted the largest *swinging* bell in existence for the new edifice of his church, St. Francis de Sales on Walnut Hills, so he ordered one from the Vanduzen Bell Foundry, to weigh 30,000 pounds. Other bells as large as this are merely tapped mechanically with a hammer, but this one was to be swung by a wheel 15 feet in diameter. It was installed, it swung — and all Walnut Hills nearly jumped out of its collective skin; the earth trembled, windows near by broke from the concussion, and when tiny bits of cement were seen falling from between the stones of the church walls, it was promptly decided that Big Joseph, as the bell had been named in honor of its donor, must never swing again. So it now hangs motionless, and is struck by a clapper in the orthodox way.

But Cincinnati continued to set marks for other cities to shoot at. Metropolitan critics pronounced her May Musical Festivals incomparable, and her annual Industrial Expositions brought exhibits even from Europe. She built a railroad 338 miles long. She sent forth a noted Arctic explorer, Charles Francis Hall (1821-71), who began as a blacksmith, then became a seal engraver and stationer and whose modest home still stands on Mount Adams. He made three expeditions to the Arctic region between 1860 and 1871, spending years in exploration, finding relics of Martin Frobisher's expedition of 1575-78 and of Sir John Franklin's in 1845, mapping much unknown territory, reaching a farthest north of 82° 16' and in '71 dying of apoplexy and being buried in Greenland. General A. W. Greely said of him that "With similar limited resources," no man had surpassed him in achievement.

Baseball after the war rapidly ousted cricket, though there were as yet no leagues, each club arranging a season's schedule as college football teams do now. Players shared precariously in the gate receipts until 1869, when the Cincinnati Red Stockings became the first salaried club in history, drawing from $1,000 to $1,500 per annum, though the players had other trades for the winter months — haberdashery, bookkeeping, engraving, marble cutting, piano-making, selling jewelry and insurance. Later there was a shortstop who doubled as Uncle Tom in *Uncle Tom's Cabin.* They went through that year '69 without losing a game; made a grand tour of the East and in the fall visited California. When they played the powerful Rockford club at Chicago, sixty people went up from Cincinnati to see the game. Their home-coming was like a Roman conqueror's triumph.

In the following year, though they were not quite invincible, losing six games, they were still idolized; but in '71 they suffered semi-collapse, and thereafter had a spotty existence. When the National League was organized in 1876, the Reds were one of its eight clubs, and started off well, but later became so bad that when on tour, the home papers sometimes didn't even notice the games of "Mr. Keck's hired muffers" — just one of the names they were called — only suggesting that the players be brought home and put to work in the pork houses.

In '69 Cincinnati was still doing the biggest river trade on the Ohio, but a decline was just around the corner. The "feeling," was optimistic, but the opening in 1870 of the new bridge by which the railroad to Louisville entered the city — though celebrated with great fanfare, with all of the Kentucky Legislature and State officials as invited guests of the city, dined, toasted and taken out in carriages to stare, open-mouthed, at the gilded palaces of Clifton — was an omen of a time of not so pleasant readjustment. Sly old Louisville, with her railroad to Nashville and beyond, was stealing much Southern business. Cincinnati had bought large blocks of stock and bonds in the Kentucky Central and the Louisville and Cincinnati Railroads, but these availed little and were unprofitable. By 1868, a movement had begun, looking to the building of a new line, bypassing Louisville and piercing directly to the heart of the South. On June 26, 1869, in a popular referendum, the citizens under the influence of such powerful arguments as bands, parades and bell-ringing, voted by a majority of 10 to 1 to issue $10,000,000 of city bonds for the construction of a railroad through Lexington to Chattanooga. Campaigns began at once for the obtaining of State charters to the southward, and for the placing of more bonds in counties along the line.

The Mechanics' Institute in 1838 promoted the first of the city's industrial expositions, which was held in Mrs. Trollope's Bazaar building. Thereafter they took place irregularly. That of 1860 was housed in the Institute building at Sixth and Vine Streets and the adjoining Mozart Hall. The young Prince of Wales visited it and tried a few shots on billiard tables exhibited by Messrs. Brunswick and Balke. In 1869 Alfred T. Goshorn, white lead manufacturer, started a movement in the Chamber of Commerce for a revival of the expositions. The Mechanics' Institute joined in the movement, as did other forces, and the first of a long series of the fairs opened in the big Sängerfest Hall, opposite Washington Park, late in September, 1870. It lasted 28 days, and Cincinnati promptly decided that it was a bigger show than New York's Crystal Palace exhibition had been.

Thereafter, the Exposition was an eagerly-awaited event each year. When the new Springer Music Hall was completed, it began to be held there. Its importance and success so increased that after the Exposition of '74, a "superlatively select complimentary banquet" was given to the commissioners, the other diners paying $12.50 a plate, a new high for dinners, which gives a hint of Cincinnati's prosperity — and that, too, in the year following the panic of '73. The Exposition of '75 opened with a parade alleged to be five miles long. At that of '79 turnstiles appeared for the first time, and the public were warned to have a quarter ready, and told how to put it in the slot and then push.

Stocky, gloriously side-whiskered, somewhat pompous but highly efficient A. T. Goshorn made such a reputation with the Exposition of '70 that when the Centennial Exposition of 1876 at Philadelphia was being planned, he was named as one of the Ohio commissioners. But his reputation was such that the central organization elected him a vice-president, and from there he quickly passed to headship of the whole big show. He went abroad to study exposition methods in London, Paris and Vienna, and all told, spend more than three years on the job, making the Exposition such a success that Philadelphia presented him with a large library, he was decorated by practically all the nations of Europe and a few others, and as a crowning appreciation by the British Government, he was, by special Act of Congress, permitted to accept knighthood from Queen Victoria, and became Sir Alfred Goshorn, an unique American figure.

But there were some things which this competent city just couldn't do. For a century, it was cursed by a particularly poor water-supply. In 1819, when Colonel S. W. Davies's private water concession, with its 40-horse-power engine was delivering river water in scant supply to a few users through bored wooden pipes, the City Directory remarked that the taste of the water was "perfectly agreeable when time is allowed for the sandy sediment to precipitate." There were no filters, no settling basins — no city had such things; just pumps. This will recall sweet memories to many persons still alive and not so very, very elderly, of days when a glass of the city's water, drawn from a hydrant in the springtime or just after a heavy rainy spell would be opaque and of a chrome-ochre color, and when you let it stand for a few minutes, a half-inch or more of yellow mud would settle to the bottom of the tumbler. The water for the Saturday night's bath was drawn hours before, and the clearer portion carefully poured off after settling. Monday morning's wash water was drawn Sunday evening and put through the same process, with not entirely satisfactory results.

For decades, the complaints of mud and bad tastes vied with those of poor pressure and sometimes complete failure of supply. The city grew so fast that a new reservoir on Mount Auburn, completed in 1851, was inadequate within 15 years. Street and back-yard cisterns and wells and an occasional primeval spring which still persisted were the chief dependence of many citizens for their drink. No wonder so many were driven to beer and booze. During the '60's several species of marine fauna, including eels, a 16-inch catfish and an 18-inch salamander strayed through the pipes and stopped hydrants from flowing. But when in '81, small snakes or worms of about the thickness and length of a darning needle were found in water from the Mount Auburn Reservoir, some people lost their latest meal when they reflected that they might have swallowed some of the varmints without knowing it. There had been a typhoid outbreak on Mount Auburn, and it was suspected, perhaps unjustly, that these reptilia had a hand in it.

In 1869 Joe Mayer, superintendent of the Water Works, reported with dry sarcasm that the city reservoir was filled and emptied twice every 24 hours, which, he said, accounted for the citizens' "getting the Ohio River water in all its peculiar freshness." In short, the Water Works slogan might have been, "From the River to You." Truth to tell, the reservoir could have been emptied four times a day if the pumps could have filled it that often. Wells and cisterns were still worked to capacity. People along lower Deer Creek were fortunate, for there was an unfailing spring near the Canal between Eighth and Ninth Streets, from which two tanneries and more than a hundred families drew their water supply. Germs were still invisible and unheard-of, and human organisms were tough.

Partial disablement of the Water Works caused a short supply again in the spring of '74, and street sprinkling was halted, awaiting repairs, which couldn't be made until the river went down! There was "an almost constantly impending water famine" raged an editor. "Muddy Water Run by Muddled Ring," was a headline. It was hoped that the new Eden Park Reservoir would allay the famine, but no sooner was it filled, late that year, than a serious leak developed, the pumps gave trouble again, and a defalcation in the Water Works accounts was discovered. A grand jury indicted three men, including Police-Chief-Water-Works-Board Secretary Snelbaker, always in office, always crooked, always immune to punishment. When the leak and the pumps were repaired, and the new pressure turned on, there were twenty breaks in the ancient mains downtown; geysers six and seven feet high rose in the streets, cellars were flooded, boxes, beer kegs and even a dray were washed away, a cave-in engulfed a street-car mule and it had to be rescued with a derrick. "The Board of Public Works expressed no astonishment at the breaks, as it was expected that these would occur."

A new Democratic leader arose in the early '70's, young John R. McLean, son of Washington McLean, long the principal owner of the *Enquirer*. With culture acquired at both Harvard and Heidelberg, John R. nevertheless came near being a professional baseball player, and only a large cash bonus offered by his father lured him into journalism. He soon bought out other interests in the paper and became sole owner. Meanwhile, he was working towards control in the local Democratic party. He confronted a Republican party which, with the triumphant close of its crusade against slavery and disunion, found itself at a loose end, needing new objectives. The industrial North tended towards conservatism, but Ohio was not yet sufficiently industrialized to sympathize with high tariffs on foreign goods. Halstead in the *Commercial* was raging in 1866 against "the infernal tariff" and "those damned harpies of Pennsylvania and New England" who favored it. Hayes, Garfield, Cox and other Ohio Republicans were still low-tariff men, but soon had to readjust their views. But before this came about, a liberal movement was born among Republicans. Disgust with the rapidly accumulating scandals of Grant's first term gave birth in free-thinking Cincinnati in '71 to a committee consisting of General Jacob D. Cox, George Hoadly, Stanley Matthews and Friedrich Hassaurek, who hoped to reform the Republican party. Halstead espoused the cause, and was joined by the *Volksblatt* and *Volksfreund*. All this led to the Liberal Republican, anti-Grant convention at Cincinnati in May, 1872, with General Carl Schurz in the chair. The "Come-outers" as they were called, opposed Grant's renomination, declared for tariff and civil service reform, for a return to specie payment and amnesty to Confederates. There was an unfavorable omen during the convention when Professor Currier's band played the Miserere from *Trovatore*. It *was* a queer selection, and one can hardly blame the delegate who sent a note to the professor, reading, "This aint a funeral. Play something lively," to which the offended maestro merely appended a line, "You are an ass," and sent it back.

It did prove to be a funeral, after all, for to the consternation of the Cincinnatians, the eccentric Horace Greeley, protectionist, disliked by the Germans and vague on civil service, was nominated. Hoadly and Matthews promptly denounced the ticket, and Hoadly eventually went over to the Democrats. As for Hassaurek, he was so Leftish that at a meeting of the polemical Friends of Inquiry in '74 we find him examining the question, "What is self government, and where should the line between government action and private enterprise be drawn?" It began even as far back as that.

That corruption and misgovernment mean little to the electorate was proven by the overwhelming reelection of Grant. Local pride may have won him some Cincinnati votes, for he was counted as one of the city's own Presidents, because his father had lived for several years in Covington, and through the naive nepotism of Son Ulysses, had become postmaster there. When Jesse Grant died in 1872, the *Cincinnati Evening Star's* four lines of delicate damnation by implication were notable: "His career as postmaster of Covington is familiar to all our readers, and does not need any enlargement at our hands. He was but mortal; he is dead."

This *Evening Star*, by the way, was decidedly leftist, favoring the abolition of National banks, of land grants to corporations and of the selling or descent of land anywhere or from or to anybody, except in limited quantities to landless persons; income taxes of $2\frac{1}{2}$ to 10 percent on "monopolized wealth;" free trade; Government ownership or control of railroads; an International Congress to settle all international disputes; a single term for the Presidency and other near-revolutionary ideas which Cincinnati readers just took in their stride. The moral quality of the *Star's* editor, that gentle dreamer, Lucius A. Hine, is seen in his defense of a rival editor, Richard Smith of the *Gazette*, whose ethical, intellectual and literary standards emphasized another side of Cincinnati than its unlovely political phase. A savant who sometimes published a whole column or more of literary news in a weekday issue — an unheard-of thing then — who headed an article on the gerrymandering of the city, "Omnes Cincinnati in Quinque Partes Divisi Sunt," whose paper from time to time published a translation by himself of one of the Odes of Horace, finely retaining the poesy and flavor of the original, Smith was sufficiently eminent to be written up in *Leslie's Weekly*, with a portrait. A Republican, he once took up indignantly the defense of a Democratic candidate, Colonel McCook, who, worn to exhaustion by a strenuous campaign, was accused by the Republicans of drunkenness. In turn, Smith was defended by Hine from the sneers of the *Commercial*, the *Enquirer* and the erratic Dana of the *New York Sun*. Hine denounced the nagging as "scurvy, indecorous, hypocritical and contemptible," and charged that the *Sun's* part of it was largely inspired by Halstead, between whom and Dana there was "mutual admiration."

Amidst the hum of factories, the ominous whirr of political machines, the brassy clangor of the saloons, theaters and honky-tonks of Vine Street and the chatter of society, music and art flourished as in almost no other city in America, and literary culture, too, more quietly. Fine libraries were numerous; not all owned by nabobs who bought them by the yard, but mostly those of men who read and loved books. Auctions of old and rare books brought good crowds and high bidding for the period. The Public Library now began to get on its feet, but soon, it too, fell under the malign influence of politics. For years it had been a neglected, struggling institution, pushed about from pillar to post, part of the time in a high school building, a strange condition for a community with so much culture at the top as Cincinnati. In the latter '6o's a different sort of Library Board, including such men as Rufus King, Henry Probasco, Henry Brown, Jr. and M. D. Hanover took over, and prepared to put it into a new building and give it a new librarian. The building was an unfinished theater on Vine Street, one of Truman B. Handy's unsuccessful ventures, which was taken over and converted — not as successfully as could be hoped — for library use. The new librarian was William F. Poole, late librarian of the Boston Athenum, and compiler of the indispensable *Index to Magazine Literature*.

But very shortly the library came under the direction of the Board of Education, and that meant politics. Poole endured it until the building had been remodelled and the books installed in it in 1874, and then, to the anguish of the book-loving public, he accepted the city librarianship at Chicago. But that there was real culture in the populace was proven by the gift of 2,466 books and 237 pamphelts to the library in 1879 by John A. B. King, a crippled "newsboy" (really middle-aged), all bought with his hard-earned savings from one of the most onerous of businesses.

Of the eleven volumes in Scribner's *Campaigns of the Civil War*, four were written by Cincinnatians. Judge Manning F. Force wrote *From Fort Henry to Corinth;* General Henry M. Cist wrote *The Army of the Cumberland* and *The Campaign of Atlanta;* and General Jacob D. Cox described *The March to the Sea*, about which Colonel George Ward Nichols also wrote *The Story of the Great March*. In Appleton's Scientific Series, Judge J. B. Stallo did the volume on Physics. Judges Force, Hoadly and Matthews wrote law treatises, S. Dana Horton and W. S. Groesbeck on money and coinage. Friedrich Hassaurek and Dr. Isaac M. Wise, in addition to works on many subects, wrote novels. William H. Venable produced a splendid volume on *The Beginnings of Literary Culture in the Ohio Valley*. Classical scholars were numerous. Judge Nicholas Longworth, grandson of the first Nicholas, did an excellent translation of the *Electra* of Sophocles.

Just as the Civil War was closing, a young man of 25 named Henry Watterson, short of stature and blind in one eye, appeared unostentatiously in Cincinnati and found a job on the *Evening Times,* then owned by Calvin W. Starbuck. He didn't want to attract too much attention, for he had recently edited a fiery Secesh newspaper at Chattanooga, called the *Rebel*. But the *Times* editor died suddenly, and when Starbuck offered Watterson the job at $75 a week, he couldn't resist accepting it. Halstead of the *Commercial* thereupon discovered his presence, and began making such scathing allusions to his wartime activities that Watterson at length went to him and asked him, as a later generation would have said, to have a heart. He wasn't going to stay in Cincinnati, he said, any longer than it would take him to find a job to southward. Halstead liked him, the attacks ceased and a warm friendship sprang up between them. After a time Watterson went to Louisville, and as editor of the *Courier-Journal*, won nation-wide fame.

Cincinnati lays claim, in one way and another, to other literary beginnings. It was from here in 1855 that a youngster named Sam Clemens, beginning his first voyage as an apprentice pilot, departed on the *Paul Jones* and heard the phrase, "Mark twain!" which he adopted as a nom de plume, to make, not the Ohio but the Mississippi River known to the uttermost parts of the world. Robert J. Burdette, editor of the *Burlington Hawkeye* and one of the famous humorists of the century, was brought up in Cumminsville.

The strangest of all the genii who had their start in Cincinnati was a little half-Greek, half-Irish, more than half-blind, painfully shy and sensitive youth who drifted in from New York penniless, somewhere around 1869-70, and slept in sheds, in boxes, in an old boiler, anywhere he could, until he found a job as errand boy-devil-janitor with the *Cincinnati Trade-List*, and slept in the shop. In 1873, Lafcadio Hearn began timidly contributing essays to the *Enquirer*, though he was terribly afraid of the managing editor, Colonel Cockrill. But when the latter read the first of his compositions, he was amazed by the quality of the writing. Soon the little gnome, huddled in a corner of the city room with his nose almost touching the paper, was writing many columns daily of smooth, vivid English and attracting new readers. His favorite themes were along widely varied lines — the beautiful and idyllic, the weird and bizarre, the slums, water-front life and characters — dump-pickers, for example, and what they found in the city dump — and the macabre — murder, horrible deaths and ghostly appearances. The "Tanyard murder" in '74 gave him an opportunity such as he loved. Two men had killed a seducer with a pitchfork and tossed his body into the tanyard furnace. Hearn dramatized the scene gruesomely, with subtitle lines in capitals, after a fashion of those days. "There is a horrible probability that the wretched victim was

FORCED INTO THE FURNACE ALIVE

and suffered all the agonies of the bitterest death which man can die. . . .

". . . the grim murderers, demoniacally pitiless, devilishly desperate, gasping with their exertions to destroy a poor human life

LOOKING ON IN SILENT TRIUMPH

Peering into the furnace until the skull exploded, and the steaming body burst, and the fiery flue hissed like a hundred snakes. . . ."

But for something really grisly, his description of the various organs of the body when found should be read. He flitted away to New Orleans in 1877, where he began to build a real reputation.

Cincinnati's stability was demonstrated in the panic of 1873, which shook the rest of the country severely. Here, currency payments were suspended by the banks for only three weeks in the autumn; there was some recession and stagnation of business for a while, though it did not continue long, nor was it as serious as it was elsewhere. The railroad strike of 1877, which brought ugly fighting, death and great destruction of property in Pittsburgh, Chicago and other cities, touched Cincinnati's serenity but lightly. A number of trains were halted, but there was no violence, no damage to property, and some railroads entering the city remained normal.

Employers were now beginning to ponder more seriously the workers' problems and welfare. Stores had always been kept open until late in the evening, though it must be said that the employer usually stayed, too. In 1858 clerks urged merchants — in most cases in vain — to close stores between 8 and 9 on Wednesday evenings, so that they might attend prayer meeting. But after the war, the custom of closing at 7:00 P.M. or earlier gradually found a foothold, and in 1877 the LeBoutillier dry goods store startled the city with the unprecedented step of closing on Saturday afternoons in summer. Procter & Gamble's in 1886 was the first factory to give the Saturday half-holiday, following this within a year with an employees' profit-sharing plan, and then with pensions and disability benefits. Other companies were soon working out these and other welfare ideas — medical care, hospitals, schools, playgrounds for young and old. P. & G. again pioneered in 1923 in guaranteeing its employees at least 48 weeks' work per year.

During the depression days of the '30's, the Cincinnati Milling Machine Company kept top experts at work, developing new products which would help to maintain employment at a good level. Other examples might be cited. Understanding and poise keep the city's strike record low, promote amicable settlements and prevent bloody, destructive strikes such as sometimes occur elsewhere. In a folksy city, it is natural that retirement rules are often violated. In 1949, "Bud" Sands, who had found a job with the Milling Machine Company when it was organized in 1884 was still working there, after 65 years. Sol Stephan's 62 years at the Zoo and Keturo Shirayamadani's 64 years at the Rookwood Pottery are hardly considered phenomenal in Cincinnati.

CHAPTER XIV

The Flesh and the Devil

WITH the election of G. W. C. Johnston as Mayor in 1873, the impulse of a new and well-oiled machine began to be felt. Republicans at first called it the "Johnston Ring," but soon discovered that a smarter hand was behind Johnston. The town was wide open. The *Gazette* said that the majority of the city council were "of the bummer element." One of them, drunk and disorderly, tried to clean out a West End saloon, and had to be taken to a police station, though of course not to jail. When the Council met with a considerable program before it, a keg of beer, with cheese, bologna and crackers, would be placed on tap in an adjacent office, to sustain the fainting spirits of the toiling legislators. On one warm day when two kegs of beer were brought, a quorum couldn't be kept in the council chamber, though there was always a quorum in the other room. Finally the Council just gave it up and adjourned noisily.

Business concerns and prominent individuals called mass meetings, appointed committees and employed an able attorney, who drew corrective bills and brought actions to curb the waste of public money; but the net gain was small and in the course of time it was nullified. Little progress towards reform could be made when voting was done orally, and so many voters were more susceptible to demagoguery and more or less open to bribery than to logic. In the election of 1876, shoals of floaters were brought in from outside — Negroes from Kentucky by the Republicans, "bummers" by the Democrats from as far away as Chicago, whither a useful citizen named Eph Holland journeyed to assemble and bring down a trainload of them. At that time the city owed $80,000 in back pay to its laborers, some of it a year overdue. It sold some property for $25,000 and slowly raised the rest of the money somehow. Meanwhile, the payoff was delayed by trumped-up technicalities, and the men had to stand in line at City Hall for hours, while their claims were being checked and audited.

McLean found it advisable to make an alliance with Thomas C. Campbell, a shyster criminal lawyer and rising Republican boss, and with the two parties thus in amiable coagency, the city was completely in subjection. Robert M. Moore, who became Mayor in 1877, had such aesthetic whimsies as carrying the stem of a rose between his teeth and serving his favorite beverage, crab-apple cider, to callers at his office, neither of which seemed to convince critics that he was what they needed as Mayor. Complaints of lawlessness and graft became so loud that the gang made a pretense of electing a reform Mayor in '79, though the *Gazette*, after a year's observation, opined that he couldn't be distinguished from the others.

In that same year a young Republican saloonkeeper named George B. Cox was elected to the City Council, almost unnoticed. His early experiences as newsboy, bootblack, butcher's boy, wagon driver, salesman and bartender had well qualified him for ward politics, and he soon showed a knack for corralling blocks of votes in district political conventions which brought him under the notice of experts. But no one could have dreamed that within a few years his name would ring across the country as the head of one of one of the worst and most powerful of municipal machines.

Important developments were taking place in the post-war years, and all had to pay toll to the machine. There had been friction and much ill-feeling over the cost of city transportation, and its inefficiency. As far back as 1855, editors were calling the Cincinnati-Covington ferry a wealthy monopoly with outrageously high fares — three cents per passenger; whereas, said the *Gazette*, you could ferry from New York to Brooklyn for a cent. The company ought at least to shovel out paths through the mud to the wharves. But when Roebling's Suspension Bridge (still trustworthy today, after more than 80 years' service) was opened in 1867 — another over the Licking, welded Covington and Newport — the ferry monopoly was broken. The Reverend A. D. Mayo preached a timely sermon on "The Suspension Bridge, Socially,

Morally and Religiously Considered." He saw points both for and against it. It would promote Sabbath-breaking, of course, but that was becoming common. When Sunday newspapers began to be published about the same time — the *Commercial* and *Enquirer* among the first — there was a considerable outcry against them, and many newsdealers in the suburbs and outlying towns refused to handle them. But not for long. The protests of the clergy in '58 against the operation of buses on Sunday, on the ground that they were used mostly by "fast men on excursions of pleasure" were now regarded as something preglacial.

The first street cars began — with a 100-gun salute — to operate in 1859 on a nickel fare. When, in '66, some of the lines tried to advance the rate to 6 cents, rebellion flared, and there were fights between passengers and crews. The passengers won that war, but when in 1871, Route 9 put on owl cars at half-hour intervals through the latter night, it collected 10 cents fare on them. All passengers acquiesced but Max Burgheim, a book-dealer; he refused to pay more than a nickel, and was thrown off the car. He had the conductor arrested, and fined $5 and costs for assault, whereupon the company ordered crews to use only the gentlest methods in ejecting passengers. Another method was demonstrated when the whole rear platform, with ten men standing on it, fell off a car one evening as it was dashing along Fourth Street.

The grades to the hilltops were too steep for horse cars, and as the buses ceased running early in the evening, there were bitter complaints that hill folk, with the exception of the swells who owned carriages, couldn't attend the theater. So the building of inclined planes began — first the Mount Auburn, rising from the head of Main Street to Jackson Hill, a 300-foot rise in 900 feet of track. When opened in the spring of 1872, it had no car or bus line connecting directly with it at either end. Soon the company completed its own car line downtown to the base of the incline, though it was a sad job. The story was told that a car once left the track at Ninth Stret and ran all the way down to Fifth on the cobbles, though the passengers said they didn't notice any difference. But these troubles were eventually ironed out.

Within three or four years, three more inclines climbed the

slopes — the Clifton, at the head of Elm Street, the Mount Adams, scaling that height to a point near Eden Park, and the Price's Hill (since shortened to Price Hill), which rose from the end of West Eighth Street. The last-named eminence was the most isolated and slowest to develop of any of the hills because of its steep slopes; an isolation which favored the writing of Timothy C. Day's fine *Letters from a Hilltop* in 1858-63. Its chief pioneer was Reese Evans Price, Welshman and vegetarian, who eschewed all liquors, tea, coffee, tobacco, animal foods and even apples, because they were the forbidden fruit of Eden. He renounced his allegiance to the United States because of its war on Mexico. But he supplied much of the cash when his son William built the incline, the steepest in the city, in 1874. The Mount Adams plane cars were open platforms, onto which street cars, wagons, any and all wheeled vehicles, were driven and hauled bodily up or down the hill. But the Price's Hill plane had enclosed cars like street cars; and as there were two daughters in the Price family named Mary and Lily, the two cars that seesawed past each other all day were named *Highland Mary* and *Lily of the Valley*. With the completion of this line, Price's Hill began a period of rapid development.

And now a new form of horseless car appeared — cars that climbed the long gradient of Gilbert Avenue to Peebles's Corner on Walnut Hills, propelled by an underground steel cable. With that, Henry Martin, a Main Street dry-goods merchant who lived on Mount Auburn, decided that his suburb should have cable service via Sycamore Street. A strict religionist, Martin disapproved of Sunday transit, but realized that as the world was then, it had become necessary. He incorporated and built his cable line, owning all the stock himself save a thimbleful which he gave to some of his employees so that he might have a board of directors. Every Saturday night at closing time, his board of directors would meet, accept his resignation as president, elect his store manager, Thiemann, to the presidency and adjourn, all within three or four minutes. The cars ran merrily all through the Sabbath under the presidency of the calloused Mr. Thiemann, while Mr. Martin went to church with a clear conscience. On

Monday morning, first thing, Thiemann would resign and Martin be reelected president.

The Republican National Convention of 1876 met at Exposition Hall and nominated Cincinnati's own son, Rutherford B. Hayes, for the Presidency. In the campaign which followed, with both parties trying to steal the election, and the Republicans proving the cleverer thieves of the two, it should be said for Mr. Hayes that the chicanery was kept secret from him, and he fully believed that he had received enough honest votes to elect him; but that tainted decision has prevented his receiving the credit he deserves for his high ability and integrity.

In the political torchlight parades as late as 1872, many partisans still carried pitch-pine fagots, a real immolation for the cause, for their hot juice was apt to run down and burn the bearer's hand painfully. But kerosene torches had appeared by that time, and thereafter, you couldn't wage a campaign without them. Important political reasoning, those parades, with their dozens of oompah-oompah bands, banners and transparencies, ward marching clubs in semiuniform, at least in Civil War caps and (usually) oilcloth capes — blue for Republicans, red for Democrats — some groups with big shields on their chests which bore defiant, exultant, insulting or instructive legends. Before 1880 the nattily dressed Lincoln Club (Republican) and Duckworth Club (Democratic), in white plug hats and carrying canes instead of torches were the dignified units in the parades. Some genius invented a mouthpiece for the torch-handle, by which the flame could be blown up to a height of three feet or more, and Republicans claimed in '76 that one Democratic parade tried with its torches to set fire to a United States flag hanging in front of Republican headquarters, but the wind always lifted the flag just high enough to save it. Every parade was a drunken brawl to the opposition newspapers. Little gamins, hidden in alleys or behind barrels, stoned the processions, aiming usually at transparencies or bass drums, and were particularly gratified if they could hit the Grand Marshal.

In a wide-open town, the gayety of course becomes gayer and wilder, and the machine's pickings larger, for without tribute duly paid, no illegal business can be expected to operate. Pugilism had always hitherto been banned in Cincinnati, and regarded with horror by better minds because of its bare-knuckle brutality and crookedness and the mobs of toughs which it drew together. A fight in 1868 in a field just across the line in Indiana, and another, also in the open, in Kentucky in 1876 were, with attendant happenings, excoriated in many-columned articles in the *Gazette*, which hoped that the battle of '76 would be the last in the vicinity of Cincinnati, but the hope was vain. With the pitch of "entertainment" rising in crescendo, boxing entered the city itself. In 1880 John L. Sullivan, then just building a reputation, knocked out another bruiser at the Pacific Garden for a mere $50. Illegality was delicately detoured by putting gloves on the boxers, to the disgust of many patrons. Five years later Sullivan was a national figure, and we see a banner flung across the top of an *Enquirer* page, "SULLIVAN AND McCAFFREY WILL FIGHT TO A FINISH."

Prostitution and street-walking were never so open and unashamed as they now became. Two narrow downtown streets, Longworth and George, had become the red-light district. The *Gazette* in '81 cited one block of Longworth, between Plum and Central Avenue which had at least twenty bagnios, and listed them by name and number. Two police sergeants who knew and often gave news tips to a young reporter friend named Green, took him one day — just for his information, not for publication — on a tour through Longworth Street. It was the machine's regular monthly tithing day, and they went down the street the full length of the red-light area, collecting the stipulated sums from every madame as casually as a landlord collecting rents. The bosses were waxing fat; and yet street-cleaning was so poorly done that in the fall of '77 Fourth Street merchants made up a purse and cleaned that thoroughfare themselves.

Perhaps the last reminder of the old, semibucolic Cincinnati was seen on a November day in 1877 when a flock of Kentucky turkeys crossed the Suspension Bridge on foot and were driven up Race Street. A noisy, gaudy, devil-may-care era was upon the city now, and was to continue at its highest tension until the end of the century, fading slowly thereafter. It is looked back upon by elderly, present-day memorists as "the good old days." It *was* a gay, insouciant period, indeed, and those folk who could forget or be oblivious of high taxes and graft and crime and bad government, and the degradation of public and private morals had uproarious times. The fun centered mostly in Vine Street, north of Fourth, and it was subdivided into two aspects — at least, for several years. Up to 1880, there was more entertainment north of the Canal than south of it, though of a simpler, more decorous character than that rapidly appearing south of the Rhine. Up there you found the old type of beer garden or wine and beer hall with the "Family Entrance," where Mamma and the children as well as Papa might go without reproach or fear of being annoyed by misbehavior; where Tyrolean warblers in native costume or even zither players were appreciated. There of an evening, slow-moving, good-natured crowds thronged the street, some patronizing the peddler who bawled, "Wiener-würst! Warm sind sie noch, meine Herrschaften!", some taking the children to see the *Kasperle-theater* (Punch and Judy show).

There were a few shoddy places up there, even in the '70's, where a three- or four-piece "orchestra" supplied the music, where the beer was poor and raddled girls were on hand to dance with the men and run up their bar bill. But there were also some like the big Loewengarten, whose Mr. Loewe had fed so many soldiers during the war free of charge, whose walls were hung with portraits of the great German composers, where a reporter dropped in one day in 1870 and heard a 50-piece orchestra ably and lovingly rendering the overture to *Tannhäuser*. Hildebrand's, Schuler's, Peters's, Kissel's, Wielert's, these were others of the older, more dignified sort which, as the '80's and '90's drew on, were slowly outmoded by the newer, more raucous type, though Wielert's outlasted them all.

In the '80's, Vine Street and immediate vicinity in the Rhineland were changing; non-Germans and Americanized Germans were introducing a new note. As the *Gazette* said, "An infusion of fast young Americanism into the inchoate character of a young German born in America produces a great change." Schwenberger's, Strang's, Hammerle's, the Apollo Garden, swam with the current. In 1875 Wielert's had had Michael Brand's "Cincinnati Orchestra Reed Band" for a long engagement. There must be music, if only a piano and violin, in every German drinking and eating place, though not for dancing. You did that in a dance hall.

You could get good German food at the better places—sausages, sauerbraten, hasenpfeffer, ham noodles, potato pancakes, excellent steaks in American style, if you preferred them, and most popular of all, *Wiener schnitzel*, which is, being interpreted, veal cutlets. It is said that if you sat down at a table in Wielert's and said nothing, didn't even look at a menu, a waiter would presently, as a matter of routine, bring you veal cutlets, German-fried potatoes, rye bread and beer. "If they had anything else," says an old-timer, "I didn't know it." But they did; much else.

South of the Canal, there was more hard liquor sold, though the Atlantic Garden, biggest of them all, just north of Sixth Street, dispensed nothing but beer, and oceans of that. The Atlantic began as a decent family place, but as pugilists, jockeys, gamblers, politicians and cheap show-folk invaded it, it became shoddy and rather tough. It had a stage where tawdry chorus girls pranced between boxing and wrestling bouts, an apparently interminable bar, a feebly tinkling fountain, and in its earlier, quieter days a small, bored deer standing or lying in a tiny grass-plot in front. Occasionally in the '90's you might see there Hy Holtgrewe, the local Hercules, who had a saloon of his own on the way to the baseball park and did amazing feats of weight-lifting. Now and then he headed a little variety company, barnstorming through the small midwestern cities, and winding up every performance by lifting a platform with the whole company of eight or ten persons standing on it.

The oceans were well represented in that neighborhood — the Pacific Garden where the Palace Hotel stands now, and the Arctic Garden which later became the Florentine Hotel diagonally across the street. The street below the Canal also became noted for good food — at Jack Frey's with the semicircular bar, at Johnny Williams's Chophouse, at Harff & Kramer's, where you selected your steak raw and saw it broiled over charcoal, at long-bearded Andy Gilligan's (favorite rendezvous of some of the greatest actors), always swathed in green on St. Patrick's Day, even the proprietor's huge beard sometimes bound near the chin with a bow of green ribbon, so that it looked like a whisk-broom. Others, on and off the street were The Stag, Foucar's, The Mecca, Bodemer's, Dave Billigheimer's, "with the largest mirror in the world," Pat Russel's Detroit Exchange, near the Court House, where a prominent jurist, scion of a prominent family, slightly elevated, once rode his horse into the bar, ordered a drink and drank it in the saddle.

Certain New York actor-playboys declared that Gotham's Broadway, Vine, and Market Street in San Francisco were the only streets in America worth knowing. Towards the end of the century, Vine was one long street of entertainment, eating and drinking—hotels, restaurants, saloons, beer gardens, theaters (legitimate to burlesque), concert halls, brothels, assignation houses, shooting galleries, bowling alleys, gambling places. The theaters were pushing northward across the Rhine before 1880. From midafternoon to dawn the street was thronged with the most heterogeneous of crowds — "rich man, poor man, beggar man, thief" — prominent business and professional men, seeking rich viands, drink and nepenthe, actors and actresses, artists, sports, touts, pimps, women of not at all doubtful reputation, confidence men, pickpockets, panhandlers, grifters, pitchmen . . . Bagdad, say you? Why, in Bagdad, many of these characters wouldn't have been permitted at large!

Sunday observance had very nearly ended by 1880. The Grand Opera House, the city's most dignified theater, began giving Sunday performances in the spring of 1877, and so did Hubert Heuck, up at Thirteenth and Vine. The Ministers' Association protested, but in vain. Ice cream vendors, pushing a freezer on wheels and blowing a fish-horn, next began to be heard on Sunday afternoons; then the barber shops began staying open until noon, cigar and fruit stands all day, and finally saloons and some merchants in certain quarters of the city followed their example. The old Sabbath was apparently extinct, though there were notable exceptions such as that supplied by Stewart Shillito, who took over the management of the big John Shillito store as his father aged, and who so disapproved even of Sunday window-shopping that the show-window shades were drawn to the bottom every Saturday night.

Virtue also appeared to be tottering. The Flesh and the Devil had only to grease the right palms, and then set their own standards. Indecency was becoming rife in the latter '70's. The Belle (sic) Union, in the old Adelphi Theatre, was given a routine raid now and then, with no apparent effect on its conduct. The manager of the Crystal Palace, on Elm Street, had had a sentence of $100 and thirty days suspended over him for so long in '79 that he wouldn't have felt natural without it, but you could not discover any effect on his show. It was proven by the record that the license of ex-police-chief Snelbaker's Vine Street Opera House had been revoked, but that did not halt its operation. Ten other places were pointed out as operating without a license, and they continued doing so. At the Gem Varieties, a tiny house on Longworth Street, said a reporter, "the indecencies were mainly confined to a man, a female impersonator." Between shows, "this person descended among the audience, and strangely enough, appeared to have some admirers among the men present."

A hearing upon immoral performances continued for several weeks in December-January, 1879-80. A prominent Cincinnati politician admitted that at two or three places, women sometimes appeared nude, but he didn't consider these immoral shows. Would he take his family to see them? he was asked. Certainly! (But no one could find that he ever did.) The hearing closed with an injunction granted against the police commissioners, preventing their closing the places under fire. So the "notorious Haymarket Varieties" on Sixth Street, went right on being notorious as did others. But Snelbaker had evidently been frightened a little, for he cleaned up his show to some extent. A reporter who visited it found nothing worse than a chorus of 14 "beauties," in white bodices and leg-tights, who danced between renditions of "A Flower from My Angel Mother's Grave," "See that My Grave is Kept Green" and "Always Keep a Smile for Mother."

Mother and the grave were invaluable properties for whatever preceded Tin Pan Alley.

Remembering the quality of the city water of that period, there are those who maintain that Cincinnati was drinking more beer in those days than water. Certainly there was far more portliness seen then than now. For decades, the standard price of beer had been three cents a glass, and some places sold two for a nickel. After the war there appeared a tendency in some bars to raise the price to five cents, causing hot argument and meetings of saloonkeepers in 1877, at which much oratory was spilled. At five cents, declared opponents of the raise, there was three cents profit in every mug. True, retorted the opposing faction, if you paid only $8 a barrel for your beer; but tastes were improving now, demanding good beer, which cost $9 and $10 per barrel. Furthermore, the growth of the free lunch fad made it imperative that the price be raised. So the five-cent price soon came to stay, and then some hosts who sold the cheaper beer began giving 21 for a dollar, serving a "wienie" with every drink, or enlarging the size of their glasses. Schuler's is said to have used steins 10 inches tall. In the '90's came the "Chicago bowl," a huge goblet with a burly leg like that of an old-fashioned square piano. Saloon signs advertised "Largest Glass of Beer in the City for a Nickel," and if you could believe the accompanying picture, it must have held from one to two gallons.

Hundreds of grocery stores had dingy bars in the rear, and near-by families "rushed the growler" (later "can"), i. e., sent a child with a tin bucket for a nickel's or dime's worth of beer two or three times a day or more. Factory workmen who brought their lunch and didn't want to wash up and change clothes at noon had their personal growlers marked with their names — Joe, Ed, Louis, Heinie, Sig — and when the noon whistle blew, a youth would hurry to the nearest saloon and bring as many as could be strung on a long, notched pole over his shoulder, completing the Oriental picture by shuffling back in a sort of gliding Chinese walk, to avoid spillage.

The *Gazette* first noticed the free lunch in 1856, saying that the tables were set between 9 and 11 each forenoon for everyone who bought a drink. "A habit of eating between breakfast and dinner is thus acquired, and doubtless many thus acquire intemperate habits." In earlier decades, and at some places always, it was a cold snack, varying somewhat, but in general including sliced bologna, liverwurst, blutwurst, dried beef, boiled ham, sometimes roast beef, dried herring, sardines, pigs' feet, hard-boiled eggs, pickles, rye bread and crackers — all things that could be picked up with the fingers, though at some spiffy places, a fork might be found on the table. And on one glass of beer you could eat as much as you liked. The hours of setting the table were gradually extended, too. For some poor fellows, it was a charity; it was their only square meal of the day. But even rich men did not disdain it. There was a saloon almost opposite John Hauck's brewery, one which sold no beer but Hauck's; and old John himself used to go over there every day, buy a nickel schooner of suds and eat a man's size — a big man's size — of the free lunch, with probably never a thought of the humor of the situation, though it did occur, wryly, to the saloon keeper.

Men who rushed the can from home or a near-by shop sometimes took some of the lunch out with them, which was considered pretty brazen; it was supposed to be eaten on the premises. But seldom was the coup complained of. How the bars could dispense such spreads seems a mystery in today's welter of fantastic prices, but of course costs of food, liquors and overhead were unbelievably low then; many drinks more costly than beer were sold, and the bars counted on many customers buying not one but several drinks.

But as competition heightened, the collation became more elaborate. Elmer Arnold remembers that at 9:00 A.M. his father would set out a lunch which included soup, sauerkraut, spare ribs, pigtails, hasen-pfeffer, boiled eggs, potato pancakes, fried green tomatoes in season and of course, rye bread. Cutlery was needed for that banquet. At some swagger downtown places like Foucar's or The Mecca, side by side on Walnut Street below Fountain Square, you might get roast goose, duck-and-dumplings — but if we carry this much further, our whole veracious chronicle will be discredited by present-day readers.

In the end, the free lunch was gradually superseded by the noon plate lunch — ten cents if you bought a drink, too — consisting of soup — which you yourself ladled out at will — meat and two vegetables.

Foucar's, by the way, a place of *ton* and good conversation, was a favorite *point de reunion* for Duveneck, Farny, the Rettigs and other famous artists of the time, some of whose canvases hung on its walls. The Mecca was a slicker, coarser, but no less opulent resort, for it was a politicians' hangout, with George B. Cox and allies frequently whispering over a table in a rear room; in fact, the Boss's headquarters were on the floor above.

Heuck took over the old Coliseum on Vine Street and opened it in '82 as Heuck's, with a seating capacity of 2,300 and perhaps the finest interior in the city. It was almost immediately the scene, on November 30th, of a tragedy which shook the composure of Cincinnati. Frank I. Frayne, melodramatic actor-marksman, who always did some fancy shooting in his plays, was appearing in *Si Slocum*, in which he, the hero, was forced by the villian to shoot an apple off his wife's head while standing with his back to her, aiming the rifle over his shoulder by looking into a small mirror. He had done the trick hundreds of times, but this time his control slipped a hair's breadth, and his leading lady, Anna von Behrens, crumpled to the stage with a bullet through her brain.

Heuck's always had a portion of the parquet reserved for Covington patrons; you could buy the tickets at the Covington street car office. Often in an aisle seat William Goebel might be seen, the Covington politician who was assassinated in Frankfort in 1899, presumably by a mountain Republican, when the Democrats were claiming that he had been elected to the Governorship of Kentucky. Heuck's old theatre at Thirteenth and Vine became a variety and burlesque house called the People's Theatre. The time was rich in dramatic entertainment. The Grand and Heuck's competed for the greatest stars and companies on the road, with circus-man John Robinson's Theatre at Ninth and Plum getting some of them, varying his offerings at times with some such number as a lecture by Edith O'Gorman, the Escaped Nun. During one week, Sara Bernhardt and Fanny Davenport, America's top-ranking actress of the day, were in town simultaneously, both playing *Camille* and *Frou-Frou*, inviting comparisons, not always to the advantage of Bernhardt. Later came the opera *La Mascotte* to both Heuck's and Robinson's at once. At times the advertising was furiously antagonistic, and the lie was passed.

A Covington boy named John H. Havlin was the youthful manager of Wood's Theatre (mostly melodrama) at that time. In '83 he built Havlin's Theatre, a decade later the Walnut, and then was likewise lessee of both the Grand and the Pike. With a partner, Stair, he controlled a chain of theaters in other cities and produced many melodramas.

Cincinnati produced some noted stage figures of its own. A child named Sarah Frances Frost, born in England in 1865, was brought to America and became known as Fanny Brough when her father changed his name. They settled in Cincinnati when Fanny was eight, and her mother ran a small hotel, while her father worked at shoemaking — sometimes. Fanny, a voracious reader, was eleven when she heard of a children's light opera company planned by Colonel Robert E. J. Miles of the Grand, whose home still stands in Kennedy Heights. She found a place with this company and showed talent, but within a year the tour was over, and nothing else offered. Her father had died, her mother had married a baker, and Fanny was now set to packing crackers in boxes, but hated it. An effort to teach her telegraphy failed, and then she began mending theatrical costumes, which brought her into the atmosphere she loved. Colonel Miles and his sister-in-law, Ada Dow, actress and coach, had kept an eye on her, and she was frequently at the Miles home, often rehearsing dramatic parts in the barn. At 17 she was sent out in *Rip van Winkle*, playing one of Rip's children, and at 18 she toured in support of Josephine Reilly, a Cincinnati aspirant to histrionic fame. Then Ada Dow took her to New York for the final training necessary to make a real star of her, and there the young lady chose her stage name, combining Julia — one of her favorite parts in *The Hunchback* — with the surname of Christopher Marlowe, to become Julia Marlowe, a name writ high on glory's page.

There was another, a pretty Irish girl named Delia O'Callahan, born on Third Street, down in the West End, and a pupil at the old St. Patrick's School, at Third and Mill, who in later years was a gorgeous leading lady in musical comedy known as Trixie Friganza. Coming forward a few lustrums, an Avondale girl named Theodosia Goodman, a clothing manufacturer's daughter, once recited "Sheridan's Ride" so dramatically in an amateur show in an attic that some of her hearers predicted a professional future for her. And sure enough, she became Theda Bara, the famous siren of the silent films. Somewhat lesser lights were a newsboy named Charlie Murray and a cross-eyed waiter in a Vine Street resort, Ben Turpin, who, in the course of time, shone in the one-reel comedies of early movie days.

Blending perfectly with Vine Street were John R. McLean and his newspaper, a far cry from the *Enquirer* of today. The sort of news that his journal often purveyed and the frankness with which it used the names of local men when it was sure of its ground are seen in an item of 1882, " . . . But little is known of the ante-cedents of the dead woman. She made her appearance in this city a couple of years ago and took up her abode with Len Thompson. She afterwards took a room with Mrs. Ireland on George Street, and about two weeks ago became an inmate of Miss Bennett's establishment. Once in a confidential mood, she informed Miss Bennett that she was of an excellent family, and that her father was once the Mayor of Baltimore. . . ."

McLean was a friend of the pee-pul, of course, and did much muckraking — of business and the Republicans; such as revealing the fact that the Gas Company directors got their coal free at the stockholders' expense, and exposing the pharmacists. A reporter took a doctor's prescription, ascertained the wholesale cost of the ingredients and packaging, then had it filled at seven drug stores, and the paper, naming and locating each store, showed that they made profits on it ranging from 1,150 to 1,900 per cent. The *Enquirer* had a daily columnist in 1881-82 whose nom de plume was "Hartshorn," who affected vernacular and who also did some frank excoriation: "I was talkin to William Epply to-day on 'Change. He's got a nice business. It's you buy oats, you sell oats, you go long and you get short — damned short — and for this privilege you pay my little fat friend $25. He has nothing up but himself and his impudence, and always looks slick."

For nearly 40 years the *Enquirer* was the voice of McLean the politician yearning for office — Governor, Senator, anything big — which he never won. He, too, always looked slick. In his first decade he often stood in front of the *Enquirer* building, stylishly dressed and good-looking, except for slightly too prominent eyes, handing out quarters to recognizable bums, half-dollars to men whom he sized up as more worthy, and dollars to needy men with families. Had it not been for the disaster of '84 he might have realized his ambitions.

One of the smartest of newspaper men, his paper catered to the well-known human fondness for salacity, without going so far as to get itself barred from the mails. Its "Personal" column was an agency for assignation. The column from New York signed by "Durandal" was, for indelicacy, compared by Will Irwin in later years with London's "Pink 'Un" and the boulevard sheets of Paris. McLean in his later years carried in a vest pocket a little notebook, containing names of people whom he particularly disliked, and which he called his "Son-of-a-bitch Book." He liked James Albert Green, who became editor of the *Times-Star*, and more than once tried to lure him to the *Enquirer* payroll. Meeting Green on the street, he would sometimes draw out his notebook, select a name and say, "I wish you would give So-and-so hell." Mr. Green and his owner might not have been inclined to agree with this extraordinary request, but if they were, they chose their own occasion for the job.

No newspaper in existence so dramatized its news, none devised such gaudy headlines as McLean's. When a steamer foundered off San Francisco's Golden Gate in 1901 with a considerable loss of life, the *Enquirer* flung across two columns a series of headlines, topped with:

FROM GOLDEN GATES OF EARTH

TO THE PEARLY GATES ON HIGH

These Startled Souls were Hurried at the Dawning of the Day

It should be reemphasized that the *Enquirer* of today, clean, dignified and not offensively partisan, to paraphrase Grover Cleveland, in no way resembles the *Enquirer* operated by McLean; in fact, is as different from it as the staid, commercial Vine Street of today is from the rowdy Vine Street of yesterday. With the death of McLean, a reform began, and in the course of time was completed.

The disaster year, 1884, saw the beginning of the end of the political power of McLean and Campbell. The year's calamities began in mid-February with the greatest flood in the city's history, surpassing the one of the previous year, which itself had been a record-breaker. The wholesale district in the lower Basin was inundated, some buildings several stories deep. The industrial Mill Creek Valley was flooded for miles and 5,000 families were homeless. Railroads from all directions were tied up. Those coming in through the Mill Creek vale made connection with the city by canal from suburbs north of the hills which were still above water. The Bee Line's advertising was typical; "Passenger boats will leave corner Canal and Main Streets as follows. . . ." The railroads that followed the river bank westward were in sad case, the Big Four being completely helpless. The Ohio & Mississippi ran a yawl ferry, a fearsome journey, across mile-wide Mill Creek for a while, but as the water rose higher, its trains could come no farther east than Aurora, Indiana, and it ran a steamboat from there.

Punishment for crime had become unfashionable by the beginning of '84. With Lawyer Tom Campbell and others of his ilk on the side of burglars, robbers and murderers, the State of Ohio, as the law laughingly calls the public, hadn't a chance. The immunity of murderers was particularly galling. Homicide was a commonplace. At the Ides of March, 23 murderers, including two wife-killers, one by butcher-knife, the other by axe, were in the county jail, many others were out on bond, and we know not how many more were at liberty, acquitted and free of taint. Among those in durance were a youth of 18 named William Berner and a mulatto who had brutally murdered their employer with a hammer because they had seen his roll of money. When Berner was brought to trial, the jury returned a verdict of manslaughter, which the presiding judge, Matthews, called "a damned outrage." He imposed the maximum sentence, twenty years; he could do no more.

On the evening of the next day, Friday, March 28th, there was a mass meeting at Music Hall with, it is said, 8,000 indignant citizens inside the building and thousands more outside. Temperate speeches, deploring the low state of justice were made by a dozen prominent men and resolutions were adopted, denouncing the Berner jury and demanding better juries and better methods of selecting them. The size of the crowd made those on the rostrum uneasy, and just before dismissal, the people were asked to return quietly to their homes. But as the throng poured into the street, a cry was raised, "To the jail! Let's hang Berner!" to which the thoughtless responded as iron filings to a magnet. Then followed nearly 50 hours of mad rioting by the worst of the city's elements, all the more senseless because the sheriff, fearing such trouble, had started Berner towards Columbus before they arrived. When they finally battered their way into the jail and beat down the sheriff and his deputies, they found Berner gone and ignored the other murderers cowering in their cells. A night of battling against an increasing force of police and militia was followed by a day of repeated attacks against the jail and adjacent Court House, for no apparent reason but a thwarted desire for vengeance. The resistance of the soldiers fanned the fury of the mob, and they began raiding hardware stores and pawnshops and smashing show-windows to get firearms. At the gun store of Powell & Clement on Main Street (and still there) they met unexpected opposition — William Powell and three armed clerks, who repulsed them with a loss of three dead and several wounded. Late that night a small group succeeded in entering the Court House, piled furniture in an office, poured kerosene over it and set it afire. Outside, the mob blocked the way of the Fire Department, and the building was destroyed. A day of skirmishing ended with one last, desperate assault upon a greatly augmented guard of militia, which was repulsed with heavy losses, and by midnight, the madness was over. The human toll had been 56 known dead — and probably many more unknown — and at least 300 injured. The property damage was heavy. The bitterest irony of the event lay in the fact that Berner, the cause of all the trouble, died peacefully in his bed many years afterward.

The Republicans, gleeful over this appalling affair, asked the Federal court for a supervisor and deputy sheriffs for the elections of that autumn. Young William H. Taft was appointed supervisor, and they put over many frauds on him, but the Republicans won the Governorship, though in the process Cincinnati lost one of its good citizens. This was Judge George Hoadly, a thoroughbred whose inwrought quality had recently been revealed when, as one of the bondsmen for a defaulter (there were no bonding companies then), he promptly asked for the amount of his obligation, and finding it to be $50,000, raised the cash, though not without difficulty, and paid it within a few days, to the astonishment of the community, who had expected that a smart lawyer would fight off payment. He had been Democratic Governor of the State for two years, but was defeated by another Cincinnatian, Joseph B. Foraker. The Democrats did their best for him. Among other devices, Mike Mullen, ward stalwart, had 152 Negroes — innately Republican, of course — arrested on fantastic charges during the night before election and held, mostly in the basement of the Hammond Street police station, until after the polls closed, but all in vain. But Judge Hoadly was so disgusted by the prevailing political rottenness that he went to New York in the following year, and there practiced law until his death. At a farewell dinner tendered him by the local Democrats, he gave his hosts some body blows. "Hamilton County Democrats," said he, "have learned the trick of changing the ballots after they have been put in the box. . . . Never again, never again allow an honorable man to contemplate, as I had to do with shame, my name accredited with 926 votes I never received in the Fourth Ward, and my friend, Judge Foraker, in Precinct A, Fourth Ward, accredited with 46 only, when he certainly received nearly 200."

His words were unheeded, of course. The city election of '85 was as crooked as ever, but this time, even with the aid of chicanery, the McLean-Campbell machine could not overcome the ill effect of the riots, and was beaten. A "reform" Mayor, Amor

Smith, was elected, and good citizens thought they saw the roseate glow of a millennium on the horizon. But it was not so to be. They still did not comprehend the caliber of that young fellow, George Cox, who was increasing his power in the Republican Party, and by 1888 was practically in control of the city. He and his two sa-traps, Rud K. Hynicka and August ("Garry") Herrmann, ran Cincinnati like a conquered province for 30 years, while the help-less minority who comprehended the implications of such rule, had to await the education of the majority by the bludgeon of experience.

Meanwhile, through all these years of political guile, a board of public-spirited citizens had brought one of Cincinnati's greatest achievements to fulfilment. In earlier, less corrupt years, an eminent judge, Alphonso Taft, had appointed five worthy men, Philip Heidelbach, Miles Greenwood, E. A. Ferguson, R. M. Bishop (afterwards Governor) and William Hooper as trustees to superintend the construction of the city's own railroad, the Cincinnati Southern. The $10,000,000 bond issue having been voted, the next hurdle was that of obtaining a charter from the State of Kentucky, then in the grip of the Louisville & Nashville Railroad. To do this, General Basil W. Duke, attorney and lobby-ist for the L. & N., had to be lured away from Frankfort by strategy, and the bill high-pressured through the Legislature in his absence.

For nine years the track crept southward from Cincinnati and northward from Chattanooga, costing more than expected, as always, the trustees nagged at and slandered by partisan critics. When in 1878 another bond issue of $2,000,000 was requested, opposition to spending more money on it was voiced; some thought it should be diverted to Knoxville to shorten the line, some wanted to halt the work altogether. A referendum on the bond issue was lost by a narrow margin, which was charged to L. & N. Railroad machination; but after much propaganda, another referendum a few months later was successful. Big banks did not take over whole bond issues then as they do now, and there was not enough loose change in Cincinnati or vicinity to buy those bonds, so Trustee William Hooper, vice-president of the First

National Bank, was sent to England to market them. He went straight to Baring Brothers, who had financed so many American projects, but found them loaded with Confederate bonds, which the United States Government had refused to recognize. They said that until those bonds, which they considered a liability of the United States, were paid for, they would back no more American projects; and they read the embarrassed Mr. Hooper quite a lecture on the obligations and the integrity of governments. He found the same attitude in Holland, and those bonds, which drew 7 per cent interest, went begging, and had to be sold in driblets at heavy discounts. For that reason, there was no great enthusiasm in Cincinnati as the completion of the road drew near. The words, "white elephant" were heard. Some business men wanted it sold at once, and one was heard to say that he was sorry it had ever been begun.

When the last rail was laid on December 9th, 1879, the road had cost $20,000,000. The first trains were operated in February, and the great celebration took place March 17th, 1880. Four special trains brought 1,500 guests from Chattanooga and beyond, including General Joe Wheeler, the Governor of Georgia and other notables. The Governors of Ohio and Kentucky were present, and Cincinnati editors believed that the "Bloody chasm" of the Civil War had been bridged. The grand banquet at Music Hall was ably handled by Balthasar Roth, of the St. Nicholas Hotel, who created incredible things in cake and sugar — a Temple of Liberty five feet tall, and a reproduction of High Bridge over a green sugar river, with steamboat and a chocolate train crossing the bridge.

The city had difficulty in handling the road for some time, and there was relief when it was leased to the Cincinnati, New Orleans & Texas Pacific Company. But hard upon this came the revelation that the secretary of the corporation had fraudulently issued and sold $400,000 in unauthorized stock. This brought on receiverships and years of litigation, with the courts finally ruling that the company was responsible for the loss. Nevertheless, when the Cox ring proposed to sell the railroad at an absurd figure in 1896, the people turned down the deal, though by only a few hundred votes. But try to get it away from them today!

CHAPTER XV

Keeping Ahead of the Joneses

A BRILLIANT ERA for society opened with the return of peace in 1865. Despite the loss of Southern trade, the war had been a profitable one for many Cincinnati industries and businesses, and with the exception of the lamented Lytle, had not ravaged the most prominent families too greatly. Now one could once more contemplate with a clear conscience the enjoyment of one's earnings and the boosting of one's favorite charities. For established society, however, there was a fly in the ointment — a parcel of Newriches who had made pots of money from war contracts — munitions, provisions, cordage—and were now feeling their oats— throwing money about, giving wine parties, racing with each other behind blooded high-steppers out Spring Grove Avenue and the Colerain Pike, to the peril of all other persons on those thoroughfares. It was evident that they must be reckoned with by society in the near future.

Sybaritism, though it now rose to greater heights, was not entirely new in Cincinnati. For example, even during the war the Cincinnati, Hamilton & Dayton Railroad had begun attaching a special car to a morning and evening local train for the exclusive use of the commuters of plutocratic Glendale, shortening the business day for some of those entrepreneurs. Of course there was no bar in this car and no whist; imaginations hadn't yet gone that far. The C. H. & D. , by the way, always an innovator, first placed Bibles in its cars for the use of passengers in 1870.

Money was cheap. Younger generations today will scarcely credit it, but you could carry gold around with you at will, and in many pockets it rubbed cheeks with plebeian silver and copper. On a winter day — probably at shivery dusk, when visibility was low and alcoholic calescence was required to ward off the cold — a gentleman buying a paper from a newsboy gave him by mistake two golden quarter-eagles instead of pennies, and was presently notified through a classified ad that he might recover them by calling at the drug store of Suire, Eckstein & Company. For the rest of the story we search the press in vain. Nor do we know whether this incident played any part in the founding of a news-boys' home in 1866, with an $800 piano in the lounge. But we do know that charities, educational institutions and the arts received much encouragement in this golden age, and that new landmarks were reared, including the beloved Fountain which is Cincinnati's heart of hearts; that the Chamber of Commerce in 1866 bought $2,200 worth of food for the people of North Georgia and Ala-bama, brought near starvation by the war, and with that, became the agency through which many thousands of dollars more were channelled southward, not only from local churches and individ-uals, but from all over Ohio.

The people who had it seemed to cherish money no more than if it had been branch-water. In the years 1868-72 one reads of ahead-of-season fruits bringing unheard of prices; tomatoes, $12 a bushel; peaches from tropical isles $2 and $3 a peck; California grapes 50 cents a pound; Alabama strawberries, $1 a quart; new potatoes, $1 a peck. The demand for Paris gowns and Bond Street clothing reached a new peak, though even in 1880, many substan-tial businessmen still wore James Means's $3 shoes; good shoes, too. When Colonel Creed of Arkansas donated a bale of cotton to the yellow fever sufferers of Memphis in 1873, it was sent from city to city and auctioned, the cash going to Memphis, though the buyer never took the cotton. St. Louis paid only $90 for the bale, Cincin-nati $2,000. Cincinnati made no boast of this; just mentioned the figures.

The building of stately mansions had long since begun, too; first, downtown, then in Walnut Hills, Mount Auburn, Clifton, Glendale and Avondale. But now a new *Saturnia Regna* trumpeted its pride in dozens more, some of them more magnificent than ever; dwellings such as Cincinnati never saw before and will never see again. To begin with the most superb group of all, Clifton, on the heights overlooking Cumminsville and the Mill Creek Valley, was to Cincinnati what Lake Forest later became to Chicago. And nowhere else in this city which preserves more of its old manorial glory than any other in the North do so many of those proud castles of the Fortunati of its giddy years still survive. An awe-stricken writer in the *St. Louis Post-Dispatch* called it "Cincinnati's world-renowned suburb."

It was built on the 600-acre estate of Charles S. Clarkson, bought by him in the 1820's and later subdivided. Flamen Ball, Eastern-born lawyer, bought one of the lots, promoted a village, incorporated it as Clifton in 1850 and was its Mayor for twenty years. The home of William Resor, the city's first stove-founder, built in 1843, is still inhabited by Resors — their greenhouse used to be famous for its orchids — and those of Alexander Lewis, (1835), Robert Buchanan, great industrialist, William F. Hulbert, Rufus King, H. W. Darby and the one occupied for nearly 80 years by the Neave family are dignified surviving relics of ante-bellum days.

Robert B. Bowler, the dry-goods magnate and Henry Probasco (hardware), bought tracts in the '50's, and Mr. Bowler erected and furnished his mansion, "Mount Storm," in time to entertain the Prince of Wales there in 1860. On his 66-acre plot, he not only had one of the finest homes in America, but ten greenhouses, with many exotic plants, trees from all over both hemispheres and a swan lake. Water for these came from a reservoir covered by a domed, Corinthian-columned structure, voluptuously christened the Temple of Love, designed by a former Austrian Imperial gardener. In this demesne the Bowlers entertained not only the British Royal heir but Emperor Dom Pedro of Brazil. After Mr. Bowler's death, his family sold the property to the city and it became Mount Storm Park.

Henry Probasco came from Connecticut in his teens to work in Tyler Davidson's hardware store, at twenty married his employer's sister, became a partner in the business and grew enormously rich. He bought two large plots of hill and dale in Clifton, and there, after the war, erected "Oakwood," considered by some the most magnificent mansion in the suburb, though externally the great stone pile, 120 by 70 feet in size, with a round tower, reminded some observers of a penal institution. In the great hall running through it, was a grand staircase of rare woods with a carven balustrade, on which Benn Pitman toiled for three years. The library — ceiling painted by Francis Pedretti, another local celebrity — contained incunabula, Aldines, Elzevirs, rare editions of Shakespeare, including the First Folio, the Dante of 1481, the Elephant Folio of Audubon's *Birds* and other treasures. Sculptures, paintings and mosaics were all over the house, and scattered through the hills and ravines were more statuary, fountains and urns. The great gates were "considered a chef d'oeuvre of Cincinnati wrought iron work." This is one of the palaces that remain, though smaller houses have been built in its subdivided grounds.

It was in 1867 that George K. Schoenberger, ironmaster, built on a 40-acre tract his third home in Cincinnati, "Scarlet Oaks"; a startling, stone-turreted mixture of Romanesque and French Gothic, 126 by 70 feet in dimensions (which seems to have become practically a standard size for top-level houses), its great drawing room alone measuring 26 by 40 feet. It is now the Bethesda Home for the Aged. Also in '67, on a 25-acre tract, Wiliam C. Neff, pork-packer, built his English castle, of almost the same dimensions as Schoenberger's. Swiss wood carvers labored three years on the interior, and gossip had it that Mr. Neff spent so much on the place that he couldn't afford to live in it, for it wasn't long until he sold it to the Sisters of the Sacred Heart, whose convent it is yet. Near by is the vast and still velvety lawn and sprawling house with one of the tallest towers in Clifton, built by Winthrop B. Smith and long occupied by Obed J. Wilson, civic benefactor, poet and bibliophile; lovingly christened "Sweet Home" by its builder, though not the sort of thing that John Howard Payne had in mind when he wrote, "Be it ever so humble." It is now occupied by Mrs. Julia Jergens Joslin, a cosmetic heiress.

In current descriptions of these luxurious edifices erected just after the Civil War, we are frequently reminded that the windows are of "French style plate glass, only two panes to a window."

Among others, Charles M. Buchanan had 44 acres, J. B. Bennett 41 acres, J. Lloyd Wayne 35 acres, William Resor 30. John W.

Ellis, Flamen Ball, C. W. Deland, James Andrews, William H. Schoenberger, S. C. Foster, Howell Gano, Gazzam Gano, William Gibson, B. B. Whiteman, A. C. Neave, the wealthy steamboat magnate Thomas Sherlock and Robert Hosea managed to get along on mere pocket-handkerchiefs of 6 to 22 acres.

Here, too, still remain the messuages of other rich men, built a little later than those named; of George W. McAlpin, founder of one of the big department stores, whose "Sunflower Place" was so named because of its carved stone sunflowers; Frank Wiborg, printing ink colossus; Sir Alfred Goshorn, the city's only knight, who, upon his return from a trip to the East, is said to have introduced Cincinnati to the eating of pie with a fork, and Alexander McDonald, Scottish-born banker and oil operator, whose "Dalray" still broods among the ornamental iron seats and fauna of its great lawn.

Such were the Barons of Clifton in the late decades of America's great century. All are gone, and most of their homes are either razed or owned by strangers or converted to other uses. With the exception of the Resor house, none is now occupied by descendants of the original owners. But Clifton is still a beautiful, well-groomed old lady, and as late as 1914 another massive and costly mansion, well qualified to stand with some of the older ones, was erected on her richest street.

Others not millionaires also came to Clifton; Francis Pedretti, the artist, whose descendants still occupy his home, Richard Smith, brilliant editor of the *Gazette*, in whose honor the adjacent street was whimsically christened Dixmyth, and John Uri Lloyd, noted chemist, who left a large business to his heirs, but who unfortunately in spare moments wrote novels which convinced the critics that he should have stuck to chemistry. And finally, there was Clifton's great disaster, its black sheep, Boss George B. Cox, who, without a by-your-leave, barged in with his beautiful wife and built a big stone house with comparatively simple exterior, though a lady who once visited it said, "I never saw such atrocious brass beds nor such gaudy colors; but some of the art work was exquisite." Of course the Coxes never "belonged" in Clifton; but as he was a Republican and so were most of his rich neighbors, they had to make the best of the situation, with such false, feeble smiles as they could muster when they met him, while their wives stonily ignored Mrs. Cox, pretending that she did not exist.

The homes of the barons could be made greatly useful in behalf of charity and good works. Mr. Bowler's whole estate, conservatories and all, was thrown open on a June afternoon and evening in 1872 for a *fete champetre* for the benefit of Calvary Church. Professor Currier's band supplied "dulcet strains," and special omnibuses ran from Fourth and Main Streets at half-hour intervals from 3:30 to 10:00 P.M. There were ample arrangements for taking care of the horses of those who drove, and eagerness to see the stately pleasure-dome of this modern Kubla Khan by those who would never otherwise have the opportunity brought large crowds, to the great comfort of Calvary Church.

One big, pinnacled stone chateau in Clifton is a reminder of Truman B. Handy, grandson of Chief-Justice John Marshall, lumber and grain speculator, builder of theaters and dwellings, who was unlucky with his homes. He remodelled a big dwelling on Mount Auburn, but before he could move in, he went broke and lost it. But he was a buoyant fellow; he conjured up another modest fortune, built another and more imposing mansion, also on Mount Auburn, and just as artisans were beginning to cut his initials, T B H, into stones over the entrance, bankruptcy overtook him again and he lost that property, too, with its beautifully wood-carved interior, one large group representing, ironically enough for Handy, "Peace, Plenty and Harmony." Later the house became the home of John Shillito, merchant prince. It is now the main building of the Conservatory of Music.

Many of the city's old mansions long outlive their families. The home of James Key, for example, founder of Mount Auburn, built in 1819, is still there, though the Keys are gone. This was called Key's Hill until, it is said, an English lady visitor in 1837 re-christened it, incongruously enough, in honor of Goldsmith's "loveliest village of the plain." In the years following the Civil War, it wasn't taking off its hat, even to Clifton. A visitor called Auburn Avenue, its main street, "Cincinnati's Fifth Avenue." Broker Albert Netter's parlors were panelled in pink and light-blue silk, which proves that Mount Auburn had some things that Clifton hadn't. And along Auburn Avenue, the residence of Anthony H. Hinkle (and after him, of A. Howard Hinkle, cotillion leader and President of the American Book Company) had an 85-foot tower; A. D. Bullock's tower was only 64 feet tall, but he had a 9-acre lawn, a dining room 26 feet long, which, plus the conservatory, made a 38-foot room, and had six bedrooms on the third floor; while Jason Evans's house had an 88-foot front; the house, remember, not the lot.

The only one of Mount Auburn's great houses still occupied by its original family is that of the Reakirts, a century old, where Llewellyn B. Reakirt was born in 1868 and died just the other day at 81. Two other Hinkle homes remain, but others occupy them now. Old houses seem to have eternal youth in Mount Auburn. Here, but occupied by alien names, are the homes of Justice Stanley Matthews, of Judge Alphonso Taft, where President William H. was born, of Captain George S. Stone, utilities executive and horse-lover, who named a colt Maud S., in honor of his daughter, saw her set a trotting record in '85 and sold her for a very pretty sum to William H. Vanderbilt; of Gorham A. Worth, built in 1819, manager of the local branch of the United States Bank; of William Corry, last Mayor of the town of Cincinnati, 1815 to 1819; of Matthew Addy, the Canadian who built the big foundry and pipe works at Addyston, down the river; of General E. F. Noyes, Governor of Ohio and Ambassador to France; of Eugene Zimmerman, oil and railroad tycoon from New Orleans, whose daughter became a British Duchess; and finally, of that rare genius William Howard Doane, industrialist, inventor, benefactor of education and composer of some of the best-loved hymns in church history. Who has not heard, "Tell Me the Old, Old Story," "Take the Name of Jesus With You" or "Jesus is Mine"? His hundreds of tunes were fitted to the words of many authors, the greatest number being those of his cousin, the blind poet, Fanny J. Crosby, who wrote "Rescue the Perishing," "Jesus, Keep Me Near the Cross," "Savior, More than Life to Me," "Safe in the Arms of Jesus" and scores of others. He was president of J. A. Fay & Company, held many patents on woodworking machinery and waged a long series of patent battles with the rival Thomas P. Egan Company, which finally ended in a merger of the two. Bars of music were painted or carved on the walls of his home here and there. It had a tower, too, in which was his study; and when neighbors saw a light up there in the evening, they said to each other, "Doane's writing another hymn." He had a remarkable collection of some 700 old musical instruments now in the Art Museum, and a fine library, including original manuscripts of some famous composers, which the Public Library has inherited.

Grandeur was not all clotted in select groups. Somewhat isolated in Westwood, Louis Werk, son of Michael Werk, soap king and viniculturist, reared for himself a majestic abode, said to have taken the Chateau of Blois as its pattern, though one suspects that the draughtsman used a slightly different scale. It had as an appurtenance, wine vaults three stories deep.

In Avondale, every estate of more than an acre extent had a more or less — not infrequently less — appropriate name, including one three-acre bower which the owners modestly called "Paradise." In the 1870's one of the chief social centers of Avondale was the home of Colonel John Kennett — it is there yet — who came of a prominent Russian family, but who was a cavalry commander in our Civil War. Here are two houses built in 1830, one long the home of William H. Doepke, department store owner, the other built by William Y. Gholson, a Virginian who became an eminent Ohio jurist, and whose quaint old farmhouse, little changed, is still occupied by a descendant. Here, too, is the big stone grange of B. H. Kroger, the wizard who expanded one little Cincinnati grocery shop into a chain of 6,000 stores. The city wanted to annex Avondale as early as 1870; but the suburb snapped back that the gang only wanted some additional revenue to pour into its Southern Railway adventure, and it stayed outside until 1896, when it came into the family peaceably. With annexation, a movement of Jews from the Basin to Avondale began, and now it is largely Jewish; a handsome suburb with costly homes and stately temples and synagogues, and much greenery.

Walnut Hills had some gorgeous homes, too, such as old Nicholas Longworth's vast, inchoate, high-towered "Rookwood," so cunningly sequestered on a little by-lane that you will have difficulty in finding it, and so named because the crows which roosted and cawed by thousands in the near-by woods sounded more refined as "rooks." In the general vicinity were the manors of old Nicholas's son, Joseph, those of William Hooper and L. B. Harrison, who progressed from a wholesale grocery partnership to control of the First National Bank, of Judge George Hoadly, with acres of hill and vale, of W. W. Scarborough, R. R. Springer, donor of the Music Hall, Timothy Walker, William S. Groesbeck, Washington McLean and Sidney Maxwell — likewise of Melville E. Ingalls, fledgling Yankee lawyer who came west in his twenties — growing a beard en route to conceal his youth — in behalf of Eastern stockholders of the Indianapolis & Cincinnati Railroad, and who built it into the great Big Four system.

Walnut Hills prided itself on ancient quality rather than ostentation — as witness the magisterial Grandin Road. Not as many fine old houses survive there as in some other even smaller areas. Among the few are Dr. Lyman Beecher's big, plain brick residence, at the site of old Lane Seminary, the homes of tragedian James E. Murdoch and Governor and Senator Joseph B. Foraker, of Caleb Shipley, machine tool manufacturer, and oldest of all, "The Pines," one of Cincinnati's picket-posts of culture, a big brick house some of whose materials came from England, built on an eleven-acre estate in 1827 by a soured bachelor Scotsman named John Hey, who walled it in. After him, it passed through the hands of two owners, including John Kilgour, who took down the wall and gave the dwelling a mansard roof, though otherwise it remains unchanged, with the stable and brick servants' quarters partly enclosing a courtyard. It has long been occupied by former Governor Myers Y. Cooper and his wife, Martha Kinney Cooper, patron of literature, chief founder of the Ohioana Library and of an annual award by which authors are enabled to write worthy books about Ohio.

Queen City plutocrats, it appeared, preferred to spend their housing money at home, for in 1871 it was remarked that Murray Shipley was the only Cincinnatian who owned a cottage at Newport.

There was a disadvantage in having society scattered over hills and Basin. At a time when even downtown streets were nothing to boast of, the roads in the hills were mostly pretty bad. When there were winter parties, rain, snow or sleet and cold winds often caused great suffering. Carriages might be mired or break down; and as a party, say on East Walnut Hills, began to wane around midnight or 2:00 A.M. on a stormy night, male guests from Clifton or Mount Auburn or downtown who had to be on the job early next morning shuddered as they thought of the long, cold ride home. But by the hospitable custom of those days — it was like Tidewater Virginia or the Blue Grass — the ladies, and such of the men as chose, could stay overnight on these inclement occasions, with the party-givers and/or some of the neighbors. Great mansions like those of the Probascos or Schoenbergers or Neffs could take care of a fairly large party under their own roofs, and had huge stables, too; but if there was an overflow, other guests who lived near by took in some of the distant dwellers. Ladies at times even found themselves marooned over another day and night.

An amusing development of this far-flung condition of society was Herman Newman's Pony Express, which may have begun in the late '70's, but certainly flourished in the early '80's, before use of the telephone became general. Quick communication and same-day reply were often necessary, especially between swains at their business or clubs in the Basin and Phyllises on the hilltops. Newman bought some fleet Western ponies and engaged two young lightweight riders, who were traditionally ready to deliver billet-doux at any time, day or night, and who rode at top speed when out of reach of the Basin police.

The youthful Telephone Company, by the way, was announcing a great reduction in rates in 1882. You could now get a "Special Wire" — that is, a private phone — for $6 a month; three on a circuit each paid $4.16 a month, five on a circuit only $3.33 a month, and dirt cheap at that, when you consider the all-day fun you could have in listening to the social and business affairs of four other families.

War, which had broken down other inhibitions, caused some slight weakening of the social barriers, too, especially for young men who had been in the army, and who exhibited rather more of a tendency to contract mesalliances. But society still upheld its canons as best it could. "One's hired girl from the country might marry wealthy," recalls a lady, "but of course she wouldn't be invited to one's parties. Our butcher's sister — a really beautiful girl — married a wealthy brewer whose family was on our calling list, but Bertha never was." Of course that brewer's family, too, had had to go through a couple of generations of purgatory to reach the stratosphere.

More attention was now being paid to genealogy — and there are not a few people in Cincinnati, it may be remarked, who may rightfully sit under the shade of tall family trees. There is one lady of German extraction whose grandfathers — great and great-great — were distant cousins of the poet Goethe, their two lines threading back to a common ancestor in the 15th Century. In one of those histories of the city, which are half or more than half biography, you may peruse the complete genealogical story of Mr. David Banning, 35 pages of it, interspersed with 17 colored plates of coats of arms of noble famiiles and 11 pictures of the *Mayflower*, its voyagers, etc. Only two examples, these. And we don't know whether it still persists, but in the '70's there was a chapter of the Anneke Jans heirs in Cincinnati, who used to meet from time to time to discuss ways and means of regaining that large chunk of lower Manhattan which slipped away from their ancestress — was it two or three centuries ago?

Household comfort and smoothness of operation increased steadily. More sewers were built, more plumbing installed. The discovery of Pennsylvania petroleum quickly substituted kerosene — coal oil, it was called — for lard oil in lamps. Of course the well-to-do used gas for illumination, but ordinary folk and even the rich who were not on a gas main had to get along with coal oil. It was a quick agency for starting the morning kitchen fire, but the numerous resulting flame-ups and explosions gave the newspaper wits a vast store of material for hired-girl-coal-oil-can jokes. It was characteristic of Cincinnati that when corncobs soaked in kerosene began to be sold for kindling, the trade name for the article was "Promethean Fire." Soon gasoline was invented, was first used in lamps and found still more dangerous. Then the gasoline kitchen stove was devised and became indispensable.

But as years passed, ladies of ton *had* to revise downward some of their luxurious habits. They had kept up after the war the long-standing practice of demanding curb service from the dry-goods stores. On a fair day a carriage would halt in front of Shillito's, Pogue's, McAlpin's, LeBoutillier's or Hopkins's, perhaps announced by the coachman with a crack of his whip. A watchful functionary would run out, ascertain in a general way the lady's wants, return and send out a clerk who would obtain fuller specifications, then run back and bring out bolts of cloth or ribbon, lace, stockings, spools of thread. If soot showered on the goods while it was in the open, that was an Act of God, not the lady's fault. The whole thing, however, began to look rather too burdensome to the merchants, and they finally discontinued it. There was indignation among the ladies, and the whole fabric of Society tottered for a moment, but survived.

Society was greatly shocked in November, 1874, by the tragic death of the old French dancing master, M. Charles Ernst, already mentioned, who had been a prominent figure for thirty years. He and his second wife, who had long done most of the hard work in his school, were boarding in the spring of 1874 at Mrs. Cadwalader's on East Fourth Street. Madame Ernst was taken ill, and her husband nonchalantly packed his bag and went to New York "on business" for three or four weeks. Returning, he heard from her physician that she could not recover. Terribly upset, apparently unable to endure the discomposure caused by her condition, he packed again and breezed off to Europe, leaving her only $30 in cash, though he had more than $6,000 in bank. When her money was exhausted, she was taken to Good Samaritan Hospital, where she died before her husband had reached Europe. Returning in November, he went to the hospital to hear the details of her illness, and Sister Anthony, the head of the institution, denounced him so scathingly that he went back to his room and shot himself. The good Sister, in the light of events, hadn't expected her rebuke to be taken so seriously.

Rev. Moncure D. Conway, the noted Unitarian minister and a

theater-goer himself, spoke out in behalf of the stage in 1860. But it was long before any other preacher would permit himself to be seen at a play, and meanwhile, shows like *The Black Crook*, which played an engagement here in 1867, did the theater no good with the clergy. But it certainly did pack the house. People came from miles around to see it; there was a large excursion run from Toledo, at $5 for the round trip. A Blue Grass lady, who went to Cincinnati with her brother for the occasion, wrote to a cousin, "Little did I think, that I would ever sit in a theatre and see almost naked women parade the stage. If John had not been with me, I think I would have sunk through the floor from embarrassment." But the "almost naked" women were in bodices and tights, and today would be considered quite decorously dressed.

The theater was being liberalized, but when a New York producer asked for an opportunity to bring a version of the Passion Play, "reverently presented," to Cincinnati, it was opposed by everybody — pulpit, press and public — and did not come. And when the girls of Wesleyan College proposed to stage *Little Women*, and had even rehearsed it at considerable length, the Board of Trustees, by resolution, "expresses its disapprobation of the projected performance" and "respectfully requests that it be discontinued"; probably not only because some of the girls were going to appear in male attire, but because the Methodist Church was not yet reconciled to the theater.

To its other aids to luxurious living, Cincinnati now began to add theater trains. The Little Miami began running such a train to outlying towns in 1876, and the advertising of Fanny Davenport in *Pique* announced that it would be held until after her performance. The C.H. & D. promptly installed a train, leaving at 11:30, but complaint was made that a street car supposed to leave Fourth and Vine at 11 to connect with it was so slow that it frequently missed it and suburbanites had to put up at a hotel for the night. Often as the car slowly neared the station, with only a minute to spare, passengers leaped from it and sprinted, either to swing aboard just as the train was pulling out or to miss it entirely. A letter writer to the *Gazette* said that he had found, however, that "The simple act of slipping a 25-cent piece into the hands of the driver and conductor stimulated the horses to such activity that the train was reached in good time."

Railroads were neighborly and thoughtful then. When Mr. and Mrs. Thomas A. Yeatman celebrated their golden wedding anniversary at their home at Riverside, five or six miles down the river, in 1877, the Ohio & Mississippi ran a special train there and back for the guests, charging only the regular fare.

With none of the antithinking boons which science has since conferred upon us — no automobiles, movies, radio or television, each reaccelerating the trend back towards illiteracy — people in those days enjoyed simpler pleasure and knew how to entertain themselves. The papers said that a circus couldn't have aroused half the interest that the eclipse of the sun on August 7th, 1869, did. Crowds were on all the hilltops. Hawkers on the streets and many kinds of stores sold colored or smoked spectacles. A man on the Post Office steps with several dozen pairs — blue, green, purple — sold out in ten minutes. Loaded excursion trains were run to the line of greatest obscuration; the Kentucky Central ran seven trains to Lexington. The steamer *General Lytle* took 300 more persons to Westport, Kentucky. *The Gazette* next day ran seven columns on the subject, including telegrams from all over the country.

Travel was enjoyed, too. The biggest and finest steamboats ran excursions to New Orleans, with richly-furnished tables, orchestras for nightly dancing and long stopovers at many places, giving the tourists not only opportunities to see the sights, but to visit friends in the vicinity.

There was much participation in entertainment, especially if with a cultural aim. Clubs like the Literary, Burns and Hawthorne met, listened to carefully prepared papers, and debated them. At least four clubs — the Shakespeare, Davenport, Clio and French — were presenting plays. The Davenport, which included many society men and women, played the best and largest theaters; it had Pike's engaged for 25 weekly performances in the winter of '78-9. The Cincinnati Chess Club played daily in a room at the Mercantile Library, while the Cuvier Club studied natural history and built up a fine collection of mounted birds and animals in their quarters. Music kept thousands more busy and happy, singing and playing, solo or in small orchestras.

In 1875, some of the churches began to have a lot of fun with old-fashioned spelling matches. The interest spread, and presently the Y.M.C.A. staged a match in Pike's Opera House, with some of the most important people in town taking part and being mowed down on such words as "cassinette" and "phthistic." The theater was packed to the roof and enthusiasm was so great that the affair had to be repeated. Then churches and clubs took up the idea, and soon a "Spelling Match Waltz" was brought out by John Church. It was a minor event, indeed, in Cincinnati, which didn't inspire a new waltz.

Ladies were becoming more interested in athletics, though necessarily in a demure manner, because of the hampering effect of corsets and bustles. They were toying with billiards as early as 1860; it is difficult to imagine how it could be played in hoop-skirts and the corsets then worn. Croquet was introduced in the 1860's, and on the vast hilltop lawns, it was considered a lively ex-ercise. Roller skating appeared in 1867, and being inexpensive, became a sport for the masses. Lawn tennis was introduced about 1876, though it had to be played without bustles, and became well-nigh the exclusive property of the elite. Archery became a fad in '78 and many clubs were formed, having about equal numbers of men and women members. The women did not find bare legs necessary in archery then, as they do now. The hazards of the sport were emphasized at a meeting of the Sagittarium, when an attendant who gathered up the arrows was wounded back of the ear by a young woman, though he was so far out of the line of fire that no one dreamed of his being in danger. It was explained that "Miss McCall of course feels very bad over the accident and regrets it exceedingly. She has been out of practice lately."

The men's sports became more strenuous. Some society men had played cricket, but when baseball replaced cricket, it became too professional for the elite. Boating became a fad, and around 1880 the Cincinnati Boat Club had many prominent names among its members. At its floating clubhouse, just above the public land-ing (and not quite far enough from the mouth of the Eggleston

Avenue sewer), were not only many handsome private skiffs but an eight-oared barge, seating 24, which was used for water parties. In fine weather it was a favorite diversion for a mixed party to leave the boathouse about 5:00 P.M., row five or six miles up the river — with some unavoidable perspiration on the part of the oarsmen — to a pleasant strand or dingle, eat a picnic supper and row back by moonlight or starlight. "Anything more informal or delightful than these parties can scarcely be imagined."

The bicycle — the old, tall bone-breaker with the 54-inch fore-wheel, at first called a velocipede — appeared in the latter '60's, and was such a curiosity that even one of them leaning against a building drew a crowd. But Cincinnati's topography did not supply an ideal playground for this machine, as cracked noses and collar-bones and plastered countenances amply testified. You couldn't climb a hill on one of them, and to try coasting down a slope was simply suicide. Nevertheless, there were cycle clubs, and men were seen in knee pants and long stockings. The real popularity of the bicycle did not arise until 1890, when the present "safety" type was invented, and it became in the vernacular, a "bike" or a "wheel."

Meanwhile, following the lead of the East, the horse became one of the favorite playthings. Even as early as 1874, there were 300 livery stables in Cincinnati. The tallyho coach appeared in the latter '70's, and young men and some young women were seen driving dog-carts with two horses tandem. A dozen other new vehicles were devised. A few years before, when some odd sort of rig appeared on the streets, small boys would hoot and throw stones at it. Now there were so many that they were regarded with lack-lustre eye. Latonia, back of Covington, outshone Chester Park as a race track, and became one of the country's most noted. On race days, long processions of landaus, coaches and what not, laden with sports, many in top hats a la Ascot or Epsom (though seldom white), flung dust over Covington folk as they sped to and from Latonia. In 1881 a news item said, "Burnet Woods is resplendent with barouches, dog-carts, T-carts, mail phaetons, Victorias, village carts, tilburys, landaus and in fact, every style imaginable."

The tallyho became such a rage in the '80's that there were two maintained by livery stables for hire to *hoi polloi*. Four horses, of course, and a horn as long as your arm to warn lesser folk of the Approach, though it wasn't supposed to be blown on city streets. The Countess de Chambrun, however, tells of a Clifton dowager who kept a small, liveried groom with a horn on her carriage, and at every corner would order, "Toot, Herman, toot!" There were several privately-owned tallyhos, and some famous drivers of them, such as Frank Gaff, Colonel Watson, Clifford and Frank Perin, Herry Kinney and Arthur Stern. One clever whip, on a dare, drove his coach through the grape-arbor of the Country Club. A favorite diversion during the Latonia meet was to gather at the St. Nicholas for lunch, then drive to the races; which brings us to a discussion of that famous hostelry.

Balthasar Roth, a Bavarian, emigrated first to New Orleans, then came to Cincinnati in 1852. A skilled chef, he and a partner ran the St. Charles restaurant for several years; then took over the big Carlisle residence at Fourth and Race Streets and remodelled it into the St. Nicholas Hotel, which, in the course of years, grew to larger size — though it was never a big hotel — and became the very swankiest in Cincinnati. A reporter saw strawberries four inches in circumference being carried into it one spring day. Presidents and titled foreigners stopped there, in a dignified elegance masked by a severely plain exterior. On a wall of the "gentlemen's sitting room," supposedly not entered by ladies, was a painting 7 by 12 feet in size — a plate on the frame said it was "by Derouge, 1811" — of Pauline Bonaparte, sister of the first Napoleon, who had a fancy — much to the annoyance of her Imperial brother — of being painted in a state of nature. This picture portrayed her in her favorite costume, seated on a sofa facing the beholder. It had been brought to America by the elder Nicholas Longworth, and after his death may have been considered too indelicate for the family gallery, so was sold to Mr. Roth.

The St. Nicholas had no large ballroom, so the old Burnet continued through the '70's to be the scene of the biggest and most gorgeous balls. Also, it remained, as it had been for decades, the Gretna Green for eloping couples from Kentucky. Elopers never thought of stopping anywhere else. It came to be the custom of the house to provide each happy pair with a fine wedding dinner, free. The young reporter, James A. Green, already mentioned, had an amicable arrangement with the hotel clerk, whereby he was promptly notified of the arrival of a runaway couple. One day such a message reached him, he rushed to the hotel, met the pair, procured a clergyman to perform the ceremony for them, acted as a witness and was invited to share the dinner with them. At table the bride became confidential, and under promise of secrecy, revealed to him that her parents had no objection to the match; in fact, her mother had helped her to prepare for the flight. Why, then, did they elope? Because, she explained, they knew everybody for miles around, they'd have had to stage a church wedding, with an expensive dress for her, and invite a mob of guests to the church and the infair — why, it might have cost them a hundred dollars, and her family just couldn't afford it! It was cheaper to elope.

"Do you suppose many of these Kentucky elopements are for the same reason?" asked the reporter.

"Mr. Green," she replied, frankly, "I guess most of 'em are."

Clubs of Harvard and Yale alumni had appeared, and in the early '70's the members of the Harvard Club contemplated, with what modesty they could muster, the fact that 23 of their number had, as undergraduates, been members of ultra-ultra-exclusive Hasty Pudding.

The first business and professional men's club of the modern sort, with its own quarters, was the Queen City Club, organized in 1876, and at once under suspicion by the clergy as intended to be a place for gambling and drinking. But the club rules permitted card-playing only in designated rooms, and in the club rules, "attention is called to Section 3, Article XII of the Constitution, prohibiting games of any kind being played for money." Also there might be no game of any sort — cards, billiards, pool or even "authors," we presume, between Saturday midnight and the opening hour, Monday morning. The Queen City Club today is as up to date as any in the city, but like all Cincinnati, it still has its old-fashioned glints; you may go there almost any day around noon and find a group of men, mostly elderly, playing dominoes.

By '76, when this club was organized, there was a little more leisure permissible; men, both old and young, might be found relaxing there for an hour or two without coming under suspicion of being loafers or ne'er-do-wells. Business, however, was still of prime importance. When old John Shillito was ready to move his dry-goods store from Fourth Street to the big new building at Race, Seventh and George (that disreputable street's name of course eventually had to be changed to Shillito Place), he didn't feel equal to the task himself, so his son Stewart — named in honor of his friend A. T. Stewart, the great New York merchant — who was in the last months of his Senior year at Yale, had to come home and superintend the job.

Society news in the papers began to appear as brief items other than descriptions of weddings, as early as 1873. For many years it was scanty and amateurish, often palpably a "handout" to the reporter by one of the *nouveau riche*. When the daughter of a West Court Street citizen was about to marry at St. Paul's Methodist Church in 1877, an item promised that "The wedding is to be on a scale of grandeur unsurpassed in the long line of similar events in that church." Of another imminent wedding and reception, it was plainly stated that "Money will not be spared to make the occasion a brilliant one." There was no reporter assigned to large parties — and he or she might not have been admitted if there had been — and some slapdash news resulted: "Mrs. Hurst's silver wedding in Clifton was a great success. Everybody was there"; and that was the sum total of an item of 1878.

The *Enquirer*, being the people's paper, mixed items about the very *creme de la creme* with bits like these, "Mr. Thomas Flaherty, foreman of the Little Miami Railroad shops, will give a birthday party to his friends on the 20th"; and "Mr. E. S. Myers, for the past three years bookkeeper for Messrs. Cochran, Lyman & Co., has resigned his position with them to accept a similar one with the Oxley Stave Company, Eastern Avenue." The first whole column of society notes appeared in the *Gazette* in the spring of

'78, headed "Social and Personal," and included the information that "Mrs. President Hayes," who had been visiting friends in Cincinnati, had returned to Washington. Later she and the President returned and were elaborately entertained by the W. S. Groesbecks, which, Mr. Groesbeck being a Democrat, was considered a broad-minded gesture, especially in view of the scandal of '76; but it proved that even the Democrats of Cincinnati did not hold Mr. Hayes responsible for that. Another fine gesture was that of Mrs. Washington McLean, mother of John R., in giving a lavish entertainment for the Republican ex-President Grant and Mrs. Grant. Here we begin to find women's gowns described in full, as in later years — Mrs. McLean appearing in "a superb costume of old gold and black satin. . . . Heavy fringes draped the tabliers and were lost in the floating drapery at the back," etc., etc.

Because of the scattered condition of social groups, calling days had to be informally agreed upon. Until 1892 they were Monday, Walnut Hills; Tuesday, East End, Pike Street, etc.; Wednesday, Dayton Street and extreme West End; Thursday, West End and Avondale; Friday, Clifton and Mount Auburn. The code decreed that you must call on a hostess within two weeks after being a guest at a dinner or party, and if you were calling in behalf of your whole family, you turned up a corner of your card. (Eventually, stationers began supplying them with the corner neatly turned by machinery.) When a lady went calling, it was not necessary for her to get out of the carriage; the coachman could hand her card in at the door. This practice led to a classic *contretemps*, which was long a topic of conversation. A lady took a visiting niece with her on a designated day for calling in Covington. The niece seized a pack of what she thought were her aunt's cards and handed them to the Negro coachman, who couldn't read. It was a drizzly day, and the ladies nowhere got out of the carriage. A week later a friend saw Mrs. J. in Cincinnati and said, "Everybody's talking about you in Covington."

"Why?" asked the startled lady.

"Those cards you left the other day were all those of dead people," was the appalling reply. The niece had gotten a packet of the cards of Mrs. J.'s friends who had passed away, and which she had been saving for sentimental reasons, some of them for years. Mrs. J.'s coachman had been recognized, and perhaps he had even mentioned her name at some doors.

Society in summer was flocking to Eastern haunts of fashion, "Saratoga and the seaside," gibed the *Commercial* in '79, "where Madame dresses and Mademoiselle coquets and Monsieur, My Lord, pays the bills to the verge of bankruptcy." For stay-at-homes, amusement promoters had done the best they could, and middle-class and even wealthy folk enjoyed the results. At the head of every inclined plane was an amusement park, with hotel or pavilion, where the best of food and drink might be had, music, fireworks and dancing. The Prices had a large picnic ground topping their plane, with refreshment stand (no alcoholic drinks, of course) and when the river went on a tear, advertised it as the best place from which to view the flood. The Bellevue House atop the Clifton Incline, had 12 acres of park around it and a 500-foot esplanade. "On sunlit Eden's blossomy plateau," the Highland House, the biggest of all, three stories high and covering nearly an acre of ground, was steam-heated so that it might be used the year 'round, and was surrounded by a vast platform, where the band concerts were held, and summer dancing might be enjoyed. All these places employed the best orchestras to be had in Cincinnati (and they were good), the Highland House at times trumping them all by having the best in America, Theodore Thomas's. Sitting there with a cold drink at his elbow, while the orchestra played a Waldteufel waltz, while sunset painted the West and faded, and the lights of three cities came out twinkling in the valley, a poet of the '80's was reminded of Vienna and the Danube:

> "Ja, die 'schöne, blaue Donau'
> Wirkt mit ihren Harmonien
> Gleich bezaubernd auf die Massen
> Hier im Highland Haus, wie Wien."

And others of the populace thought that Cincinnati had at last attained the ultimate in year-'round happiness.

Cincinnati let no other city do anything that she wouldn't at least attempt. A Mardi Gras was staged in 1876, but here the city fell below its usual high standard of success. An annual dog show was started by some of the best people, but there was a mishap in '77 too terrible even to be mentioned afterward — the prize for Best Dog in Show Exhibited by a Lady was found to have been won by a madame from George Street.

In September, '83, pageantry was again attempted, this time by the so-called Order of Cincinnatus, in imitation of St. Louis's Veiled Prophet gala. Cincinnatus, Rex and Momus, with queens, were the star characters. On the opening morning, a procession of steamboats went downstream to meet Rex, who was supposed to have risen from the river somewhere beyond Si Keck's stink factory, and who was awaiting them on the *City of Madison*, one of the biggest boats. "The narrow stream still dignified with the name of river" (*Enquirer*) was low, and the channel therefore so constricted that maneuvering was difficult. In fact, the *Vint Shinkle*, with Cincinnatus himself on board, collided with another boat, to the considerable damage of both and of some expensive costumes, to say nothing of scaring a lot of people half to death. They finally got back to the city, and then ensued the grand parade, with elaborate and gorgeous floats. The Burnet House was the Royal Palace and the Gibson was the Palace of Momus, being lavishly decorated for the occasion, while complaint was made that the Burnet didn't decorate at all. Cincinnatus, just a plain Roman farmer, had no palace. Entertainments alternated among these two hotels and the Highland House, where the grand ball, ending the frolic, was given. Evening dress was rigidly specified here, and many who came attired otherwise were turned away. One of these was a man from Indianapolis, an invited guest, who appeared in a frock ("Prince Albert") coat, but was turned down. His wife was considered to be properly dressed, but she wouldn't go in without him, and they returned sadly to Indianapolis.

Current music gives a hint of a change in attitude towards life, intangible but real, which was taking place most noticeably in those two decades. The old, gloomy type of religion which acquired such sway in America had a definite influence on some of the people's songs. True, there were plenty of merry and romantic ones extant, but a large segment of church folk considered them too frivolous, even meretricious. They thought it more in keeping with the real solemnity of life to wail

> "The long, long, weary day
> Has passed in tears away,
> And by my window still I'm weeping"

and so forth, or one of those two Cincinnati good sellers of around 1870, "Mother, Let the Angels In" and "Whisper Softly, Mother's Dying." The last one of this type that we have seen was a lugubrious thing of 1878, "Georgie, Raise Me from my Pillow," though by that time, such dirges were going out of fashion, and a light romanticism was more noticeable among the song writers. Oldsters still alive remember some of the pretty popular songs of the 1880's — "Sweet Violets," "White Wings," "My Nelly's Blue Eyes" — and the tenors who sang them in the halls.

By 1880 society was at a new high pitch of gayety. "Nothing satisfies it long," declared an editor. To meet its demands for novelty, there had been devised "kettle-drums, polo, drags, routs, germans, lawn tennis, archery, teas at ten o'clock in the morning, and dinners at eight o'clock at night." Gossips said that infidelity (domestic) was on the increase. The *Enquirer* on July 15th, '83 remarked, "Elopements with brothers-in-law are becoming a familiar feature of the season's eccentricities." No names were mentioned, and we are left in a delightful dither of surmise.

New York, of all places, had the nerve to accuse Cincinnati of being purse-proud. A New York paper asserted that on the stone pillars on each side of the carriage gate of a wealthy man's estate on Walnut Hills a dollar mark stood out in bold relief, naked and shameless. Of all imaginable unblushing boasts, all gauche flauntings of one's own success, the New Yorker thought this example stood alone and unrivaled. After some startled embarrassment, an explanation came from Cincinnati. The property, it was said, was that of John Simpkinson, a prosperous boot and shoe manufacturer. In all innocence, he had had his initials, J. S., entwined in a monogram, cut on the entrance pillars in high relief; but some scampish joker with a mallet and cold chisel had stolen thither by night and removed the tail of the J, leaving a palpable dollar sign.

Cincinnati entertained royalty twice in the 1870's — the Grand Duke Alexis of Russia and Dom Pedro de Alcantara, Emperor of Brazil. By the time King Albert of Belgium and his Queen arrived, years later, most of the great mansions of which we have spoken in this chapter had passed from the hands of their original owners, and the Belgian royalty were guests in a newer manor, that of Levi A. Ault, printing ink manufacturer, and Mrs. Ault.

Long before that time, the inevitable had happened; wealthy Cincinnati girls were being sought in marriage by European titles. There were a number of such noble alliances. Judge J. B. Stallo gave the hands of two of his daughters to princes; and there were others. Even a Covington girl, Miss Kleiner, married a prince. Of French counts there were several, such as de Choiseul, who married Mary Hooper; d'Adhemer, whose bride was Josephine Cromwell and the Vicomte de Chambrun, who married Clara Longworth, great-granddaughter of the first Nicholas. Helena Zimmerman's husband, the Duke of Manchester, was considered by many to be the biggest catch of all. One need not list them all, nor tell all that one knows or hears. There was one heiress, said to be a hard swearer herself, whose noble son later came to Cincinnati on a visit, and left an unpaid hotel bill. "But she wasn't from one of our old families, my dear. She was an outsider."

The temperance crusade of the 1870's struck a hard blow at the old custom of New Year calling, for many hostesses now abjured alcohol, replacing it with coffee, which alienated men whose chief pleasure in calling had been the wines. Only at the more elegant resorts on George and Longworth Streets, which were giving "fashionable" New Year at homes before 1880 could men who were so disposed get all the drinks the market afforded. But in good society the custom died slowly. The *Enquirer* for December 31st, 1880, printed fourteen columns of names of hostesses in the city and suburbs who would keep open house on the morrow. Calling then did not begin until around noon or one o'clock; and what with cold cuts, salads, cakes, ices, coffee, tea (occasionally) and more or less alcoholic fluids, the caller need eat no meal but breakfast at home on that day.

There had always been year-ends when some families, because of bereavements or illness — but for no other reason, so sacred was the obligation considered — did not receive on New Year's Day. They drew down the shades and retired to the rear or upper levels of the house, leaving an "elegant" basket hanging to the front doorknob or standing in the vestibule to receive the cards of those who chose to leave them. "Nearly all baskets were decorated with bright ribbons, and some, a few, where a death had recently occurred in the family, were tied with black ribbons"; which must have struck the observer as being in faultless taste.

The migration to the suburbs and the decrease in the liquor supply operated not only to decrease the old custom noticeably but to bring about changes in technic. There was a growing practice among the young men who could afford it, of driving about in carriages, and sending their cards in by the coachman, especially if it was a house where nothing but coffee and chocolate were apt to be on tap. By 1880 some were sending their cards by mail or a District Telegraph messenger boy.

"Calling on New Year's Day was not general," remarked the *Enquirer* on January 8, 1882. Most gentlemen either remained at home or spent a portion of the day at the clubs. The number of ladies who made elaborate preparations for receiving were very few. "Many persons spent the day out of town, and the hotels looked vacant and empty. There was perhaps less drinking than on any previous New Year's Day for many years."

But as late as 1885, in the most select surviving district of the Basin, including Pike, East Fourth and Fifth streets and lower Broadway, the old pleasant custom continued, though much altered. The reception hours had shrunk, but the menu had swollen beyond recognition. For example, to be bidden to call between 5 and 7:00 P.M. at 131 Broadway, the home of Alfred Gaither, a big-bodied Marylander who loved good eating, was to be invited to a banquet. The house was always lavishly decorated with red ribbons, red candles, holly, bittersweet and partridge berries and General Jacqueminot roses. Huge chafing dishes held hot terrapin a la Maryland, broiled quail, escalloped oysters and oysters fried in olive oil. Then there were ham, chicken, turkey in aspic, lobster, sweetbreads, salads, fruit cake and cookies; while for knick-knackery there were preserves, jams, jellies, pickles, nuts, candies, big bowls of all the fresh fruit the market afforded. Whitecapped Negro technicians carved and served the meats, and maids went about with silver baskets of tiny, hot buttered biscuits. On side tables you found your coffee, tea, chocolate, hot punch or egg-nog dipped from a venerable three-legged bowl, a Virginian colonial relic.[1]

The continued migration to the suburbs, leaving the old Basin mansions the lonely, pathetic things they are today, the lack of good suburban streets and roads in the pre-motor age, these finally put an end to the custom once so formal and pleasant and lavishly hospitable. By or before 1900 it may be said to have almost completely passed away.

[1] Interview with Dr. Alfred Gaither, Jr., by Marie Dickore, *Cincinnati Times-Star*, Jan. 1, 1942.

CHAPTER XVI

The Ardor of Creation

BELIEF in Cincinnati's taste may totter slightly when one reads a news item of 1850 to the effect that Mrs. William Shires "has molded a splendid shell and pebble monument," which was acquired by Philip Grandin, Esq., who placed it on the lawn in front of his residence, where, surmised a reporter, it would no doubt attract thousands of sight-seers. And in 1874, "all Cincinnati" was flocking to see a head, "Dreaming Iolanthe," sculptured in butter by a Mrs. Brooks who, only last summer, "was living on a farm nine miles from Helena, Arkansas, in a destitute, almost uncivilized country." She sold butter of her own production in town, and being "a lady of culture and native taste," she modelled it in beautiful forms until she presently blossomed as a real sculptor.

There is always a public for this sort of thing; there probably was in Athens in the time of Phidias. Cincinnati had the better sort of art, too, and acquired fame thereby. It produced some great painting and sculpture, including the most talked-of statue in nineteenth-century America—whether it was the best was another question — and it certainly operated the most artistic pottery in the Western Hemisphere. There was a time, too, when amateur artistic fervor — not dilettantism; it was too earnest for that — raged among its women, resulting in the production of much mediocre work, it is true, but also some that was really admirable.

Cincinnati began to be introduced to the arts when it was just a frontier fort. George Jacob Beck, a scout who came with Anthony Wayne's army in 1792, was a painter with a dominant interest in landscapes, though none of his work remains. His widow opened a school for young ladies in 1812, as did one Edwin B. Smith, who taught portraiture, landscape, miniature painting and ornament. Artisans and artists in other lines are heard of — silversmiths, potters, cabinet makers, sculptors in wood. By 1820

Allen & Bridges were making ornamental wall paper, besides importing the fine French product, picturing landscapes and classical scenes. Short-lived museums of the arts began to appear and disappear.

An early example of taste in Cincinnati is the home of the immigrant, Martin Baum, who had likewise come with Wayne's army, who rapidly made a fortune here and built this mansion on Pike Street in or near 1820. A fine example of eighteenth-century Americanized Georgian, gracefully simple externally, beautiful within, attributed — though without authority — to Benjamin Latrobe, it remains today as the Taft Museum, one of Cincinnati's treasures.

In 1826-27 sculpture was introduced, with the advent of Frederick Eckstein, a German of fine artistic background, who is believed to have given the city's noted sculptor, Hiram Powers, some lessons, though Powers is also reported to have studied under another, almost legendary figure, Gottfried Schadow, a victim of the cholera epidemic of 1832. Powers was a Vermonter, one of nine children of a poor blacksmith-farmer who settled near Cincinnati and soon died of "the ager." Young Hiram found a job with a clockmaker, which experience was useful to him in his later designing of mechanical gadgetries for the Western Museum. Early in his stay at Cincinnati, he saw a bust of Washington, the first sculpture he had ever encountered, which enthralled him and determined his career. After some lessons from Eckstein or Schadow or both, he found a subject, a little girl who gave him two sittings daily, and made a bust of her. Meanwhile, he was working for Dorfeuille, of the Western Museum, designing and actuating Hell and Heaven, with their population, but probably doing some more serious work as well. It is likely that he was the creator of the group mentioned in a card to the public in 1829, which explained that "the contemplated exhibition of the likeness of General Jackson will be delayed for a short time, in order to place in the attitude of crowning him with laurels, a most splendid wax figure of the

BEAUTY OF CINCINNATI

which is now in preparation, and which as a specimen of the Fine Arts, will at least equal the best productions of the Italian artists."

Powers attracted the attention of Nicholas Longworth, who, as riches came to him, conceived the noble desire to cultivate talent as well as grapes. He offered to send Powers to Europe for study, but the young man's ambition at that time extended no further than the thought of making busts of American statesmen. So Mr. Longworth sent him to Washington, where he produced busts of Jackson, Marshall, Webster, Calhoun, Van Buren and John Quincy Adams. There was some criticism of him because he did not prettify them enough, actually showing Van Buren *au naturel*, with one eyebrow higher than the other. Now his vision expanded, he longed for bigger things, and another patron, wealthy General Preston of South Carolina, sent him to Italy in 1837.

Another farm boy, Shobal V. Clevenger, began doing plain stone-cutting at 15 on the locks of the Ohio Canal. Drifting down to Cincinnati, he saw a "female figure" on a market-house (those classical Cincinnatians! Could it have been Ceres? — or Persephone?) and his vision of *his* career was spread before him. For several years he worked for a monument maker, cutting lettering and figures in low relief on gravestones, but at last did a bust which attracted the attention of Mr. Longworth. He sent Clevenger to Paris and Florence, where he did notable work for three years, but was stricken by tuberculosis and died at 31.

Another young Cincinnatian, Nathan F. Baker, was studying in Rome at the same time, and a letter from there in 1843 remarked that he had completed "a model of a ball player in the act of throwing the ball," which was "very highly spoken of." It does not say "baseball player," and much to our grief, there is no record of the fate of this work, executed six years before Doubleday is alleged to have "invented" baseball, which of course he didn't do. Baker also did a statue of Cincinnatus, which long occupied a niche on Fourth Street in the sculptor's home town and then was placed in City Hall, but which has long since disappeared, no one knows where. One fine piece of Baker's work which survives is a statue of Egeria on an island in Spring Grove cemetery.

Meanwhile, Powers's reputation was rising in swift crescendo. The most extravagant praise of him came from — you'd never guess — Mrs. Trollope! Writing from Florence in December, 1843, she rhapsodized over this "truth-inspired sculptor from Ohio," the "Transatlantic Apelles," declaring that "no studio in Florence so well deserves repeated visits as his." She had seen the great Thorwaldson's eye kindle at the mention of Powers, and heard him exclaim, "I consider the birth of this young man as an epoch in the art of sculpture." Mrs. Trollope raved on that Powers "sets all praise at defiance. . . . Nature and truth speak for him in his own eloquent marbles. He is in sculpture what Shakespeare is in poetry," and so on and on. He had developed a flair for nudes, and after doing a figure of Eve, had carved "The Greek Slave," which was the talk of two continents, a figure whose beautiful curves were a golden mean between Rubens embonpoint and twentieth-century emaciation. It created such a furor that six copies had to be made of it for various museums.

Among the very early painters who stopped at least briefly at Cincinnati was Auguste Hervieu, the Frenchman who came in Mrs. Trollope's train in 1828, and while there splashed upon a vast canvas, 16 by 12 feet in size, a dream picture of the landing of LaFayette at Cincinnati, which was the most densely populated phantasmagoria in all art, picturing many persons who weren't there, and some of whom had never been there.

A many-sided character in Cincinnati art was Thomas Buchanan Read. Pennsylvania-born, his father died when the boy was only ten and he was apprenticed to a tailor. Harshly treated, he ran away, worked in a grocery store a while and began to learn cigar-making in Philadelphia. But at 15 he walked to Pittsburgh, and three years later went to Cincinnati, where he found shelter with a married sister and earned a living by rolling cigars, carving tombstones, painting canal boats and doing odd jobs. He next set up as a sign painter, meanwhile practicing drawing and writing verse for the local papers. Then he toured Ohio, dashing off oil portraits, stopping at Dayton long enough to play female roles in a stock company, which he could do very nicely, being only about five feet tall and delicate in face and figure. The watchful Mr. Longworth had observed him, and now enabled him, when he was a mere precocious youngster of 16, to set up a studio in Cincinnati, where he promptly received an order for a portrait of General Harrison. "A sad daub," Read called it later, but it gave him useful publicity. Yet no more than a year had passed before he was painting his way eastward to New York and Boston, where he met all the great literary figures of the day and was soon thriving, aided by his indefatigable industry, for he thought nothing of standing eight hours at his easel. Thereafter, he divided his time between New York and Cincinnati until his untimely death in 1872 at the age of 50. A minor figure in the arts, perhaps, Read nevertheless did some highly meritorious work, both in painting and poetry; and that with no instruction whatsoever in the former, and no schooling after his tenth year to account for his vocabulary or the beauty of expression in such poems as "Drifting" and "The Death of Autumn." There must have been art in his blood, for he had a sister, Mrs. Harriet Hosea who was a sculptor.

Another one of the several aided by Mr. Longworth was William Henry Powell who, after some study in painting in Cincinnati, he sent to New York for further instruction, and among whose many works was the great mural, "The Discovery of the Mississippi by De Soto" in the rotunda of the National Capitol.

Painters had begun appearing, along with the early sculptors. Outstanding among the pioneers were James H. and William Beard and the Frankenstein brothers. Of the latter, brought to Cincinnati in early childhood by their German immigrant parents, Godfrey was regarded by some as the best portrait painter in America in his time, though both he and his brother John did landscapes, too. Miss Martineau in 1835 considered the work of James H. Beard the best she had seen in America. An Academy of Fine Arts, organized in 1838, with Godfrey Frankenstein as president, held an exhibit in the following year, in which were 150 works of foreign and native artists, most of them Cincinnatians.

In the early '50's one begins to hear gossip of many artists — Bingham, White, Griswold, Sloop, Eaton, Kellogg, Duncanson, Sonntag; Miller doing miniatures, Spinning designing for wood engraving. Several were studying in Europe. Whittridge was at Dusseldorf in '51, and McConkey just returned after two years abroad. Eccentric Theodore Jones was not only doing fine portraits, but writing poetry and comic skits such as "The Harp of a Thousand Strings," which convulsed our great-grandparents. Henry Worrell, English painter-musician who settled here, was largely responsible for the birth of the famous Sketch Club. As late as the '60's, its members came with drawing board and pencils to the monthly meeting after having all read some classic poem such as Milton's "Comus," Longfellow's "Skeleton in Armor," Gray's "Elegy in a Country Churchyard" or Goldsmith's "Deserted Village," and during the evening each would make a drawing, illustrating the work. The varied conceptions of the central incident or thought of each poem must have made an intriguing collection.

A notable artist of the ante-bellum period was Robert S. Duncanson, a young quadroon, son of a Scotch father and a mulatto mother, who first appears in the City Directory as a "daguerreotype artist," at 28 West Fourth Street. Like many others, he began his painting with portraits, and progressed to other things, developing a delicate beauty of style all his own. In the main hall of the Baum-Taft mansion are eight mural landscape panels, probably idealized Ohio River scenes, and two overdoor designs of fruit and flowers, all attributed to Duncanson. Nicholas Longworth owned and occupied the building for 35 years, and he is believed to have commissioned this work. After his time, probably while the druggist Suire briefly owned the place, wall paper was pasted over these panels and varnish added. When Mrs. Charles P. Taft came into occupancy of the house, she noticed through a torn place in the paper that there was some valuable painting underneath. Eventually, the paper was removed and the murals happily rediscovered. Duncanson spent some of his later life in England, where his work was highly regarded.

The artists of that period considered their proper fields to be portraits, landscapes, historical, classical and legendary subjects. The landscapes were almost all rural — farm, village, mountain, seashore. It did not occur to them that cities, with their traffic, shipping and smoke, were "artistic" subjects, as painters and etchers, even Whistler, discovered, years later. Godfrey Franken-stein, with the assistance of his brother and family, worked off and on for years on a great panorama of Niagara Falls and the Whirl-pool Rapids, "to take Niagara to those people who could not go to it," he explained to Kossuth in 1852. Artists pictured city street scenes and buildings only when commissioned to do so for illustra-tive or commercial purposes, some of them learning to draw on the wood block or work in lithograph. Martin Rettig, the last of the great artists' group of the latter nineteenth century now left alive, says that the Strobridge Lithographing Company was responsible for bringing some fine artists to Cincinnati, declaring that they paid as high as $10,000 per year to some of the best; and incredible as it may seem that such salaries were paid 80 years and more ago, the company modestly confirms it.

The pioneer fresco artist in the Middle West, Italian-born and-educated Francis Pedretti, came to Cincinnati in the early 1850's to fresco the Burnet House. He married an Anglo-Saxon girl, Miss Maitland, settled down and started an Old Family which is in the city yet. Other excellent workmen were appearing in mid-century Joseph O. Eaton, Chester Harding, and Henry Mosler—who drew war pictures for *Harper's Weekly*, and then went on to become one of the city's greats — his "Prodigal's Return," a Breton peasant scene, is said to have been the first American painting to be bought by the French Government; and in 1859, Henry F. Farny came to town, a colorful figure in its artistic history.

Mrs. William Peter — brilliant, eager, dynamic Sarah Worth-ington, daughter of Governor Worthington, whose first husband had been Edward King — now appears as a practical patron of art. Her home was a cultural center, a salon. She and a group of women friends organized in 1854, describing themselves as "An associa-tion of ladies for the purpose of founding and maintaining an Academy of Fine Arts." At first, they hoped to do no more than collect copies of great paintings and sculpture for the encourage-ment of art and the improvement of public taste. Between that time and her death nearly a quarter-century later at the age of 77, Mrs. Peter made five trips to Europe to buy copies or originals.

She had been delegated to this work in her latter years by the School of Design (opened in 1868) of McMicken University, soon to become a part of the University of Cincinnati. The Civil War had snuffed out Mrs. Peter's Women's Academy in 1864; but several members of it reorganized in 1877 as the Women's Art Museum Association; so that little group of '54 may in some degree be regarded as the germ of the city's present great Art Museum.

From the close of the Civil War to 1890 or 1900 is sometimes spoken of as Cincinnati's Golden Age of art. An infusion of highly talented youth had begun appearing around war-time. Frank Duveneck, a Covington boy, was 22 in 1860; Mosler and Farny were slightly younger. Some began calling Cincinnati the Paris of America, and as may be imagined, it did not disdain the epithet. It became a famous teaching center, with a hard-headed leaning towards factuality. Except for ordered murals, the vogue of the historical and classical was gone. But that coterie was considered to have a certain manner of its own; Farny, of French stock, coming from the East, was said to have fallen under its spell. Charles Dudley Warner, after a visit, wrote in 1889 that the art of Cincinnati had "the air of being indigenous," and "For a long time, the city has led an independent life in art and music"; while others call the city's art highly traditional. Did some of its famous pupils follow the early impulses given them here? Sir Moses Ezekiel, for example, a Virginian who spent more than half his life latterly in Europe with great distinction, being knighted by both Germany and Italy — came to Cincinnati for his earliest lessons. Kenyon Cox, an Ohioan who became not only an eminent mural and figure painter, honored on both sides of the Atlantic, but a critic, author of books on art, member of the National Academy of Art and the American Academy of Arts and Sciences, had his youthful art schooling in Cincinnati. Perhaps it is straining a point to say that it might be expected of a man who began his study here, that Cox would be a staunch upholder of tradition in an age of artistic incoherence.

Eaton, Kellogg, Noble, Breuer, Webber and Lily Martin, painters, and Louis T. Rebisso, sculptor, were in middle age as this post war period began, and younger fry were rapidly appearing.

Charles T. Webber opened a school in 1869, and it had 300 pupils
and a wide reputation when young Frank Duveneck, who had
been studying under Wilhelm Dietz in Munich, returned in '73
with a number of canvases, including one of his best known, "The
Whistling Boy," in which pundits saw the influence of Franz
Hals, and which was declared by some to have introduced a new
era in American art. Duveneck, at 25, began teaching in the school,
among his earlier pupils being Kenyon Cox, Robert F. Blum, John
H. Twachtman and Joseph DeCamp, all names destined for glory.
Others were springing up as the years passed, many of them native-
born — the Rettig brothers, John and Martin, William Forsyth,
William J. Baer (miniatures), Joseph Sharp, Edward H. Potthast,
Louis H. Meakin, Edward Volkert, Charles Kaelin, Robert Henri
and others. These men, just as do artists nowadays, had to turn
their hands to many tasks in earlier years, in order to eat. Twachtman was painting flowers and curlicues on window shades, a current fad for the home, when he joined Duveneck's class. Even in
mid-career, when he once fell into the doldrums, he took the job
of doing a cyclorama of the Battle of Gettysburg in Chicago,
which put him back on his feet again. Farny did circus posters
and that huge panorama of the pork-packing industry for the
Vienna Exposition of 1874. Winsor McCay, who came along a
little later, and who became a famous New York cartoonist, did
not disdain in youth to letter streamers advertising Kohl & Middle-
ton's Dime Museum and whoever else needed such graphs. Several
throughout their careers, notably Blum and Farny, did magazine
and book illustrating when it was offered. John Rettig, a creator of
fine portraits and beautiful landscapes, was also noted for his
theater curtains and scenery. He did the great curtain for the
Music Hall when he was 21. He also painted the gigantic scenery
for those outdoor spectacles with fireworks that were staged in
early autumns in the '80's — "Rome Under Nero," "The Last
Days of Pompeii,," "The Fall of Babylon," "Moses, or the
Bondage in Egypt."

Duveneck was a great teacher, beloved by his pupils; his round
head, big mustache and eyes gleaming through spectacles were
like those of a German professor of philosophy, though he had an

unprofessorial joviality, a love of a baseball game or a long hour of talk over beer and a bite at Foucar's. He did every sort of painting well, though he had a particular fancy for figures — "Woman with Forget-Me-Nots," "The Circassian," "The Professor," "The Blacksmith," "Turkish Page," "Woman in Black Scarf" — that sort of thing. In his earlier period, he worked mostly in the brown tints of the seventeenth-century Dutch masters whom he so greatly admired; but after a visit to the brilliant skies and florid scenes of Italy, his work became more colorful, and this newer manner continued throughout his life. No less an authority and fellow-artist than John Singer Sargent said of him, "He is the greatest talent of the brush in this generation."

Of the three or four leading sculptors produced by Cincinnati in that period, Clement Barnhorn, another Covington boy, and Charles H. Niehaus, both had their early study under Cincinnati's Louis Rebisso, whose equestrian statue of General Harrison is an example of his favorite type of work. At the Academy of Design in Munich in '79, four young sculptors, former students at Cincinnati's School of Design. won medals, Niehaus taking the highest honors for a group in clay, which the Academy asked permission to copy in bronze. A third among the city's great sculptors was none other than Duveneck. There were those who mourned the domination of painting in his life, believing that in sculpture he might have equalled or exceeded his work with the brush. The noble bronze memorial which he created for the grave of his wife in Florence, where she died in 1888, after only two years of happy wedded life (the original model is in the Art Museum at Cincinnati), gives proof of his genius in that branch of art. Other notable examples are the bust of President Eliot of Harvard and the seated statue of Ralph Waldo Emerson, also at Harvard, which he did in collaboration with Barnhorn. When St. Mary's Roman Catholic Cathedral was built in Covington, Duveneck contributed murals and Barnhorn a sculptured portal, both in honor of their mothers, which well-informed tourists cross the river to see.

After two years of painting and teaching in Cincinnati, his canvases selling and his reputation soaring rapidly, Duveneck returned to Munich, taking with him Twachtman, who later became an impressionist, and whose patrons loved best his winter landscapes. In Munich, Duveneck soon had a class, at times numbering 60, mostly Americans, and so devoted that when he moved to Italy, the majority of them folowed him. He returned to Cincinnati in '81, to loose a blast at the city for its neglect of its artists, mentioning Twachtman, Blum and Breuer as examples; said wealthy folk still went East to buy their paintings, and local painters and sculptors were never consulted in art movements. He was evidently referring to the current promotion of the Art Museum and Art Academy, in which, it is true, professional artists seemed to have little part. It was remarked a few years ago that the only artist ever elected to the Museum's Board of Directors was Henry Farny, and he was placed on the Committee on Real Estate — about the last subject that one would think of in connection with Farny.

Duveneck was one of the earliest to see beauty in grimy manufacturing cities; he liked his home town best in fog and smoke. "There are," said he, "atmospheric effects to be found in Cincinnati that few cities afford." For many Cincinnatians, this threw a new light on their smoke. They had called it by various other names, but they had never thought of it as a valuable accessory to art. But when a group of California artists came this way in 1918, they were delighted with it. Their spokesman, H. Bennett Abdy, thought Cincinnati "regal, . . . enthroned on noble hills." Best of all, it was "paintable." The water front was "a color-poem of soft greys," and he was enthusiastic about the view of the close-packed city and Covington from Mount Adams, "all of it veiled in a paintable haze of smoke."[1]

Henry Farny, the most colorful of the nineteenth-century art community, was a painter of fine talent, but a Bohemian playboy, irresponsible and inevitably popular. His favorite subjects were Indians, of whom he created many notable pictures. Theodore Roosevelt once told him that "The Nation owes you a great debt. You are preserving for future generations, phases of American history that are rapidly passing away." But the gayeties of Vine

[1] H. Bennett Abdy, *On the Ohio*, (New York: 1919)

Street and the studios occupied so much of his time that he didn't paint as much as he might have. People who wanted him to do pictures for them sometimes thought to hasten the process by giving him a check in advance — but that was a sad mistake. Instead of working on the commissioned picture, he worked on others for which he hadn't yet been paid. He didn't intend to cheat anyone; somehow, that check seemed to make that particular picture for him a closed incident, and only by the most persistent bedevilment could the customer get Farny started on the job. But once begun, he was capable of working with a furious energy and speed which turned out the finished product in surprisingly quick time, yet beautifully done.

He once agreed to do a series of illustrations for Harpers, but for weeks kept postponing the task, while the publishers urged and pleaded. Finally, one Saturday evening, Alexander Hill of Robert Clark & Company, book-dealers, received a telegram from Harpers, asking his aid in inducing Farny to do the drawings. Hill started up Vine Street, and after much inquiry, found that Farny was taking part in an amateur performance over the Rhine. In the role of Samson, he was, as Mr. Hill arrived, just pulling down the temple of the Philistines at Gaza — pasteboard cylinders like hat-boxes representing the sections of the stone columns. Crawling out of the wreckage after the curtain fell, he was confronted by Hill with the telegram, demanding action, but he positively refused to leave the place before the night's fun was over, about 3:00 A.M. Then he went to a restaurant, drank numerous cups of black coffee, proceeded to his studio and dashed off the drawings within a few hours.

Farny always kept at his studio in the Pike Opera House building — where Duveneck and others also worked — a supply of a certain red wine made at a monastery in the hills back of Newport, and if you were invited to dine at his place, the menu might sometimes be cheese and crackers and that red wine. But for all his oddities and shortcomings, his fellow-artists held him in such high esteem that when they organized the Art Club in 1890, with a two-year term for presidents, they elected John Rettig as their first executive, and Farny in '92 as their second. That club, by the way, after using rented rooms for a while, bought an old residence on East Third Street, opposite Lytle Park, and in course of time, paid off and burned the mortgage on it, with much ceremony and loud cheers; at least, they thought they did, but someone discovered five years later that with true artistic inadvertence, what they burned must have been the deed to the property, for the canceled mortgage was still among their papers. That clubhouse is thought by some to have changed the least of anything in Cincinnati. A recent president has remarked satirically that the club "has made a gallant fight against progress." Furnishings, pictures, relics, all remain as they were; and the custodian is an ancient retainer so deaf that an outsider, when no members are there, may ring the bell for hours and she will never hear it.

In the early '80's, women's names were becoming more numerous in the art news. Mary Spencer was already a veteran painter. Mrs. Thomas L. Nichols (later Mrs. Storer) and Clara Chipman Newton were designing china at the Rookwood Pottery, and Laura H. Fry was the most noted of the numerous women woodcarvers. Some young painters were coming on, and they, with some male artists, made up a colony, a little Montmartre, on the heights at the upper end of Vine Street. Some fine talent developed among them — Henrietta Wilson, Kate Reno Miller, Ida Holterhoff, Dixie Selden, Elizabeth Nourse, the last two attaining international fame. They sounded the men's Art Club on the matter of admission to that body, but the men were inhospitable, so the women organized their own club in 1892, and it still functions.

One of the late nineteeth-century crop of young artists, David Rosenthal, whose work had been hung in the galleries of America and Europe, died the other day at 73. But he and Paul Jones and John D. Wareham, director of the Rookwood Pottery and others of that brood still surviving, were and are all younger than Martin Rettig, the last survivor of the Old Guard who gave the Golden Age its glory. The genial, well-preserved Mr. Rettig, now in his eighties, still paints in his austere studio, up a curious, corkscrew stairway in a centenarian building on Third Street. His two highceilinged rooms were once the law offices of Rutherford B. Hayes; in the back room, a big, built-in vault with a huge lock and doors edged with wrought ornamental border, once held Mr. Hayes's books and valuable papers. High up on the wall of the front room, close to the ceiling, your eye is caught by a row of painters' palettes, each of which once rested on the thumb of one of the masters of those golden years, each marked with the name of its long-dead owner — Mosler, Twachtman, Duveneck, Farny, Noble, John Rettig, Blum, DeCamp, Hammond, Bussbaum, Madrazo, Van Loo, Baer, Cox, Webber, Potthast, Mrs. Storer. What a gallery of beauty has sprung from those palettes! And a humbler note is seen in a photograph on the wall of Long John Reilly, first-baseman of the Cincinnati Reds in the '80's, who was also a commercial artist and cartoonist.

In this story of Cincinnati's art belongs the story of the Fountain which is one of its treasures, the jealously-guarded ward of its artists. As a memorial to his beloved brother-in-law, who died in 1866, Millionaire Henry Probasco presented to the city the Tyler Davidson Fountain. It happened that in Bavaria, August von Kreiling of Nuremberg had designed just the thing he wanted, and Ferdinand von Müller's Royal Bavarian Bronze Foundry was ready to cast it.

Where to put it was the question, and the Council decided that the greatly widened stretch of Fifth Street between Vine and Walnut, on the site of the market house, was the ideal place. That unkempt old shambles, stinking of fish and spoiled meat, made the shopping district look countrified and smell worse, and was no longer greatly needed, anyhow, as more people were moving away from the Basin. But the market people thought otherwise, and there was a roar of protest, especially from the butchers, who sued and got injunctions and writs of mandamus and certiorari, if those are the right words, and cut up rough; and when they lost the legal battle, announced that, law or no law, they weren't going to vacate. That made it necessary to tear the roof from over them. On a February day in 1870, when the market was not in session, the Council instructed the street cleaning superintendent to proceed to the spot with his entire force and all necessary picks, axes, crowbars and ladders. Truth to tell, knowing that the order was coming, he was already there. Within ten minutes after the passage of the resolution, workmen were swarming over the roof, and within two hours the building was in ruins.

After a slight delay, caused by the Franco-Prussian War, the great castings arrived, together with porphyry from the mountains of Saxony for the base. The dedication, on October 5th, 1871, was the biggest thing that had happened since the War. Governor Rutherford B. Hayes was the principal speaker. That night all Cincinnati came to see the fountain, illumined by calcium lights and red and green fire.

The design of the group, portraying the blessings of water to the human race, set in the midst of a city which had never had enough good water, had its touch of pathos. The 43-foot structure — how tall it seemed then! — is topped by the draped figure of a woman, the Genius of Water, facing East with arms outstretched to North and South and water spraying down from the hands. Just below her, four figures or groups dramatize the principal uses of water: a mother leading a naked little boy to the bath; a farmer praying for rain; a girl offering a drink of water to an old man; and a man on a burning housetop begging for water to quench the fire. Around the rim of the basin, boys are mounted on various fauna — turtle, dolphin, bird, snake — from whose mouths water pours, and entablatures picture some of the pleasures derived from water.

The plaza around the Fountain leaves what the twentieth century regards as only a narrow street on each side, though it was big enough then. The plaza has a few trees which do not flourish any too robustly, and benches which are favorite meeting and resting places. Pigeons and starlings make nuisances of themselves, roosting on the sculpture. The pigeons seem to think it makes a fine effect when they perch there in threes, one on the head of the Genius, one on each outstretched hand. Booths for war bond sales, for charity at Christmas and other times, open-air art shows — the place is beloved by artists — are here upon occasion, and on one day in each year there is a curious ceremony. That space in Fifth Street was originally set aside for a market place forever; and lest that old law may not have been fully quieted, a little flower stand is set up and the Mayor buys a flower, officially keeping up the pretense that it is still a market.

The Fountain was cleaned in 1874, to make it nice and shiny for the Exposition, but much to the disgust of the art colony. This happened two or three times, though there is a legend that Vincent Nowottny, well-known citizen and a big fellow physically, once blocked such a vandalistic attack single-handed; but this is apocryphal. But when the news flashed about the city in the spring of '93, "They're going to scour the Fountain again!" the members of the Art Club, shouting weird war cries, rushed to the clubhouse and pledged their determination to die on the barricades, if necessary. A committee was appointed — the records name the veteran Charlie Webber and Matt Daly, though rumor has it that President Farny went along, which seems not improbable. There is even a version which has him pointing a stern finger at the head of the Park Department — another variant says the Mayor — and thundering, "Dare to lay a finger on that Fountain, and we'll get an injunction!" Completely mystified, the politicians, who may never have heard the word "patina," conferred and decided to postpone action. It seemed from the ravings of these fellows that a dirty Fountain was considered more artistic than a clean one, and they weren't going to have Cincinnati accused of being inartistic.

In these latter days there are motorists and high blood pressures who deplore the Fountain as an obstruction to traffic, and suggest moving it elsewhere; but so far, their hints arouse such storms of disapproval that Authority dares not take action. Perhaps it is also aware of outside opinion such as that of the artist, H. Bennett Abdy, already quoted, who saw "time-mellowed and smoke-toned Fountain Square" as "a bit of Paris, a dainty French lozenge dropped into the vast mosaic of our mellowing Middle West."

The rejuvenation of the Women's Art Association in 1877 set in motion the machinery which created an Art Museum. For some time they exhibited art objects borrowed from private collectors; one showing drew 13,000 people and put $10,000 into the association's treasury. Then in 1880, Charles W. West, who in 40 years

had made a fortune in merchandising in Cincinnati, offered
$150,000 towards the building of an Art Museum if a like amount
could be raised otherwise. It was little sooner said than done. M.
E. Ingalls, the railroad magnate, gave a dinner to 53 plutocrats
at $1,000 a plate; David Sinton pledged $75,000, Joseph Longworth $37,000, Reuben R. Springer and Julius Dexter other large
amounts. The Museum building, a Romanesque structure, was
placed in one of the most beautiful possible locations, in Eden
Park. The University's School of Design was transferred to the
Museum Association in '84, and endowed by Joseph and Nicholas
Longworth II and Messrs. Sinton, Springer and Ingalls. Mr. Sinton contributed the Academy building, which adjoins the
Museum, the latter being dedicated in 1886, the Academy in the
following year. Duveneck spent the last 25 years of his life in
service to the two, and left the Museum 40 of his paintings at his
death. Barnhorn, Sharpe and others of the city's great were also
teachers there.

Meanwhile, the joy of creation had two great manifestations
among the amateurs, The first was wood carving, which epidemic
continued for some 20 years and was at its height in the '70's. It
left Cincinnati with literally hundreds of buildings, public and
private, more or less decorated interiorly with carven wood.
Many, especially among private homes, are in evidence yet —
some still occupied as homes, some now public institutions and
some unhappily nearing the end of their story. One of the latter is
in the West End — once a gracious mansion, now alongside a big
printing plant and serving as its office building. Much of the carving has been torn out in remodelling, but some remains. One large
and particularly impressive panel over a mantel, you see at a glance
pictures the taking of the wooden horse into Troy. As usual, the
horse doesn't look as if it could hold enough men to capture a city,
but that's the fault of the legend, not the sculptor.

There were two schools of wood carving in Cincinnati, that
of the Fry family and that of Benn Pitman. Three generations of
the Frys — Henry L., William H. and Laura Ann — worked in
wood. In the Church of the New Jerusalem on Walnut Hills are
a pulpit, pulpit chair, communion table and pair of candlesticks

carved by William Fry when he was a mere lad of 95. Both William and his rival, Benn Pitman, taught for long periods at the Art Academy. Pitman, an eccentric and versatile genius who came to Cincinnati in 1853 and introduced his brother-in-law, Sir Isaac Pitman's system of shorthand in America, also invented the process of electroplating engravings, tinkered with stained glass and china painting and wrote a couple of books. His home, at the foot of the hills, overlooking the river, up Pendleton way, is a fearful and wonderful exposition of his several skills. The exterior mingles carved wood and stone, while the interior, the work of many years — great mantels, doors, panels, wainscoting, ceiling beams — was carved by the master's pupils at the Academy, with the exception of one mantel, which he himself did. The Nourse sisters, one of whom he married — the other being Elizabeth, the painter — did some of the carving. There are stained glass windows, old and modern, and Pitman inlaid some hammered silver filigree work into the wood carving, even putting silver alloyed hinges on the front door. Fry's home also remains, well graced with carving, though not so elaborate.

The carving on the front of the great organ in Music Hall is largely the work of the pupils of these two men, many of them prominent socially. The newspapers mentioned them all. Three principal panels were "Morning," a flight of birds upward, by "Mrs. Dr. Williams"; "Noon," butterflies fluttering around a sunflower, by "Mrs. Judge Force"; and "Night," descending swallows and a crescent moon, by Mr. Fry. There were many smaller bits, mostly panels honoring composers and musicians, usually a flower piece with the man's name done in early English type. The *Gazette*, on May 11th, 1878, published a list of 112 of the sculptors, a large majority of them women, with the subject of each — "Rossini, grapevine, Miss Isora Collard; Wagner, thistle, Misses Hattie and Mary Johnson; Gluck, acanthus, Miss Jennie Philips; Haydn, morning glory, Mrs. S. M. Barrett," and so on; a pity there is not room here for them all. Miss Laura Fry herself did Mendelssohn. Work on the towers and wainscoting was done principally by the "ladies of the School of Design." The organ is not often seen by today's audiences, and when it is, this intricate carving in dark wood is not visible from the auditorium. But it is pleasant to go behind the scenes, close to the great structure and envision the many hours of toil by the devoted hands of those women — and some men — of long ago, all unpaid save for $500 in prizes given to a few by Mr. Springer, the donor of the Music Hall; and all worthy, too, for neither Fry nor Pitman would have tolerated any bad work. Lacking the muscular strength to drive the carving tools entirely with the heel of the hand, the women used small wooden mallets very skilfully.

Fry and Pitman followed this up with exhibits of their pupils' work at the Centennial Exposition in '79, which drew a critical but generally approving article in the *American Architect*, entitled, "Women Wood Carvers — the Movement in Cincinnati." Barring some slight tendency towards over ornament, the writer was greatly pleased with the studies, "handled with great vigor and precision." He particularly praised Mrs. Force's corner cupboard, Mrs. Dodd's Gothic table; the several exhibits of Miss Pitman; a prayer book by Miss Collard; a bedstead designed by Mr. Fry and executed by Mrs. Dr. Williams. Miss Louise McLaughlin's hanging cabinet, "entirely her own design," was "one of the finest exhibits"; while on the footboard of the bed carved by the Misses Johnson was "one of the most beautiful and delicate pieces of carving we have ever seen, a convolvulus in intaglio." Even if this were only a passing fad, the writer saw permanent cultural inspiration remaining from it.

The pottery rage had its beginning in 1875 when Benn Pitman procured from the East some overglaze colors and invited a few Cincinnati ladies of artistic tendencies to form a class in china painting, which they did with praiseworthy results. Miss M. Louise McLaughlin, already known for her wood carving, was deeply impressed by the Limoges Faience that she saw at the Centennial. She came home and after much experimentation, it was announced that she had succeeded in producing enameled ware exactly like that of Limoges. The newspapers called it "Cincinnati Faience." A group of women gathered around her to form a Pottery Club, with herself as president. They rented a room as a studio, with the president and Mrs. George Ward

Nichols, another member, at first paying the expenses. And here a new and towering figure enters upon the scene. Mrs. Nichols, daughter of Joseph Longworth and granddaughter of Nicholas, had already won distinction in Cincinnati's art world by the part she played in the promotion of the May Musical Festivals. She now threw herself with equal vigor into the production of pottery. But she was not so much interested in the Pottery Club as in doing something on her own. The Club built two kilns for firing its own product, but never prospered greatly. Three other ventures in pottery, all unsuccessful, were made within a few years — one producing a ware called Avon, another known as Kezonta, and a faience in Moorish design put forth by Matt Morgan and some fellow-artists.

Meanwhile, Mrs. Nichols, who had been intrigued by some Japanese ware she saw at the Centennial, took over an old suburban pottery and began molding and painting her own. The kilns, however, were not suited to the sort of ware she had in mind, so she began all over again, in an old schoolhouse — her father, a devoted patron of the arts, after a plaintive question, "But wouldn't it be cheaper to buy vases for painting?" supplying the needed cash. She engaged a staff of artisans and plunged into the work with her characteristic energy. From Munich she brought a Bavarian master-potter, and through the American minister to Japan she engaged the services of a Satsuma expert, the Pottery Club ladies urging her to insist that he wear native garb when he came, "and the more rococo it is, the better."

The first kiln was fired in November, 1880, and Mrs. Nichols christened it the Rookwood Pottery, honoring her grandfather's home on the hills, though for some time the newspapers continued to refer to it as "Mrs. Nichols's Pottery." A small announcement in March, '81 by John A. Mohlenhoff, on Fountain Square, read, "ROOKWOOD POTTERY. Goods of Mrs. Maria Longworth Nichols, made at these works, are now on exhibition and for sale. You are kindly invited." Her father must have poured no little cash into the venture in its earlier days, but not many years had passed before it became profitable. Within the first year it was producing breakfast and dinner services, vases, pitchers and plaques, all graceful in form and most of them decorated. "Mrs. Col. Nichols" herself designed the new dinner service installed by the Queen City Club in the fall of '81. "A feature of the decoration is the Club's monogram, impaled upon a spray or two of wild oats"; a delicate suggestion or perhaps a hope that the Q.C. members had sown theirs and settled down.

The first of the pottery's famous finishes, "Tiger Eye," was developed in 1884. Mrs. Clara Chipman Newton came into the company and then William W. Taylor, who finally took over the business in 1889, when Mrs. Nichols had, by her second marriage, become Mrs. Bellamy Storer, Jr., her husband being the son of the old Judge. It is by this name, rather than her previous one, that she is always remembered as the great promoter of art pottery and music. It was about that time that Charles Dudley Warner visited Rookwood and remarked that it was "the only pottery in this country in which the instinct of beauty is paramount to the desire of profit." But though it was never a great money-maker, it did for many years take care of itself handily.

New famous finishes were developed—the limpid "Gold Stone," the opalescent "Sea Green" and the light and delicate "Iris." Mr. Taylor built the comely half-timbered factory which doesn't resemble a factory, where the Diehl Fireworks plant had been, at the head of the Mount Adams incline. (The iron gates of its yard today were those of the old court house yard, the one destroyed in '84.) Taylor brought a superintendent from England's — or as some of us like to think of them, Arnold Bennett's — Five Towns, and assembled a group of able artists to shape and decorate the product. Among them were A. R. Valentien, Artus van Briggle, Matt Daly, Edward T. Hurley — some of whose hundreds of lovely etchings of Cincinnati and vicinity he has put into little books which are treasured by art lovers — and the lovable Japanese Ketaro Shirayamadani, whom Mrs. Storer engaged in the winter of '83-4, and who worked until his last illness, 64 years later, in 1948. Of him John D. Wareham, the art director of the pottery, said, "Sweet and gentle in character, understanding, with a keen sense of humor and a mind of high culture, he occupied a position in the art history of Rookwood which cannot easily be filled." Hurley is the only one of this great coterie left alive.

At the very start, Mrs. Storer decreed that of the finer art creations, such as decorated vases, there should never be any duplication, and no piece in the slightest degree defective should ever be sold. And so, if you have a Rookwood, an exquisitely shaped and painted thing on soft, mellow finish, you have something that is unique in all the world. Meanwhile, the vow of perfection was filling a closely-guarded yard with broken shards of beauty, no smallest scrap being permitted to escape. For half a century these ideals were cherished and Rookwood was worldfamous. Then the general recession of taste and the rise of imitations sold on roadside stands and in dime stores threatened it with ruin. Many of these cheap pieces flaunted on their under sides something as near the Rookwood trademark as the fakers thought they could get away with; and people bought them. Rumors of difficulty at Rookwood were heard around Cincinnati, and in 1941, for the first time, the plant ceased operations, and a small notice in the papers offered it for sale.

But there were Cincinnatians who could not endure the thought of seeing this cradle of beauty and art, so long the city's pride and joy, pass out of existence; they incorporated, bought the plant, reinstalled Mr. Wareham as art director, and it has gone on. But it cannot hold its head as high as it once did; it can no longer be entirely idealistic. To pay production costs and overhead, that cursed element which has become an Old Man of the Sea to all businesses, professions and arts, it must now compete to some extent with the less tasteful products of pure commercialism.

CHAPTER XVII

The New Vienna

WITH its large German population, it was inevitable that Cincinnati would be a music-loving city; but it began lisping the universal language before the Germans came. It heard its first strains from the regimental band in Fort Washington; then at least as early as 1814, it had a little brass band of its own. Books of songs were put forth by local printers in 1815 and '16; and in the latter year, a local correspondent of the *Boston Courier* wrote that there were "Pianofortes by the dozen in Cincinnati," but a dearth of tuners. Before 1820, instruments were being advertised by local shops which indicate the existence of small orchestras. In 1817 M. Philibertus Ratel and his wife, French emigres, settled here, the versatile Philibertus teaching several instruments, while his wife specialized in the piano. Later chroniclers were of opinion that the Ratels had much to do with setting Cincinnati's feet on the road to musical eminence.

In 1819 two singing societies appeared and gave an occasional concert of more or less religious music by composers who, save for Haydn and Handel, are now almost or quite forgotten. With the exception of the worldly Episcopalians, the early settlers from the East were apt to look with disfavor upon secular music, and would tolerate no instruments, not even an organ, in church services. But the Germans, as they came, were troubled by no such inhibitions, and the Catholics, Lutherans and Swedenborgians accordingly used organs as rapidly as they could be built. We have already noticed the early appearance of German organ builders, and in 1819 George Chartres appears in the directory as a piano-maker.

A young violinist of mixed descent, Joseph Tosso, who came up from New Orleans, assumed leadership in 1827 of the small orchestra of the Cincinnati Theatre, and presently became Cincinnati's leading musical figure. He built up a small symphony orchestra, sold pianos, played the organ and assembled an excellent choir at St. Xavier's Church, and was Professor of Music at Dr. Lake's Female Seminary. He and various partners long operated a dancing school on an upper floor of Mrs. Trollope's Bazaar, and as a sideline, he opened a "Music and Fancy Store." He eventually laid claim to having written the words and music for that popular old rustic American fireside skit, "The Arkansaw Traveler," a comic colloquy between a horseback wayfarer and a backwoods cabin dweller, with scraps of a hoedown dance tune scattered through it. The impossibility that a foreigner who, so far as can be discovered, never saw the wild hinterland, and who couldn't pronounce the rustic dialect, let alone write it, could conceive a thing so earthy, so palpably bred in the hardscrabble American frontier, is apparent, yet many people believed Tosso's claim, and as his years increased, he probably came to believe it himself.

When the Philharmonic Society gave its first concert in 1847, Tosso conducted. He continued to be active for years thereafter, as soloist and conductor, leading the orchestra at most of the big hotel balls, and playing numerous benefits during the Civil War. Even at 79 he toured Ohio with a small concert company. There are persons still alive who remember him in his latter years at his Covington home, with long white hair and velvet coat, scraping his violin and quavering the lines of "The Arkansaw Traveler," always emphasizing the statement that it was his own work.

The Eclectic Academy of Music, founded in 1834, and when incorporated, with that busy participant in many things, Judge Jacob Burnet, as its president, developed a 24-piece amateur orchestra under the direction of the Swede, Victor Williams, who also gave the young city its first opportunity to hear some of the great oratorios. Meanwhile the Germans, as we have seen, were flocking into Cincinnati and filling it with singing societies, small orchestras and brass bands. Noted soloists were coming, to educate Cincinnati's taste in something other than sacred music — Henri Vieuxtemps, violinist and composer, some of whose lovely music is still played, appeared in 1844, when he was only 24, and returned 14 years later with the pianist Thalberg; Ole Bull, who made the first of several visits in '44; William Vincent Wallace, composer of *Maritana* and other operas, came in 1850, also Strakosch, the pianist, and Remenyi, Hungarian violinist. That was a busy year. The French Opera Company of New Orleans, halted here en route to New York, and introduced Cincinnati to the profane form of entertainment, "grand" opera, by presenting several programs of excerpts. Louis M. Gottschalk, New Orleans composer, whose "The Last Hope" was a favorite of several generations, was another visitor. The most noted soloist of the era was of course Jenny Lind, who, through the industrious ballyhooing of her impresario, Barnum, became impressed upon the public mind everywhere as the "greatest soprano of all time," though we of today would prefer an audition before subscribing to such encomiums. She gave two concerts in Cincinnati in 1851 to packed houses at $16 top price, mingling operatic arias with religious and folk songs.

Cincinnati had now begun to send out its own musical entertainers, too. In 1850 the Misses Ludlum, known professionally as Mlles. Augusta Victoria and Appoline, pianist and guitarist respectively, toured the Middle West with Mr. Bishop, the vocalist, evoking, no doubt, unfavorable comment at home on the highly unconventional proceeding.

In the 1840's there were two houses — and then John Church made three — that were publishing songs and piano pieces ground out by local bards and melodists, who seemed ready to dash off an opus in celebration of almost any current topic. The great contribution of Messrs. Howe and Singer to domestic economy was commemorated by the Sewing Machine Polka in 1860, while the discovery of Pennsylvania oil in '59 evoked the Petroleum Galop, by "Oily Gammon." We do not grasp the significance of the Cradle Schottische, dedicated "Aux Demoiselles Anna E. Cromwell and Louise Hazzard," but pretty social compliments were paid, as with the piece, "'Tis Midnight Hour, Composed for the Piano Forte and Respectfully Dedicated to Miss ELIZABETH LEWIS of Cincinnati by an AMATEUR," or "The Music of the Footfall, Composed and Sung with Unbounded Applause by MME. CAR-

OLINE RIVE, Written and Respectfully Dedicated to Miss Maggie LeBoutillier by Mrs. Mary Farrell Moore."

One of the song writers who timidly offered a manuscript to a publisher now and then was a young chap named Steve Foster, who spent his daylight hours on a high stool in the office of Irwin & Foster, steamboat agents, at Number 4, Cassily's Row, on the water front. One of the partners, Dunning Foster, was Stephen's elder brother. Stephen a native of Pittsburgh, had first visited Cincinnati in 1833 at the age of seven, with his mother and sisters, when they were guests at the home of Michael P. Cassily, prosperous dry-goods merchant, and family, old Pittsburgh friends of the Fosters. As Stephen mooned dreamily through his teens, he wasted so much time on music that the folks decided to send him to his brother's office in Cincinnati, to see if something useful couldn't be knocked into his head. Stephen, living at a boarding house, was shy and did not make acquaintances readily, but gradually came to know a few literary folk such as William H. Lytle, William D. Gallagher and E. D. Mansfield; some steamboat captains and agents; and through the Cassilys, some younger folk. His early love ditties, published in Cincinnati, were sometimes dedicated to young women of his acquaintance there. He was at first ashamed of his Negro songs, and gave them to blackface singers without thought of recompense. But in March, 1848 the Mason-Colburn house announced the publication of his "Uncle Ned, arranged for Piano Forte, Solo and Quartette," and on June 22, one of his most famous, "Susanna" (later called "O, Susanna") was published by Field-Peters, who were running a series, "Songs of the Sable Harmonists." As it was written, there was nothing about the West in this piece; the singer said, "I came from Alabama," or, as sung over the Rhine,

"Ich kam von Alabama,
Mein Banjo auf dem Knie ——"

The Oregon emigration, in full swing in '48, seized upon the song, changed it to "I'm going out to Oregon," and in the following year the Forty-Niners used either Oregon or California. That rush spread it around the world. It was translated into many languages, including Chinese — and it must have seemed a bit mysterious to the Celestials. Bayard Taylor heard it in India.

Foster's "Nelly Was a Lady" was published in 1849, and "Camptown Races" in 1850. He returned about that time to Pittsburgh where he met and married Jane McDowell — "Jeanie with the Light Brown Hair." In 1858, famous but still not wealthy, though he had written songs which seem as nearly destined for immortality as any that we have, he returned with his wife to Cincinnati for a visit. One evening, in company with an old friend, Billy Hamilton, he went to call on some friends. On their way home, they heard a quartette parked in a yard on Broadway, serenading a young lady, and oddly enough, singing "Jeanie with the Light Brown Hair" — or trying to, for Hamilton and Foster didn't think their work was quite up to the mark. So, as a slight corrective, they crossed the street and joined in the vocalization. The original singers were indignant, and wanted to know, how come this impertinent interference? Hamilton introduced the composer, and of course was not believed. But after his identity had been established, the six of them went about the residence areas, serenading, for another hour or so. A day or two later, Stephen left Cincinnati for the last time.

It has been said that he joined in serenading during his more youthful years in Cincinnati, which can easily be believed, for that was a favorite sentimental pastime of the age. The singers were sometimes accompanied by a flute — the favorite instrument of melanch'ly lovers since long before Dick Swiveller's time — or strings. Serenading was for a time under police displeasure. One night when the Washington Fire Company fell into internal discord and their loud brawling and cursing aroused the neighborhood, no police appeared to quiet them; but the *Gazette* editor was convinced "that if three or four sentimental noodles had been blowing a harmless flute or singing a love song under a sweetheart's window, five or six able-bodied watchmen would have rushed upon them, carried them off to the watch-house and locked them up."

But this oppression of romance and harmony could not go on in a city so mindful of those ameliorations of life, and it wasn't long before serenading came into its own again. In '58 a citizen came to the Mayor with a complaint that a young lady living near him was so popular that she was serenaded two or three times weekly by troubadours who, with characteristic inconsistency, alternately besought her to "Open Thy Lattice, Love" and to "Sleep, My Pretty One, Sleep" — which the complainant said he found it impossible to do while the concert was in progress. Was there no relief for the innocent bystander? The Mayor pondered the problem seriously, but could think of nothing other than the helpful suggestion that the sufferer move out of the neighborhood. So harmless and felicitous a diversion as serenading "the fair sex" must not be stinted.

The 1850's were an eventful decade in music. The Germans, by the dozen, bands and orchestras, kept assiduity at a high pitch throughout the year; and many of their performers also participated in the activities of other organizations below the Rhine. In '52 the Philharmonic Society (vocal) was organized and Smith & Nixon's Musical Hall was opened, the first in the city to be on the ground level, thus allaying the fear of fire. It became much in demand for all sorts of entertainments, including lectures and such novelties as Rarey, the tamer of vicious horses, "Winchell the Drollerist" and Robert Heller, "the Unrivalled Conjurer, Pianist and Conversationalist." Another Philharmonic Society, this time an orchestra, aimed to be large and permanent, "like the New York Philharmonic Society," appeared four years later. "At last," exclaimed the *Gazette* in January, '57, "we have an orchestra here — thanks to our German friends and lovers of classical music — that proposes to treat us to No. 1 as a commencement." "No. 1" was Beethoven's *First Symphony*, which began the first program, and was followed by not-too-difficult things by Mozart, Schubert and Weber. The *Gazette* was outraged because only 300 people were present to hear "a programme which could not have been surpassed at Leipsic or Boston." The fact was that Cincinnati was still mostly interested in brass and vocal music and in the personality of soloists; it still required education in the subtler, finer cadences of a symphony orchestra. The Philharmonic persisted, however, and gave three concerts in the late winter and spring, during which it progressed through the more difficult *Pastorale Symphony* to the mighty *Eroica*, and won many plaudits. In the fourth concert of the following season, however, it waded into water too deep for the friendly critic, who praised the concert with the exception of the symphony, which he didn't name, but which he called "more tedious than entertaining. It may have been intensely scientific, but not calculated to please a public audience." Which reminds us of a later organ recital by an eminent performer, whose final encore was "some flowery piece, utterly unadapted to an organ and unworthy of his own taste and celebrity. We could not discover what it was, but the music had a blue cover."

In 1857 Samuel N. Pike, a successful distiller, began the erection of an opera house on Fourth Street between Vine and Walnut. Mr. Pike — who had a corsair mustache and a dull, fishy gray eye, and whose father's name had been Hecht, of which Pike is a translation — had decided, despite the disapproval of some church folk, that Cincinnati was ready for opera, and he was right. His opera house had a big auditorium, 100 by 140 feet in size, and was gorgeously appointed. It extended back to a narrow lane called Baker Street, and as the ground fell away rapidly from Fourth Street, there was space under the auditorium for a large prosperous oasis, the Do You Smile Saloon, opening on Baker Street, with of course a way of easy access from the auditorium.

Moralists still inveighed against opera and refused to support it, but as the opening of Pike's drew near, it was evident that they were outnumbered. The building was "dedicated" on Washington's Birthday, 1859, with a "festival" and ball given by the citizens in honor of Mr. Pike, which was attended by thousands at an admission fee of $10 per couple! The opera opening took place on March 15th, with Max Strakosch's Italian company presenting *Martha*. There had been 3,500 tickets sold in advance for the engagement, and with the first performance, the city went opera-mad. Cincinnati's musical age was now well under way. Even domestic servants, white and black, sat in the galleries at concert and opera and often became competent critics, discussing performances with their employers. The salaries allegedly received by the stars were mentioned with awe — Brignoli, $1,500 a month; Amodio, $1,000; Junca, $800; Squires, $750; Barilli, $600; Madame Pauline Colson, $2,000; Cora de Wilhorst, $1,600; Teresa Parodi, $1,500; Amelia Strakosch, $1,000. The minor singers' salaries were not made public but it was estimated that the chorus, orchestra, general staff, advertising and traveling expenses added $6,000 per month more.

But disaster struck Mr. Pike and the city in March 1866. Shortly after a performance of *A Midsummer Night's Dream*, fortunately after the audience had left the theatre, a gas explosion backstage set fire to the building and it was quickly destroyed, together with several adjacent buildings, including the plant of the *Enquirer*. Mr. Pike, stoically smoking a cigar, watched the disaster from the roof of the Burnet House. His loss was given as $1,000,000 mostly uninsured. He wanted the city to help him in rebuilding, but got no support, and pettishly threatened to leave Cincinnati without opera. He presently replaced the building with a concert hall, which opened in '68, with the Harmonic Society presenting Haydn's *Creation*. But Cincinnati wanted an opera house, so Pike finally built a stage into the hall and reopened it in 1871. He died in the following year.

And now Cincinnati's musical Renaissance, her Golden Age, was at hand. In 1867, young Fraulein Clara Baur came from Stuttgart to found the Cincinnati Conservatory of Music and to make it, during the 58 years of her management, one of the most famous musical colleges in the nation. Anton Rubinstein said that nowhere else in America had he found such adequate teaching. It was during her regime that the Conservatory removed to Mount Auburn and took over the former Handy-Shillito mansion as one of its buildings. After Clara's death, her niece, Bertha Baur, carried on with the same selfless devotion as did her aunt, taking — like the older woman — from the receipts only enough money for her own simple needs, and using the rest to aid young musicians. Music was being taught in the public schools, and in the middle '70's, the examinations were stiff.

Young Cincinnatians were also going abroad for musical study

— to Berlin, to Vienna (at least one under Liszt), to Italy. Miss Laura Woolwine went to Italy and came back Signorina Laura Bellini (well, she had to do something about that name, hadn't she?). Never were the German singing societies so numerous or more active. There were 21 of them in 1869, besides many not German, and new ones being born frequently. The Orpheus Club's *Sommernachtsfest* was an important event. The public were admitted free to the Mozart Club's rehearsals once a month. The Harmonic Society, under a talented conductor, Otto Singer, procured Christine Nilsson, Annie Louise Cary and other soloists from Strakosch's company to sing with it in oratorio in '71; and Strakosch in the same year brought a notable company, including Nilsson, Cary, Brignoli, Verger and Vieuxtemps, the violinist-composer, to the city in opera.

The war had produced several new military bands, and concert bands — Currie's, Seidensticker's and especially Michael Brand's — were reaching higher levels of artistry. They began after 1870 to add woodwinds to the brass, which was such an innovation that only 10 to 12 clarinets and flutes sufficed to give one the designation of "reed band." Orchestras were in the making, too. Signor A. Jannotta began a series of symphonic concerts in '69, but had strong competition, for the man who became Cincinnati's favorite musician, German-born Theodore Thomas, first appeared with his 50-piece orchestra from New York in Cincinnati that year and regularly thereafter, sometimes twice annually. By '71 he had so won the heart of Cincinnati that he could play a whole week's engagement there. Early in '72, that indomitable woman, Mrs. Maria Longworth Nichols, and her husband, Colonel George W. Nichols, invited Thomas to dinner one rainy Sunday at their home on Grandin Road. During the afternoon, Mrs. Nichols showed the guest some programs of the Birmingham (England) Music Festival, and asked why something of the sort couldn't be done in Cincinnati. Thomas thought it could. "Why not next spring?" asked Mrs. Nichols. That, too, might be possible.

Thereupon, peppery little Colonel Nichols took charge, as he had a habit of doing, a committee was appointed, and soon the movement which was to bring Cincinnati perhaps the greatest glory it had yet known was in full swing. By autumn, $30,000 had been subscribed to the guarantee fund, and $50,000 seemed in sight. The Festival was to be held in May in Exposition Hall, an adjunct to the Industrial Exposition, on Elm Street, near Fourteenth, where Music Hall stands today. It was a plain frame affair, with seating for 4,600 in the auditorium; cane-seated chairs on the lower floor, benches in the balconies. There would be "standing or camp-stool room" for 300 more, space for a 120-piece orchestra and for a thousand singers, if desired, on the stage. The orchestra sat on those same kitchen chairs, the chorus on benches. The house was lighted by 500 gas jets.

The committee conferred with Thomas at Schurman's Hall, over the Rhine, in October, sitting around a long table dotted with steins of beer. There were Colonel Nichols, George W. Jones, John Church, Jr., John Shillito, C. F. G. Adae, Bellamy Storer, Jr., also some prominent local musicians. Three or four of the committee were officers of the Harmonic Society Nichols being president of that, too. Thomas asked if all choral societies in the city — they then numbered 36 — would cooperate, and was assured that they would. Had he seen the hall? someone asked. "Yes," he replied, "and it is really splendid. The acoustic properties, I am sure, are good. . . . Gentlemen, we have no such hall in the East. You of the West are ahead of us in the happiness of possessing so good a place for a musical festival." Rehearsals, he said, should begin at once, the societies working separately until late in March, when they should begin rehearsing together. He thought a chorus of 600 would be enough.

There was so much music immediately preceding the Festival that one would have thought the city's taste would be sated, but it wasn't. Thomas was back for some concerts in March, at one of which Anton Rubinstein in person conducted his own now forgotten *Ocean Symphony*, which we should like to hear at least once. His conducting was unique; he began with his left hand in his breeches pocket; then, as the music became more animated, he used both hands, but at times lowered the baton and kept time with his foot — sometimes the right, sometimes the left. In April,

Pike's was packed, night after night, to hear beautiful Pauline Lucca and Clara Louise Kellogg in opera.

As the festal opening day, May 5th, 1873, drew near, the whole musical world of Cincinnati and vicinity was keyed to concert pitch. Purely for policy's sake and not because they were needed, small groups of chorus singers had been recruited from near-suburban Hartwell, from Milford, Middletown, Hamilton, Xenia, and even from as far away as Middleport, Urbana and Mansfield. These rehearsed at home until a few days before the first concert, when they came to Cincinnati to join the big choir under Otto Singer. Local musicians had been added to Thomas's orchestra to swell it to the number of 150, and he, too, was in the city for days before the opening, giving far more time than he was paid for to bring the big machine as near to perfection as possible. And when you played for Thomas in those days, you had to work, as he did. Just before an important engagement like this, the orchestra would assemble, for example, on Sunday at noon and rehearse until 4 o'clock; go across the street for a beer and a bite, then come back and hammer away again until 8 that evening, and all on their regular salary. Try that on your orchestra today.

In the hall, 800 more gas jets had been installed. "A coat of whitewash gives the interior a neat appearance," said the *Daily Times and Chronicle*, while the organ had been "neatly draped in front with blue muslin." The rest of the country had become aware that something big was on the fire. *Leslie's Weekly* sent an artist several days in advance to begin making sketches. The Associated Press detailed a reporter to the job, while music critics came from the *New York Tribune* and three Chicago papers.

There were to be four evening concerts, three matinees and a final Grand Fete Musicale. They took their music seriously in those days. The evening programs began at 7:30, and the audiences were gathering long before that time. All reserved seats for the first concert had been sold in advance. Unreserved seats, a dollar each, were sold at the door by tail-coated members of the Festival committee, each with an arm encircling his silk hat, into which the dollar bills were dropped. Here you dealt with eminences — Shillito, Storer, Pierson, Adae. When Thomas took the podium, the house seemed full, but they were still coming, until all standing room was jammed.

The first part of the program was devoted to that massive endurance test, the *Dettingen Te Deum*, composed by Handel to celebrate the Battle of Dettingen, in which fat little George II's horse ran away with him, but the French outblundered him, and the English won, anyhow. The soloists in the oratorio numbers were Mrs. H. M. Smith, soprano, Annie Louise Cary, who became one of Cincinnati's darlings, contralto, J. F. Rudolfson, baritone and Myron W. Whitney, basso. Mrs. Emma R. Dexter, Cincinnatian, contributed some independent solos, but the critics were not greatly impressed by her. After the *Te Deum*, there was a long intermission, when quantities of solid food, coffee and ice cream were consumed in the adjacent refreshment room. In the second half of the concert were Beethoven's *C-minor Symphony*, a tenor solo and the Haydn chorus, "The Heavens are Telling."

After the second concert the *Chicago Times* critic wrote, "Poor Boston! Who shall recover her laurels? Westward the star of musical empire has taken its way, and it will never go back." After the third evening, when Beethoven's *Ninth Symphony* was performed — the *Chicago Inter-Ocean* called it "the greatest musical event of the age" — the pundits simply went overboard. "To have performed this symphony alone would have justified the Festival," said the *Chicago Times*. "It was nothing less than an extraordinary achievement. At the close of the performance the house rose and cheered, as on some tremendous occasion, when all the highest and deepest sentiments are stirred. Thomas was called for with as much enthusiasm as Beethoven would have been at the first performance of the symphony in Vienna." Upton of the *Chicago Tribune* thought the Festival would have an important effect upon music in the West. It was a bombshell which should break up the lethargy and clannishness of Western musical people. There was no better place than Cincinnati to begin this work. St. Louis was too conservative, Chicago too cosmopolitan. All the materials were at hand here. One of the effects of the festival would be to "make Gilmore jubilees impossible—"a slap at Boston, where P. S. Gilmore had led orchestras and choruses of Gargantuan size in concerts punctuated by cannon fire, a stunt imitated by San Francisco, at all of which Cincinnati shuddered audibly.

After the fourth concert, when hundreds stood in the rear of the house or knelt or sat in the aisles, and hundreds more were turned away, when local trains were held over to accomodate people from as far away as Hamilton and Dayton, the *Inter-Ocean* declared that "Cincinnati has exhibited an energy and a discrimination in musical matters which have proved her audiences to be among the most enlightened in the country." That the Festival was a success financially was proven when the entire guarantee fund was returned to subscribers. Riding high on the ecstasy of conscious achievement, a little dizzied by praise, Cincinnati now resolved to have a Festival every spring and to make them progressively bigger and better. But there were long, hard years of struggle ahead. In autumn when they should have been preparing for the next spring's job, the pall of the panic was over the land, a brief bank holiday was on in Cincinnati, and businessmen, alarmed and gloomy, did not think it wise to attempt anything in '74. Even Thomas's orchestra engagement was rather poorly patronized that fall, as was Clara Louise Kellogg's own opera company, which came to Pike's Opera House (then under the management of C. D. Hess and Maurice Grau) for a week's engagement; though on the night of Miss Kellogg's benefit, the house was jammed, with hundreds, including many women, standing. And when the city's three best dramatic societies, the Allemannia, Phoenix and Eureka (German, Jewish and Anglo-Saxon) combined in a presentation of *The Marble Heart* for the benefit of the yellow fever sufferers in Memphis, the response was generous.

The events of May, '74 seemed to indicate that if the Festival had been staged, it would have been well supported. Strakosch's Opera Company, with Lucca and Cary, packed them in, and the Harmonic Society gave a two days' festival, with nearly all the big names in the city as patrons, with most of the Festival soloists, Michael Brand's Cincinnati Orchestra and a chorus of 200. They did the *Dettingen* again and other pieces, and drew full houses. So musical had Cincinnati become that a three-column review of a Cincinnati Orchestra program in the *Gazette* reproduced bits of the music here and there to illustrate the discussion.

For the May Festival of '75 the city was lavishly decorated. Vine Street was an embowered avenue of flags and green festoons to the hill-foot; many gas lamps had colored globes, Chinese lanterns hung on Fountain Square and in the parks, and the Fountain was illuminated by colored calcium lights. In the decoration of Festival Hall, it was noted that the names of all the musicians honored were German. The Chicago critics were there in force again, as were others from New York, Buffalo, Baltimore, Louisville and St. Louis. Music lovers came from as far away as St. Louis and Pittsburgh, and there were 50 from Chicago.

There were two sopranos, two tenors, and the two contraltos were Annie Louise Cary, without whom there couldn't have been a Festival, and Cincinnati's own Emma Cranch. On the first evening, the first part of the performance went off well. The second part was to begin with the *Lohengrin Vorspiele*, for which twelve trumpets had been added to the big orchestra. But just as Thomas raised his baton for the opening note, the heavens were opened and the rains descended. The uproar was terrific; the hall had a tin roof! ! !

After two or three bars, Thomas halted the orchestra, turned and shouted to the audience, "I will leave it to you to say whether we shall go on or not." "Wait! Wait!" cried those who could hear him. "I will wait fifteen minutes," he promised; but he had to wait nearly half an hour before he could resume. When the crowd emerged from the hall at ten minutes after 11:00 the sky was clear.

The second evening was given over to Mendelssohn's *Elijah*, which won unstinted praise. Of its great chorus, "Thanks Be to God," the *New York Tribune* critic said, "I have heard this many times in Europe and America — often when numbers and discipline had brought the singers to a high standard of perfection — but the effect of these 800 Western singers surpassed all previous experience." During the last evening program, Otto Singer had the well-merited honor of conducting two Liszt numbers. As he first took the podium, the whole chorus rose, the audience cheered, and he was showered with bouquets until the rostrum was heaped high with them. Thomas gave him most of the credit for the excellence of the singing, though he said the musical taste and enthusiasm of the community had much to do with it. *The Philadelphia Times* said, "If the managers of the Centennial wish to make the musical feature of our celebration one of which the country may be proud, they need go no further than to Cincinnati to find out how to do it."

But that rain on the roof had made it unpleasantly clear that no Festival was safe from interruption in that hall. Two days after the last concert, Reuben R. Springer, Kentucky-born merchant who had made a fortune in Cincinnati, suggested that a musical auditorium might be built for $250,000, of which, he said, he would contribute one-half if the other half could be raised elsewise. Mr. Shillito and the committee accepted the offer with alacrity, and began soliciting at once. Some in their enthusiasm dreamed that it might all be accomplished in time for a festival in the following year. But that was not to be.

In June, band concerts in Burnet Woods, made possible by a $50,000 endowment by William S. Groesbeck, began, with Brand's "Reed Band" supplying the music. During the first concert, Mr. Springer rode up on his well-known old white horse and sat under a tree for a while, listening, the observed of all observers. Concerts began almost simultaneously in Eden Park. In fact, summer band music had now become Cincinnati's regular fare. The pavilions at the heads of the several inclined planes all had their music of sorts, though each strove to have what we would now call a "name band" for at least a part of the summer.

"Many of our good citizens," said the *Gazette*, "are disturbed in mind by the prominent association of beer with music in the attractive summer entertainments of the city." They deprecated its influence upon manners, the editor went on, the fostering of loose principles as to drinking, and the encouragement of drinking habits among the young. But what did they propose? This talk of separating music from all coarse influences was the same sort of wish-fancy as that of a religious theater. The naked fact was that "In all America and Europe, as in this city, beer supports music. . . . The difficulty of supporting music without beer is that the great part of the class who are by principle opposed to beer care but little for public entertainment." At Price's Hill Park, where no alcoholic liquors were sold, such folk had "opportunity to support a teetotal cause." But here, notwithstanding the beautiful park and pavilion, the best of music and unequalled scenic splendor, Mr. Price "has so far received but a feeble support from citizens who hold these high principles."

The Music Hall Association was organized, with such men as Shillito, Springer, Longworth, Lincoln, Dexter, Harrison, Mitchell and Goshorn as Trustees. In the spring of '76 plans were still being debated. Contracts were let that fall and it was discovered that the building could not be constructed for anything like the original guess which, after much discussion, led to a reduction in its size, and thereby, more delay. To aid the cause, Springer, Shillito, Schoenberger Nichols, Florence Marmet and A. Howard Hinkle organized a separate $30,000 corporation to buy the organ. Finally, work began on the building, and Mr. Springer was called upon to hand over his promised cash. As work went on and costs continued to exceed expectations, he gave other sums; in November, it was remarked that "Mr. Springer is spending a thousand dollars a day on the new Music Hall. He enjoys seeing it grow." In January, '78, he put up another $20,000, which, he remarked, "will just about exhaust me, and in a manner, use me up." In the end, his contributions to the Hall and organ amounted to $190,500 — "and he still has some left in the old sock," remarked an envious citizen. Of course there could be no other name for the building than Springer Music Hall.

Meanwhile, Cincinnati revelled in rich musical fare, what with its own bands and orchestras, with Thomas coming at least twice a year, Strakosch appearing every season, always with the favorite Cary and the also well-liked Kellogg, Mrs. James A. Oates's light opera company, another Cincinnati favorite, doing *Girofle-Girofla*, *The Daughter of Madame Angot*, *The Grand Duchess of of Gerolstein*, *The Princess of Trebizond*, and in '76 giving the city its first taste of Gilbert and Sullivan; soloists — pianist Hans von Bulow in three recitals, Teresa Tietjens — who found her first orchestra conductor (at Hamburg in 1840) living over the Rhine— Emma Abbott, soprano, Annette Empoff, Russian pianist; both the Musical Club and the Cincinnati Conservatory giving highly-praised chamber music concerts, the Cincinnati Choral Society — commended by a critic as the only one in the city organized for purely musical ends — and the Arion Club doing oratorio (though it also presented *Maritana*), the all-Jewish Phoenix Club staging Flotow's *Stradella*, winning great praise, not only for its soloists, but for the "chorus of well-dressed, well-drilled men and sweet-faced, fresh-voiced women," while the 26-piece orchestra under Professor Neunbach "was head and shoulders above the bands of the itinerant companies." Signor Janotta's amateur production of *Fra Diavolo* was a splendid success until its final moment, when the bandit star was fleeing up the mountain-side just as the curtain fell, and the carbine which was to slay him missed fire — where-upon, he clapped his hand to his bosom and fell behind the rocks, anyhow, apparently dying of a heart attack.

A great testimonial was given to Cincinnati's sweetheart, Annie Louise Cary, at Pike's in May, '77, Thomas's orchestra supplying most of the music. The theater was lavishly decorated with flowers and garlands. Miss Cary sat in a georgeously festooned box with friends between her own vocal numbers, and when she sang, was almost smothered with flowers.

And at last! — as the crocuses and snowdrops of '78 crept out from the frosty earth, the Music Hall was nearing completion, and the May Festival was assured. Chorus rehearsals were incon-veniencing business and society. The great organ was being in-stalled, and there was none-too-quiet satisfaction over the fact that it had 763 more pipes than the Boston organ. Fry, Pitman and the women wood carvers were toiling day and night to complete the most elaborate and artistic organ-front in existence.

The whole Middle West and South — far too many of them — wanted to attend the Festival. Two months before the opening day, 30 music-lovers in Florence and Tuscumbia, Alabama, had engaged tickets for it and reserved passage on the steamer *Laura*

L. Davis, which plied between Florence and Cincinnati via the Tennessee and Ohio Rivers. The *Charles Morgan* brought a large party from New Orleans, and other cities and villages contributed so whole-heartedly that Cincinnati was swamped with the multitude. Railroads and excursion steamers brought in thousands on the opening day. Most of the hotels had been almost filled by mail and wire reservations; now they were packing in thousands more — several in a room, some on billiard tables, on cots, on the floors, and turning many away. Public halls, gymnasiums, the upper floors of large buildings were filled with cots; all homes downtown and on the hills had out-of-town guests. Most of those who came by river slept on the boats, as did others. Hundreds, perhaps thousands of disappointed folk could not get into the Hall, and a multitude of them stood or sat on whatever they could find outside the building at every performance.

John J. Piatt had written an ode celebrating the opening of the Hall and Singer had composed a cantata. There was an all-Cincinnati chorus of 700 and an orchestra of 100. In addition to Emma Cranch, another Cincinnati girl, Louise Rollwagen, just returned from study in Berlin, was added to the soloists. Cary was there as usual, as well as another stand-by, Myron Whitney, he of the big bartender mustache and thunderous bass. This Festival, too, went over with great praise and encomiums for the new Music Hall, which was found to have well-nigh perfect acoustic properties, such as are seldom found elsewhere. Experts came, even from abroad, to measure and study it, trying to discover its secret.

Now other cities began demanding to be told why they couldn't have such music, too. "What has Cincinnati that we haven't?" "The comparison," said the *St. Louis Post,* "between Cincinnati enjoying the full flush of splendor of her musical festival, and St. Louis playing a very faint second fiddle, so to speak, is one of the most odious we can imagine." And then the editor couldn't forbear adding a quite irrelevant gibe, "It is no consolation to reflect that Cincinnati owes $16,000,000 for an unfinished railroad leading to nowhere." The time came when Cincinnati could laugh at that sneer. The *Baltimore Gazette* said, more equably, "The thing for Baltimoreans to do is to strive with generous emulation to make our city an art center of the East as Cincinnati is of the West."

Cincinnati might now say, with Wolsey (according to Shakespeare), "I have touched the highest point of all my greatness"; but ambitious Colonel Nichols wasn't yet satisfied. He wanted the city to become the musical center of the world by establishing here a musical university which should make Miss Baur's Conservatory and other efforts look small (and perhaps adding another presidency to those of the Festival Association and the Harmonic Society, both of which he held). Enlisting a number of moneyed men, he launched the College of Music in '78, with Thomas engaged to head it artistically at $10,000 annual salary, though Nichols, with a passion for dictatorship which boded ill for the project, was elected president of the corporation.

The two temperaments, artistic and commercial, were at cross purposes from the start. Thomas wanted a larger endowment, so that none but talented pupils might be received, while Nichols and some other directors thought the school should begin being self-sustaining at once — a dollar and a half income for every dollar of expense, was Nichols's formula — accepting any who could pay the price, even the dumbest or least musical of youngsters, whom fond parents wanted to see caracoling over a costly grand piano keyboard or chirping would-be coloratura. And so college affairs quickly came to a boil.

In an article in the *Musical World*, headed "Music Jobbery," H. E. Krehbiel, one of the faculty, later a noted critic, accused the College of peddling musicians and trying to monopolize the local music market. George Whiting, noted organist, had been lured away from Boston, said the writer, by a $4,000 salary, but it was found that he couldn't be made profitable to the College of Music, so they tried to farm him out to some church, as they also tried to do with Professor Andrus, a piano teacher. Whiting and a quartet were offered for $1,000 a year or Andrus and a quartet for $1,600, much as a baseball manager would offer another club a good outfielder and three rookies in exchange for a star pitcher. Choir singers were on the bargain counter at $50 each per year. Of course Krehbiel had to resign from the faculty immediately, but other revelations that instructors and pupils were being pushed around summarily, soon followed. Several instructors resigned, and as the crowning blow, in March, 1880, Thomas himself resigned, though promising that this would make no difference in his direction of the May Festival. The whole country was interested in the scandal, and listening greedily for the latest bits of gossip. The *St. Louis Post-Dispatch* heard that cables had been sent to both Brahms and Liszt, no less, in the hope that one or the other of them might be persuaded to fill Thomas's place.

Lou Ballenberg of the Brand-Ballenberg orchestra, was Thomas's warm supporter and said he didn't know a musician in the city who wasn't. Chicago wanted Thomas, and Ballenberg, who made a visit to that city as an emissary, reported that it had no musical taste worth mentioning, but had money and wanted to do big things. But it did not get Thomas until it had its own symphony orchestra, in 1891. Thomas took over then, with the understanding that he was to continue directing the Cincinnati May Festivals, which he did until his death in 1905.

While the Festival of 1880 — after '78 they were staged semi-annually — was in progress, J. R. G. Hassard of the *New York Tribune* observed that the discords in the College of Music had not affected the quality of Festival music. Thomas was directing a 156-piece orchestra and the noted tenor, Campanini had been added to the soloists, with the familiar Cary, Cranch and Whitney among the other names. A six-day walking match was in competition with the Festival, but those who go to stare at that dreary iteration would not be interested in good music, anyhow. At the close, Hassard spoke only in superlatives: "No American music festival has ever been held with such a stupendous programme, such noble forces and such complete preparation. . . . The orchestra is by far the largest and finest ever collected in America for the performance of any serious work. . . . It was the chorus that carried off the honor. Its fine attack, its clear, full, rich tone and its absolute steadiness can hardly be praised too highly. . . . Musicians who are here in large numbers from Boston, New York and other distant places are often heard to declare that there has never been anything like it in America, and that no better chorus singing can be heard in the world." Of Beethoven's *Missa Solennis*, Upton of Chicago said, "It was the chorus's own night, and its magnificent performance of that colossal work has placed it beyond all cavil at the head of all vocal organizations of this country. It was one of those great, incomparable performances to which words cannot give expression. . . . I question whether such singing was ever heard in this country before."

As other cities developed musically, less attention was paid by them to Cincinnati's May Festivals, which nevertheless continued and still continue, a permanent institution, with unflaggingly high standards. There was no difficulty over guarantees in early years; Stewart Shillito, who succeeded his father on the Board, used to say that he could always find unfailing backers among the wealthy Jews and Germans of the city, even if there hadn't been others. It is characteristic of Cincinnati that a place in the chorus became a coveted honor and a heritage; those who sang under Thomas and Singer were often pridefully succeeded by their sons and daughters, and they by grandchildren and great-grandchildren, even to this day. And it was also to be expected that when they celebrated the 75th anniversary of the Festival founding in 1948, they would sing the old *Dettingen Te Deum* again, as they had done on that first evening in 1873. Thomas's place is worthily filled at this writing by Fritz Busch.

It was in the early '80's that the city broke out in a rash of "opera festivals." In 1879 "Her Majesty's Opera Company of Covent Garden"—an unauthorized grandiloquence of that shrewd impresario Colonel Mapleson — came, headed by Etelka Gerster, for a series of five operas. In February, '81, it appeared in an "Opera Festival," a whole week of it, with Gerster, Cary, Belocca, Campanini, Del Puente, Valleria and half a dozen other stars, and for conductor, the noted composer, Luigi Arditi. Miss Cary in *Aida* practically stopped the show; Arditi had to hand so many floral tributes over the footlights to her that he sagged noticeably under the strain. Sara Bernhardt, who was to be playing in the city during the Festival, engaged seats for herself and one or two of her company for *Mefistofele*, and an ad of the Festival screamed: "20 seats adjoining those of Sarah Bernhardt." Here, unfortunately, began the journalistic practice of describing the gorgeous gowns worn by feminine gentility at such affairs, revealing why some ladies attend the opera, and why some others read the reviews of it. For weeks preceding the Festival, Eastern cities had been flooded with circulars and news handouts, and there was some jeering in response. "A common season of opera," said the *Philadelphia Times*, "might do for New York or Philadelphia, but it is useless to offer the Western Athens anything less than an 'operatic festival!'" though the *Times* couldn't detect the difference. The *Cincinnati Gazette* printed a whole column of such delicate disparagement under the heading, "What the Envious Barbarians of the East say in their Jealousy."

During Christmas week, '81, the May Musical Festival Association took a flyer by presenting *The Messiah*, with the top-ranking operatic star of the age, none other than Adelina Patti, in the soprano lead, with Cary, Whitney, the May Festival chorus and Thomas as conductor. The choicest seats were sold at auction. Patti having thus been introduced to Cincinnati, she returned two months later in another of Mapleson's Opera Festivals, and again in '83. These affairs were staged at Pike's Opera House, and new scenery, the finest ever used, of course, was painted for them by John Rettig and two other local artists.

The opera festival of '84 was a memorable one. With an impressive roster of soloists — the aging Nilsson, young Marcella Sembrich, Scalchi, Lablache, Valleria (but alas! no Cary), Campanari, Del Puente, Capoul, Novara and others — the Abbey Opera Company came to town in mid-February, just as the Ohio River was rising to the highest flood-stage in the city's history. The gas plant was inundated, electric lights had not yet really arrived, and Cincinnati's only dependence for light were the several candle factories still working and a good stock of kerosene — neither one sufficient for a good opera performance. But on Sunday afternoon, the 17th, while the flood was at its height, the troupe gave a concert at Music Hall for the benefit of the thousands of homeless. As it lasted until after dark, in the homes along Elm and cross-streets in the vicinity of Music Hall, as some old-timers remember it, candles or oil lamps were placed in the second-story windows to help light the streets for the home-going audience.

The program, which consisted of solos and scenes from opera, was pleasantly informal. As an encore, Mme. Sembrich played a piano solo. As her encore, Mme. Nilsson had the piano drawn nearer the audience and played her own accompaniment to "Please Give Me a Penny," a particularly appropriate selection, to come just before a collection for the flood-sufferers. Mmes. Nilsson, Sembrich, Scalchi and three other women stars went through the audience with gayly decorated baskets, and contributions were generous. A tiny girl stepped into an aisle and dropped a coin into Nilsson's basket, whereupon the latter kissed her, bringing a round of applause. At that, a second little girl popped out to contribute, Nilsson kissed her, too, and the applause was deafening. When Mlle. Valleria pointed out a third child in the diva's path, Nilsson kissed her likewise, and the popular enthusiasm fairly rocked the building.

That was the last of the opera festivals, though New York's Metropolitan and other companies always visited Cincinnati when they went a-touring. As the end of the century neared, their programs were more heavily weighted with Wagner, whom Cincinntai had understood from the first, looking with cold contempt upon *Puck* and other lowbrow humorists of the '80's who ridiculed the great, crashing, Wagnerian orchestral climaxes as mere noise. When Maurice Grau and others were bringing West around the turn of the century those stupendous aggregations of talent — Nordica, Melba, Eames, Sembrich, Calve, Gadski, Schumann-Heink, Homer, the de Reszkes, Salignac, Alvary, Bispham, Campanari and Plancon, to name only some of them, marking an era which, with young Enrico Caruso just coming on the scene, included more great voices than any other in history — Grau remarked that "Cincinnati numbers more lovers of classical music in her population than many cities twice her size." There was a Schumann-Heink Club in the Conservatory of Music, which strove to be present en masse whenever that noted contralto sang.

Meanwhile, Lou Ballenberg had gone to New York, and the orchestra which he had aided Brand in developing, became, under the promotion of Misses Helen Sparrman and Emma Roedter and Mrs. William H. Taft, the Cincinnati Symphony Orchestra, the fifth of its kind to appear in the country. The three ladies started with $15,000 capital, gave their first series of concerts in the spring of '95, took in other ladies and organized the Association of Fifteen Women, which for several years operated the orchestra. Frank van der Stucken, its first conductor, served until 1907. During the first two seasons, it played in Pike's Opera House, then removed to Music Hall. Mrs. Taft resigned the presidency of the Association in 1900 and was succeeded by Mrs. Christian R. Holmes (Bettie Fleischmann), who served 13 years. Then Mrs. Charles P. Taft took over and was president until the reorganization in 1929. Through the earlier years, the small operating deficits were easily covered by a guarantee fund. But as costs rose and plans became more ambitious, the problem of keeping heads above water became an onerous one. Then the Musicians' Union arose and presented such demands that the orchestra disbanded in 1907 and remained dead through 1908.

A guarantee fund of $50,000 for five years was raised by subscription, the orchestra was reorganized in 1909, and a young conductor named Leopold Stokowski was brought from Europe — just one of Cincinnati's many gifts to America. Elderly ladies remember that he "swore dreadfully at the musicians" in broken English, and he was at times taken sharply to task by local critics for unorthodox readings of classics. In a drawing room in Avondale, you may see a leather-upholstered chair in which he would sit and shed tears of vexation sometimes over harsh criticisms levelled at him. He departed in 1912 to take over the Philadelphia Orchestra, and was succeeded by Ernst Kunwald, whose contretemps at the beginning of the First World War has been mentioned. Eugen Ysaye, Fritz Reiner and Eugene Goossens followed him in turn, which brings the story down to young Thor Johnson, the present incumbent. The most triumphant refutation of the charge that Cincinnati is hidebound by tradition is found in the fact that in 1927, as already related, it "discovered" and engaged for half the season that great virtuoso, Victor de Sabata, more than 20 years before any other American city heard him.

The Symphony Society received a great lift in 1915 when that human atomic bomb, Martha Cora Dow, died. Daughter of a small West End druggist, with a passionate desire for a musical career, nevertheless, when orphaned in her teens, she took over her father's business, ate and slept back of the store, did everything, including janitor work, slashed prices and started branches. She was fought by other druggists, and as she related in after years, was "sued, blacklisted, hounded, threatened, boycotted, slandered, followed by detectives and even sentenced to jail." But nothing daunted her unconquerable spirit. She had ten stores when she died at the age of 47, and now there are more of them. She bequeathed her entire estate – the Symphony management won't tell how much it was, but guesses run all the way from $700,000 to more than a million – to the orchestra. The estates of Mrs. Nicholas Longworth and Mrs. Victoria Hoover added more money to the endowment.

But mounting costs after the First World War soon had managerial brows furrowed with anxiety again. It was then that those public-spirited citizens, the elder Mr. and Mrs. Charles P. Taft, conceived the idea of an Institute of Fine Arts, which should be sufficiently endowed to take care of the orchestra, their own home as art museum, and to give aid to schools of art, music and the drama or any activity in connection with the arts. Towards such a fund they offered $1,000,000, on condition that $2,500,000 be contributed by others. This was done, and in the spring of 1929 the orchestra was taken over, functioning since that time without too great worry on the part of the management.

Another activity which Cincinnati has maintained against heavy odds has been its summer opera, and in the queerest setting imaginable – the Zoological Garden. The whole thing grew out of a band shell in the garden, which was remodelled to provide dressing rooms for soloists, and then in 1919-20 had an extension built on its front to complete a stage, on which it had been decided to try light opera. Over the 400 chairs which had been occupied by listeners to the concerts, a roof was hastily thrown, and an eight weeks' season of six full operas per week opened in June, 1920, with some "name" soloists, but most of the company from home talent. Cincinnati's idea of light opera meant things like *Martha, Barber of Seville, Don Pasquale* and *Hansel and Gretel.* But public response was immediate and enthusiastic, a demand for heavier opera arose. In the following season, the program was expanded, eight operas being given, with *Tales of Hoffman* the lightest, and Verdi's *Otello* the one calculated to appeal only to highbrows. *Lohengrin* drew a first-night audience of 4,000, the vast majority of whom of course had to stand or sit on the grass. The popularity of the opera was so great that more noted singers were added yearly and the plant was expanded, a clubhouse and a restaurant being tacked on, and during pianissimo passages, you could hear the dishes being washed. Fortunately, termites were discovered under the restaurant, and it was removed. An ice show in another part of the garden supplied competition, and it became the custom to have a 45-minute intermission somewhere in the opera to permit auditors to see the skaters, if they so desired.

Director Ralph Lyford, broken in health, resigned in 1924 and the opera blacked out. It was revived in 1926 by the Zoo management itself, which brought Isaac Van Grove to the podium, and later added full management to his job. He remained eight years, and added greatly to the program. He staged the first performance in America of *Falstaff* in English, and three years later achieved a thing unique in summer opera history — presented the colossal *Parsifal*, beginning at 5:30 P.M., with time out for dinner, and with the May Festival chorus singing on the clubhouse roof. He added first a week and then two weeks of operetta to the regular season. But after the debacle of '29, the opera languished, audiences fell away at times to a mere 600, the season was shortened, and despite the strenuous efforts each year of a long-standing supporter, Attorney Robert L. Black, to raise a guarantee fund, it seemed, early in '34 that the opera was done for.

In this crisis, Anthony Stavaniello, the stage director, Reuben Lawson of the Cincinnati Symphony Orchestra and Oscar F. Hild, president of the Cincinnati Musicians' Association, determined upon a revival. They and other musicians incorporated a Summer Opera Association, and scoured the community, seeking stock subscriptions and additions to the guarantee fund started by the Musicians' Union. Since that time the opera has functioned under the management — an amazing paradox to strangers — of that quiet connoisseur, Mr. Hild, head of the Musicians' Union, who has been accepted and supported by Cincinnati society and music lovers as the man for the job. The seating has long since been enlarged to 3,150, most of which is covered by roof. For years, not only the soloists but the chorus have been brought from the Metropolitan Opera, and in turn, the Zoo opera has developed and sent to the Met some fine singers, such as James Melton and Jan Peerce. The orchestra has always been drawn from the Cincinnati Symphony. Fausto Cleva, its conductor for 17 years, has now become one of the conductors at the Metropolitan.

The opera fell upon evil days in the summer of 1949, when a combination of unfavorable circumstances, including increasingly higher costs of everything, seemed about to close it in mid-season. The Thomas J. Emery Foundation, Hulbert Taft and his paper, the *Times-Star*, the Musicians' Union and several others came to the rescue with substantial sums, which enabled it to complete the season. Then in the following April it suffered another staggering blow when Oscar Hild, its presiding genius (without salary) for sixteen years, died. But carrying on the tradition, Mr. Hild's successor as head of the Musicians' Union, Robert L. Sidell, was also chosen to manage the opera, and it will continue.

At Music Hall on New Year's Eve, 1883-4, there was a "concert of Negro minstrelsy, the tunes of Christy and Foster." "Music Hall," said the *Commercial-Gazette*, "is not associated in the popular mind with Negro minstrelsy, but there was no desecration in the singing within its walls of the old plantation melodies as they were sung last night." Desecration, quotha! What would that editor think if he saw some of the signs displayed outside Music Hall today — "Basketball, U. of C.," "Wrestling Friday Night;" "Art Mooney, Topper Dancing." Well, the old Hall must live, and in an age when everything costs far more than it is worth, if there isn't enough filet mignon procurable, it must e'en fall back on tripe. It came dangerously near being sold at one time, and only heroic measures by the friends of music saved it. It seems to be — at least, one hopes it is — reasonably safe at the present moment, save perhaps from those who deplore its architecture. But suppose it is old-fashioned externally; grant that it has too many pinnacles; they'll never be able to build another with better acoustics than, if as good as, that of its big, roomy, kindly interior. New Yorkers with knees calloused from sitting in the theaters and concert halls of the metropolis can relax here. where there are inches of space between their knees and the seat in front. The foyers, upstairs and down, and the corridors encircling all floors, have the vastness of an age which did not have to pinch space or pennies.

The May Festivals are of course always sung here. And the popularity, with youth as well as age, of the Cincinnati Symphony Orchestra concerts on Friday afternoons and Saturday evenings in the Hall through a long season, is an earnest of the virility of the city's great musical tradition. The women's committee always sells more season tickets in advance here than are sold for any other orchestra in the country. The rapt attention of a loving and understanding audience, palpably aware of what it is hearing, where, one fancies, a casual mention of "the C-major Symphony" would be instantly identified by almost anybody within hearing as Schubert's incomparable Ninth, makes a Symphony evening an interesting experience to a stranger. The intermission, with the big foyers and corridors all thronged and humming with talk, are the pleasantest scenes imaginable, for almost everybody seems to know almost everybody else. Meanwhile, in the lower lobby, as is quite fitting, the two tutelary deities, frock-coated Reuben R. Springer in marble (by Preston Powers) and Theodore Thomas in bronze (by Clement Barnhorn) stand looking benevolently upon these later generations who are the fortunate inheritors of their great legacy.

CHAPTER XVIII

Battlers for Ideals

It is not only in music and art that Cincinnati has built monumentally. Less spectacular but quite as noble has been the work of certain valiant souls who, through vast toil and travail, created two other institutions in which the city takes particular pride — the University of Cincinnati and the Cincinnati General Hospital, now in harmonious union under the municipality. Their story is a melodrama a century and a half long.

John P. Foote, the bookseller-type-founder, who, like most other early nineteenth-century Cincinnatians, also wrote books, remarked that "A history of the Medical College of Ohio may not inaptly be styled a history of the Thirty Years War." Foote, long a trustee of that college, found that the medical profession was "remarkable for the belligerent propensities of its professors." Efforts were made to discover scientifically some reason why professors of medicine quarrelled so violently, but in vain. Dr. Daniel Drake seemed to think that if medicine had some "ultimate tribunal" to settle controversies, as law did in the Supreme Court, peace might be more easily attained. Drake didn't realize it, but one of the major reasons for the turbulence in the Cincinnati arena was his own peppery temperament. He was a great scientist for his period, one still revered by scientists, but high-strung, impatient with opposition and incompetence. He had some favorite opponents, especially one Dr. John Moorhead, who were well-nigh as difficult as he was.

When Daniel Drake, then a boy of 15, was brought from his Kentucky farm home to Cincinnati for study in 1800, Dr. William Goforth was the town's chief physician — a lovable, well-schooled man for his day, who went about with powdered hair in a pigtail and a tall gold-headed cane, and who was keener at collecting fossils and Indian arrowheads than the fees owed him. His pupil, young Drake, was his accountant, pharmacist and general handy man, as well as studying the simple medicine of the time by making town and country visits with him, observing what he did with three or four primitive instruments and a parcel of herbs and tinctures. His charges for country visits were 25 cents per mile ridden, or half that if the horses were fed. If he collected at all, it was often in the form of a bushel of potatoes or a razorback hog on foot, so that he was frequently short of money, while Daniel sometimes went for months without a copper in his pocket.

Dan was "going on 20" when Dr. Goforth did the best he could for him by giving him a "diploma" as "Surgeon-General of the First Division of the Ohio Militia — a hollow and preposterous honor. Soon afterward, with his father's help, the youth went to Philadelphia for some real medical study with specimens and paraphernalia. He returned in 1806 when Goforth migrated to New Orleans, leaving his practice to the pupil. This nerved him, within another year, to take a wife and start a family.

He had the current itch to write, but he was one of the few who had the ability to produce worth-while writing. His first two books, historical and descriptive things about Cincinnati, are still of value. He became owner of a drug store — also selling groceries and hardware — and there installed the town's first soda fountain. His activities seemed numberless; he was one of the founders and trustees in 1815 of the Lancastrian School, which grew into Cincinnati College, whose medical department Drake founded 20 years later. He promoted the organization of the first Episcopal congregation in the city. He was one of the promoters of a Library Society, he started a Debating Society and a so-called School of Literature and Art. He dashed off to Philadelphia for a few months to complete his medical course and came home with a real diploma. Then he turned his drug store over to his father and brother Benjamin (also a budding author) and built a new home on the brow of the northern hills, which, with wry humor, he christened Mount Poverty.

But he had been at home again scarcely a year when he was invited to join the faculty of Transylvania College at Lexington,

Kentucky, and as he also had an urge to teach, he accepted, leaving his Cincinnati practice to an associate. But he found dissension in the college faculty and he didn't like it there, so after one winter he resigned and returned to Cincinnati. He and two other physicians soon began delivering a series of lectures on medical subjects, but this didn't satisfy Drake. He wanted a college, and early in 1819 it was chartered, with the three lecturing doctors, Drake, Rogers and Slack, and a fourth, Samuel Brown, as incorporators. But a strange and unexplained rift arose immediately; Rogers and Brown were dismissed, and Drake and Slack with two others launched the college, with 20 students, in an upper room over the Drake drug store, in November, 1820. In the following spring it graduated a class of 7.

Again dissension flamed, and in 1822 Drake was ousted by a majority vote of the little faculty (in whose hands the charter had placed such power), men who owed their jobs to him. But this aroused such a roar of protest in the city, where Drake had become a famous citizen that the cowed professors reinstated him, whereupon he promptly resigned. Another year of practice and he was once more bidden to Transylvania, where he remained three years. But his dearly beloved wife died in Lexington, a great blow to him, and once more he returned to Cincinnati. Ten years later one of his colleagues at Transylvania called his departure "a stroke from which the college has never recovered." Almost immediately after his return to Cincinnati, he fell dangerously ill, and one of his Lexington confreres rode 80 miles on horseback to attend him, remaining with him until he was convalescent. Curious what extremes of love and hatred the man aroused!

In 1827 Drake, in partnership with a Dr. Cobb, opened the Cincinnati Eye Infirmary. He also took over the editorship of the feeble *Western Journal of the Medical and Physical Sciences* and gave it a start on a long and useful career. In its pages, early in 1830, appeared the first account printed in America of a Caesarian section, though the operation, it seems, had been performed in this country before that time. The story is one of those sublimely heroic sagas of pioneer life which fiction can never rival. Dr. Drake had noticed the janitor of the medical college standing humbly in the door of the hall, listening to his lectures. He questioned the man, found that his name was John Lambert Richmond and that he had somehow succeeded in acquiring a considerable amount of book-learning, despite the handicaps of a family of ten children and bitter poverty. His chief ambition was to become a physician, and to this end Drake promptly aided him.

Richmond settled in Newtown, a hamlet just east of the city, near the Little Miami River, whose best recommendation must have been that living was cheap there. One cold night in early spring, when all streams were high, he was called to attend a young pregnant Negro woman who was suffering greatly, and who lived in a log cabin then so nearly surrounded by flood waters that the doctor had to be rowed to it across a submerged cornfield. The cabin was new and the wind blew so lustily through its unstopped crevices between the logs that quilts had to be held up around the bed to prevent its blowing out the candle which was the doctor's only light. He quickly decided that there could not be a normal birth; he would have to take the child by Caesarian. He had only a few simple instruments, no anaesthetic, no antiseptic; but he did the job so well that the woman was up and at work 24 days later. The simplicity and modesty with which Richmond describes the episode, not stressing the difficulties, make it a profoundly moving story.

In 1830 Jefferson Medical College in Philadelphia called Drake to its faculty and he accepted, retaining the editorship of the *Western Journal.* But he could no more be kept static than can a globule of mercury; in February, '31 he resigned and returned to Cincinnati, taking with him a galaxy of medical illuminati which struck terror to the Medical College of Ohio. He soon announced the creation of the Medical Department of Miami University. Ohio Medical knew that it could not prevail against him and asked for terms. With the easy mutability of the times, the Miami connection was promptly severed like a thread, and Drake and his Eastern stars plus a Kentuckian, Dr. Henry, were added to the Ohio Medical faculty, those who had taken part in ousting him being, at his instigation, tossed out to make room for the newcomers.

Drake's Eastern colleagues persuaded him to compromise by retaining one antagonist, Dr. John Moorhead, Irish-born, heir to a baronetcy in his own country, an able though rough and intolerant man, often privately called "Old Hydrarg," because of his strong belief in the virtues of such potent stuffs as "blue mass" (mostly mercury) and calomel. Now Drake was back in a practically impossible position, with Moorhead glowering at him on the faculty and the trustees of the college more or less hostile. There had been cold wars through the newspapers ever since 1819, all pseudo-anonymous, nearly every doctor in town being involved, and now they came to what might be called a shooting war. Drake and Moorhead met on the public landing one day while the former was waiting to board a boat, swapped insults and then fell into a clumsy, amateurish fight, in which Moorhead had an eye blacked and his scalp laid open. A little later, Brother Benjamin Drake and Moorhead had another fisticuff. The college was in a stew most of the time; it was charged that some of the professors went armed, and the rancor inevitably affected the students, who took sides and sometimes brawled amongst themselves. The trustees, after trying in all imaginable ways to keep the two chief fighting cocks apart, finally promulgated rules intended to keep Drake from invading Moorhead's province. Drake had already been angered by the discharge of his friend Henry, the Kentuckian, and at this new indignity, he resigned and returned to private practice again.

Meanwhile, the college trustees and faculty were trying hard to improve conditions. They invested $1,000, a fearful expense for the time, in chemical apparatus, manikins, etc. Grave-robbing by the students to obtain cadavers for dissection had become a scandal, so the faculty sought to have the practice handled more skilfully by adding a professional "resurrectionist," an elegant term for a ghoul, added to the staff. The impossibility of teaching medicine and surgery without human subjects for dissection and the absence of legal methods for obtaining such subjects kept medical colleges in hot water for more than a century. Dr. Goforth had had to leave New York because of being involved in such trouble.

Drake, now living on Vine Street between Third and Fourth,

had never an idle moment. When not attending patients, he was fighting strong drink and cholera epidemics, boosting the proposed railroad to Georgia, lending aid to the College of Teachers, founded in 1833, and other educational dreams, nagging at the Medical College, as in an article of 1835 for the *Whig and Commercial Intelligencer,* so long that it had to be printed as a supplement, giving much attention to social-intellectual affairs, bossing the literary parties at his home, introducing his motherless daughters to society, entertaining visiting celebrities such as Miss Martineau. Harriet Beecher wrote of him about this time:

"Our family physician is Dr. Drake, a man of a good deal of science, theory and reputed skill, but a general mark for the opposition of all the medical cloth of the city. He is a tall, rectangular, perpendicular sort of body, stiff as a poker, and enunciates his prescriptions much as if he were giving a discourse on the doctrine of election. The other evening he was detained from visiting Kate, and sent a very polite, ceremonious note, containing a prescription with Dr. D's compliments to Miss Beecher, requesting that she would take the enclosed with a little molasses at nine o'clock precisely."

In the meantime the Medical College of Ohio fell into bad repute. Its collapse seemed imminent in 1835, and some of its officials appealed to Drake to save it. As might have been expected, he said he would return if they would jettison Moorhead; but they were unwilling to lose so able a man, and refused. Drake, his blood stirred by this rebuff, proceeded to organize the Medical Department of Cincinnati College, bringing some excellent men from the East for his faculty. In its second year, his school had more students than Ohio Medical. Seventy years later, Otto Juettner, Drake's biographer, called this "the greatest medical school the West has ever seen," adding that it had a faculty equalled by only two others in the nineteenth century.

Again there was war to the knife. Ohio Medical contested the right of Cincinnati College to operate a school of medicine under its charter. Both sides filled the air with dialectic, polemic, and plain and fancy slander. Students of the two schools traded buffets now and then, and once there came near being armed conflict.

Major Daniel Gano, of the old Cincinnati family of that name, who was then living in the Brighton neighborhood, told the story. Mrs. Gano, by the way, had become a disciple of Samuel Thomson, Yankee theorist who, though no doctor, had revolted against such current medical practices as bleeding and extravagant dosage, especially of such dangerous drugs as mercury, jalap, calomel, arsenic and laudanum. He favored herb remedies, emesis, enemas and steam baths.

One cold winter evening, when there was a frozen crust of snow on the ground, a young Ohio Medical student known to the Ganos knocked on their door and whispered hoarsely, "Major, there are some friends at the gate wishing to see you." Mr. Gano went out and found a group of students, the college resurrectionist, officially known as the janitor, and "Professor S - - - -," minus hat and cloak, with a handkerchief tied around his head and suffering much pain. The group had been fired upon with a shotgun while unearthing a corpse from the Potter's Field, not far off, and the professor was the only one hit. He was of opinion that they had been attacked by a party from Drake's rival college.

Major Gano invited them into the house, saying, "My wife is a good doctress. She will do everything possible for you." She washed off the blood and found three flesh wounds, in the eyelid, ear and neck, probably by birdshot. She applied a bandage, "saturated with Thompsonian third preparation of lobelia, gave him hot composition tea," and relieved him somewhat. The "other gentlemen" — students and resurrectionist — were given wine. Major Gano hitched up his horse and drove downtown, where he found that one student, fleeing the resurrection scene, had carried the news to other members of the class, and they were arming themselves with guns, pistols, clubs and swords, expecting to join battle with the Drake forces. Fortunately they were persuaded to postpone the war.

Some time later, Major Gano, in conversation with one Dennis Kelly, who operated a brickyard near the cemetery, mentioned this incident. "Oh, that was the way of it, eh?" exclaimed Kelly. "Why, my brickyard boys did that. They shot at the doctors to frighten them and stop their digging up the dead; and they went

to the grave, and seeing a dead man and a cap and cloak laying together, they thought they had killed a doctor, and so ran away,
and they've been afraid to speak of it since."

After four years of struggle to survive without endowment,
Drake and his staff were forced to give up, and Cincinnati College's medical department was no more. But as a physician and
fighter for his causes, he still held high rank in the city's estimation.
When the fiftieth anniversary of the founding of the city was
celebrated during Christmas week, '38, he was asked to deliver the
principal address, and he gave them their money's worth — three
hours and twenty minutes of it. In 1840 he was lured to Louisville,
where there was an excellent and comparatively peaceful Medical
Institute, and there he seemed settled for life.

During that decade, other new medical institutions were born
and died in Cincinnati, though two survived — the Eclectic Medical Institute, founded in 1843 by Dr. T. V. Morrow, who had previously had a small college in upstate Ohio; but when the body of
a citizen was found in its dissecting room, he had to leave town in
a hurry, with his dwelling in flames behind him. The College of
Dental Surgery, chartered in 1845, is said to have been the first
dental college in the world to occupy a building especially erected
for it. For many years it gave a Bible to each graduate, along with
his diploma. The Cincinnati College of Medicine and Surgery,
founded in 1851 by Alvah H. Baker, for a time tried to undermine
the Ohio and Miami (organized 1852) medical schools by giving
free tuition. Under an abler man, R. Stockton Reed, it was the
first medical college in the West to admit female students, and
continued to function until 1902. First and last, some 20 medical
schools, three of them for women alone, have operated more or
less briefly in Cincinnati.

The Medical College of Ohio was more acridly than ever
embroiled internally in 1849-50. Again Drake was called upon to
save from total ruin the school he had founded, and this sentimental reason alone moved him to accept the bid. Moorhead and others
who had been his chief opponents were now gone and the skies
seemed fairer, so he left the excellent institution where he had not
had too much trouble and returned to the problem child. He had

won great acclaim that year with the publication of the first volume (900 pages) of his *Systematic Treatise on Diseases of the Interior Valley of North America,* the fruit of 20 years of study and travel. Professor Silliman of Yale called it "an enduring monument of American genius," while Humboldt considered it "a treasure among scientific works." When the American Medical Association met at Cincinnati that year, the book was one of the chief topics. Drake was led to a seat on the rostrum, among the celebrities, and so much ado was made over him, to the tune of so much applause and cheering, that he was moved to tears and could not speak a word. Friends wanted to propose him for the presidency of the Association, but — with a curious humility, contrasting with his firm belief in his rightness when in controversy with his colleagues — he refused, pleading unworthiness. He also refused to visit Europe, where he was well known, fearing that he would be no credit to America among the old continent's highly trained scientists.

As always, he had a long and eloquent inaugural address ready to deliver when he opened the college term, but he soon found that he was back in the same old caldron of trouble. There was a new element in the broth now. The secretary of the Board of Trustees, had a smoothly-working spy system, by which the private sayings and doings of his faculty were duly reported to him; information which he used to damage the reputation of those of whom he did not approve. Before the end of the season, Drake resigned and was promptly called back to Louisville. But scarce two years more — this may begin to sound incredible, but it seems to be true — the brawling outfit in Cincinnati begged him to come back and subdue it; and once more, fatuously letting himself be convinced that all that was needed was a firm hand, he obeyed. The closing scene of the drama was tragedy as thrilling as any playwright could desire. At the very first faculty meeting after Drake's return, a violent quarrel broke out, in which nearly everybody joined. Drake, stricken to the heart, tottered away and took to his bed with a high fever, to which his overwrought system had long been liable. He never arose from it; his spirit was broken at last. "Medical schools have consumed me!" he muttered to those at his bedside, and they were in agreement. How much his agony and that of his colleges could have been eased had he been less contentious himself, it is impossible to say. On November 6th, 1852, the man who has been called the Franklin of Cincinnati and the Father of Medicine in Ohio, died at the age of 67.

To pick up another thread which was, after a century, woven with that of the city's medical instruction, General William Lytle suggested in 1818 that the Lancastrian Seminary be "elevated into a respectable college," and offered $11,500 towards the endowment of such an institution. Dr. Drake took fire at once, threw himself into the cause, and enough more was raised to bring the fund up to $40,000. Cincinnati College was chartered in 1819, with Reverend Elijah Slack as its first president, and an enrolment of about 60. You had to be a real student if you wanted to attend a Western college in those days, To enter the Freshman class at Cincinnati, you must not only have studied Latin and read two books of the *Aeneid*, but you must know "the Greek grammar and one or two of the Evangelists and the Greek Testament." And as another sample, in the Junior class, mathematics included surveying and navigation. It was no place for dilettantes.

But an English visitor of 1823 did not think it was likely to be well patronized until it was better regulated. He was "much shocked at the want of decorum exhibited by the students, who sat down in their plaids and cloaks, and were constantly spitting tobacco juice about the room."

It was not due to this indecorum, but rather to the depression of the 1820's that the college declined, and in 1827 all departments ceased to operate except a primary school, which kept the charter alive. The trustees hoped that the Mechanics' Institute, the Lyceum and the Public Library "may be induced to connect their exertions with the College," but they did not. Nevertheless, in 1834, the depression having been shaken off, a movement for revival began. When Ohio Medical's attempt to reengage Drake failed, he proposed that in rejuvenating the College, it take on a medical department. The story of that brilliant four-year connection has already been told. The Cincinnati Law School, founded in 1833 by Timothy Walker, John C. Wright and Edmund King, also merged with the College. William H. McGuffey, who came as President in 1836, was just putting forth the first two of his readers, and brought glory to the institution thereby, though he could be induced to stay only three years.

The College pioneered in several ways. It established the first chair of music seen in any American college, and one of the very early courses in civil engineering. Professor Ormsby M. Mitchell, as we have seen, persuaded the citizens to finance an observatory. The College building burned in 1844, and when it was shortly rebuilt, the academic department was dropped, leaving the Law School, most virile of the departments, to carry on and flourish. After the Civil War, it produced some notable men of law, such as President and Chief Justice William H. Taft, Vice-President Charles G. Dawes, Supreme Court Justice Willis Van Devanter, United States Attorney-General Judson Harmon, Senators Atlee Pomerene of Ohio and Richard P. Ernst of Kentucky, Speakers of the House of Representatives Champ Clark, Joseph G. Cannon and Nicholas Longworth.

In 1803 a 21-year-old Pennsylvanian named Charles McMicken, whose sole earthly possessions were a horse, saddle and bridle, rode into Cincinnati, and in the course of a few years, had established a shipping business down-river. Taciturn, a lifelong bachelor, he acquired considerable properties in Cincinnati, Louisiana and elsewhere. At his death in 1858 he bequeathed the greater part of these holdings, believed to be worth a million dollars, to the City of Cincinnati, for the founding of an institution to instruct in "all the higher branches of learning except denominational theology." Here was the real beginning of the University of Cincinnati.

The City Council at once appointed a Board of Trustees for McMicken University, but long and tediously static years were to intervene before it became more than a name. To begin with, Louisiana refused to recognize McMicken's bequests of his property in that State, which was a serious blow. The income from his Cincinnati properties fell so low during the war that it did not pay the taxes and the annuities specified in his will. But after the war, the annuities began to be terminated, and careful handling by the Board, headed by Rufus King, brought the income up to

$35,000 in 1868. The Trustees proposed a consolidation of McMicken with Cincinnati College and other institutions, the College then having property on Walnut Street worth a quarter million and an annual income of $13,000, though its critics charged that "it is doing nothing in the way of education." But the union could not be brought about at the time, and the College continued to exist in name, a dry shell, only its law school really functioning. The *Gazette* was merry about its annual meeting in 1880, calling it "Mr. McGuffey's annual election" of the "ancient college," and reporting that "the old regular party, the staunch defenders of law and order and scholastic dignity, conquered all opposition" and reelected the old Board of Trustees, on which were a score of the biggest names in Cincinnati. Of course there was no opposition whatever, the election being a cut-and-dried affair.

The only thing that could be accomplished by the McMicken trustees in 1869 as a starter was the creation of a school of design. In 1870, with a change of name, the University of Cincinnati was chartered, being the first to be born under the earliest municipal university statute in the United States, just passed by Ohio. A city bond issue in 1872 made possible the erection of a recitation and laboratory building, a slender, four-story, red brick affair on the steep hillside back of McMicken's modest cottage and close alongside the Clifton Inclined Plane. The first president was General and ex-Governor Jacob D. Cox. In 1877 the first three graduates received their diplomas. In 1889 the Council authorized the appropriation of the south end of the big park, Burnet Woods, to become the University campus; and there its great array of buildings has developed, some of whose names reveal their donors — Hanna, Cunningham, Van Wormer, Nippert (stadium), Kettering, etc. Gifts of more than a million from Francis H. Baldwin and two million from Mrs. Charles P. Taft the elder, plus bond issues and collective donations from many citizens have made possible the busy campus of today, with its 25 buildings and 12,000 students, under the able presidency since 1932 of Dr. Raymond Walters. Among its distinctions are the originating of the cooperative system of technological education in 1906. Old Cincinnati

College was finally absorbed in 1918, though it still exists as a corporation.

One of its accessions in recent years, a part of a great auxiliary group northeast of the main campus, is a storied institution whose building was an epic equal in heroism and human endurance to that of Amadis of Gaul. Danish-born Christian R. Holmes, brought to this country in his teens, clerked in stores, polished furniture and did draughting in railroad shops, finally contriving at 29 to win a medical doctor's diploma from the Cincinnati College of Medicine and Surgery. After a brief internship, he entered private practice, and by publication of articles, illustrated with his own fine drawings, made such an impression that only three years after his graduation, he was elected president of the local Medical Society at the age of 32.

He married Bettie Fleischmann, of the distilling and yeast-making family, and presently opened his own private hospital. But he was driven relentlessly by dreams of a great modern hospital, a better medical school and a more learned medical profession. In 1900 he became a trustee of Cincinnati Hospital, which was a fire trap, screenless, unsanitary, poor in equipment, criminally slipshod in operation. Most of its trustees were opposed to any change. Holmes was at first aided in his crusade against it by the fact that his brother-in-law, Julius Fleischmann, became Mayor of the city in 1901, and by an opportunity to air his views in a series of articles in the *Times-Star*, then owned by Charles P. Taft, who continued a valiant ally until death.

Holmes's drive at length brought the authorization of a $550,000 bond issue, but he shocked his critics by spending too much of it, they thought, for a 20-acre site in Avondale. There work began on a building for contagious diseases, the first of his plans, but when three-fifths of the half-million had been spent, a new Mayor, Dempsey, took office in 1906, and he and the Board of Public Service proposed to spend the rest of the money in patching up the old hospital.

But Holmes had sold his vision to the citizens too well for that. The public roar of protest startled the politicians; the newspapers excoriated the Board and the people did so at public hearings. Yet still there was delay until early in 1907 when Holmes asked for a writ of mandamus to compel continuance of the work. At that, the Board yielded, and the building went on. In the autumn, the Council authorized a $2,000,000 bond issue — later raised to $2,500,000 — overwhelmingly voted by the citizens, and under a new Mayor, Leopold Markbreit, proprietor of the *Volksblatt*, who had always been on Holmes's side, the skies seemed brighter.

But the elderly Markbreit's health failed in two years, and a new Mayor came in who was not so friendly. There is not space to tell of Holmes's long battle by day and by night against every sort of harassment to achieve his ideal. Politicians and theorists beset him at every turn; his plans were too grandiose, he had his head in the clouds, he was throwing money around like water, such were the comments. Even some of his staunch friends who battled at his side at times wavered a little, wondered whether all his dreams were practical. But he fought them through, the great plant slowly rose, and on December 1st, 1912, he had the happiness of seeing a long article in the *New York Times*, headed, "The Finest Hospital in the World in Cincinnati." The world was taking notice, too — even London and Berlin. Buffalo, contemplating a new hospital, sent a commission to learn how to "build like Cincinnati." The *Buffalo Express* used the word "perfection." Detroit papers also ran lengthy articles. "Detroit should build as did Cincinnati," said one editor, and it did — adopted plans which were almost a duplicate of Holmes's. St. Louis sent an emissary to study what other authorities were calling the world's finest. In January, 1914, it became an adjunct of the University of Cincinnati, Holmes being installed as Dean in a notable ceremony, with University President Dabney presiding, and medical eminences from afar in attendance.

The old College of Medicine and Surgery had died in 1902, leaving (beside an eclectic and a homeopathic school) only the Ohio and the Miami Medical Colleges. In 1906 the Ohio faculty considered the Miami school "gangrenous," but Miami's opinion of Ohio was still lower — it was a "corpse." Yet within three years the two united as the Ohio-Miami Medical College, and this shortly became an appanage of the University. Now Holmes wanted a new medical college plant. Mrs. Mary M. Emery gave $250,000, asking that it be duplicated. Harry M. Levy, Mrs. Charles Fleischmann, William Cooper Procter and the Charles P. Tafts each gave $50,000, and the remainder came in only slightly smaller donations, including $10,000 from Mrs. Holmes. When they were in difficulties again during the First World War, Holmes wrote of them to Mrs. Emery, then in the East, asking for $25,000, and she promptly wired $50,000. She could always be depended upon.

After Holmes's death, hastened by overwork, in 1920, Mrs. Holmes built a hospital for private patients as a memorial to him and for years took care of its annual deficit. It has not been mentioned that the planning of the main hospital's kitchen arrangements and of the nurses' building were largely hers. Now came the Carnegie Foundation with a belated gift of $250,000 to the medical college, while William Cooper Procter added a princely bounty, $3,000,000, for a pediatric foundation. A score or more of cities have frankly patterned hospitals after Cincinnati's, and it can no longer claim preeminence, but there are still none better. It remains unique, in that it is a branch of the University of Cincinnati, which in turn, is controlled by a Board appointed by the Mayor; but in Cincinnati, with the sort of government that it has had for a quarter-century past, this gives rise to no fears that the big medical center will become a political jungle.

It is notable, among other things, as the workshop of great scientists such as Dr. Gustave Eckstein, he of the canaries and the brilliant books, Dr. Clarence Mills, high authority on the physiological effects of climate and weather, and Dr. Martin Fischer, physiologist, linguist, artist, author, whose students seek places where he is scheduled to speak and beg for admission, whose corner of the building is rich with wood-carven walls of his own design, whose lecture room is one of the sights of the city, the wall back of him containing a full reproduction of an apothecary's shop shelves in Renaissance Italy, filled with beautiful majolica jars for drugs, herbs, etc., the Professor himself delivering his lecture from the apothecary's small marble-topped counter.

CHAPTER XIX

The Domestic Giraffe, The Fighting Jackass And the Lonely Pigeon

LIFE IN CINCINNATI had vivid spots of color for small boys sixty years and more ago, when you could walk along a certain street and see a giraffe loafing in a back yard as casually as a pony, but lunching off tree-foliage far higher than a pony could reach; or where you might be bowling along a road on the outskirts of town and see an elephant or two in harness, plowing the glebe just like a mule. Cincinnati was better accustomed to exotic animals than most cities, for it was the home of a circus which scattered them about the town, and in 1875 the city began to enjoy its own zoological park, which had at least two distinctions that made it unique in the world.

Cincinnati's own circus magnate, John Robinson, was the son of a Scotch soldier in the British army during the American Revolution. The father, like many another redcoat, settled in the United States after the war, and became a blacksmith in upstate New York, where John was born, somewhere around 1802 to 1806. The boy was intended for his father's trade, but he stayed only long enough to begin the development of some powerful muscles, then ran away and joined a circus. He served with one and another of the small tent-shows of the day, becoming a bareback rider and a doughty fighting man. The legend is that his first circus ownership came to him as the result of a mutiny among the hands of a small show, which he put down, with considerable damage to the mutineers, and as his reward, took over a half share in the outfit. He had various partners, but eventually the show became John Robinson's alone. Old John, as he was being called, and as he called himself when he was in his fifties, made himself solid in the South before the Civil War. He regarded it as his own private territory, and resented the invasion of other circuses. He even became a Southern champion, pitting "Southern men, Southern women, Southern horses and Southern enterprises against the world."

Nothing was unfair as between circuses, if you could get away with it. Advance bill-posters covered up each other's sheets, pasted strips over the competitor's dates, "postponing" its appearance, and pulled any other trick they could think of, Old John letting no one outdo him in this respect. He had his winter quarters at Cincinnati long before the War, though winter didn't last as long with circus folk then as it does now; every season Robinson would still be trouping around the Southern States in November and December. In fact, in January, 1878, when Old John had retired from the road and his son John F. was manager, the show was still touring northern Alabama. In November, 1873, when it was wagoning through Texas and five days behind its schedule — a not uncommon thing in such out of the way parts; the country folk just kept coming to town day after day until the circus appeared — Old John at his office in Cincinnati received news of a serious "clem" (attack by rowdies) at Jacksonville, Texas. There was so much damage to equipment and personnel that young John cancelled the two remaining weeks of bookings, extending up into Kansas, and brought the show home. In Texas in those days it was nothing uncommon for a tough to shove a pistol through a ticket window and ask, "This good for a ticket?"

Robinson's circus became a deep-rooted Cincinnati institution. His wagons, cages, costumes, all equipment were made there. All his posters and other printing were done by the *Enquirer* job department until the plant was burned, along with Pike's Opera House and all of Robinson's paper for the season, in 1866. He then bought the *Enquirer's* job business and set up a plant of his own, which he put under the care of two young Civil War veterans named Russell and Morgan, who had been printers before the War. From that beginning came Russell, Morgan & Company, one of the nation's great printing concerns, which eventually bifurcated into the United States Printing Company and the United States Playing Card Company.

After the War, the Robinson circus made a practice of opening the season in April with a week's stand in its home town. In '71 it gave the city a novelty, an indoor circus, playing that week in a big roller skating rink — a presage of the Ringlings' annual opening engagement at Madison Square Garden. But critics thought the bareback riding below standard, "probably due to the effect of the wet, rheumatic weather outside upon the men and horses." Old John wanted to lease the Industrial Exposition building for winter quarters and performances, but the directors would not permit it.

Imitators — James Robinson, Yankee Robinson, "the New Robinson Circuses," came around, trying to confuse the public, but getting nowhere with Cincinnati. When Barnum began advertising his as "the Greatest Show on Earth," Cincinnati knew better than that; it could be no more than second to "John Robinson's Great World's Exposition, embodying in one Grand Travelling Exhibition more Genuine Usefulness, General Information, Greater Curiosities, more Object Teaching, Rational Amusement and Inimitable Show Demonstrations than were ever congregated together by the will of MAN, backed by Millions of Capital." It had a "Special fleet of Steamers for Transportation, employs 2,000 (!) Men and Horses, 100 Male Performers, 20 Lady Celebrities, 42 Cages of Wild Beasts . . . 3 solid Miles of Procession, $12,000 South African Giraffe, $30,000 Hippopotamus from the Baher-el-Azreh or Blue River Nile . . . Giant Ostrich, 15 feet high, not an Emu, as is usually palmed off by confidence operators, African Harte Beest, often advertised but only seen in Old John's collection." Best of all, it was a Strictly Moral Circus.

Barnum sought novelty with a balloon, giving a volunteer couple an aerial wedding in connection with an afternoon performance in '74. The balloon obligingly took the wedding in a semicircular course over the Kentucky suburbs and back over Walnut Hills; but its drag-rope pulled down a batch of police, fire and private telegraph wires in the hills, and when the superintendent of the fire-alarm telegraph drove up there to survey the damage, his horse became entangled in the wires, ran away and broke its neck. The rotund Mr. Barnum, perspiring only slightly, paid for the damage, and four days later sent four young ladies, one of them a daughter of Benn Pitman, and all dressed in their very best, up in the balloon. But in the upper air they ran into a terrific shower of rain, which ruined their dresses; they descended in the country, dried themselves by a farmhouse fire and were driven back to the city more or less unhappily.

Old John scorned all such monkeyshines. They weren't circus business; they weren't ethical.

His first winter quarters were in the West End, but you were apt to find his animals 'most anywhere. His home was on Seventh, at the corner of narrow little College Street, which ran back of the *Enquirer* office. It was there that the $12,000 giraffe sometimes spent a few weeks in the barn and back yard. Old John built a theater, already mentioned, at Ninth and Plum Streets, and in winter kept some of the animals in its basement. Auditors in the theater are said to have had at times a faint notion that there must be a livery stable somewhere near by, but people of the '70's were accustomed to that sort of thing.

Mr. Robinson also built a country home (still there) in what came to be Terrace Park, just east of the city, and there, from time to time, entertained many exotic and often distinguished guests from all parts of the world. Some of the animals were kept there at times, too, and it was there that the elephants were given exercise by doing plowing and other chores. He built a Protestant church on the edge of his estate, and was a regular attendant there when in residence. His own private pew was on one side, and he sat in it squarely against the wall. He had a little door made in the wall there which was an object of wonder to the builders, but congregations soon discovered its object. He was an inveterate tobacco-chewer, and he wanted an outlet which, no matter how cold or stormy the weather, he could open momentarily and spit through.

He was ever open-handed, and gave, regardless of creed or color. Trouping through the Shenandoah Valley after the Civil War, he found that even some country churches had been destroyed in Northern scourges, and he gave money to rebuild them. The thunderous profanity with which he had grown up could not be curbed, no matter in whose presence. Two nuns once solicited his aid for a certain large charitable project, timidly mentioning $500 as his possible contribution.

"Five hundred dollars!" he boomed. "What the hell can you do with a God-damned $500? God damn it, make it a thousand!" and he made it a thousand.

What was mentioned as a nonpartisan committee, though it had a strong Republican odor, met at Turner Hall in the spring of '75 and nominated Hon. John Robinson for Mayor, with Bellamy Storer, Jr., put up for City Solicitor. They couldn't have picked a better-known citizen as their Mayoralty candidate, and his fine old bearded face under its low-crowned soft felt hat looked as well on campaign literature as it did on the circus posters; but he was easily beaten in this, his only excursion into politics, by the incumbent Democratic Mayor, Johnston.

His eldest son, John Franklin, who became known in the family as The Governor, carried on the tradition for eccentricity. The house at Seventh and College became one of five or six stories, and as each child married, it was given a floor, a suite complete, with kitchen. Each family ate what it liked and didn't cater to others. If brother John the Third's family invited Gil's family to dine, and the latter didn't like the brand of coffee John used or the way it was brewed, the guests brought their own. This choosiness in some cases even caused the guests to bring their own meat.

Under John F. and then John G., John Robinson's Ten Big Shows Combined was really one of the big ones of circusdom, having at one time, it is said, 800 employes. John G. was one of the first to take performers to hospitals and orphanages to entertain children. The younger Robinsons went more and more into other businesses, and the fourth generation passed out from under the big top forever. Some of the Robinson animals became actors in the Selig jungle pictures of early movie days. The last appearance of the elephants as Robinson's was as Republican symbols at the inauguration of Governor John W. Bricker of Ohio.

There was another man who did much to bring Uganda and

Araby and Ind to the small fry — and large — of Cincinnati. Andrew Erkenbrecher, a boy out of Saxe-Coburg-Gotha, acquired a small gristmill near Cincinnati at 22, and presently began making starch there. In middle life he had the largest starch factory in the West. He became concerned about the inroads of caterpillars on American trees; it seemed to him that American birds were not taking care of the situation as birds should, so he decided to import birds from Europe to handle the job.

He organized in 1873 the Association for the Propagation of Rare Birds, with the notion that he could people America with the feathered fauna of the whole world. Membership was to cost $10, and each member was to receive his share of the foreign birds, which he was to set free in his own property, and which supposedly would settle there, they and their descendants, and thereafter be his choir. But few people seemed to be interested in the $10 Bird Club, so presently a new organization, the Cincinnati Acclimatization Society was evolved, with Mr. Erkenbrecher as president, and some solid citizens, who could put up real money, behind him. The secretary, Armin Tenner, made several trips to Europe, returning with not only sparrows and starlings, but larks, linnets, finches and others, mostly insectiverous, but none of which throve here save the English sparrows and starlings.

Leaving St. Bernard, where he had built up his starch business, Erkenbrecher now moved into Avondale, where he constructed an aviary in his yard. He had begun in 1868 to talk of another project — a zoological garden. He retired from business in order to give all his time to it, with the cooperation of such men as Otto and Florence Marmet, William Resor and Julius Dexter. It was finally opened in 1875, with a limited collection of animals and a staff of the rawest of amateurs to operate it, with no end of troubles resulting. Even before the Zoo opened, the lioness escaped from her cage and had a desperate battle with a donkey, which the latter was judged to have won on points, though he was so badly clawed that he died later. But he had the glory of having been written up and editorialized from coast to coast as the jackass who had stood up and slugged it out with the king, or rather, the queen of beasts. The lioness fled the park after the melee, and for a day and a half held all the western hills house-bound, in a state of terror. The pursuers did not know how to catch her, so it was reluctantly decided to shoot her. The skin was mounted, as was that of a leopard which died a few months later. When this was followed in death by a seal, a newspaper bard swept the strings of his lyre and sang,

"The elephant moves mournfully 'round,
The band plays the Dead March in Saul.
The smell of the living, the stench of the dead
Hangs over the Zoo like a pall."

And an editor inquired, "Isn't the collection of stuffed animals at the Zoological Garden getting unpleasantly large?"

When the formal opening took place in the fall of '75, the crowds were enormous. The Mount Auburn Inclined Plane sped up its schedule, and the buses from the incline to the Zoo were so overloaded that four horses each could scarcely drag them. Streams of people on foot filled the sidewalks. This kept up for weeks, the disasters which punctuated the pageant probably being good publicity. Somebody made a baboon ill by giving it chewing tobacco — though it recovered — and one of the alligators escaped from its pool one night and after a frantic search, was found to have moved over into the more commodious swan lake, which the swans promptly vacated. Then the ostrich, considered the Zoo's most valuable specimen, died in midwinter, from under-heating of its quarters, it was believed.

The superintendent was fired, but not until the new elephant man began to get his fingers on the controls did real order appear. The Zoo's first elephant, Conqueror by name, was bought from a circus which was at Dayton at the time, and its keeper, Sol Stephan, brought it down to instal it in its new home. Having led it into the house prepared for it and given instructions as to its care, Stephan said, "Well, good-bye, Conqueror," and with a pat on the big fellow's trunk, he went out and started towards the gate of the park. Left alone, Conqueror looked about him and a panicky feeling shot through him. Stephan had left him often before, but always there were other elephants to keep him company. Now he was absolutely alone — no Sol, none of his own kind. His resolution was formed in an instant; he must find Sol. He pulled stakes and went out through the nearest door, regardless whether it was big enough for him or not.

Stephan had not reached the gate of the park when he heard shouts behind him. Turning, he saw a man running and waving his arms.

"Come back!" the man implored. "That elephant's broke loose!"

Stephan ran back and found Conqueror standing outside his house, whimpering and looking wildly about for his friend. With evident joy, he hurried to meet Sol and put his trunk around his neck.

The superintendent was afraid to let Stephan go. "Can't you stay just a few days," he pleaded, "until he gets used to his quarters?" and Stephan agreed to do so. The days lengthened into weeks. He resigned from his position with the circus, took over the care of other Zoo animals, eventually became head keeper and general manager. When he retired in 1937 at the age of 88, he had been with the Zoo for 62 years and done much towards building one of the great animal collections of the country. Meanwhile his son, Joseph A. Stephan, now general superintendent, has completed more than half a century with the Zoo. As this is written, Joseph's son, Dr. Sol G. Stephan, is the Zoo's veterinarian, besides having an animal clinic of his own. On April 3d, 1949, old Sol's one hundredth birthday was celebrated with great eclat, and late in October, he died.

The Zoo's popularity was threatened in the summer of '77, first, when it was reported that they were charging 10 cents a glass for ice water at the Zoo refreshment stand, and secondly, when the Lookout House, at the head of the Mount Auburn Incline, gave advance notice of the coming of a white whale. Herman Melville was then in literary eclipse and the promoters had probably never heard of him, else they would have advertised this as the original Moby Dick. W. C. Coup, later a circus owner but then manager of the New York Aquarium, started with the whale via the Erie Canal, and sent publicity bulletins of their progress from Syracuse and Rochester, but the whale died at Cleveland. Another was then shipped, "by express," we are told, though this is difficult to believe. It was reported in good health at points in New York and Ohio, but lived only one day after reaching Cincinnati. A third was procured, and it, too, lived but a few days. Each successive whale was smaller than the preceding one, and the tank in which the last one came, the *Gazette* reported, had "shrunk to the size of a coffin." Its body was embalmed and put on exhibition at the Lookout House, but within 24 hours an odor arose which necessitated a hasty call for Si Keck, and then for fumigation of the building.

Not two decades had passed after Mr. Erkenbrecher imported his first English sparrows before some Cincinnatians were cursing the day he was born. Roosting by thousands in the mazes of telegraph and telephone wires then overhanging the downtown streets, they were a menace to the habiliments of everybody on the sidewalks. One day a group of sports who frequented Jack Frey's cafe on Vine Street procured police permission to fire several shotgun charges into their overhead assemblies along that street, and brought down some hundreds of them, though with no telling how much damage to the wires. The tiny fowls were baked into a pie in Frey's kitchen and eaten by the boulevardiers with vengeful relish, though, as may be surmised, with no noticeable effect upon the sparrow multitudes.

Two Clifton millionaires, Robert R. Bowler and George Schoenberger, liked blackbirds, and provided food for them for years, with the result that thousands of those wise grackles chattered in the trees of the two great estates, not always to the content of neighbors. Mr. Bowler even provided in his will a sum for their sustenance after his death, and this was carried on through fifty years, until the blackbird relief agency was abolished by court order.

The Zoo has had more than its share of ups and downs, especially downs. For several years, Messrs. Erkenbrecher, Dexter and the Marmets guaranteed its expenses. But as they died, one by one and the collection of animals increased, the institution seemed threatened with extinction. Then John Hauck came to the rescue, paid off all debts, bought the ground on which it stands for $135,000, and leased the property to the Cincinnati Zoological Company with privilege of purchase at any time. In 1901 the Cincinnati Traction Company bought a controlling interest in the Zoo and operated it for 16 years. Finally, rising costs again threatened it, and in 1917 the street car people wanted to get out from under. In this crisis, those sterling citizens, Mrs. Charles P. Taft the elder and Mrs. Mary M. Emery — what would Cincinnati have done without them? — each offered $125,000, provided other citizens would contribute a like sum, which was done; the city never failed to stand up to such a challenge. Once more the Zoo staggered to its feet and kept going for 15 years; but in 1932 it was on the ragged edge again, and there was talk of selling the animals and turning the land into a realty subdivision. At that, the people with one voice, cried out against the proposed abandonment; the municipality bought the Zoo outright for a public park, and gave the management of it to the Zoological Society of Cincinnati, so that it now seems safe forevermore.

We mentioned that the Cincinnati Zoo has two distinctions which make it unique in the world. One is that it is the only zoological park in which grand opera is performed. The other is that in it lived and died the last representative of a now extinct species. In its earlier years, the Zoo always had a cageful of those beautiful American passenger pigeons, most graceful of all birds, which flew over Cincinnati by millions in the long ago, and which often roosted in the very beech groves where the Zoo now stands, drawn there by their love for the tiny beech-nuts. In the 1870's the enormous flocks were no longer seen, but new specimens could still be procured, though their numbers were decreasing alarmingly. Some couples of them occasionally reared young in their cage, though this, too, was becoming less frequent. When a pair of them hatched a setting of eggs in 1888, Superintendent Stephan regarded it as an important event, for it had become no longer possible to find any wild specimens at large. The species was dying, and dying rapidly. That brood of '88 was the last reared in captivity. One by one, its members died until only one was left, a female which they had christened Martha. Stephan scoured the continent for a mate for her, but none could be found, though the Zoo would have paid handsomely for one. Inexorably, the conviction settled upon naturalists everywhere that this was the last passenger pigeon left on earth.

As ten, fifteen, twenty years passed, Martha became perhaps the zoological world's greatest celebrity. Her beautiful bluish and faint mauve tints faded, her plumage grew ragged, but ornithologists from all over America came to see her, and occasionally, one from across the seas. Her dulled eyes regarded them indifferently. She was just waiting — waiting for the summons to join the moa and the dodo and the quagga, the great auk and the heath hen, in that Valhalla of God's creatures which have been unable to endure the presence of man upon earth. She might have hastened the end, if she had known how, through sheer boredom. The time came when she could no longer fly up to the perch which had once been so easy for her, and they lowered it a little. It was not long before that was too high for her, and they lowered it again . . . and again . . . and again. At last, the feeble wings could no longer raise her even an inch; her appetite failed entirely, and on September 1st, 1914, her head sank to the floor and she died at the age of 26 — the last of a mighty race which had once numbered probably hundreds of millions. The Smithsonian Institution had long since made a request for her body for mounting, and there it may be seen today.

CHAPTER XX

Families

IT CAME to pass in the latter nineteenth century that the question, Who were the First Families of Cincinnati, those who came to it by land or those who came by water? was for a time ardently debated. But there could be only one possible answer. In point of time, certainly Symmes, Stites, Ludlow, Lytle, Gano and the other very first adventurers who camped on the wildwood site of the future city arrived by the Ohio River. And close after them came such names as Burnet, Taylor, Harrison, Anderson, Allison, Cummins, Corry, Howell, Dennison, Gest, Baum, Mansfield, Piatt, Langdon, Spencer, Drake, Smith (of course), Kilgour, Faran, Wade, to name only a few. And so — although this was taken none too seriously by most folk, although Lawsons, L'Hommedieus and others who came by land stood just as high in the community — it was whimsically decided that the real F. F. C.'s, those taking precedence over all others, were those whose ancestors floated down the Ohio in flatboats, arks and broadhorns, midwestern fluvial *Mayflowers*, bringing with them their oxen and asses and heirlooms, their ploughshares and kettles and spinning wheels, not to mention some elegant and beautiful furniture and creature comforts.

Early and repeated intermarriages, as the descendants of the first families contentedly remained in the circle of the hills have made practically all of the prominent old stocks, what are left of them, cousins, and give point to a favorite joke which some of them now and then chuckle over. It is of a young matron in the first year or two of Fort Washington's existence who was outside the stockade one day with her baby in her arms when Indians appeared unexpectedly, as they had an annoying habit of doing, from the surrounding woods. Warned by shouts from the men on guard, she ran at her best speed towards the stockade gate through a shower of arrows. When it appeared that she might not be able to reach it in time, she resolved to save her baby at least, and so tossed it over the stockade. Nobody caught it, and the veracious chronicle records that it alighted on its head. The mother won the race to the gate, after all, and was saved, while the infant survived the high dive, and in due time became an Ancestor. But from that day to this, any mental or psychological vagary, real or seeming, which may appear in any of the variously-named posterity, is humorously ascribed by other cousins to that cranial jolt, *circa* 1790-92.

Perhaps one may touch lightly upon a few family connections and prominent representatives of old stocks without being expected to compile a Cincinnati genealogy. As intermarriage wove its colorful pattern and created probably more hundreds of "kissing cousins" than any other city of its size has known, some old family names have been perpetuated, even to this day, while some others, through a preponderance of girl-babies and those bludgeonings of fate noted in genealogical tables as "d.young" and "d.s.p.," were eliminated. Some, through fortune or achievement, have kept themselves in the public eye, always a part of the pageant of current history; others, less acquisitive or less intense in action, are no longer in the news, perhaps even forgotten. Ask where are the Symmeses, the Ludlows, the Ganos, the Lytles, the Yeatmans, the L'Hommedieus, and faces are blank and heads are shaken. "Must be all gone" is a surmise at hazard, though some may be only in eclipse or *in absentia*.

The daughter of John Cleves Symmes, the founder, and his wife (a New York Livingston) married young William Henry Harrison, later General and President, to become the ancestress of many worthy Cincinnatians, as well as of another President. Two honorable names in the colony were those of Dr. Goforth, already mentioned, and William Goforth, the first territorial judge. The Judge's daughter Mary, who married Major-General John S. Gano, had "a highly cultivated mind and much force of character. In the wilderness she dispensed hospitalities with the grace and elegance of the best society of Eastern cities." She and Bella Ludlow, who married Judge McLean, Anna Sheffield, who married Major Ziegler, Cincinnati's first German citizen, and Mrs. Philip Grandin, were a prominent quartet of friends and social leaders in early days. Goforth is one of the vanished names.

Time was when Burnet was a name to conjure with in Cincinnati; when Judge Jacob Burnet's mansion sat in the midst of a demesne covering a whole block, and the Judge's brother, Isaac G. Burnet was usually Mayor or something else high up in the city government. They were a handsome family. Caroline, the Judge's youngest daughter, married General Nathaniel C. McLean (and died at 36) and Murat Halstead declared fifty years later that such were her beauty and charm that it were better to omit the refreshments from a party than to have her absent. A son and a daughter of the Judge married a daughter and a son of John H. Groesbeck, of a family whose eminence in Cincinnati annals continued throughout the century. Another Burnet daughter married Vachel Worthington. The prominent Neff family received a considerable infusion of Burnet blood, for Peter Rudolph Neff married Caroline, a granddaughter of Judge Burnet, and when she died, married her sister Josephine. Josephine's daughter married Lawrence Mendenhall, whose father a doctor, sometimes attended the Beecher family, and whose household is said to have contributed characters to *Uncle Tom's Cabin*.

Judge Burnet's daughter Elizabeth married William S. Groesbeck, attorney, one of Cincinnati's most distinguished citizens, with service in both the State Legislature and Congress, famed for having made the greatest speech in the impeachment trial of Andrew Johnson, with offers of judgeships and a nomination for the Presidency, but refusing them all, donor of the free summer concerts still heard in Burnet Woods, scholar who, in his latter years, daily read the Greek and Latin classic originals for recreation. His sons and daughters married into other old families — Perry, Ludlow, Goddard, Cox — and one married an Englishman, Sir Kenelm Digby.

The Groesbecks were another comely race. In mid-nineteenth century, the Misses Olivia Groesbeck and Sally Carneal were spoken of as the two most beautiful girls in Cincinnati. A portrait of Olivia by Thomas Buchanan Read, in the home of a kinswoman in New York, confirms not only the fact of her beauty but of Read's fine ability as a painter. She visited England once, and met the Duke of Wellington, evidently making a distinct impression upon that old connoisseur; for there is a legend that when, long afterward, he tasted some of Nicholas Longworth's wine, and praising it, asked where it came from, "Cincinnati!" he repeated. "Ah, that is where Miss Groesbeck lives." Like some other beauties, Miss Olivia was so flattered and besought by a legion of admirers that she was unable to choose among them, and so presently found herself in middle age and still a maid. But still beautiful, she was courted and won by the dashing Civil War soldier, General Joseph Hooker, himself then rising of 50. They were married in 1867, but she lived only two years thereafter.

Major Silas Howell, an officer of the Revolution from New Jersey, was an ancestor, through female lines, of many Cincinnati family names not his own. One of his daughters married Thomas D. Carneal, the capitalist whom we have mentioned as rearing many mansions about the city, one of them still standing in Covington, and they were the parents of the beautiful Sally Carneal, one of the two toasts of the town in the '50's. Another Howell daughter married Nicholas Longworth, of whom we shall hear more. A granddaughter married first John H. Piatt and then David E. Gwynne, being his second wife. Gwynne's son, Abraham, married Lettie Flagg, sister of William J. Flagg, who married Nicholas Longworth's daughter Eliza; and Abraham's daughter Alice, on a summer sojourn in Newport, met young Cornelius Vanderbilt II, married him, and for forty years after his death at 56, reigned in solitary state in the enormous French chateau which he had reared on New York's Fifth Avenue, so completely the acknowledged and imperious head of the family that no identification of her was needed and none used other than just "Mrs. Vanderbilt."

Among those who came down river a few years after the founding was a plain, skinny, undersized youth of 20 named Nicholas Longworth; a name which became perhaps the best-known in nineteenth-century Cincinnati, not only because of wealth and beneficence but because he and his descendants were so often engaged in some activity which won headlines. His family, New Jersey loyalists, had been impoverished by the Revolution, and young Nicholas had been apprenticed to the shoemaker's trade. But his vision was too big for that, and he had no sooner landed in Cincinnati than he looked about for something else. Getting into Judge Burnet's office as a law student, he was presently declared an attorney, and practiced desultorily until about 1819. But in the meantime he had embarked in the sideline which made him the city's topmost capitalist — trading in realty. In the redoubling city, he bought many a lot for $10 and sold it later for hundreds.

His only venture into politics was his very early campaign for and election to the post of fence-viewer. John Kilgour was his associate in office, and a doggerel verse of the time pictures them at their duties, Kilgour, who was tall, looking over the fence, while little Nick could only peer through the crack through which the pigs crawled. Gorham A. Worth, the United States Bank manager at Cincinnati, said of him, "He did not claim to be a scholar, either in his profession or in the walks of science or literature. His books were nothing, for he never read them; the same may be said of his office, for he was never in it. He carried his law in his head and his papers in his hat. . . . When I first knew Mr. Longworth (1817), I doubt whether he was worth $5,000. He is now (1851) said to be worth five millions" (an overestimate).

One of his best strokes was made while he was still practicing law. A client whom he had wrested from under a charge of horsestealing lacked cash, and offered his attorney two copper stills in payment of his fee. Shrewd Nicholas presently traded them for 33 acres of scrubby-looking land bordering on Western Row (now Central Avenue), which he lived to see worth more than a million dollars.

But young Nicholas was no mere granite-faced go-getter; he enjoyed life in many ways. Among other activities, he was a member — along with Peyton Symmes, Arthur St. Clair, Jr., Benjamin Drake and others — of The Thespians, a local dramatic club or Little Theatre affair, though we do not know what parts he played. He was only 23 and still a fledgling lawyer when he married a young widow, Susan Howell Conner, whose father, Major Howell, as a Revolutionary war veteran, had acquired a thousand acres of land on East Walnut Hills, along an Indian trail which became the winding, aristocratic Grandin Road of a later day; and this, in turn, accounts for the later colonization of Longworths in that area.

For a few years the young couple lived modestly, but as the city mushroomed and the husband's realty turnover reached enormous proportions, the time came soon enough when they need skimp no longer. Nicholas was even playing with a hobby, which he characteristically turned into a business — the grape-growing and wine-making introduced by the early German-Swiss settlers around Cincinnati. He actually became the leading wine-maker in America, was world-famous, and made Cincinnati a center of the wine trade, for many others there engaged in it. From his favorite grape, the old American red variety Catawba, he made all manner of still and sparkling wines, including a champagne which the British traveler, Charles Mackay, pronounced equal to France's. "The Western Bacchus," as Mackay called him, "a man whom the Greeks would have apotheosized," employed mostly French wine-makers, and his cellars were one of the sights which few visitors to the city failed to see. Charles Richard Weld, who went through them in '55, found the stowage of casks and bottles, the removal of sediment, the flavoring and corking "identical with the practice in Epernay. Indeed, all the men employed in the cellar are from that neighborhood." He said that Longworth's champagne was then selling as high as Moet's.

Mr. Longworth remarked in later life that he never advertised his wine. Perhaps not, but he did not scorn publicity, and anyone who knew him was liable to be called upon to assist in it. Cincinnati friends who went East usually had to take some bottles of his wine along to give to prominent people. A case was sent to Henry Wadsworth Longfellow, in acknowledgment of which that bard sat down and knocked off a three-stanza jingle, alleging among other things that

> The richest and best
> Is the wine of the West
> That grows by the beautiful river,
> Whose sweet perfume
> Fills all the room
> With a benison on the giver.

Painters and sculptors who went to Italy for study told of receiving cases of Longworth's wine, which were to be distributed among prominent personages, American and Italian. Results are seen in a letter from Hiram Powers to his patron in 1857, which tells how greatly the family enjoyed the wine, and adds that the Marquis Ponciattica wished a barrel of the dry Catawba sent to him, with the bill.

A contemporary said of him that "He was very shrewd, quick-witted, with great common sense and acquisitiveness. He had little dignity or learning, but had a quiet good humor and a readiness at repartee which made him very popular." Another tells us that despite his wealth, he was "haunted at times with the dread of dying in the poorhouse." In 1830, as his daughters were growing up and needed a more elegant setting, he bought Belmont, the mansion on Pike Street which Martin Baum had built and lost, and which had lately been occupied by Mrs. James Wood's "respectable female school." Here, in rough garb, with unkempt, stringy hair hanging almost to his shoulders, he tended the lawn and shrubbery, and was not infrequently mistaken for a gardner by strangers who wanted to see the wealthy Mr. Longworth's estate. He used to say that he sometimes received a dime tip for showing visitors about the grounds, and on rare occasions as high as a quarter, which he accepted with thanks, preserving his anonymity. Here, too, he once concealed a fleeing slave, hotly pursued, lied to the pursuers, took the grateful Negro into his service and left him a small legacy at his death.

Although frugal and a sharp hand at a trade, he was not stingy, as his liberal aid to painters and sculptors bears witness; he even financed the publishing of a book of poems for a Mrs. Rebecca Nichols, who otherwise would never have been seen in print. As his son Joseph and his daughters married and settled for a time in spacious Belmont, producing sons and daughters, Grandfather Nicholas, who hated being pestered for money, placed every morning in a drawer of his desk a sum of cash in various denominations, regarding which the established dictum was, "Let everyone take what he wants, and don't bother me." On Monday mornings for several years, he distributed food to the poor. He often spoke of himself in the third person, "There's Longworth; it takes $30,000 a year to pay his taxes, and it keeps him poor to raise the money." In the '50's, it was said that he was second in America only to John Jacob Astor as a taxpayer. In 1858 he paid $37,570.56 in taxes on 366 parcels of land, most of which had at least doubled in value since he bought them.

He liked to promote home ownership, and is said to have aided hundreds of families to acquire homes by selling them lots on easy payments and being patient with them. William D. Gallagher, the rising young author, had scrimped and saved a few dollars, and at 21 bought a lot on easy terms from Longworth, hoping some day to make it a home for his widowed mother. "Billy," said Mr. Longworth to him, "I want you to build your mother a home; can you raise money to buy the lumber?" Billy thought or hoped he could, somehow. "All right," said the capitalist. "Get the lumber, I'll build the house and you can pay me when you are able." That was his way, to give others the help without which they could not help themselves.

When Professor Mitchell promoted the Observatory in the '40's, Mr. Longworth donated four acres on Mount Adams for its site. He frequently offered to sell the city land at a very low price for a park. In 1856 he made another offer, a whimsical one, of land for a park or a much-needed workhouse, on long-time notes, the interest to be paid eventually, "one-half to the most worthless and needy vagabond that could be found, the other half to such of the Longworth descendants as may at any time be reduced to poverty." The offer went unaccepted.

Joseph, the only son of Nicholas, married Annie Rives, daughter of a Virginia aristocrat, Dr. Landon Rives, and sister of Margaret Rives, who married Rufus King, grandson of the Revolutionary patriot and son of Edward King and Sarah Worthington, philanthropist and art patron. Old Nicholas by this time had tired of living downtown and built his country home, "Rookwood," on the ancestral Howell property bordering the Grandin Road, where a colony of Cincinnati's best-known names was coagulating — Burnet, Douglas, Goodman, Grandin, Groesbeck, Harrison, Hooper, LeBoutillier, Sibley were some of them. Joseph took another piece of the Howell land for his home. Of Nicholas's three daughters, Eliza mated with William J. Flagg; Catherine with Larz Anderson, son of a Revolutionary officer and brother of the general who defended Fort Sumter, and became the mother of nine sons, of whom the eight still living when their father died in 1878 were his pallbearers, and who, to trace the family pattern further, married respectively girls named Kilgour, Worthington, Force, Nettleton, Mendenhall, Hinkle, Herron and Wallingford. Mary, the third daughter of Nicholas, a precocious child who, at the age of thirty months, so her father wrote to a friend, could recite "the 39 stanzas of Goldsmith's poem, 'The Hermit'" (did she forget the fortieth?), married John Stettinius, and produced another John, who married Eloise Olmstead, and on another slice of Rookwood, built his estate, "Oatfield."

Joseph Longworth, a stocky, scholarly person with bushy sidewhiskers, was never greatly active in business, and remarked with gentle ruefulness that he would be remembered only as the son of his father and the father of his son. The truth is that today he is hardly remembered at all. But he should be held in the city's grateful memory as the man who made almost a free gift of the present Eden Park to the city after blight had destroyed the vineyards there which had been his father's joy, who made the largest original contribution to the founding of the Art Museum in that park, and who financed his daughter in the promotion of the Rookwood Pottery.

His brilliant son and daughter were not so easily forgotten; the dynamic, overpowering Maria, who, as Mrs. Nichols and Mrs. Storer, did so much for Cincinnati, and Nicholas the Second, a brilliant, many-sided but slightly erratic lawyer with a big, King Humbert mustache, a boyish magistrate before he was 30, judge of the Common Pleas Court at 32 and of the Supreme Court of Ohio at 37; a sparkling conversationalist, an excellent amateur photographer before kodaks were invented, a writer of good poetry and translator of Greek classics. He married Susan, daughter of Judge Timothy Walker, whose wife was Ellen, daughter of that Mrs. Wood who had the "respectable female school" at Belmont. Of Ellen's two sisters, one married Edmund Cranch, the Semi-Colon wit, the other, Olivia, wedded U. P. James and mothered that dynasty of bibliopoles.

Judge Longworth died in 1890, aged only 45. Of his three children, Nicholas III became a distinguished and beloved Congressman, was married in 1906 to Alice, daughter of President Theodore Roosevelt, in the White House, and like his father, died much too soon. His sister, Annie Rives, married Buckner Ashby Wallingford, iron merchant, whose Christian names indicate Southern ancestry; as this is written, she still lives on the Grandin Road. The other sister, Clara Eleanor, was married at Rookwood in 1901 to Count Adelbert, the son of the French Marquis de Chambrun, and who, in turn, himself became the Marquis. The Countess Clara resides in Paris, an able historian and litterateur who has written more than a dozen volumes, some in French, some in English, and some published in both languages.

When his daughter Maria married Colonel George Ward Nichols, a peppery little Maine Yankee and Civil War veteran, Joseph Longworth built a home for them, with some fine interior wood carving by Piatt, on a portion of the Rookwood property fronting on Grandin Road. Mr. and Mrs. Nichols were two high explosives whom it was dangerous to bring into conjunction. Each had a head popping with ideas and a determination to put them over, regardless of opposition. Acquaintances and associates often found them difficult, especially the Colonel, whose troubles with Theodore Thomas have been mentioned, as have his wife's services to music and art. Eventually the Colonel's galvanism became too much for his wife, or perhaps it was because she had fallen in love with handsome Bellamy Storer, Jr., middle-aged son of the old Judge, for there was a divorce in 1886.

But the prospective Mrs. Storer, who owned the home in which they lived, did not propose to turn her ex-husband out into the cold. Instead, always original, she did a thing unique in social history; she built a new house for herself not 25 feet from the old, and lent the older one to Nichols for use during his lifetime. The children of the couple were to live with her, but visit their father as often as they wished. To facilitate this, the two houses were connected, not only by an underground tunnel, but by a bridge at the second story. But before the rearranged establishment could begin functioning, Colonel Nichols died. With twin houses on their hands, the Storers are said to have lived most of the time in the older one.

Mr. Storer, a prominent attorney, went into politics, served four years in Congress in the '90's, and aided William McKinley in reaching both the Governorship and the Presidency. In Washington he and Mrs. Storer became acquainted with the effervescent Teddy Roosevelt (then in Civil Service) and his wife, and presently "Dear Bellamy," "Dear Maria," "Dear old Fellow," and other loving epithets were flecking their letters. When McKinley was made President, Roosevelt wanted a post under him, and because of McKinley's obligation to Storer, he asked the latter to recommend him. Storer spoke, and Roosevelt became Assistant Secretary of the Navy, while Storer himself became Minister to Belgium for two years, and then Minister to Spain. The family friendliness was intensified. "What trumps you two blessed people are!" Teddy wrote at one time.

But trouble was on the way. The Storers had become Roman Catholics in 1896, and now began to push the idea with Roosevelt and others that their friend, Archbishop John Ireland of Minneapolis ought to be made a Cardinal. With Mrs. Storer it became another cause, a promotion like that of the May Festivals and the Rookwood Pottery. Roosevelt agreed with them and wrote letters to that effect which were produced in evidence later. After he became President through McKinley's assassination in 1901, he continued, under Mrs. Storer's prodding, to assist in the campaign. She was probably responsible for Bellamy's journey to Rome from Spain to take the matter up personally with Pope Leo — which did Archbishop Ireland no good.

But now that "Dear Theodore" was in the White House, the Storers had a new "must" — a top-ranking ambassadorship for Bellamy, preferably either London or Paris, though both posts were occupied at that time by able men. Mrs. Storer gave nobody any rest, either on this subject or on the Cardinalate. "I must, I suppose, poison off one of our ambassadors," said the President, plaintively to Mgr. Ireland. "Mrs. Storer has written me an awful letter. She gives me no time. Try, I beg of you, to calm her."

But there was no stopping her; she kept on hammering. In the fall of 1902 her husband was named Ambassador to Austria-Hungary, the best that Theodore could do, and from Vienna she continued the bombardment about the Ireland affair. Roosevelt was now in a difficult position. It had not been so hazardous for him to meddle in a Catholic church appointment when he was a Government underling or even Governor of New York, but as President of a predominantly Protestant country, he began to see that he didn't want to appear in any such imbroglio. So he was now trying to curb Mrs. Storer's activities and mentally veering towards the point of denying that he had ever had anything to do with the matter. In July, 1904, he confessed that "Mrs. Storer is an awful trial. I wish to Heaven she would either quit her professional sectarian business or get Bellamy to leave public life." From there, it was only a step to his peevish request to Storer, "For God's sake, tell your wife to shut up!" Finally, late in 1905, the irreparable break came and the President removed Storer from his post. Mrs. Storer came home, wrote a pamphlet entitled, "Roosevelt the Child," giving her side of the story, to which he retorted, electing the Storers, in a favorite newspaper whimsy of the day, to his "Ananias Club."

That was Mrs. Storer's last public activity. Her husband died in 1922 and she sold the Grandin Road property. The new and well-to-do owners did not want a Siamese twin dwelling-house, so they razed the new one, which they considered in "atrocious" taste; a curious reflection, that an artist and a promoter of art should create such a thing.

Nicholas Longworth III, Congressman, Speaker of the House and husband of Alice Roosevelt, was the last of his name in the direct line from Nicholas the founder. He did not marry until he was 37, and left only one child, a daughter, Paulina. A merry as well as an able man, liked by both Democratic and Republican colleagues, he was also honest and independent. When the Roosevelt-Taft breach occurred in 1912, and the ambitious Rough Rider opposed his old friend for a second term, Nick Longworth, though he was a Roosevelt son-in-law, loyally supported his friend Taft, whom he considered wronged.

Today, old Rookwood still stands, the last of the Longworth manors; but Mrs. Alice, who cares little for Cincinnati, drops in only occasionally, and then not for long.

After the first Mrs. Nicholas Longworth died, the family had no further use for the too-spacious Belmont, on Pike Street, and it was sold in 1866, reputedly for $100,000, to F. E. Suire, a druggist, and the second of its owners who, like Martin Baum, flew too high. The Suire-Eckstein pharmacy at Fourth and Vine Streets was the finest in the city, it did the biggest soda fountain business, and it paid its chief pharmacist, Edward S. Wayne — who had, at various times, held two professorships in medical colleges and one in a college of pharmacy — the unheard-of salary of $7,000 a year, with the result that he was the Beau Brummel of his profession. But the pace was too hot; Suire-Eckstein failed, and Belmont was sold in 1873 to a new colossus, David Sinton, a self-made man if ever there was one.

Born in Ireland, he was brought to America in infancy. His parents settled in a small Ohio town, and David, with only the sketchiest of schooling, was working in a store in his teens. At 18 he made his way to Cincinnati, and with a few dollars of savings and a young partner, he tried to operate a small commission business. He remarked in later life that there was then no place of relaxation open to a young man in the city but the saloons and brothels, and he wanted none of either, so he spent his evenings in his small, bare room, reading a history of England. This was not for long, for he and his partner presently lost their all, and he tramped up-river to the Hanging Rock iron region, near Ironton, where he found a job at a furnace. But Dave Sinton was never content to work for someone else. He and a friend leased a small furnace, and presently he had one of his own — and then another — and another. He was producing only a few tons a day, but it was the best iron that could be made.

He removed his office to Cincinnati in 1849. Seeing the approach of war in '61, and knowing that it would send the price of iron soaring, he ceased selling pig, but continued making it as fast as possible, which rapidly exhausted his ready cash. He paid his workmen in flour, molasses and salt pork, which he bought on credit from Harrison & Hooper, wholesale grocers. One of the partners, L. B. Harrison, later founder of the First National Bank of Cincinnati, became concerned over the debt, and went up to Hanging Rock to look things over. There were the furnaces, and there were big piles of pig iron on the river bank, perfectly safe because nobody would try to steal it, and the river couldn't wash it away. But Mr. Harrison decided to take possession of a quantity of it as collateral, much to Sinton's annoyance. It was brought down to Cincinnati on a barge and stored in Harrison & Hooper's cellar. When, in 1864, the price of iron had risen to an enormously inflated figure, Sinton sold, and Harrison & Hooper received their money with full interest, but none of the profit which they thought they should have shared in. Hence there was a coolness between Sinton and Harrison ever after.

From that date, Sinton was a capitalist, poking his fingers into various pies. He was one of the chief financiers of both the Cincinnati and Cleveland Gas Companies, and with General Andrew Hickenlooper, President of the Cincinnati company, was undoubtedly responsible for keeping electricity out of the city for several years after it should have arrived. He became one of the Queen City's legendary characters. Blunt in speech, careless in dress, he, like many another rich man, pinched pennies but disarmed criticism by giving away large sums to charity and good causes. Whisky sold at two drinks for a quarter in the post-bellum period, and it was Mr. Sinton's habit to go into a saloon in the morning, take a drink and say, "I'll get the other this afternoon." That wasn't the way the saloonkeeper intended it, but he was Dave Sinton and he could get away with it. But remembering those bleak youthful evenings of his in the city, he gave $33,000 to the Y.M.C.A. and $100,000 to the city's great waterfront charity, the Union Bethel, in 1874.

One day some years later, he visited the *Times-Star* editorial room, where James Albert Green was then managing editor, and saw a staff member, the dramatic critic, smoking a cigar.

"What do you pay that man?" he asked of Mr. Green.

"Twenty-five dollars a week," which was a fair salary for the '80's.

"And he smokes cigars!" exclaimed Mr. Sinton in shocked amazement. He took a small piece of plug tobacco from his pocket, where it reposed amid the usual lint and debris of such receptacles. "See that?" he said, "That's all the tobacco I can afford; ten cents' worth a week." Well, reflects Mr. Green, he had the better of the argument in the end; the dramatic critic died poor and Sinton a millionaire.

His daughter and only child, Anna, was being courted by a scion of one of the city's wealthiest families, and society expected to hear of their engagement at any time. But the young blade, thinking to dazzle his inamorata, lighted a cigar one day in her presence with a crackling new one-dollar bill. (A strain of Scotch ancestry manifested itself even there.) But his tactic was deplorably bad. Anna Sinton, her father's own daughter, wanted neither truck nor traffic with anyone who threw away even a dollar like that. She dropped the young showoff with a thud that shook society to its foundations, and presently married Charles Phelps Taft in her father's home, the former Baum-Longworth mansion. "The world of fashion was fully represented," wrote a reporter. "One of the most elegant suppers that has ever been spread in the city was furnished by Keppler," a fashionable restaurateur.

The Tafts took up their abode with Mr. Sinton, he being at that time a widower. It has been gossiped that he didn't think much of his son-in-law; but we have been unable to learn what the son-in-law thought of Mr. Sinton. However, the trio lived together until the father-in-law died in 1900.

The name of Taft was brought to Cincinnati in 1839 by a big-framed, genial Vermont Yankee named Alphonso Taft. Like most farm boys of his day, the barrier he had to overcome was not poverty, but lack of cash. After drinking dry his own village fount of knowledge, he had two or three sessions at Amherst, paying expenses by teaching school betweentimes. He entered Yale at 19, walking the nearly 150 miles between his home and New Haven every time he made the trip. Having gotten all he could afford of Yale's classical learning, he again taught school for four years, then graduated from the Yale Law School at 28, headed westward and hung out his shingle in Cincinnati. Five years later he married his Vermont sweetheart, but she lived only eight years thereafter, and passed away, leaving two sons, Charles Phelps and Peter Rawson Taft.

Alphonso Taft was always an important factor in the community. He did much to promote the railroads of the city, and was particularly useful in validating the bond issue necessary to build the Cincinnati Southern. He and his friend Thomas Spooner organized the Cincinnati unit of the new Republican party in 1856, and were delegates to the convention which nominated Fremont for the Presidency. It was Judge Taft (for he had served eight years on the Superior Court of Ohio) who enabled the executors of Charles McMicken to carry out that gentleman's will and thus make the University of Cincinnati possible. His services in liberalizing the public schools' attitude towards Bible reading have been cited. In taking this stand, he sacrificed any possible chance of nomination to higher office.

When he resigned from the Superior Court in 1873, the card of A. Taft and Sons, Attorneys at Law, Nos. 1 and 2 Masonic Temple, was already appearing in the papers. The Sons were the two elders, Charles P. and Peter R. Four more children had been born to the Judge's second wife, Louise Torrey, in their Mount Auburn home (which still stands); William Howard (president), Henry W., a distinguished New York attorney, Horace D., founder and headmaster of the Taft School for Boys in

Watertown, Connecticut, and Fannie, who married a California physician.

Judge Taft had been brought up a Baptist, but the Unitarian cult which flourished in Cincinnati in his younger days claimed him as one of its adherents. Independent and individualistic, he was not afraid to be different. He was nearly 50 when he became Benn Pitman's first shorthand pupil in Cincinnati, after Pitman had failed to convince New York and Washington that his system was not a fake. The Judge's second wife was the chief promoter of Cincinnati's first free kindergarten, which functioned in the old Spencer House. For many years she was a leading partisan of such schools.

The Judge's stand on the Bible in the schools did not prevent his becoming, first, Secretary of War and then Attorney-General in Grant's cabinet, nor from serving later as Minister to Austria-Hungary and then to Russia. His long and useful life came to an end in 1891. According to his schedule, his five sons had all been destined to follow him into the law; only Horace broke away from it and went into education.

His son, William Howard, began life as a typical American schoolboy — trudging several blocks along Mount Auburn streets to a district school, skating on the canal, acquiring elegance at M. Ernst's dancing school, which he temporarily forgot when fighting alongside his boy neighbors against gangs from Reading Road and Little Bethlehem, playing marbles and sandlot baseball, which last he did so well, despite his increasing weight that, according to legend, as he neared maturity, he could have had a contract with the Cincinnati Reds as catcher if he had wanted it. "Big Lub" was his teen-age nickname, but a personal item in the papers in Holiday week, 1877 tells us that "Howard Taft is at home from Yale for the Holidays." His first job after leaving college was as a law reporter on the *Times* and *Commercial*. He became assistant prosecuting attorney for the county in 1881 and served two years. He showed his mettle at an early age by waging a fight to disbar Thomas C. Campbell of the Cox gang.

Leaving public office in '83, he was in private law practice for four years, and during that time married Helen Herron. The

Countess de Chambrun quotes a number of the intermarriages of old families in those late nineteenth-century years which prove how closely knit society had become and remained; Albert Chatfield and Helen Huntington; Joseph Neave and Emma Harrison; Charles Harrison and Bertha Webster; Edmund Harrison and Caroline Andrews; Davis Carneal Anderson and Annie Wallingford; Vachel Anderson and May Chambliss; Harry Woods and Katharine Anderson; Charles Anderson and Jane Herron; William Howard Taft and Helen Herron; William Herron and Jane Espy; Arthur Espy and Lily Seely; Arthur Stern and Mary Halstead; George Dana and Clarissa Halstead, and so on. To marry out of town was highly unusual.

In 1887 at the age of 30, William Howard Taft became a boyish-looking judge in Ohio's Superior Court. His steady rise from that post through Solicitor-General of the United States, a Federal judgeship and other places to the highest honor the people had to offer need not be traced in full. On a summer day in 1908, he stood perspiring on the steps of old Belmont, his half-brother Charlie's beautiful home on Pike Street, in the presence of a crowd that packed the lawn and overflowed from Pike into neighboring streets, and formally accepted the nomination for the Presidency. The remainder of the story — his election, his one term, troubled by the increasing problems of a changing age and Roosevelt's quarrel with him, his eight years as law professor at Yale and nine years as Chief Justice of the Supreme Court, these are all recent in memory.

He left two sons and a daughter (Mrs. Manning), of whom the eldest son, Senator Robert A. Taft, is one of America's most honest and distinguished statesmen, whose ability has not yet received its due recognition. The other, Charles Phelps Taft II, lawyer and prominent churchman, president of the Federal Council of Churches, startled the World Council of Churches at Amsterdam in 1948 by drawing up, in collaboration with some more or less pinkish parsons, a report on "The Church and the Disorder in Society," in which both communism and capitalism were denounced as being inconsistent with the Christian way of life; a strange emanation from one of this traditionally conservative fam-

ily. It was even too strong for the Council, which modified it
before spreading it upon the record.

The elder Charles P. Taft forsook the law for journalism —
bought the *Cincinnati Times* in '79, to become its editor and
publisher, added the *Star* to it in '80, to make it the *Cincinnati
Times-Star*, as which it has been an influential evening paper ever
since. Charles, for years was also one of the owners of the *Volksblatt*. His brother, Peter, who died in 1889, left one son, Hulbert,
who is now the owner of the *Times-Star*.

Besides operating his newspaper, Charles P. did much public
service, as long-time, efficient Sinking Fund trustee, many terms
treasurer of the May Festivals, and supporter of the Symphony
Orchestra, the Zoo and other things necessary to the city's cultural
life. Mrs. Taft also gave liberally to these activities, and we have
heard how she and her husband — having no sons, and their two
married daughters being well provided for — gave their home with
its magnificent art collection and $2,700,000 in cash to the city in
1932. Here, in one of the most beautiful of settings, you may see
paintings by Rembrandt, Steen, DeHooch, Hals, Hobbema, Van
Dyck, Corot, Millet, Daubigny, Rousseau, Ingres, Goya, Turner
(12 of his) Reynolds, Lawrence, Constable, Gainsborough, Rae-
burn, Hoppner, Romney, Duveneck, Farny and many more, as
well as sculpture, ceramics, crystals, jewelry.

A remarkable family which has spanned a century and a quarter
in Cincinnati with only three generations is that of the Emerys.
Thomas Emery, born in England, came to America in 1832, bringing his wife and little son, Thomas Josephus, to which another son,
John Josiah, was soon added. In Cincinnati Thomas first appeared
as an "estate and money agent," and made a specialty of "country
seats, situated from one-half a mile to eight miles from the city,
not surpassed for elegance of buildings, gardens and orchards in
Hamilton County." One of these, with 16 acres of land, winsome-
ly named Eglantine Cottage, situated a quarter of a mile beyond
Cheviot (always pronounced Chiviot in Cincinnati), was spoken
of as a "cottage ornee."

Thomas Emery also embarked, rather rashly, in the manufacture of lard oil and candles, suffered a bankruptcy, from which

he doggedly arose and fought his way up to prosperity. His lard oil factory on Water Street was flourishing by 1845, and its queer, sourish odor, unavoidable in such processes, sometimes invaded even the elegant parlors of Broadway and Pike Street. When Thomas fell through a hatchway of this plant and was killed in 1851, the two sons, Thomas J. and John J., then in their twenties, were already keen hands at a bargain. Trustees were left in charge of the estate, but it is said that they soon realized that the boys were smarter businessmen than they were, and so gave them practically free rein. There were two sisters, Kezia and Julia, who shared in the fortune, but Kezia died, leaving her all to Julia, and Julia bequeathed hers to the Salvation Army of England.

It wasn't many years until Thomas Emery's Sons, Incorporated, were building hotels, business and apartment houses all over the place. Their Hotel Emery, completed in 1877, had an arcade running through it from Vine to Race Street, with stores fronting on it and offices above, a great novelty at the time. The arcade had its own steam heating, electric and ice-making plants. Very nearly if not quite the first apartment building in the city – "flats," they called them then – was erected by the Emerys in 1881, and the young William H. Tafts were for a time tenants there. The brothers displayed their love for medieval history and geography in the naming of their apartment houses. Lorraine, Lombardy, Brittany, Saxony and Normandy were the first five; then came Warwick, Somerset, Cumberland, Essex, Clermont, Navarre, Verona, Madrid, Suffolk, Granada, Seville, Garonne, Aragon, Castile and several more. They extended their activities to many other cities, even owning properties as far away as New York and San Francisco.

One of the brothers, Tom, waxed indignant in the latter '70's because he considered that the leading hotels in the city, the Burnet, Grand and Gibson, were profiteering; they were charging guests $3 and $3.50 per day, American plan, which of course included both food and lodging. "Two dollars a day is enough," he declared; and at his behest, Emery Brothers built a hotel to prove it – the eight-story Palace, the tallest building in the city when it was opened in 1882. Two dollars a day, including meals, was the rate for every room. "As long as the sun shines," asserted Tom Emery, "the Palace will be a two-dollar hotel." How futile is prophecy! But be not decived; the Palace was a good hotel. For two dollars you enjoyed good food, comfortable rooms with walnut furniture, body Brussels, Moquette and Wilton carpets, while "engravings hung in the rooms give the hotel a homelike air," said a news item. True, it then had only one bathroom (public) and toilet on a floor, but that was nothing unusual then, and that condition was corrected long ago. Today, nearing three-score and ten, the Palace is still functioning, having but recently undergone the latest of several face-liftings, and looks quite youthful again.

Thomas's widow, Mary Hopkins Emery, who survived him by 21 years, has been noticed herein as one of the city's great benefactors. Losing her only two children, both sons, in their youth, she opened her heart to many causes in her home town. She erected a building for the Mechanics' Institute, including a 2,200-seat auditorium which for several years was the home of the Cincinnati Symphony Orchestra. She gave a building extension and a $3,500,000 collection of paintings to the Art Museum. She built Mariemont, a model suburb for people of modest means, east of the city, with underground electric, telephone, telegraph, fire alarm and central heating services which are even yet a step in advance of any other American community, and added a school, a hospital, an inn, a community church and a theater. Her saving of Holmes's great hospital project has been mentioned (she gave it $700,000 in all), but there is not space to tell of all the money she poured into the Community Chest, the Red Cross, the Children's Hospital on Mount Auburn, the Colored Orphan Asylum, the May Festivals, the Zoo and its opera, the Conservatory of Music, the Christ Church parish house and other causes, much of it under the eye of her adviser, Charles J. Livingood, now president of the Thomas J. Emery Memorial, which was her $20,000,000 estate, for this Lady Bountiful died in 1927 at the age of 83.

Her nephew, John J. Emery, Jr., also specializes in hotels, but not in two-dollar ones; far from it. Now probably Cincinnati's leading capitalist, builder of the 48-story Carew Tower, the city's tallest building, also of the Netherland Plaza and the new and startling Terrace Plaza Hotels, he appears to be a worthy scion of this amazing dynasty.

Look for elders among the old family names now, and what you find are for the most part elderly widows. The men of their generation, under the greater stress and strain of business and profession, besides being less durable than the women, have in great numbers succumbed to life's toils, some of them without leaving any males of their name to carry on.

CHAPTER XXI
Social Dictator

On October 11th, 1948, the *Cincinnati Enquirer* spread a head-line across two columns, "Death Takes 'Tsarina' Marion Dev-ereux, Long Arbiter of Cincinnati's Social Life." The word "arbiter" is to be understood in its more positive sense, and "Tsar-ina" was almost an understatement. No autocrat of all the Russias ever dictated the social life of his well-to-do subjects so com-pletely as this tiny woman did the people of her own particular domain for some thirty years. And unlike the Tsars, she finally and suddenly laid down her scepter, and for nine years before her death, remained in total eclipse. There has never been any-one else quite like her in America, and Cincinnati for one fervently hopes there never will be again.

The Devereux domination of Cincinnati society did not begin with Miss Marion. Her parents came to this city from New York at some time after Marion's birth in 1873. The father, Arthur F. Devereux, a Civil War brigadier, entered the Government engi-neering service after the war and was stationed at Cincinnati. The family lived on East Fourth Street, not far from the home of Murat Halstead, editor and publisher of the *Cincinnati Com-mercial*. Mr. Halstead found Mrs. Devereux to be a woman of education and culture, and somewhere around 1880 he diffidently asked her if she would do society reporting for his paper. The needs of five children, now mostly in their teens, were evidently becoming a problem, and the General and his wife, though no doubt shuddering at the thought of her becoming a salaried hire-ling, yet must have recognized that it was a highly respectable position, such as a gentlewoman might assume without too great discredit, especially in view of the fact that her name would not appear in connection with it.

Pure society reporting was still in its infancy, and in a column headed "Personal" you might, as we have already remarked, find the doings of Clifton and Mount Auburn mixed with those of bookkeepers and shop foremen. Mrs. Devereux looked with horror upon this sort of thing, and set about correcting it in her column. But the more old-fashioned portion of society had not yet grown accustomed to having its doings chronicled in the newspapers, and no doubt antagonized by the bourgeois type of reporting just mentioned, thought such activity rather vulgar. Mrs. Devereux, when she called at some of these ultraconservative homes for items, was not even seated in the parlor, but had to wait in the hall until the lady of the house chose to go down and speak to her. But ah! as years passed, the time came when positions were reversed, and ladies either called her by telephone or went to the extreme of calling in person at her office.

As the city's social activity became more complicated in the latter nineteenth century, a social secretary was needed to prevent clashes in dates of the more important events. Mrs. Devereux — Madame Devereux, as she came to be called, because of her French-sounding name — gradually worked herself into this position, and as she became necessary to the social machine, she assumed more and more an air of authority. When in 1892, in collaboration with a Mrs. Avery, she published *Who's Who; A Society Register . . . for Cincinnati*, she set about correcting the overlaps in the days for calling.

"With the beginning of the new year," announces this Blue Book, "there has been a proposed change in reception days. . . . The following is submitted. . . . The first two Fridays in the month are Clifton at home days, the last two are set apart for Mt. Auburn. The first two Thursdays of the month are at home days for Avondale, the last two for West Sixth and Fourth Streets. The first two Mondays for East Walnut Hills, the second two for the West Hill. Tuesday, the Burnet House, St. Nicholas, East Fourth and Pike, Broadway and the East End generally. Wednesday, Dayton Street and Covington."

The complete reorganization — probably not to the entire satisfaction of everybody — of the calling day schedule gives

a hint of iron-hand-in-velvet-glove to the word "submitted."
Anyhow, the program became official.

Mrs. Devereux continued with the *Commercial-Gazette* until
1897, when she resigned. But when that paper was taken over
by the *Enquirer*, three years later, the publishers of the latter
induced her to return to the society page, in which post she
continued almost until her death in 1910. As she became more
imperious in her latter years, she developed animosities, and ladies
did not risk her displeasure unscathed. An example of her punishment of such temerity reveals a technic similar to that practiced
by her more famous daughter in the succeeding reign. A lady
who was at the moment out of favor with her had suffered a
bereavement and was in mourning, but felt constrained to attend
one session of the Horse Show because her son, a notable performer on horseback, was to be one of the stars. She was all in
black, but the society column noted Mrs. H.'s presence in a box
"in a gorgeous red toilette."

Upon Mrs. Devereux's death, her daughter Marion, who had
long been her assistant, readily if not eagerly assumed the vacant
chair and began her fantastic career. Now thirty-seven, Miss
Devereux had had early polish and burnishing in two fashionable
schools in Cincinnati, and years of experience in society reporting. She had developed the Devereux style of writing to the point
where for lacy, embroidered rhetoric, it surpassed even that of
her mother. In her lexicon, debutantes were almost invariably
"rosebuds" — two of them brought out simultaneously on one
occasion were "twin rosebuds on the parent stem" — a table was
a mahogany, a large dining table being the central mahogany,
and she prolonged the life of the nineteenth-century word toilet
or toilette for a woman's dress. Society ladies collectively were
Femina — as for example, on the occasion of a particularly gorgeous party, "For this supreme occasion, Femina had resplen-
dently arrayed herself in some of the most scintillatingly exquisite
creations evoked by the couturier's wand of enchantment."

She had a taste for power, which she exercised steadily to
strengthen her hold upon the city's society. From the mere
arranging of a winter's calendar, so that the larger events might

not clash, she went on to become more than an arbiter — an actual dictator to the social world. She named the hotel or club at which parties, balls, wedding breakfasts and dinners were to be held, and her word was final. Gradually but unwaveringly the society department of the *Enquirer* became one of the more important, if not the very most important, in the paper. As this situation developed, all limitations as to her space and her handling of her materials ceased. It would be hard to find another journal in the country in the present century which would devote three or four close-packed columns to a description of one ball or wedding not involving royalty. At the height of the season, a single week-day's social news might fill sixteen columns — two pages. And remember that in those days the society page was not half or three-quarters pictures, as it is now; in fact, during the most of Miss Devereux's incumbency, there were no pictures at all — just singing, faintly coruscant prose, like the tinkle of small, sweetly-attuned bells in a mauve-tinted, heliotrope-scented atmosphere. And the women of Cincinnati, down to the lowest income level, in popular phrase, "ate it up." Her manuscript became inviolate; no impious editorial pencil would venture to touch a word or phrase. It was as if "stet" had been writ large on every page with invisible ink.

It was not long before the management of one of the city's leading hotels, the Sinton, conceived a bright idea; they handed over to Miss Devereux a suite for her own living quarters, rent-free. After that, you may be sure that the Sinton got its share of the big social affairs, though it must be admitted that other places were not really slighted. Nor did the Sinton's decor and service suffer for lack of notice. The Bachelors' Cotillion Club — her notice of it upon its organization as "a group of young celi-brates" for whom tail coats would be "*de rigeuer*" may have been just a couple of typographical errors, though the *Enquirer* staff later swore that that was her exact copy, and they dared not correct it — gave its second ball in November, 1929, and her article about it began with a rhapsody upon the setting, of which only fragments can be quoted:

"In the long, lofty ballroom of the Hotel Sinton, framed in

the replicas of Eighteenth Century panels, gold-bordered, lighted by stately, sparkling chandeliers of faceted crystal placed among the Bourcher clouds and cupids of the ceiling a la Louis Seize, the second of the Bachelors' Cotillions took place with such success as to seem to the guests the ultimate in entertainment. . . .

"Drooping tendrils of Southern ivy veiled the electroliers of the walls and garlanded in delicate spirals of green the intricately carved railing of the balcony, an occasional golden chrysanthemum peeping through these vines. . . ."

In such an atmosphere a dance could scarcely avoid being a success, and it was:

"Never did dance rhythms seem so dulcet to the meticulous ear, never was perfect congeniality a greater factor in the success of a dance, and never were partners so numerous and so attentive. . . .

"If those who contend that chivalry is dead could surreptitiously have gazed upon this gallant scene, they would have realized incontestably that their own pet theories alone were moribund at this most charming of balls."

The writer appeared almost intoxicated by "the dazzling fashion-plate figures which Femina seemed in the whirling beauty of the ball-room floor." She was seldom seen taking a written note at these affairs, but her amazing memory preserved many personal pictures: "Mrs. Hiram Quackenbush was one of the loveliest of the dancers, her gown of pale blue being lovely with her bronze hair"; "Miss Eleanor Rapp was a great belle, her gown being of gray-blue satin, most becomingly designed in long, slim lines."

When her editor-in-chief's daughter was married in 1933, Miss Devereux of course put on paper one of her choicest confections in turgid English. The event was "of wide importance," the fathers of the young couple being "nationally known." (The bridegroom's father was a Cincinnati attorney.) After the overtures, Miss D. drifted into one of her typical wedding-church-interior scenes: "Into the hush of this ambient twilight came the bridal procession, the feathery green of tender laurel that wreathed choir stalls, pulpit and rood screen, and the curving fronds of a few giant palms massed in the chancel pointing the way to the altar, where the snowy chalices of tall Easter lilies were sentineled by blazing candelabra, seven-branched. . . .

"Very pretty, with lovely light brown hair and gray-blue eyes, the bride's youthfulness suddenly seemed to take on a certain queenliness as she swept from end to end of this line of light. Her gown of soft white, crinkly crepe was the essence of simplicity, and therefore the perfection of chic. . . ."

Even the bride's veil seemed to throw Miss Devereux into a sort of swoon; "Held closely to her well-poised head, her fair hair visible through its delicate mesh, this airy unsubstantial fabric drifted in long, broad folds for yards behind her, as fragile as a mist, enmeshing her tall figure, concealing her face, and in its upturned brim that circled her shapely head, forming the semblance of a halo, that gave her the air of one of the saints or angels that, in color, looked down from the gorgeous memorial windows on every hand."

Her memory and accuracy received their severest tests during May Musical Festival week, when the *Enquirer* often carried five or six columns of society news every day, sprinkled with personal glimpses and ladies' seminary French: Mrs. Harry Eistner Talbott of Dayton "wore her pearls and diamonds in her ears"; Miss Elizabeth Rogan was "a dainty charmer"; Mrs. Charles Dana Gibson was "as always, very distinguee"; Mrs. Henry Probasco was "very Grande Dame"; "the Hinkle box was a scene of constant va and vient."

Obviously, all this tremendous wordage could not be written by one woman, though she was indefatigable and her output prodigious. The less important scripts were written by one and later two assistants, who must first realize that society reporting, as jestingly defined in newspaper offices, is the art of saying the least in the most possible words, and must learn to imitate though not to surpass their chief's rococo style; for she permitted herself an occasional tantrum, and was capable of hurling a manuscript across the room if it did not suit her.

Her days were much longer than those of most toilers; she seemed to live only for her work. A morning newspaper, as is well known, is written in the afternoon and evening, some of it far along in the night. But this little dynamo, who seemed to need less sleep than most people, began her day in her own room in the morning, and when she reported at the office in the afternoon, had already turned out what would be a day's work for some writers. If she had any interesting private life, no detail of it ever reached the public. When it is remembered that she must attend many social events in person, must have numerous telephone calls and occasional office interviews with anxious mothers and hostesses, her day's writing achievements seem incredible. Her only daily exercise consisted of a half hour's brisk walk from her hotel across the Suspension Bridge and back. Her summer vacations were spent in Europe, where no doubt she sought as close views as possible of Old World society.

She had a definite reverence for Old Families — as old as Cincinnati had — and great wealth, and a scion of any such family, no matter how unattractive he or she might be, was given the tenderest of treatment. She was accused of showing particular favoritism for "the Grandin Road crowd" (old aristocracy), the ultra-rich "Glendale crowd" and those of the East End, the original, downtown, Longworth-Sinton-Taft-Lytle-Dexter, etc., area, on whose fringe she herself had lived in childhood, and which she liked to refer to as the Court Quarter or the Court area of town. She abhorred climbers and gave them no assistance, though sometimes they attained eminence without her help and forced her to countenance them. She found it hard to accept the German-Americans who had risen to wealth through beer, pork, soap, starch or machinery, though many of the Anglo-Saxon old families whom she so reverenced had — starting a little earlier — come up by quite similar avenues. Jews she scarcely recognized at all, though Cincinnati has long had many of wealth and eminence.

Visitors to her office never forgot it; the thick-piled rugs, General Devereux's sword hanging on the wall, the large-flowered chintz covering her desk under the glass top, the blonde, slowly graying little woman behind it whose countenance could exhibit all degrees of consistency, from adamant to cream puff. She had lowered her guests' chairs by having two or three inches sawed off their legs; and it is difficult for one to be dignified or forceful when looking at the dominant dignitary in a strange office over one's knees. She was adept in skirting the edges of libel, and when some indignant person dared to invade her sanctum with complaint or threat, her blue eyes could look as touchingly naive and innocent of wrong intent as those of a child of three.

But her language on such rare occasions and the honeyed froth of her newspaper page were quite in another category from her spoken words in the role of a social potentate as resolute and relentless as Catharine the Second. When she had looked over the field in early autumn and decided on the number of debutantes that would be permitted to emerge during the season, remonstrances were of little avail. She did not hesitate to say flatly to a hopeful mother, "Your daughter is not eligible for a formal debut"; or "I don't think your daughter would enjoy coming out this season — the crowd this year is so different from her own," thus forcing a postponement, with no assurance that you would get a date next year. And if she didn't want you to have your dance at the Queen City Club or the Hotel Gibson, you just didn't have it there, that's all. Protest was useless, and strenuous protest only got you into her black book. Cincinnati society used to wonder how it ever permitted itself to get into such a coil, but could never quite explain it. And yet many who deplore her methods will admit that she had a certain salutary influence; her standards were high and she kept society up to them.

True, there were rarely occasional uprisings against her rule. There was the case of a wealthy radio manufacturer and his wife, for example, whose daughter was soon to be married, and who chose to have the wedding party at the Netherland-Plaza, a big, new, elegantly appointed hotel. Miss Devereux was not yet quite reconciled to the Netherland-Plaza, and knowing that this particular plutocrat could and probably would put on the most gorgeous affair of the season, she ordered that it be staged at the Sinton. The parents of the bride were quite firm in their determination to have it at the new hotel. Miss Devereux, after a debate which grew heated, told them in effect that if they persisted in their stubborn course, they must take the consequences. They indicated that they were quite prepared to do so. The outcome was that not one word about the wedding or the attendant festivities appeared in the *Enquirer*, for which retaliations the family cared not a rap. Miss Devereux cut but a poor figure in this episode — considerably less dignified than that of Ajax defying the lightning. She had tackled a force too big for her. Everyone knew why the glaring omission was perpetrated, and also that the social prestige of the ignored family was not impaired in the least by her would-be slight.

Another case was that of a lady — call her Mrs. X — whose husband's name is inseparable from that of one of the best known household necessities. Some years ago she organized what she called the Satin Slipper Club among her woman friends, and in the course of time ventured to give a rather large party in the clubs' name without asking permission. This brought a telephone call which fairly made the wire smoke. "How dare you give a party without consulting me?" demanded Authority. "Don't you know that I am the social arbiter of Cincinnati? What do you mean?" etc., etc. In this tirade, like many others vented by the autocrat when angered or defied, her utteranecs sounded little like those of a lady of refinement, qualified to rule society. She even called Mrs. X. a "social highway robber," and closed by warning her that she would regret her rash act. Thereafter, when three of Mrs. X.'s children, one after another, were married, the weddings were completely ignored by the *Enquirer*. Any possible repercussions in the matter of advertising could not be taken into consideration. The advertising department would just have to explain embarrassedly to manufacturers that no one ever uttered the word "must" to Miss Devereux.

One of her favorite methods of torturing ladies who had violated her rules was to rout them out of bed at three or four o'clock in the morning to deliver her diatribes. Onlookers thought at times that she found a sadistic pleasure in hounding women who offended her. She also showed signs in her latter years of relishing her power in the office. There were times when she would telephone for a copy boy to come from the other end of the long building, and when he arrived, tell him to open a window, poke his head out and see if it was raining. But there was one thing that she couldn't do, though she tried it more than once; she couldn't stop the presses in the latter hours of the night, perhaps when thousands of copies had already been run off, so that she might alter or add to her material. The luckless functionary who had to say No to her might do so with fear and trembling, but there the organization doggedly took a stand; that was Verdun.

She had ways of punishing women not in her good graces which, to her victims, seemed little short of fiendish; such items, for example, in the report of a great reception or ball as, "Mrs. A. appeared in her customary brown"; "Mrs. B. wore the green toilet in which she always looks so well"; "Mrs. C. appeared in the blue dress which has graced several previous occasions" — any or all of which might have been flagrantly false, though there was never any retraction. More than once she remarked that "Mrs. So-and-so wore a string of pearls" or "appeared in a lovely bead neckless," which costume might have been a la mode, as she would say, at certain Greenwich Village Bohemian balls in years past, but never in Cincinnati. There were snippy little barbs such as "Miss I. W. arrived with two or three swains who were constantly in her train. Her frock was white, simply fashioned." She could be mischievously unsubtle in touching upon a delicate subject, as when noting that a popular young matron was absent from a party, "but of course she is not going out in any large way at present." When two people in their sixties were married and started for Florida on their wedding journey, she remarked that "Mr. and Mrs. S. on their honeymoon will follow the trail of Ponce de Leon in his quest for the Fountain of Youth."

Matrons and mothers who were not of her inmost circle of regard believed that it kept them in reasonably good standing if they sent Miss Devereux some silk stockings, lace handkerchiefs, fine perfume or other feminine whatnots around Christmas time. Parents with daughters whom they hoped to bring out or give in marriage during an impending season sometimes sought to gain the favor of the supreme power by opening a charge account for her at one of the large department stores, perhaps with a prudent stipulation that the credit be limited to $500. The gossip that she at times accepted actual cash is not believed by those best qualified to know. A lady would not do anything so coarse.

It has been remarked of her by those who followed her career that she could do some of the finest and some of the meanest things within human imagination. Her entries on the credit side of the ledger, though fewer, should be given passing notice. A lady who had three daughters, not in society but wanting to be, appealed to a prominent citizen, a former journalist, to intercede for them with Miss Devereux. The family, though gently born, was not wealthy, though it could sustain a modest social position fairly well, and the daughters were personable. Miss Devereux was under some obligation to the former journalist, and when he laid the case before her, she agreed to act. She "requested" several ladies to put the girls on their invitation lists, and presto! they were In.

And there was the *Enquirer* reporter who, beginning as a mere boy, for years escorted Miss Devereux home from the office every night — only two or three blocks, it is true, but in the small hours of the morning she was timorous and wanted protection. When the inevitable day came for that young man himself to be married — to a saloonkeeper's daughter, by the way — Miss Devereux was present and hurried back to the office to unlimber some of her plushiest altiloquence in description of the affair; you would have thought it was a union of two old families in the upper brackets. Grand ladies on the hilltops may have shuddered at finding these plebeian unknowns elbowing them on the society page, but who were they to raise an eyebrow when Miss Devereux was requiting an obligation?

Slowly as the years passed, she grew more wizened and seemingly smaller, though there was no dimming of her fire, though there were moments when hand and brain faltered a little, and her sentences had a touch of the inexplicable, even preternatural. The staff puzzled mightily over a paragraph dashed off during a May Musical Festival week:

"In nothing to the Philistine are the May Festivals more intriguing than in the boxes and the Audience. Last night these themes of and corridor and foyer were paramount to the carnal-minded devotee of these two yearly events."

"What does it mean?" editors and copy readers asked of each other. There were palpable evidences of muddlement. But at the mere suggestion that she be asked to explain the paragraph, tough, leathery cheeks in the city room blanched; the question went unvoiced and the item appeared as written.

Miss Devereux's exit from the scene of her long reign was as strange as her career had been. One day in 1939 she walked out of her office to consult a physician about a small pimple on her cheek. She never came back. It was found that she had no less than four serious ailments, and for a time they threatened her life; but with characteristic indomitability she survived them all, though physically she was never quite the same again. In complete retirement from the public eye, she gradually assumed the aspect of a legend. After nine years of retirement, death came to her quietly in a hospital at the age of seventy-five; but she had given her paper a certain dominance in the local scene which it has never lost.

CHAPTER XXII

The Changing City

CINCINNATI would like to forget — at least, it wishes that others might forget — its Dark Age, the years when it was one of Lincoln Steffens's Horrible Examples. It may seem inexplicable, the long reign of Cox and his evil allies in a city of such eminent achievement, apparently so cultured and intelligent; but to experienced political observers, it is just another case history, proving that there is no wholly successful form of government, not even democracy. In the most advanced of cities, there is, always has been and will be, far beyond any now conceivable era, a great mass of uninformed, thinkless voters; and inertia's clammy hand will long continue to hold motionless, as in the past, many folk who should know better.

To visiting muckrakers like Steffens, Cox prated the usual vaunts of the bosses — "gave the city government, honest government, never took a dollar of graft," etc., yet the city remained in a state of near-bankruptcy, taxes were high, and Cox and his chief lieutenants, Rud K. Hynicka and Garry Herrmann, grew steadily wealthier. They gave Cincinnati a new water-works — which might have been better, at that — and in 1912 they built several hundred yards of a subway which was to enter the Basin from the Mill Creek valley and enable interurban electric cars to traverse the downtown area. But by that time, the vogue of the interurban car was beginning to fade before the advance of the automobile; and after a $6,000,000 bond issue had been expended, work on the subway was halted. You may see its remains out towards Cumminsville today. (It may yet be completed.) They tried to sell the city's Cincinnati Southern Railway in 1896 for a sacrifice price, and in the referendum on the question, were defeated by only 538 votes — a close call which makes the citizens of today shudder at the thought of such a near-loss of a valuable heritage.

The story of Cincinnati's regeneration is one of many years of chipping away at the foundations of the machine's seemingly impregnable fortress by a few, steadily increasing to many, patriots and reformers. Back in the early '80's, E. W. Scripps started a little spitfire newspaper, the *Post*, yapping at the gang, while other papers remained on speaking terms with it or just temporized because there didn't seem anything else that could be done at the time. But after the turn of the century, the sound of the chisels grew louder, journalistic attacks were more virulent, and cracks began to appear in the structure. The machine lost the mayoralty in 1905, but kept the Council. State legislative investigating committees in 1906 and 1908 revealed putridity in city affairs, but friendly courts saved the malefactors, though they were compelled to disgorge $214,000 in interest on public funds which they had absorbed. A reform prosecuting attorney, Henry T. Hunt, lodged an indictment against Cox in 1911, but was defeated by a venal court. Hunt went in as Mayor that fall, but could do little for reform, and was defeated for reelection in 1913. Cox was on trial again that year, and again was saved by the courts. He retired in 1915 and died a year later, while his equally vicious lieutenants, Hynicka and Herrmann, carried on.

In 1917, with public attention diverted by the World War, the Ring put over a "home rule" charter, which made independent voting impossible. But after the war, a revolutionary spirit electrified the air; people were saying that the city had been in bondage long enough and too long. Captain Victor Heintz, who had served in Congress and overseas in the war, organized the Cincinnatus Association, some 50 young business and professional men to discuss and act on municipal problems. They revealed that Cincinnati's per capita indebtedness was the fourth largest among the nation's large cities. They began stirring up the animals. In 1923 the machine sought to put over a bond issue to take care of a steadily increasing deficit, and Cincinnatus fought it. A speech made before the Association by a businessman, Murray

Seasongood, a stalwart worker in the cause, won space in the press, and was influential in defeating the bond issue in a plebiscite. The gang savagely retaliated by turning off street lights and starving all municipal services, but this only hastened their downfall. A survey of the city government by Dr. Lent D. Upson of the Detroit Bureau of Governmental Research and his staff in 1924 was fatal to machine politics. Amendments to the city charter by a committee of nine, including two women, provided for a city manager and porportional representation in the City Council, was approved by the voters in November of '24. Then Robert A. Taft, Robert N. Gorman and Henry Bentley wrote a whole new charter for the city, embodying the reform ideas, and in 1925 it was approved by the citizens by a majority of more than two to one.

The old machine was utterly routed, smashed, macerated, never to rise or be seen again in politics. Murray Seasongood was elected as the first Mayor of the regenerated city, and Colonel C. O. Sherrill was called as the first City Manager. There have been other City Managers since then, but no lapse in the city's liking for its form of government, its pride in its distinction as perhaps the best-governed American city. The better, the real Cincinnati took the driver's seat in 1924 and proceeded to prove its quality. The new regime showed so complete a reversal of form from the old that it left observers dazed. A reporter for the *New York Daily News*, touring the largest cities of the country in 1933, when the depression was at its worst, was so startled at what he found here that he headed his article, "Cincinnati Must Be Heaven!" "What a town!" he wrote. "Money in the bank. A balanced budget. A steadily decreasing bonded debt. Lowest tax delinquency in America. No defaults. No scrip. No deficits.

"Operating on a pay-as-you-go basis, with the cash in hand for every obligation. The only city I've encountered on this tour that isn't crying depression as an alibi for blundering leadership. The only city whose government has measured up to the emergency." He found that tax delinquencies in Cincinnati in 1932 had been only 4.29 per cent, while in other cities they ranged all the way from 20 to 42.43 per cent. A study by the National

Municipal League in 1944 brought forth the facts that Cincinnati had one of the highest credit ratings in the country and one of the lowest tax rates. The report called the Cincinnati government "an instrument as effective as has yet been devised for carrying out the will of the people in municipal affairs."

Ever since the new birth there as been a Charter Party — with Charles P. Taft II usually at its head — to contest control of the Council with the Republicans, who are the dominant force in Cincinnati. Sometimes one has a majority in the Council, sometimes the other, but you can't tell the difference in the functioning of the municipality. Both desire the public good, and the fact is that there are many Republicans who are as staunch supporters of the Charter as the most ardent Charterite. As illustrating the public spirited, nonpartisan attitude of the Council, composed entirely of Republicans and Charterites, it has, as these lines are written, elected a Democrat, Albert Cash, as Mayor of the city.

It is characteristically Cincinnatian that this highly efficient city government flouts one of the modern efficiency expert's most cherished rules; it does not shelve elderly employes at a fixed age, as is present-day practice, but keeps them on as long as they are capable. In a non-partisan regime, there is little fear that political considerations will influence this custom.

With her municipal house cleaned and no prospect of its becoming untidy again, Cincinnati resumed her wonted serenity — though truth to tell, she had never quite lost it. Indeed, her troubles had been the result of too much serenity. Even her Great Reform was put through without a seismic upheaval. Perhaps it could have been accomplished more quickly if there had been convulsions, but that isn't Cincinnati's way. Slowly, thoughtfully is the method here, just as she is going about her new city plan. It is a curious paradox, that Cincinnati, most devoted to tradition, should be first in the land to decide that she needed to be, to a certain extent, replanned. Without demur, she has spent $100,000 on a master plan, and when it is put through, this won't be the old Cincinnati. A series of six-lane highways is to spray out, up and down river and through the hills, with intent to separate industry and home areas, giving the latter, it is dreamed, a sort of small-town isolation with city advantages — a beautiful con-summation, if it can be made workable. There is even a vision of a Cincinnati waterfront as prim and prettified as Chicago's; which will be another prodigy, if it can be done with an errant, inebriate river which one cannot conceive as ever being reformed to the sobriety of Lake Michigan.

Anyhow, there will be a partly new, a somewhat rearranged Cincinnati where traffic, a major consideration in a motor-mad age, will function more slickly, but it will not, despite all efforts to the contrary, preserve all the serenity and mellow charm which visitors still see in the Cincinnati built on the late Georgian pat-tern. It is like an old dwelling in which generations have been born and reared, which was home in the days when wars were few and insignificant and taxes were the least of our worries, when no one had heard of nuclear fission and life moved at a gentler, easier pace. New dwellings and apartments with all modern gad-getry facilitate living in an age of speed, but older, nostalgic memories will look back lovingly, even to the inconveniences of the old home. The peace and contentment of that vanished age are so inseparably connected in the mind with the time-worn dwelling that it seems to have had a hand in producing them. And how they were and are loved here! One recalls the last of the family to live in the old Jacob Strader mansion in the "court quarter," just before it was to be razed, lighting it up — every room — from top to bottom, then calling a cab and driving away with one long, backward look, seeing it for the last time as it used to be in the evenings that were halcyon.

Millions of dollars in new industries are coming, bringing new people, new affluence, new social factors. Society is changing; many of the old families once dominant are receding into the farther background now, or are quite gone, and new names are daily in the news. Some veteran observers speak gloomily of a "revolution," and say that already Cincinnati society is, with a few exceptions, scarcely recognizable as an extension of that of yesterday. But isn't that the story of all cities? Money is spent more lavishly; the cost of a debutante ball at one of the big hotels may run into many thousands, but decorum is still respected, and

less drinking is done at such parties than is popularly supposed —
much less than in the 1920's. Joe Garretson of the *Enquirer*, who
gets about and should know, says that champagne is always on
tap, but that more beer is drunk than champagne — tchk, tchk,
not a word from you about that Teutonic influence! — that surprisingly many glasses of tomato juice, coke and even milk are
drunk by younger guests, and that there are no wrecked cars
after the parties.

Perhaps Cincinnati's serenity will be a casualty of the near
future. Poise is increasingly difficult to maintain in a global scientific arena. But it is to be hoped that this social moderation and
the city's knack of and preference for good government will not
be lost with it.

Acknowledgments

PERSONAL and family recollections—my parents lived in Cincinnati for a time in their youth, and I was there years later — and correspondence supplied some factual material and atmosphere for this chronicle. Much more came from libraries and present-day Cincinnatians, and no author ever had more willing and able collaborators. Those two great metropolitan treasure-houses, the New York Public Library and the New York Historical Society, have not only nearly all the books necessary, but such vast quantities of old Cincinnati newspapers, going back to the very first one, in 1793, that they must be seen to be believed in. I spent many months in poring through them. In Cincinnati, Carl Vitz, librarian of the Cincinnati Public Library, Virginius C. Hall, director of the Historical and Philosophical Society of Ohio, Harry Pence, librarian of the *Cincinnati Enquirer* and John J. Rowe, historically-minded president and Miss Marie Dickoré, librarian of the Fifth-Third-Union Trust Company (I told Mr. Rowe that it seemed almost as much of an historical society as a bank), put everything they had at my disposal, lent me books, even when I was in New York and left no stone unturned if they or I thought there was a fact under it that I needed. Miss Dickoré, local historian and antiquarian, the scholarly Mr. Hall and his staff, and in the Public Library Miss Ethel L. Hutchins, research chief and Mrs. Alice S. Plaut, head of the art department were valued allies who, at my every inquiry, would patiently dig to the bottom of the subject and write me long and dependable letters, giving me the last word available in their collections, as well as what they could gather by other means; clipping many newspaper items for me, too. I could not have written this book without their aid and that of three or four others whom I shall name.

James Alfred Green, retired journalist, local historian, authority on William Henry Harrison, Public Library trustee for fifty years and with a head full of civic and social memories, would sit down at his

[419]

desk every few days, get his old black pipe going and scribble off for me several pages of priceless lore, most of which cannot be found in print. E. Leo Koester, of the Chamber of Commerce, was an able and willing aid in the matter of business and industrial information both when I was in Cincinnati and in New York, and once took me on a memorable drive through Clifton, Spring Grove Cemetery and other areas. Attorney Michael G. Heintz was a lively source of historical facts and stories, both orally and by letter, and one afternoon escorted me on a long walk in the West End, pointing out many historic buildings and important trends. Some unforgettable hours, punctuated by sandwiches and beer, were spent in the remarkable Medical College workshop of that many-sided genius, Dr. Martin H. Fischer, who also gave me some of his finely-written books. S. Percy Wells, one of the city's elder merchants, sat through most of an afternoon, reeling off for me a panorama of places and peoples of the past, and wrote me more later. I had only to touch the right spring in Harry Pence, veteran librarian of the *Enquirer*, to bring forth rare gems of memory; and when he was on vacation, his daughter, Mrs. Dorothy Royer, went to bat for him. Miss Jane Finneran, society editor of the *Enquirer*, was another valued coadjutor, as was Miss Caroline Williams, who draws those beautiful pen-and-ink pictures of Cincinnati landmarks, which later are made into books; she gave me one of them and some indispensable clippings. My friend, E. Y. Chapin of Chattanooga who knew Cincinnati long ago, contributed many reminiscences.

Among others, too numerous to list in full, who gave me of their time and resources were the New York representatives of the *Enquirer* and *Times-Star*, Lee Evans and Albert Parker; in Cincinnati J. Herman Thuman, Miss Beatrice Shillito and the late Oscar F. Hild on music; Edgar Friedlander, Fred Tuke and W. R. Skirvin on realty and building and loan associations; Martin Rettig on art; N. S. Hastings and Joseph A. Stephan on the Zoo; John G. Robinson of the city's famous circus family; David Dupee, Louis Coffin and A. F. Stanley of the United States Playing Card Company; Hulbert Taft, owner of the *Times-Star;* Emil Bauer, Eric Schulte, Frank Grammer, Elmer Arnold, Walter W. Tangeman, Dr. Otto P. Geier, George P. Stimson, Philip Hinkle, Mrs. George Hoadly, Mrs. James Morgan Hutton, Mrs. Frank H. Stevenson, Mrs. Howard Wurlitzer, Mrs. J. Walter

ACKNOWLEDGMENTS

Freiberg, Mrs. Minnie L. Chalfin, Mrs. Lewis Earl Lee, Mrs. Alfred C. Shepherd; also Mrs. Charles W. Pierson of New York. Clark B. Firestone of the *Times-Star*, author of delightful books, would have given me aid of inestimable value — he did send me clippings — but I make it a practice never to ask another author for material which he might sometime use himself.

Bibliography

As WILL be discovered from a reading of this book, much material was garnered from Cincinnati newspapers of the past, which have been conned at great length, beginning with the very first one, the *Centinel of the Northwestern Territory*, in 1793. They are among the finest of original documents.

BOOKS

ANON. *Biographical Cyclopedia and Portrait Gallery of the State of Ohio. Cincinnati*, 1883.

—— *Cincinnati and Hamilton County, Ohio; Their Past and Present*. Cincinnati, 1894.

—— *Cincinnati, Past and Present*. Cincinnati, 1872.

—— *Cincinnati, the Queen City, Pictorial and Biographical.* 2 vol. Chicago and Cincinnati, 1912.

—— "Literary Cincinnati," *Literary World*, vol. 13, p. 249.

—— "Porkopolis," *Colburn's Magazine*, vol. 103, p. 139.

ASHE, THOMAS. *Travels in America in 1806*. London, 1808.

ATWATER, CALEB. *A History of the State of Ohio*. Cincinnati (1838).

BAKER, AVIS. *Cincinnati as a Western Outpost of Boston Liberalism.* MA thesis, University of Chicago, 1916. Typed ms. New York Public Library.

BIRKBECK, MORRIS. *Notes on a Journey in America*, etc. London, 1818.

BISHOP, MRS. ISABELLA BIRD. *An Englishwoman in America*, London, 1856.

BIBLIOGRAPHY

BISHOP, J. L. *History of American Manufactures*, Philadelphia, 1868.

BRACKENRIDGE, H. H. *Recollections of Persons and Places in the West.* Philadelphia, 1834.

BUCKINGHAM, JAMES SILK. *The Eastern and Western States of America*, London, 1842.

BURGHEIM, MAX. *Cincinnati im Wort und Bild*, Cincinnati, 1888.

BURNET, JACOB. *Notes on the Early Settlement of the Northwestern Territory*, New York and Cincinnati, 1847.

CHAMBERS, WILLIAM. *Things as They Are in America.* London and Edinburgh, 1857.

CHEVALIER, MICHEL. *Society, Manners and Politics in the United States.* Boston, 1839.

CIST, CHARLES. *Cincinnati in 1841*, etc. Cincinnati, 1841.

—— *Cincinnati Miscellany*, Cincinnati, 1845-46.

—— *Sketches and Statistics of Cincinnati in 1851*, Cincinnati, 1851.

—— *Sketches and Statistics of Cincinnati in 1859*, Cincinnati, 1859.

CLARK, EDNA MARIA. *Ohio Art and Artists.* Richmond, Va., 1932.

COGGESHALL, WILLIAM T. *The Poets and Poetry of the West*, Columbus, O., 1860.

CONWAY, MONCURE D. *Autobiographical Memories and Experiences of Moncure Daniel Conway.* 2 vol. Boston and New York, 1904.

COOKE, GEORGE WILLIS. *Unitarianism in America.* Boston, 1902.

(DAWSON, JAMES W., comp.) *Picturesque Cincinnati.* n.p. (1883).

DAY, SARAH J., *The Man on a Hilltop.* Philadelphia (1931).

DE CHAMBRUN, CLARA, COUNTESS. *Cincinnati; Story of the Queen City*, New York, 1939.

DERBY, J. C. *Fifty Years among Authors, Books and Publishers.* New York and London, 1886.

[423]

DICKENS, CHARLES. *American Notes*, London, 1842.

DRAKE, BENJAMIN, AND EDWARD D. MANSFIELD. *Cincinnati in 1826*, Cincinnati, 1827.

DRAKE, DANIEL. *Notices Concerning Cincinnati*. Cincinnati, 1810.

— *Picture of Cincinnati*, Cincinnati, 1815.

EMERY, JOSEPH. *Thirty-five Years among the Poor and Public Institutions of Cincinnati*. Cincinnati, 1887.

FIRESTONE, CLARK B. *Flowing South*. New York (1941).

FLEXNER, JAMES THOMAS. *Doctors on Horseback*. New York, 1937.

FOOTE, JOHN P. *The Schools of Cincinnati and its Vicinity*. Cincinnati, 1855.

FORD, HENRY A. AND MRS. KATE B. *History of Cincinnati*, Cleveland, 1881.

FROTHINGHAM, OCTAVIUS BROOKS. *Memoir of William Henry Channing*. New York, 1886.

GOSS, CHARLES FREDERICK. *Cincinnati, the Queen City, 1788-1924*. 4 Vol., Chicago and Cincinnati, 1912.

GOULD, GEORGE M. *Concerning Lafcadio Hearn*. Philadelphia (1908).

GRAYSON, FRANK. *Pioneers of Night Life on Vine Street*, Cincinnati, 1924.

GREVE, CHARLES T. *Centennial History of Cincinnati and Representative Citizens*. Chicago, 1904.

HALL, A. C. "Faience Pottery of Cincinnati," *Potters' American Monthly*, vol. 15, p. 357.

HEARN, LAFCADIO. *An American Miscellany*, 2 vol., New York, 1924.

HEBBLE, CHARLES R. AND FRANK P. GOODWIN. *The Citizens' Book*. Cincinnati, 1919.

HOFFMAN, CHARLES FENNO. *A Winter in the West*. New York, 1835.

BIBLIOGRAPHY

HOUSTOUN, MRS. *Hesperos; or Travels in the West.* London, 1850.

HOWE, HENRY. *Historical Collections of Ohio.* 2 vol., Cincinnati, 1907.

HOWELLS, WILLIAM DEAN. *Literary Friends and Acquaintances.* New York and London, 1902.

HUDSON, FREDERIC. *Journalism in the United States from 1690 to 1872.* New York, 1873.

JAMES, DAVIS L. "Judge James Hall, a Literary Pioneer of the Middle West." *Ohio Archaeological and Historical Society Quarterly,* vol. 18, p. 468.

JUETTNER, OTTO. *Daniel Drake and His Followers,* Cincinnati, 1909.

KENNY, D. J. *Illustrated Guide to Cincinnati.* Cincinnati, 1893.

KING, RUFUS. *Ohio, First Fruits of the Ordinance of 1787.* Cincinnati, 1888.

KLAUPRECHT, EMIL. *Deutsche Chronik in der Geschichte des Ohio-Thales,* etc. Cincinnati, 1864.

KÖRNER, GUSTAV. *Der Deutsche Element in den Vereinigten Staaten von Nordamerika.* Cincinnati, 1880.

LEONARD, LEWIS ALEXANDER. *Greater Cincinnati and its People.* New York, Cincinnati and Chicago, 1927.

LOGAN, OLIVE. "Cincinnati." *Harper's Magazine,* vol. 68, p. 245.

LYELL, SIR CHARLES. *Travels in North America in the Years 1841-42.* London, 1842.

—— *A Second Visit to the United States of North America,* London, 1849.

MANSFIELD, EDWARD D. *Memoirs of the Life and Services of Daniel Drake, M.D.,* Cincinnati, 1855.

—— *Personal Memories, Social, Political and Literary.* Cincinnati, 1879.

MARRYAT, CAPTAIN. *A Diary in America.* (First and second series.) London, 1838-39.

(MARTIN, ISAAC M.) *History of the Schools of Cincinnati and Other Educational Institutions.* Cincinnati, 1900.

MARTINEAU, HARRIET. *Retrospect of Western Travel.* London and New York, 1838.

MAXWELL, SIDNEY D. *The Suburbs of Cincinnati.* Cincinnati, 1870.

MINNICH, HARVEY C. *William Holmes McGuffey and His Readers,* New York and Cincinnati (1936).

MURRAY, CHARLES AUGUSTUS, *Travels in North America in the Years 1834, 1835 and 1836.* 2 vol. London, 1839.

MURRAY, CHARLES B. *Life Notes of Charles B. Murray,* Cincinnati, 1915.

MURRAY, HENRY A. *The Lands of the Slave and the Free.* London, 1857.

NICHOLS, THOMAS LOW. *Forty Years of American Life.* London, 1874.

OHIO ANTI-SLAVERY SOCIETY. *Narrative of the Late Riotous Proceedings Against the Liberty of the Press in Cincinnati,* etc. Cincinnati, 1836.

OHIO WRITERS' PROJECT, WPA. *Cincinnati.* Cincinnati, 1943.

—— *City Hall; the Story of Government in Cincinnati.* Cincinnati, 1940.

OLDMIXON, CAPTAIN. *Transatlantic Wanderings.* London, 1855.

PARTON, JAMES. "Cincinnati." *Atlantic Monthly,* vol. 20, p. 209.

RANDALL, E. O. AND D. J. RYAN. *History of Ohio,* New York, 1912.

REID, WHITELAW. *Ohio in the War.* Cincinnati. 1868.

RHODES, DUDLEY WARD. *Creed and Greed.* Cincinnati, 1879.

ROURKE, CONSTANCE M. *Trumpets of Jubilee.* New York, 1927.

BIBLIOGRAPHY

SMITH, SOL. *Theatrical Management in the West and South for Thirty Years.* New York, 1868.

STORER, MARIA LONGWORTH. *In Memoriam, Bellamy Storer.* n.p., 1903.

STOWE, CHARLES EDWARD. *Life of Harriet Beecher Stowe, Compiled from Her Letters and Journals.* Boston and New York, 1890.

STOWE, HARRIET BEECHER. *The May Flower and Miscellaneous Writings.* Boston, 1855.

STOWE, LYMAN BEECHER. *Saints, Sinners and Beechers,* Indianapolis, (1934).

TASSIN, ALGERNON. *The Magazine in America.* New York, 1916.

TENNER, ARMIN. *Cincinnati Sonst und Jetzt.* Cincinnati, 1878.

THOMSON, WILLIAM. *A Tradesman's Travels in the United States and Canada in the Years 1840, 1841 and 1842.* Edinburgh, 1842.

TOPE, M. *A Biography of William Holmes McGuffey.* New York, 1929.

TUNISON, J. S. *The Cincinnati Riot.* Cincinnati, 1886.

UPTON, G. P. "The Musical Festivals of Cincinnati," *Lakeside Magazine,* vol. 9, p. 472.

VENABLE, WILLIAM H. *The Beginnings of Literary Culture in the Ohio Valley.* Cincinnati, 1891.

WAITE, HENRY M. "Transportation History of Cincinnati." Literary Club paper, ms. Cincinnati Public Library.

WARNER, CHARLES DUDLEY. *Studies in the South and West.* New York, 1889.

WELD, CHARLES RICHARD. *A Vacation Tour in the United States and Canada.* London, 1855.

WHO'S WHO: A SOCIETY REGISTER CONTAINING THE NAMES OF CINCINNATI FAMILIES, ETC. Cincinnati, 1892.

WILLIAMS, CAROLINE. *The City on Seven Hills,* Cincinnati, 1938.

—— *Mirrored Landmarks of Cincinnati.* Cincinnati, 1939.

WITTKE, CARL, editor (Beverley W. Bond, Jr., William T. Utter, Francis P. Weisenburger, Eugene H. Roseboom, Philip D. Jordan and Harlow Lindley, authors). *History of the State of Ohio.* 6 vols., Columbus, 1941-4.

(WORTH, GORHAM A.) *Recollections of Cincinnati from a Residence of Five Years, 1817 to 1821,* etc. Albany, 1851.

WRIGHT, HENRY C. *Bossism in Cincinnati.* Cincinnati, 1905.

INDEX

Index

CRYSTAL PALACE